RISEN INDEED?

EARLY CHRISTIANITY AND ITS LITERATURE

Shelly Matthews, General Editor

Editorial Board:
Ronald Charles
Jennifer A. Glancy
Meira Kensky
Joseph A. Marchal
Anders Runesson

Number 31

RISEN INDEED?

Resurrection and Doubt in the Gospel of Mark

Austin Busch

SBL PRESS

Atlanta

Copyright © 2022 by Austin Busch

All rights reserved. No part of this work may be reproduced or transmitted in any form or by any means, electronic or mechanical, including photocopying and recording, or by means of any information storage or retrieval system, except as may be expressly permitted by the 1976 Copyright Act or in writing from the publisher. Requests for permission should be addressed in writing to the Rights and Permissions Office, SBL Press, 825 Houston Mill Road, Atlanta, GA 30329 USA.

Library of Congress Control Number: 2022942252

Contents

Acknowledgments vii
Abbreviations ix

Introduction 1
    Weighing Death and Resurrection in Mark's Gospel   2
    The Skeptical Impulse of Mark's Treatment of Resurrection   9
    Mark as Dialogue and *Commentarii*   16
    The Paradox of Resurrection in Mark   26

1. Ambiguous Resurrections 29
    Risen Indeed? A Careful Reading of Mark 16:1–8   29
    Figurative versus Literal Resurrections 1: Mark 5   43
    Figurative versus Literal Resurrections 2: Mark 9:14–29   69
    Dialogizing Resurrection Faith   73

2. A Dialogue about Resurrection (Mark 12:18–27) 75
    The Questions Debated   75
    The Answers Proposed   82
    From Debate to Dialogism   89

3. Jesus's Demand for Faith and the Disciples' Doubt 97
    The Disciples' Skepticism about Resurrection in Mark 8:27–9:29   98
    Jesus's Demand in 8:31–9:1   111
    The Scope of Jesus's Demand   116
    Mark 13, the Disciples' Second Chance to Die and Rise
        with Jesus, and the Readers' Flight   125
    Mark and Martyrdom   135

4. Faithlessness Condemned or Redeemed? 139
    Peter's Failure   140
    The Failures of James and John   160

Mark's Exploration of Faith's Failure ... 170

5. A Ransom for Many 177
   "A Ransom for Many" ... 179
   The Centurion and Legion: Mark 15:39 and 5:1–20 ... 185
   Legion and Polyphemus: Mark 5:1–20; 16:1–8; and *Odyssey* 9 ... 192
   Jesus's Deceptive Weakness ... 203
   Jesus's Death as an Anthropophagic Meal ... 208
   Jesus's Deceptive Redemption in Early Christian Writings ... 213
   Peter's Redemption ... 216

Conclusion: The Redemption of Doubt 231

Bibliography 235

Ancient Sources Index 259
Modern Authors Index 273
Subject Index 279

Acknowledgments

I wish to thank my undergraduate friends from San Francisco State, with whom I first encountered Mark in small group Bible studies whose exhilarating sense of exploration and discovery I try to re-create in my own classes today. I remain grateful to my mentors from Indiana University, especially David Brakke (now of Ohio State), Herb Marks, and the late Eleanor Winsor Leach, whose generosity and scholarship continue to inspire me. Finally, thank you to Shelly Matthews, general editor of Early Christianity and Its Literature, and the anonymous readers, whose insightful criticism has made this a better book than it would otherwise have become.

I dedicate it to my wife, Joy.

Abbreviations

1 Apol.	Justin, *Apologia i*
1 En.	1 Enoch
1 Macc	1 Maccabees
2 Bar.	2 Baruch
2 En.	2 Enoch
2 Macc	2 Maccabees
4 Macc	4 Maccabees
AARSR	American Academy of Religion Studies in Religion
AB	Anchor Bible
ABD	Freedman, David Noel, ed. *Anchor Bible Dictionary*. 6 vols. New York: Doubleday, 1992.
ABRL	Anchor Bible Reference Library
Acts Paul	Acts of Paul
Acts Paul Thecl.	Acts of Paul and Thecla
Aen.	Virgil, *Aeneid*
Aeth.	Heliodorus, *Aethiopica*
Aj.	Sophocles, *Ajax*
A.J.	Josephus, *Antiquitates judaicae*
AJP	*American Journal of Philology*
AnBib	Analecta Biblica
Ann.	Tacitus, *Annales*
Apol.	Tertullian, *Apologeticus*
Att.	Cicero, *Epistulae ad Atticum*
b.	Babylonian Talmud
BAGD	Bauer, Walter, William F. Arndt, F. Wilbur Gingrich, and Frederick W. Danker. *A Greek-English Lexicon of the New Testament and Other Early Christian Literature*. 3rd. ed. Chicago: University of Chicago Press, 2000.
BBB	Bonner biblische Beiträge

BBR	*Bulletin for Biblical Research*
BDF	Blass, Friedrich, Albert Debrunner, and Robert W. Funk. *A Greek Grammar of the New Testament and Other Early Christian Literature*. Chicago: University of Chicago Press, 1961.
BETL	Bibliotheca Ephemeridum Theologicarum Lovaniensium
BHT	Beiträge zur historischen Theologie
Bib	*Biblica*
BibInt	*Biblical Interpretation*
BibInt	Biblical Interpretation Series
B.J.	Josephus, *Bellum judaicum*
BM	Biblical Monographs
BNTC	Black's New Testament Commentaries
Brut.	Cicero, *Brutus*
BSGRT	Bibliotheca Scriptorum Graecorum et Romanorum Teubneriana
BTB	*Biblical Theology Bulletin*
BZAW	Beihefte zur Zeitschrift für die alttestamentliche Wissenschaft
BZNW	Beihefte zur Zeitschrift für die neutestamentliche Wissenschaft
Catech.	Cyril of Jerusalem, *Catecheses*
CBQ	*Catholic Biblical Quarterly*
CCS	Cambridge Classical Studies
Cels.	Origen, *Contra Celsum*
Chaer.	Chariton, *De Chaerea et Callirhoe*
CJ	*Classical Journal*
CML	Corpus medicorum Latinorum
CML	*Classical and Modern Literature*
Comm. Matt.	Origen, *Commentarium in evangelium Matthaei*
Comm. Rom.	Origen, *Commentarii in Romanos*
COQG	Christian Origins and the Question of God
CSNTCO	Claremont Studies in New Testament and Christian Origins
CTJ	*Calvin Theological Journal*
CurTM	*Currents in Theology and Mission*
CW	*Classical World*
DCLS	Deuterocanonical and Cognate Literature Studies

Dial.	Justin, *Dialogus cum Tryphone*
EBib	Etudes bibliques
ECL	Early Christianity and Its Literature
ECLectures	Edward Cadbury Lectures
Ed.	Edduyot
EKKNT	Evangelisch-katholischer Kommentar zum Neuen Testament
Ep.	*Epistula(e)*
Eph.	Xenophon of Ephesus, *Ephesiaca*
ER	*Ecumenical Review*
ETL	*Ephemerides Theologicae Lovanienses*
ExpTim	*Expository Times*
FCNTECW	Feminist Companion to the New Testament and Early Christian Writings
Fid. orth.	John of Damascus, *De fide orthodoxa*
Flor.	Apuleius, *Florida*
frag(s).	fragments
Fug.	Tertullian, *De fuga in persecutione*
Geogr.	Strabo, *Geographica*
GNO	Gregorii Nysseni opera
Gos. Phil.	Gospel of Philip
GP	Gospel Perspectives
GR	*Greece and Rome*
GRBS	*Greek, Roman, and Byzantine Studies*
Haer.	Irenaeus, *Adversus haereses*
Herc. fur.	Euripides, *Hercules furens*
Hist. eccl.	Eusebius, *Historia ecclesiastica*
HR	*History of Religions*
HTR	*Harvard Theological Review*
HUCA	*Hebrew Union College Annual*
IBS	*Irish Biblical Studies*
ICC	International Critical Commentary
Id.	Theocritus, *Idylls*
Il.	Homer, *Iliad*
Int	*Interpretation*
JBL	*Journal of Biblical Literature*
JQR	*Jewish Quarterly Review*
JR	*Journal of Religion*
JRS	*Journal of Roman Studies*

JSJSup	Supplements to the Journal for the Study of Judaism in the Persian, Hellenistic, and Roman Period
JSNT	*Journal for the Study of the New Testament*
JSNTSup	Journal for the Study of the New Testament Supplement Series
JSOT	*Journal for the Study of the Old Testament*
JTI	*Journal of Theological Interpretation*
JTS	*Journal of Theological Studies*
Jul.	Suetonius, *Divus Julius*
KJV	King James Version
l(l).	line(s)
LCL	Loeb Classical Library
LD	*Lectio Difficilior*
Leg.	Plato, *Leges*
Leuc. Clitop.	Achilles Tatius, *Leucippe et Clitophon*
LNTS	The Library of New Testament Studies
LTT	Library of Theological Translations
LXX	Septuagint
m.	Mishnah
Mart. Pet.	Martyrdom of Peter
Med.	Celsus, *De medicina*
MGS	Montanari, Franco. *The Brill Dictionary of Ancient Greek*. Edited by Madeleine Goh and Chad Schroeder. Translated by Rachel Barritt-Costa et al. Leiden: Brill, 2015.
MnemSup	Mnemosyne Supplements
Moral.	Gregory the Great, *Expositio in Librum Job, sive Moralium libri xxv*
Mos.	Philo, *De vita Mosis*
MT	Masoretic Text
NA[28]	*Novum Testamentum graece*, Nestle-Aland, 28th ed.
Nat.	Pliny, *Naturalis historia*
NDST	Notre Dame Studies in Theology
NedTT	*Nederlands theologisch tijdschrift*
Neot	*Neotestamentica*
NGS	New Gospel Studies
NHMS	Nag Hammadi and Manichean Studies
NIGTC	New International Greek Testament Commentary
NIV	New International Version

NovT	*Novum Testamentum*
NovTSup	Supplements to Novum Testamentum
NPNF	Schaff, Philip, and Henry Wace, eds. *A Select Library of Nicene and Post-Nicene Fathers of the Christian Church*. 28 vols. in 2 series. 1886–1889.
NRSV	New Revised Standard Version
NTL	New Testament Library
NTS	*New Testament Studies*
OACL	Oxford Approaches to Classical Literature
OCT	Oxford Classical Texts
Od.	Homer, *Odyssey*
Oed.	Seneca, *Oedipus*
OG	Old Greek
Or.	Libanius, *Orationes*
Or. cat.	Gregory of Nyssa, *Oratio catechetica*
OrChrAn	Orientalia Christiana Analecta
par(r).	parallel(s)
Pass. cruc. Dom.	*De passione et cruce Domini*
PG	Migne, Jacques-Paul, ed. Patrologia Graeca [= Patrologiae Cursus Completus: Series Graeca]. 162 vols. Paris, 1857–1866.
PMS	Patristic Monograph Series
PNTC	Penguin New Testament Commentaries
praef.	*praefatio*
PRSt	*Perspectives in Religious Studies*
PT	*Poetics Today*
PWHMM	Publications of the Welcome Historical Medical Museum
Quom. hist.	Lucian, *Quomodo historia conscribenda sit*
RB	*Revue biblique*
Res.	Tertullian, *De resurrectione carnis*
RevExp	*Review and Expositor*
RMCS	Routledge Monographs in Classical Studies
Rom.	Plutarch, *Romulus*
RSV	Revised Standard Version
RTR	*Reformed Theological Review*
SAC	Studies in Antiquity and Christianity
Sanh.	Sanhedrin
SBLDS	Society of Biblical Literature Dissertation Series

SBLSP	Society of Biblical Literature Seminar Papers
SC	Sources chrétiennes
Scorp.	Tertullian, *Scorpiace*
SE	*Studia Evangelica I, II, III*
SemeiaSt	Semeia Studies
Serm.	Augustine, *Sermones*
SJLA	Studies in Judaism in Late Antiquity
Smyrn.	Ignatius, *To the Smyrnaens*
SNTSMS	Society for New Testament Studies Monograph Series
SP	Sacra Pagina
StBibLit	Studies in Biblical Literature (Lang)
STDJ	Studies on the Texts of the Desert of Judah
StPatr	Studia Patristica
STR	*Southeastern Theological Review*
Str-B	Strack, H. L., and P. Billerbeck. *Kommentar zum Neuen Testament aus Talmud und Midrasch.* 6 vols. Munich, 1922–1961.
Strom.	Clement, *Stromateis*
SVTQ	*St. Vladimir's Theological Quarterly*
Ta'an.	Ta'anit
TB	Theologische Bücherei: Neudrucke und Berichte aus dem 20. Jarhundert
TDNT	Kittel, Gerhard, and Gerhard Friedrich, ed. *Theological Dictionary of the New Testament.* Translated by Geoffrey W. Bromiley. 10 vols. Grand Rapids: Eerdmans, 1964–1976.
TED	Teología: Estudios y Documentos
Theod.	Theodotion
Theog.	Hesiod, *Theogony*
THL	Theory and History of Literature
Trid. spat.	Gregory of Nyssa, *In tridui spatio*
TynBul	*Tyndale Bulletin*
Urb. cond.	Livy, *Ab urbe condita libri*
UTPSS	University of Texas Press Slavic Series
VC	*Vigiliae Christianae*
VCSup	Supplements to Vigiliae Christianae
Vit. Apoll.	Philostratus, *Vita Apollonii*
VT	*Vetus Testamentum*
WBC	Word Biblical Commentary

WGRW	Writings from the Greco-Roman World
WTJ	*Westminster Theological Journal*
WUNT	Wissenschaftliche Untersuchungen zum Neuen Testament
ZAC	*Zeitschrift für Antikes Christentum/Journal of Ancient Christianity*
ZNW	*Zeitschrift für die neutestamentliche Wissenschaft und die Kunde der älteren Kirche*

Introduction

On initial consideration, a book on resurrection in Mark's Gospel seems incongruous. Mark devotes only half a chapter to Jesus's resurrection (16:1–8)—far less than any other New Testament gospel—and the risen Jesus never appears. The only other recent book on the topic, Paul Fullmer's *Resurrection in Mark's Literary-Historical Perspective*, devotes more attention to *comparanda* than to Mark itself.[1] A handful of relevant articles have appeared,[2] but one more often encounters scholarly claims that Mark assigns meager importance to Jesus's resurrection, especially in comparison with his death, than scholarship probing resurrection's meaning in the Second Gospel. This study aims to fill that lacuna by arguing that Mark represents resurrection so as to invite skepticism about it and by exploring the literary implications and theological significance of the doubt Mark promotes.

This study argues for a new way of reading Mark faithfully. To the extent that Mark locates skepticism at the center of its good news about the resurrections of Jesus and of others, readers may find their response to the Second Gospel reflected in the father of the demon-possessed lad whom Mark's Jesus restores. When Jesus challenges this man's skepticism about whether he can help his endangered son, the father responds with a qualified declaration of faith that acknowledges doubt's persistence: "I have faith; help my lack of faith" (πιστεύω· βοήθει μου τῇ ἀπιστίᾳ, 9:24).[3] His

---

1. Paul Fullmer, *Resurrection in Mark's Literary-Historical Perspective*, LNTS 360 (London: T&T Clark, 2007).
2. E.g., Robin Scroggs and Kent Ira Groff, "Baptism in Mark: Dying and Rising with Christ," *JBL* 92 (1973): 531–48; Andy Johnson, "The 'New Creation,' the Crucified and Risen Christ, and the Temple: A Pauline Audience for Mark," *JTI* 1 (2007): 171–91; Richard C. Miller, "Mark's Empty Tomb and Other Translation Fables in Classical Antiquity," *JBL* 129 (2010): 759–76; Andrew T. Lincoln, "The Promise and the Failure: Mark 16:7, 8," *JBL* 108 (1989): 283–300.
3. Throughout this study, I cite and translate NA^{28}.

statement's internal dialogization finds an echo in the report of the boy's healing. Witnesses declare that Jesus's restoration of the lad constitutes a resurrection, but the narrator neglects to affirm that view, leaving readers to wonder whether Jesus really can defeat death (9:25–27). I discuss this passage in detail in chapter 1, anticipating that treatment here to identify the stakes of my argument: Mark thematizes both faith in and doubt about resurrection, and it prescinds from resolving that tension in favor of faith. This tendency comes into relief when Mark's narrative is compared to the other gospels, which deal with resurrection more straightforwardly. Though it may seem a counterintuitive response to the good news about Jesus's restoration to life that Mark presents, the Second Gospel raises questions about resurrection that it will not resolve. Reading Mark faithfully thus involves exploring the possibility of trust in resurrection, but also understanding the skepticism that Mark's narrative authorizes.

Weighing Death and Resurrection in Mark's Gospel

Notwithstanding some voices in opposition,[4] the idea that Mark places extraordinary emphasis on the death of Jesus represents the standard view, which often overlooks the Second Gospel's complex thematization of resurrection. This study challenges that perspective, arguing for resurrection's centrality to Mark's theology and ideology. I therefore begin by probing the arbitrariness of scholarly claims that Mark emphasizes Jesus's death. Despite its earlier influence, I pass over work positing that Mark privileges Christ's suffering and death over his resurrection glory in reflection of christological disputes supposedly underlying early ecclesiastical conflicts.[5] The popularity of these theories has waned,[6] yet even without their framework, scholars still insist that Mark highlights Jesus's death at the expense of his restoration to life.

---

4. E.g., Robert H. Gundry, *Mark: A Commentary on His Apology for the Cross* (Grand Rapids: Eerdmans, 1993); Holly J. Carey, "Is It as Bad as All That? The Misconception of Mark as a Gospel Film Noir," in *Mark, Manuscripts, and Monotheism: Essays in Honor of Larry W. Hurtado*, ed. Chris Keith and Dieter T. Roth, LNTS 528 (London: Bloomsbury, 2015), 3–21.

5. E.g., Theodore J. Weeden, *Mark: Traditions in Conflict* (Philadelphia: Fortress, 1971); Joseph B. Tyson, "The Blindness of the Disciples in Mark," *JBL* 80 (1961): 261–68.

6. For an early death knell, see Jack Dean Kingsbury, "The 'Divine Man' as the Key to Mark's Christology—The End of an Era?," *Int* 35 (1981): 243–57.

Now that scholars increasingly view Paul and his letters as influencing Mark,[7] the same insistence on Mark's emphasis of Jesus's deadly suffering sometimes surfaces in this newly prevalent literary-critical context, which is less speculative since it allows for Mark's treatment of Jesus's death and resurrection to be measured against Paul's. Joel Marcus, perhaps the most influential scholar on Mark's Gospel in recent history, in positing Paul's influence on Mark notes:

> Both Paul and Mark lay *extraordinary* stress on the death of Jesus.... In both Paul and Mark the death of Jesus on the cross is understood as an apocalyptic event, the turning point of the ages.... Jesus's subsequent resurrection *confirms* this eschatological change, but does not supersede it.... [Mark] prescinds from describing resurrection appearances [and] shapes his narrative in such a way that it climaxes with the point of apocalyptic revelation at which a human being for the first time recognizes Jesus's divine sonship—which is precisely the moment of his death (15:39).[8]

For Marcus, Jesus's death is the central eschatological event of Mark's Gospel, as it is for Paul (Marcus cites 1 Cor 1–2; Gal 6:14 as proof). Jesus's resurrection merely corroborates his death's apocalyptic significance. Scot McKnight also places Paul's Christology in dialogue with Mark's and is similarly impressed by the latter's emphasis on the cross over resurrection. However, according to McKnight, Mark diverges from Paul: "if Paul has a 50/50 relationship of death to vindication ... Mark has a 75/25 relationship. For Mark, the cross gains a heavy emphasis."[9]

Though this comparative approach offers a putative basis for gauging Mark's emphasis on Jesus's suffering and death against an established reference, interpretations employing it are sometimes more impressionistic than carefully measured, as McKnight's makeshift ratios suggest. Yet

---

7. See especially the important collections Oda Wischmeyer, David C. Sim, and Ian J. Elmer, eds., *Two Authors at the Beginnings of Christianity*, part 1 of *Paul and Mark: Comparative Essays*, BZNW 198 (Berlin: de Gruyter, 2014); and Eve-Marie Becker, Troels Engberg-Pedersen, and Mogens Mueller, eds., *For and Against Pauline Influence on Mark*, part 2 of *Mark and Paul: Comparative Essays*, BZNW 199 (Berlin: de Gruyter, 2014), cited throughout.

8. Joel Marcus, "Mark—Interpreter of Paul," *NTS* 46 (2000): 479–80, emphasis original.

9. Scot McKnight, *Jesus and His Death: Historiography, the Historical Jesus, and Atonement Theory* (Waco, TX: Baylor University Press, 2005), 356.

scholarship relying on a more thorough assessment of textual evidence to draw the same conclusion displays similar problems. Take as an example Darrell Bock's article "Son of Man" in InterVarsity Press's *The Dictionary of Jesus and the Gospels*. It adopts a conventional interpretive approach in its synthesis of relevant scholarship.[10] Since so many of Mark's Son of Man sayings deal with Jesus's death and/or resurrection, it presents a useful case study.

Bock employs statistical analysis in support of his view that Mark

> highlights Jesus as the suffering and rejected Son of Man. With nine ... passages [mentioning the Son of Man: 8:31; 9:9, 12, 31; 10:33, 45; 14:21 (2×), 41], Mark has three times the number of suffering sayings as he does the other two categories [i.e., about Jesus's "present ministry" (2:10, 28) and "apocalyptic sayings" (8:38; 13:26; 14:62)].... The bulk of his references in the core of his Gospel involve the prediction of the Son of Man's suffering.[11]

The tripartite scheme Bock employs to support this conclusion, though common,[12] lends itself to manipulation. Three logia included within the category of "suffering sayings," whose purpose is to "highlight ... the suffering and rejected Son" (8:31; 9:31; 10:33–34), actually culminate in a prophecy of resurrection. Can one reasonably claim that statements assuring the Son of Man's restoration to life within days of his death highlight his suffering and rejection at all? Would not deliverance from death as suffering's terminus necessarily be the emphasized feature?[13] Bock's categories enshrine a convention so grounded in scholarly tradition that it may seem unfair to call out his reliance on them ("suffering saying" is a

---

10. Cozier calls the first edition of this widely used reference book "an excellent source for surveying primarily English-speaking scholarship on Jesus and the Gospels that leans towards more conservative conclusions." See Clint L. Cozier, review of *Dictionary of Jesus and the Gospels*, ed. Joel B. Green, Jeannine K. Brown, and Norman Perrin, *JSNT* 49 (1993): 125. For a similar assessment of the second edition, see Paul Foster, "A New Dictionary of Jesus and the Gospels," *ExpTim* 126 (2015): 195.

11. Darrell L. Bock, "Son of Man," in *Dictionary of Jesus and the Gospels*, ed. Joel B. Green, Jeannine K. Brown, and Norman Perrin, 2nd ed. (Downers Grove, IL: InterVarsity Press, 2013), 899.

12. See Heinz Eduard Tödt, *The Son of Man in the Synoptic Tradition*, trans. Dorthea M. Barton, NTL (Philadelphia: Westminster, 1965) and standard reference books, e.g., George W. E. Nickelsburg, "Son of Man," *ABD* 6:137–50, esp. 143–44.

13. See George H. Boobyer, "St. Mark and the Transfiguration," *JTS* 41 (1940): 124.

synonym for the ubiquitous "passion prediction"), but the consequential imprecision should be avoided.[14]

Bock's decision to include Mark 9:9 among the suffering sayings raises particular questions, for this verse refers only to the Son of Man's resurrection, without any reference to his rejection, suffering, or death. If this is not a mistake, since Bock understands 9:9 to lead into the prophecy of the Son's murderous contempt in 9:12 (ἐξουδενηθῇ), he may view the verse's prediction of resurrection as a shorthand allusion to the Son's suffering and death culminating in restoration to life. In this case, his insistence that 9:9 emphasizes suffering it does not even mention would complement his categorization of 8:31, 9:31, and 10:33–34 as suffering sayings although they end in resurrection prophecies.

Bock's decision to count 14:21 as two separate suffering sayings because that verse twice mentions the Son of Man raises similar concerns. Mark 14:21 seems to be a single saying with complementary clauses, as the μέν ... δέ construction suggests. Bock may believe Mark combined two Son of Man sayings that circulated independently, though this seems not to be the standard view,[15] and in any case Bock never presents it as his reasoning. If this is not evidence of interpretation slanted toward a presupposed conclusion, Bock's decision to count the verse twice may also represent an error.

Bock's analysis of the Markan Son of Man sayings, on which he bases his conventional interpretive claim that Mark "highlights Jesus as the suffering and rejected Son of Man," overcounts references to the Son's suffering and death. Some of the complications troubling his analysis may be traced to overreliance on standard classifications. Others may amount to the kind

---

14. Other scholars, though their conclusions about the Markan Son of Man sayings basically agree with Bock's, do not write resurrection out of these passages, as Bock approaches doing. Bultmann, for instance, categorizes sayings as those "which speak of the Son of Man ... as suffering death and rising again." See Rudolf Bultmann, *Theology of the New Testament*, trans. Kendrick Grobel (New York: Scribner's Sons, 1951–1955), 1:30. Tödt (*Son of Man*, esp. 144–49) and Nickelsburg ("Son of Man," 143–44) are also more nuanced.

15. See Barnabas Lindars, *Jesus, Son of Man: A Fresh Examination of the Son of Man Sayings in the Gospels in the Light of Recent Research* (Grand Rapids: Eerdmans, 1984), 74–76. Collins's explanation of the verse's origin as an elaboration "of a traditional saying preserved in Luke 17:1b-2 and Matt 18:6-7" is more convincing. See Adela Yarbro Collins, *Mark: A Commentary*, Hermeneia (Minneapolis: Fortress, 2007), 652.

of inadvertent analytical error that occasionally besets us all. Others still point to legitimate though questionable interpretive judgment calls. However, underlying the entire endeavor lies a fundamental problem like the one troubling Marcus's and especially McKnight's comparative approaches to Jesus's death in Mark vis-à-vis the Pauline epistles. Bock's analysis begins with an impression about Mark's emphasis on Jesus's suffering and death over against his resurrection and reign, and then categorically describes the text in ways supporting that presupposed impression, even when the categorization stands in tension with the passages analyzed.

When I analyze the same sayings Bock treats employing analogous interpretive methods, though without reliance on a categorical scheme biased toward the Son's suffering and death, I arrive at a different tabulation of Mark's Son of Man sayings. Only slightly over half (seven) of Mark's thirteen discrete passages containing the phrase "Son of Man" (counting 14:21 once) mention the Son's betrayal, suffering, or death (8:31; 9:12, 31; 10:33–34, 45; 14:21, 41). Of those seven, three culminate in prophecies of vindication through resurrection (8:31; 9:31; 10:33–34). Four additional verses mention the Son's resurrection and/or eschatological reign without reference to his suffering or death (8:38; 9:9; 13:26; 14:62). Two more emphasize the quasi-divine authority Jesus exercises in his ministry (2:10, 28). That leaves only four of Mark's thirteen discrete sayings about the Son of Man to mention the Son's betrayal, suffering, and/or death, as opposed to his eschatological glory or earthly authority, without immediately moving to predict his rapid resurrection: 9:12; 10:45; 14:21, 41. These four out of thirteen verses, then, would constitute the body of suffering sayings left to support the conclusion that Mark "highlights ... the suffering and rejected Son of Man."

Perhaps it would be better to conclude that while the Second Evangelist acknowledges the Son's horrible death, Mark emphasizes his vindication through resurrection and eschatological reign. This emphasis, anticipated in the authority over demons, illness, and death itself that Jesus exercises throughout his ministry, may be so profound as to unmask the Son's suffering and death as inconsequential hindrances on a destined path of glory. Robert Gundry comes to such a conclusion in his commentary on Mark's Gospel, with the subtitle *Mark's Apology for the Cross*. According to Gundry, Mark pits Jesus's

> successes [i.e., his attraction of crowds, exorcisms, miracles, authoritative teaching and debating prowess] against [his] suffering and death,

and then uses the passion predictions, writes up the passion narrative, and caps his gospel with a discovery of the empty tomb in ways that cohere with the success-stories ... [to] make the passion itself into a success-story.[16]

My interpretation of resurrection in Mark is more complex. Though it has implications for the much-studied problem of what Mark and other New Testament writings mean by referring to Jesus as the "Son of Man," the focus of Bock's article, that question lies beyond the scope of this work. The point I make here is more general: claims about Mark's emphasis on the suffering and death of Jesus, the Son of Man, which surface throughout New Testament scholarship, tend toward arbitrariness, whether they involve thorough textual analysis employing standard interpretive categories (as Bock's) or are elaborated as more impressionistic suggestions (as McKnight's and to a lesser degree Marcus's).

In claiming that Bock's treatment of Mark's Son of Man sayings, alongside the other assessments of Jesus's death discussed above, aims at supporting an impression of the Second Gospel's thematization of Jesus's death and resurrection that Mark does not finally bear out, I do not suggest that the impression lacks any textual basis. In comparison with the other gospels, Mark's treatment of Jesus's resurrection is subdued, even anticlimactic: no angels, no earthquakes, no risen Christ's commission of the disciples. The risen Christ does not even appear in Mark, a detail Marcus points to in support of his claim that Mark lays "*extraordinary stress*" on Jesus's death.[17] Mark treats Jesus's vindication through resurrection tersely, devoting to it only a handful of verses in the final chapter (16:3-8), in contrast with Jesus's betrayal, arrest, interrogations, trials, condemnations, execution, and interment, all recounted in detail (14:43-16:2). The same situation obtains in miniature in the Son of Man saying from 10:33-34 and, to a lesser degree, in the remaining Markan Son of Man passion and resurrection predictions as well.

Marcus's treatment of the announcement of resurrection in Mark 10:33-34 makes explicit the equation of rhetorical brevity with insignificance that promotes the interpretive impression of Mark's emphasis on Jesus's death over his resurrection. After arguing that the pericope in which this saying is embedded assimilates the Son of Man to Deutero-

---

16. Gundry, *Mark*, 2-3.
17. Marcus, "Mark—Interpreter of Paul," 479, emphasis original.

Isaiah's suffering servant, whose death God wills, Marcus elaborates the prophecy's final few words: "and after three days he will rise." He observes that resurrection's "significance seems to be dwarfed by the massiveness of the suffering that precedes it" but acknowledges that not death but resurrection has "the last word ... in all three passion predictions." Marcus admits that Mark presents resurrection as "the ultimate and determinative reality," so that the saying constitutes "an effective response to the terror that the disciples ... displayed in 10:32."[18]

While the admission stands in tension with his view of Mark's emphasis on Jesus's death over his resurrection, it does not affect the interpretive trajectory Marcus's initial impression of the passage's rhetoric establishes. Marcus forestalls its ability to check that approach by provocatively conflating suffering with victory, so that resurrection does not so much resolve the problem of the Messiah's humiliating death as reimagine it. "In the next passage, the Markan Jesus will call on his disciples to share in this victory by being 'baptized' into the messianic suffering that brings it to pass."[19] I am not interpreting Marcus reductively here: it is the crucifixion that reveals Jesus's triumph and divine glory; resurrection represents a confirmatory afterthought.[20] This section of Marcus's commentary instantiates the broader hermeneutical approach to the theme he adopts in the article quoted above. In Mark, "the death of Jesus ... is understood as an apocalyptic event, the turning point of the ages.... Jesus's subsequent resurrection *confirms* this eschatological change, but does not supersede it."[21]

I would construe the Markan passage's rhetorical progression less paradoxically. In a brief prophecy such as Mark 10:33–34, which details the Son of Man's suffering and death but culminates in resurrection, the abrupt declaration "after three days he will rise again" is not "dwarfed" by the longer prediction of suffering and death that it follows. It rather recoils on that previous discourse, cutting it off, as it were, and threatening to render it insignificant as a description of genuine suffering and death. Something similar happens in Mark's brief narrative of Jesus's resurrection following the elaborate account of his death. When the women of chapter

---

18. Joel Marcus, *Mark 8–16: A New Translation with Introduction and Commentary*, AB 27A (New Haven: Yale University Press, 2009), 745–46.

19. Marcus, *Mark 8–16*, 746.

20. See esp. Joel Marcus, "Crucifixion as Parodic Exaltation," *JBL* 125 (2006): 73–87.

21. Marcus, "Mark—Interpreter of Paul," 479, emphasis original.

16 coming to anoint Jesus's body learn his corpse is not in its tomb, they flee in amazement. The resurrection claim has rendered irrelevant their understanding of all they observed as they watched Jesus die, and of what they thought they knew about death. Since they mean to anoint Jesus's decaying corpse, their presence at his tomb is superfluous; they should leave and proclaim that Jesus lives, as the young man says (16:6–7). They fail to follow his directive (16:8), but Mark's Gospel itself still ends with an announcement of resurrection no less abrupt and destabilizing than does the passion prediction from 10:33–34, and no less oriented toward undermining the apparent significance of what Mark has just written about Jesus's death.

The limited attention Mark devotes to resurrection, as measured by rhetorical or narrative amplification, presents a genuine problem. It requires an interpretive solution more robust than the one I have preliminarily offered or the one Gundry's commentary provides. Yet it seems shortsighted to infer from that problem's existence that Mark's emphatic focus remains on Jesus's suffering and death rather than on the evangelical claim that he has exceeded death's bounds by rising. This study is concerned with explicating Mark's treatment of resurrection and with laying bare the literary, theological, and ideological significance of its claims about Jesus's vindication from death. The reading of Mark it presents shows that resurrection constitutes a more significant theme than much relevant scholarship leads one to expect. In that regard, it is contrarian, though I hope not polemical. Mark's neglect to provide elaborate and authoritative details about Jesus's resurrection, and other characters' restorations to life as well, points not to resurrection's lack of significance but rather to a critical feature of the Second Gospel's conceptualization of it. Reserve or even skepticism about resurrection lies at the heart of this theme and theologoumenon's meaning within Mark.

The Skeptical Impulse of Mark's Treatment of Resurrection

The two opening chapters of my study deal with the resurrections (figurative and literal) that Mark's Gospel seems to narrate, as well as with the dialogue about resurrection in which Jesus and the Sadducees engage. Equivocation characterizes Mark's treatment of resurrection. Mark never makes clear whether resurrection actually occurs—either Jesus's or anybody else's (ch. 1)—and Mark invites readers to question whether Jesus's scripturally interpretive argument in support of resurrection in 12:18–27 is as persuasive as the Sadducees' argument opposing it (ch. 2). The next two chapters connect this equivocating impulse to the Markan disciples' responses to Jesus's commands that they follow him to death in expectation of resurrection. The disciples find their master's directives untrustworthy and confusing (ch. 3). Not only do Jesus's students refuse to follow them, but the master himself may in the end fail to believe his prophecies that God will vindicate him through resurrection, and Mark countenances the readers responding with flight to the possibility of death in Jesus's name (chs. 3–4). My study's final chapter builds on these interpretive observations and arguments to construct a theological interpretation of the Second Gospel's literary treatment of Jesus's death and resurrection that contextualizes them within its comprehensive narrative development, as well as in intertextual dialogue with Greco-Roman mythical-literary traditions. Allusions to the latter also surface in later ancient Christian writings elaborating the same apocalyptic myth of redemption that underlies Mark's account of Jesus's ministry, crucifixion, and resurrection from the dead, and I briefly consider this literary and theological tradition that Mark helped to originate.

Chapter 5 shows that Mark's theologically resonant treatment of resurrection has the potential to resolve some of the ambivalence my study's earlier chapters disclose and to explain some of the troubling examples of faithlessness that surface throughout Mark, including Jesus's. But there is no getting around the fact that resurrection acquires its significance in the Second Gospel by being subjected to an inquiry featuring vigorous adversarial interrogation. The hope associated with resurrection in Mark that my final chapter explores thus does not so much obviate as redeem the doubt that Mark exposes, especially in its representation of the faithless disciples and Peter. I reflect on this interpretive dimension in my study's brief conclusion.

The urgent questions about resurrection to which Mark gives voice never find resolution within the Second Gospel's confines, though Mark points to solutions that later writers will develop. Other New Testament writings treat Jesus's resurrection differently. Paul insists that Christ has risen: hundreds of people have seen the risen Lord to spread word of his resurrection, including Paul himself (1 Cor 15:1–11). The other gospels all pair Jesus's empty tomb with disciples' direct encounters with the risen Christ (Matt 28; Luke 24; John 20), sometimes including details that stress the resurrected Jesus's materiality (Luke 24:30, 39–42; John 20:27), apparently lest observers take him to be an apparition instead of an embodied person risen from the dead. Mark, in contrast, will not authorize unequivocal faith in Christ's resurrection. No one sees the risen Jesus within Mark's pages. Death in Mark—Jesus's above all—is inevitable and brutal, both physically and emotionally, and Mark does not shy away from that reality. Resurrection, and more broadly any form of personal survival after death, represents a provocative possibility that threatens to undermine death's significance, but it always remains just that—a possibility, rather than a necessarily persuasive solution to the problems death poses. If Jesus's empty tomb and the young man's claim that he has risen gesture toward Jesus's resurrection as undermining death's decisiveness in Mark, his female disciples' fearful flight and refusal to repeat the young man's unconfirmed announcement raise questions about that gesture's accuracy.

Other New Testament writings also evince skepticism about resurrection, though scholars often interpret the relevant passages as proto-orthodox caricatures of heterodox belief—critiques of faith in something other than a particular view of bodily resurrection that Mark and certain other Jesus-believing authors hold. Take 1 Cor 15 as an example. Paul begins by castigating the Corinthian congregation for denying resurrection (15:12–13), but his argument includes a technical discussion of what sort of body resurrection entails (15:35–54). This suggests to scholars that at least some Corinthians' "denials" of resurrection were narrow. They responded not to the possibility of personalized life after death that resurrection synecdochically represents but rather to Paul's conceptualization of an "enspirited body ... designed for and thus enable[ing] body-spirit coherence in heaven" or to related theological positions Paul holds.[22]

Yet not all of Paul's extended discourse about resurrection should be viewed as subtle theological dispute of this sort. The chapter contains another strand of argumentation open to a more expansive interpretation, suggesting at least some Corinthians might not have been offended by possibly misunderstood details about the nature of the risen body. Instead they were skeptical about this teaching's broader corollary—namely, that death is not final but temporary, as Paul affirms by employing for it the euphemism of sleep, but in such a way as to encompasses the possibility

---

22. Frederick S. Tappenden, *Resurrection in Paul: Cognition, Metaphor, and Transformation*, ECL 19 (Atlanta: SBL Press, 2016), 119. James Ware surveys the scholarship and proposes an innovative solution to relevant interpretive problems. See Ware, "Paul's Understanding of the Resurrection in 1 Corinthians 15:36–54," *JBL* 133 (2014): 809–35.

of awaking. "If Christ has not been raised, your faith is in vain.... Then even those having fallen asleep [κοιμηθέντες] in Christ have perished [ἀπώλοντο]. If in this life [ἐν τῇ ζωῇ ταύτῃ] alone we hope in Christ, then we are to be more pitied than all people" (1 Cor 15:17–19).

Paul brings his discourse about resurrection to a close by reflecting on the fundamental idea that Christ's resurrection implies death's defeat and guarantees immortality to all (15:54–55), or at least all who trust in Christ. Although Frederick Tappenden's cognitive-linguistic approach to the problem has superseded Dale Martin's understanding of how Paul conceptualizes the risen body in 1 Cor 15,[23] Martin remains convincing on this point: some Corinthians would have found not only Paul's notion of an afterlife involving enspirited bodies odd and off-putting but any notion at all of a personalized life after death incredible.[24] The world-weary cynicism characterizing some Roman imperial sepulchral inscriptions confirms that acceptance of life's impermanence was common in Paul's world: n. f. n. s. n. c. (*non fui non sum non curo*; "I was not, I am not, I don't care") or, somewhat more gently, s. t. t. l.: *sit tibi terra levis* ("may the earth lie on you lightly").[25] It is this sort of generic skepticism about claims of personal life after death that Mark often reflects.

With respect to the Fourth Gospel, Gregory Riley has taken the figure of "doubting Thomas" to represent not skepticism about Jesus's restoration to life, let alone about the possibility of personalized eternal life for all. Thomas rather represents belief in a particular mode of eternal life that differs from the evangelist's view of bodily resurrection. This would be something akin to the survival of an immortal mind or soul, roughly corresponding to the view found in Thomasine Christian literature that, according to Riley, inscribes the teachings and traditions John's representation of the disciple Thomas polemically caricatures.[26] Riley's interpretation of John remains provocative, especially its treatment of 20:24–29, where Thomas says he will only believe Jesus has risen if he can handle his res-

---

23. Compare Tappenden, *Resurrection in Paul*, 97–121, and Dale B. Martin, *The Corinthian Body* (New Haven: Yale University Press, 1995), 117–36.

24. Martin, *Corinthian Body*, 107–8.

25. For relevant discussion and citation of inscriptions, see Martin, *Corinthian Body*, 108–9, and Ramsay MacMullen, *Paganism in the Roman Empire* (New Haven: Yale University Press, 1981), 56–57.

26. Gregory J. Riley, *Resurrection Reconsidered: Thomas and John in Controversy* (Minneapolis: Fortress, 1995).

urrected body and probe the wounds that must have somehow healed over.[27] Riley's reading of even that passage may require adjustment in light of April DeConick's argument that the Fourth Evangelist critiques not a particular understanding of Jesus's resurrection but an understanding of salvation privileging visionary encounters with Christ the mystagogue over faith in the risen Lord.[28] However, in certain Johannine passages, the disciple Thomas seems to serve a thematic function altogether different from the one either DeConick or Riley assigns him.

In John 11:1–16, Thomas evinces cynical skepticism aimed not at bodily resurrection but at any kind of life after death whatsoever. Lazarus has fallen ill and died, and Jesus invites his disciples to "have faith" (πιστεύσητε, 11:15) that he will "awaken" his friend from death (ἐξυπνίσω, 11:11), using the same euphemism Paul employs in 1 Cor 15:18. Since Lazarus lived in Bethany, just east of Jerusalem (John 11:1), Jesus's resolution of the man's death entails a journey with his disciples to the region of Judea, whose inhabitants had recently been planning to stone him (see 10:31). The disciples all hesitate to return with the master on so unlikely and dangerous an errand (11:8, 12), but Thomas goes a step further. As soon as he understands that Jesus's plan involves an improbable challenge to death's power over Lazarus, which could itself threaten the lives of Jesus and his disciples, he speaks to his fellow students with sarcastic cynicism: "Let's go, too, so that we may die with him" (11:16).

The view Thomas expresses in this section of John has nothing to do with questioning teaching about resurrection per se, nor would it seem polemically to cast an alternative Thomasine soteriology as a lack of faith. It is not until much later in John that Thomas's imprudent demand to probe and prod Jesus's body may suggest that he is moti-

---

27. Riley, *Resurrection Reconsidered*, 100–126.

28. April D. DeConick, "'Blessed Are Those Who Have Not Seen' (Jn 20:29): Johannine Dramatization of an Early Christian Discourse," in *The Nag Hammadi Library after Fifty Years: Proceedings of the 1995 Society of Biblical Literature Commemoration*, ed. John D. Turner and Anne McGuire, NHMS 44 (Leiden: Brill, 1997), 381–98; DeConick, *Voices of the Mystics: Early Christian Discourse in the Gospels of John and Thomas and Other Ancient Christian Literature*, JSNTSup 157 (Sheffield: Sheffield Academic, 2001), 77–85. DeConick interprets Thomas's desire to probe Jesus's wounds with reference to the Greco-Roman *topos* of the hero, including the hero's shade (see Virgil, *Aen.* 2.270–279), identified by his wounds. Thomas's need to see and probe them (John 20:25) signals his desire for a direct, prolonged encounter with Christ, akin to a mystical vision. This is what the Fourth Evangelist critiques.

vated by a misunderstanding of what embodied resurrection entails, or else by an urge to apprehend the heavenly through direct visionary encounter as opposed to faith. In this earlier episode, on the contrary, urgent questions regarding God's capability of resolving the problem of death through any kind of eternal life at all come to the fore. In fact, in this episode it is only when Martha, not Thomas, confronts Jesus that subtle distinctions arise. Jesus insists, against her confession of belief in the eschatological resurrection of the dead, that the resurrection he promises is not reserved for the future but can be apprehended in the present by everyone who puts faith in him (πιστεύων εἰς ἐμέ, 11:24–27). That understanding of resurrection, and all it implies for John's soteriology, finds immediate affirmation in Jesus's raising of Lazarus from the dead (11:38–44).

The main issue in Thomas's cynical response to Jesus's plan that his disciples follow him to danger so that he might restore Lazarus is not nascent doctrinal controversy about resurrection (embodied or not; solely eschatological or somehow realized in the present) or about the risen, heavenly Lord (apprehended through faith or through visionary encounter). At issue is sweeping skepticism about God's willingness or ability to save any after they have died. According to Thomas's point of view, one can evade death for a time—that is what Jesus did when he fled those who tried to kill him in Judea (John 10:31, 39–40)—but of course one cannot defeat it. Death must be respected, even feared. That is one point of Thomas's fixation on Jesus's damaged body in chapter 20, for bodily ruin and decay are the most obvious signs of death's power, as Lazarus's decomposition likewise affirms (see 11:39–40).[29] Jesus's refusal in chapter 11 to accept this obvious state of affairs is

---

29. According to DeConick, Thomasites believed that salvation was attained through premortem visionary ascents to heaven guided by Jesus the mystagogue, while the Fourth Gospel instead ties salvation closely to faith in the crucified and risen Jesus ("Blessed Are Those"). These visions seem to have anticipated a postmortem spiritual ascent to heaven, but the Thomasites may not have had clear beliefs about life after death, and seem not to have emphasized salvation from it. See April D. DeConick, "John Rivals Thomas: From Community Conflict to Gospel Narrative," in *Jesus in Johannine Tradition*, ed. Robert T. Fortna and Tom Thatcher (Louisville: Westminster John Knox, 2001), 305; DeConick, "Blessed Are Those," 396. Partly for this reason, the Fourth Gospel, in critiquing Thomasine Christianity's fixation on premortem visionary experiences, represents Thomas as skeptical and confused about life after death in general and about Jesus's resurrection specifically.

nothing short of ridiculous. He aims to return to Judea, where he will put his own and his disciples' lives at risk to help a man who, by virtue of already being dead and decomposing, lies beyond assistance. Thus, Jesus's plan is subject not merely to Thomas's skepticism but even to his scorn.

Chapter 2 of this study will point to another textual complex that scholars have interpreted in such a way as to elide from the early Christian literary record skepticism about God's ability or willingness to guarantee personal eternal life (2 Tim 2:17–18). I will also argue that Mark's Sadducees in 12:18–27 give voice to the same objection the pastoral epistle attributes to Paul's opponents, with Mark's Jesus failing to defeat the Sadducees' scripturally sensitive skepticism. Even at this point, though, it should be clear that some early Jesus-believers, like others in the Roman Empire, found incredible the idea of death's defeat by means of any personalized life after death—perhaps especially but not exclusively resurrection. Certain members of Paul's congregations and those believers whom the Fourth Gospel's Thomas represents were not receptive to it and would have responded with skeptical interrogation or dismissive scorn.

Of course, Mark's Jesus does privilege embodied resurrection, and Mark depicts subtle debate between Jesus and those holding alternative points of view, as I will show. Moreover, Mark situates resurrection in an eschatological context and is willing to brave the shoals of obscure controversies relevant to it. But the Second Gospel does not primarily conceptualize resurrection as a coherent concept involving detailed specifics about how to understand the risen body, as does 1 Cor 15 and perhaps John 20:24–29 or even Luke 24:28–43. Statements about resurrection in Mark primarily signify God's willingness and ability to defeat death by offering persons eternal life; they are only secondarily invested in the form that eternal life takes. In fact, one passage crucial to Mark's development of the resurrection theme uses terminology assimilable to belief in an immortal soul (8:35–37). When viewed against the backdrop of skepticism about personally individualized life after death that many in the Greco-Roman world possessed, resurrection in Mark may be interpreted as a synecdoche for a person's divinely granted eternal life, rather than opposed to alternative conceptualizations of personal life after death. If Mark's readers feared—justifiably or not—violence and death in connection to their identification with Christ, as many scholars now believe, the evangelist's examination of this general theme and conviction might have been urgent indeed, and its results consequential.[30]

Mark as Dialogue and *Commentarii*

Mark's interrogation of teaching about resurrection presses this gospel toward a stylistic and ideological position close to the novelistic discourse Mikhail Bakhtin identifies as polyphonic and unfinalized. Such discourse consists of different voices, in the form of characters speaking from specific ideological positions or socialized personal experiences, or as the narrative voice focalized through such characters. These voices participate in a sustained dialogue, as it were, but without any one emerging to dominate the others, and without even the author's voice exercising hegemonic control.[31] According to one of Bakhtin's more expressive descriptions of polyphonic or dialogic narrative,

> this dialogue—the "great dialogue" of the novel as a whole—takes place not in the past, but right now, that is, in the *real present* of the creative process. This is no stenographer's report of a *finished* dialogue, from which the author has already withdrawn and *over* which he is now located as if in some higher decision-making position: that would have turned an authentic and unfinished dialogue into an objectivized and finalized *image of a dialogue*, of the sort usual for every monologic novel. The great dialogue ... is organized as an *unclosed whole* of life itself, life poised *on the threshold*.[32]

---

30. Some interpreters view persecution as an (anticipated?) experience of the Markan readers. See Bas M. F. Van Iersel, "The Gospel according to St. Mark—Written for a Persecuted Community?," *NedTT* 34 (1980): 15–36; Paul S. Pudussery, "Discipleship: A Call to Suffering and Glory; An Exegetico-Theological Study of Mk 8,27–9,1; 13,9–13 and 13,24–27" (PhD diss., Pontificia Università Urbaniana, 1987); Hendrika Nicoline Roskam, *The Purpose of the Gospel of Mark in Its Historical and Social Context*, NovTSup 114 (Leiden: Brill, 2004); Adam Winn, *The Purpose of Mark's Gospel: An Early Christian Response to Roman Imperial Propaganda*, WUNT 245 (Tübingen: Mohr Siebeck, 2008); and Brian J. Incigneri, *The Gospel to the Romans: The Setting and Rhetoric of Mark's Gospel*, BibInt 65 (Leiden: Brill, 2003). See also Joel Marcus, *Mark 1–8: A New Translation with Introduction and Commentary*, AB 27 (New York: Doubleday, 2000), 28–29; Collins, *Mark*, 96–102 (esp. 102).

31. See, e.g., Mikhail M. Bakhtin, *The Dialogic Imagination: Four Essays*, trans. Michael Holquist, UTPSS 1 (Austin: University of Texas Press, 1981), 262–63.

32. Mikhail M. Bakhtin, *Problems of Dostoevsky's Poetics*, ed. and trans. Caryl Emerson (Minneapolis: University of Minnesota Press, 1984), 63, emphasis original.

I have written elsewhere about Mark as dialogic in a Bakhtinian sense,[33] and I apply a related hermeneutic in chapter 2 of the present study. This view of Mark supports a modified version of the argument about the Second Gospel's genre that Matthew D. C. Larsen recently proposed in *Gospels before the Book*, in which Bakhtin's ideas also play a role.[34] Larsen suggests Mark was written in such a way as to prime readers' expectations for what I argue that it offers them: an open-ended exploration of resurrection faith that is polyphonic or dialogic in a broad though still recognizably Bakhtinian sense, as opposed to a dogmatic treatment of the resurrection theme.

Larsen argues that Mark constitutes a ὑπόμνημα or ὑπομνήματα, or, in Latin, *commentarii* (the plurals are more often used in antiquity)—unordered, unfinished, unpolished (stylistically plain), and even unauthored collections of notes (not unwritten, of course, but not attributed to an authorizing writer). These were meant not to be read as finalized books but instead to be expanded, supplemented, and explained by writers employing them in their own literary endeavors, and by authoritative teachers with specialized knowledge on which they could draw to clarify ambiguities, resolve contradictions, and elaborate in ways helpful to auditors. Larsen offers several examples of works of this sort, some of which will be familiar to students of classical literature.[35] A key example is Cicero's no longer extant *commentarius* or ὑπόμνημα about his consulship (Cicero uses both the Latin and Greek terms), which he wrote up and circulated to see whether anyone would develop it into a formal history (see *Att.* 1.19; 2.1). Others are less well-known: for instance, the original version of Galen's *On Anatomical Procedures*, which is no longer extant, though Galen refers to it in the opening sentences of a surviving (version of the) work he wrote later and gave the same name.[36] In this case, the same author developed his own *commentarii* into a more formalized literary work.

---

33. Austin Busch, "Questioning and Conviction: Double-Voiced Discourse in Mark 3:22–30," *JBL* 125 (2006): 477–505.

34. Matthew D. C. Larsen, *Gospels before the Book* (New York: Oxford University Press, 2018), 121–22, 135–36.

35. Larsen, *Gospels before the Book*, 11–36. See Lucian, *Quom. hist.* 48, for discussion of the relationship between ὑπομνήματα and formal historiography.

36. Charles Singer, ed. and trans., *Galen on Anatomical Procedures: De anatomicis administrationibus*, PWHMM, NS 7 (London: Oxford University Press, 1956), 1, discussed in Larsen, *Gospels before the Book*, 29–34.

Larsen's generic identification finds confirmation in a view of the Second Gospel that surfaces among early Christian writers and explains much of what Mark's Gospel itself offers. Some ancient Christians label Mark as ὑπομνήματα (see, e.g., Eusebius, *Hist. eccl.* 2.15),[37] and Mark certainly appears unfinished and unpolished. Later writers elaborated, explained, and finalized Mark, as the manuscript tradition surrounding its conclusion reveals. Moreover, biblical scholars agree that the gospels of Matthew and Luke (if not John) amount to larger-scale expansions and emendations. Discrete rhetorical features of the Second Gospel complement Larsen's generic identification of it as ὑπομνήματα. For instance, Mark's literary style is lively and straightforward to the point of abruptness, and Mark includes a liberal use of non-Greek "barbarian" language. The latter constitutes a generic feature Cicero expresses anxiety about in his discussion of his own *commentarius* at *Att.* 1.19.[38]

Larsen, though, groups what may amount to a somewhat different mode of writing in the generic category he discovers/constructs to explain Mark. Also called ὑπομνήματα or *commentarii* in antiquity, this type of writing might be distinguished from the texts discussed above as secondary *commentarii* rather than primary, on the model of the distinction between two types of epic C. S. Lewis draws in *Preface to Paradise Lost*.[39] According to Lewis's schema, primary epic's poetic form emerges from and reflects its original performative context. As a written record of oral poetry, or even a transcript of an oral performance, a primary epic's notable formal and stylistic features represent characteristics of improvised oral narrative poetry. It instantiates complex poetic traditions whose mastery was passed on from one balladist to another. These include heroic epithets and similarly stylized diction and rhetoric (e.g., extended similes), regular narrative sequencing with consistent employment of stock themes, and related formal patternings. A secondary epic, on the other hand, constitutes an originally written work that adopts and elaborates (even exaggerates) these and other formal features of primary

---

37. On ancient Christian descriptions of Mark that support Larsen's view, see *Gospels before the Book*, 79–98.

38. Discussed at Larsen, *Gospels before the Book*, 13.

39. C. S. Lewis, *A Preface to Paradise Lost, Being the Ballard Matthews Lectures, Delivered at University College, North Wales, 1941* (London: Oxford University Press, 1942).

epic to evoke in the reader an aesthetic and emotional experience akin to the one primary epic generates, while at the same time compensating for the absence of an authentic oral context. Though the relationship between primary epic's performative function and secondary epic's literary form is distant and derivative, this does not imply the inferiority of the latter (examples of which include Virgil's *Aeneid* or Milton's *Paradise Lost*) to the former (e.g., Homer's *Iliad* and *Odyssey* or *Beowulf*). It merely acknowledges that secondary epic develops in self-consciously literary ways generic expectations that originally emerged in oral traditions and performance settings not directly relevant to secondary epic's own compositional context.

Analogously, some ancient ὑπομνήματα or *commentarii* seem to have been primary, with formal features reflecting a functional compositional context similar to those Larsen identifies in chapters 1–4 of his study. Such works, often written by interested parties well-connected to the events they describe, constitute archival notes, transcripts, informal memoirs, and the like. They were produced with the expectation that they would later be explained, elaborated, and finalized by authoritative authors and teachers, including historians, philosophers, and physicians. But other works labeled *commentarii* seem not to fit this functional description, even though they adopt some of the formal features primary ὑπομνήματα or *commentarii* display and may even go by the same name. A key example is Aulus Gellius's *Attic Nights*, whose preface repeatedly uses the label *commentarii* (see *praef.* 3, 13, and passim) for the work it introduces (a kind of commonplace book, or collection of anecdotes about philosophers and other learned men drawn from Gellius's reading). A careful reading of this work's preface supports the bifurcated generic categorization I propose.

Gellius distinguishes *hi commentarii*, the work he is publishing, from *illis annotationibus* (*praef.* 3), which he identifies as notes he took in order to aid his memory when studying and on whose basis he composed the *commentarii* proper. As a partial result of this compositional origin, his (secondary) *commentarii* retain some of the apparently haphazard order, episodic variety, and rhetorical urgency of the (primary) *annotationes*. However, unlike the genre of *commentarii* that Larsen discusses, Gellius's are most definitely not unpolished notes (that would be what Gellius calls his *annotationes*), and they are not unauthored. On the contrary, the work's preface, as Wytse Hette Keulen argues, constitutes a rhetorically complex attempt to position Gellius's authorial voice as didactically authoritative and philosophically exemplary.[40] The strong authorial voice in *Attic Nights*—hardly what one would expect from *commentarii*, in Larsen's conceptualization—turns out to bear a close relationship to a feature of this literary work that one would expect from the generic designation for which Larsen argues: namely, it remains unfinished. Though twenty books long at the time of the publication its preface imagines, Gellius insists he will keep adding to his *commentarii* for as long as he lives: "Therefore the number of books will increase, provided the gods graciously help, in accordance with the progressing steps of life itself, however few they may be. Nor do I wish to be given me a longer duration of living than so long as I will be sufficient to this faculty of writing and of composing *commentarii* [*scribendi commentandique*]" (*praef.* 24; see also 23).[41] This suggestion that Gellius's *commentarii* are coterminous with Gellius's life seems not to have been meant merely as a straightforward declaration of the author's long-range compositional plans. In any case, twenty books are all that has survived of the *Attic Nights*. The statement amounts to hermeneutically significant insistence on Gellius's intent that his work remain open-ended in a different sense.

The openness of *Attic Nights* entails a responsibility not only for the author but for readers as well. The difficult labor Gellius has already put into his composition, and will continue to put into it even after releasing it to the world (laboring late into the long winter nights in his few hours of leisure to discover, rework, and add philosophical anecdotes; see *praef.* 5, 10), should inspire his readers to undertake their own intellectual activity in engaging with his *commentarii*. Ideally, the result will be that his work "might lead ... to the desire of noble learning and the contemplation of useful knowledge" (*praef.* 12).

Gellius explicitly calls on his readers to make sense of the difficult and sometimes contradictory statements his *commentarii* incorporate. They must wrestle with obscure, unexplained, and otherwise confusing aspects of his work, which involves understanding it as a dialogue of authorities articulating distinct points of view on the subject matters it treats. Readers

---

40. Wytse Hette Keulen, *Gellius the Satirist: Roman Cultural Authority in Attic Nights*, MnemSup 297 (Leiden: Brill, 2009), 17–35.

41. Translating Peter K. Marshall, ed., *Aulus Gellius noctes atticae*, 2 vols., OCT (Oxford: Oxford University Press, 1968). Translations of ancient texts are my own, unless otherwise noted. (With respect to the Bible, I make no effort to deviate from widely used translations [esp. RSV, NRSV], whose language I surely echo.)

ought not to dismiss anything they read in *Attic Nights* because it appears to privilege ideas they do not comprehend or viewpoints they tend to resist; instead, they should pursue those ideas and attempt to make sense of the controversial opinions and judgments Gellius incorporates.

> But let [the readers] judge that those things left ... less than fully explicated, I ask, were written not for the sake of teaching but rather for bringing to mind [*non docendi magis quam admonendi*] and, as if content to be shown a path, let [the readers] trace them afterwards, if they like, by means of either procured books or teachers. But those things which they will have thought worthy of reproach, let them, if they dare, burn with anger at those from which we have received them. However, to those things which they might have read written elsewhere differently, let them not right away thoughtlessly object, but let them consider the reasons for these matters [*ne iam statim temere obstrepant, sed et rationes rerum ... pensitent*] and the authoritative judgments of the men whom those writers and whom we have followed. (*praef.* 17–18; see also 13–16)

The dialogically open quality of Gellius's book—its unfinalizability, in multiple senses of the word—is a function not only of the author's relationship to his own writing but also of the response to it he expects his readers to adopt.

Attic Nights clearly displays some formal features of the *commentarii* genre, but it deploys them independently of the functional context of primary *commentarii*. Gellius is not writing up *commentarii* as notes for himself or other authors to incorporate into formal philosophical writings, or for authoritative teachers to adapt into lectures, or for anything of the sort. He has already done that in the *annotationes* lying behind what he calls his *commentarii*. He seems rather to have approached the *commentarii* genre in much the way Apollonius of Rhodes or Virgil approached the epic genre associated in antiquity with Homer. These later poets deployed and elaborated some of (primary) epic's formal features for purposes at one remove (at least) from the functional performative context underlying the generic models Homer's epics offered. In his secondary *commentarii* Gellius adopts some of the generic conventions of primary *commentarii* in order to produce a work that is not so much unfinished as unfinalized in an aesthetic and ideological sense, especially in its requirement of readers' interpretive mediation and independent research to "complete."

Something similar would seem to obtain for other texts labeled *commentarii* in antiquity—for instance, Julius Caesar's famous *commentarii* on the Roman civil war. Cicero evaluates these writings in a way analogous to Gellius's discussion of his own, though Cicero focuses more on literary style than on content. He notes that Caesar's *commentarii* are plain and unfinished, but not in the sense of needing rhetorical adornment or literary refinement. They are rather stark in the way a nude body may be beautiful: "bare, upright, and graceful [*nudi ..., recti et venusti*], with all rhetorical ornament—just like a garment [*tamque veste*]—removed" (*Brut.* 262).[42] Like such a nude, Caesar's work is not incomplete but rather elegant in its (rhetorical) austerity. In fact, Cicero compares fools (*inepti*) who would attempt to ornament or otherwise "finish" Caesar's writings to those who, when faced with a nude model for artistic representation (context makes it clear that is the kind of nude Cicero has in mind), fail to admire its beauty. Instead, they dangerously fumble about with a hot iron in a stupid attempt to curl the model's hair (*qui volent illa calamistris inurere, Brut.* 262).[43] Cicero's point may be reformulated using the generic categories I have been considering. Caesar's writings about the civil war are in a sense *commentarii*—that is, unfinished annotations for later writers to elaborate and complete—but they manage to transcend that function to become aesthetically powerful in their own right. Thus they make historians attempting to finish them look like fools in their misguided attempts at embellishment and elaboration. They constitute secondary rather than primary *commentarii*.

Moving from rhetoric to subject matter, the obvious lack of finish Caesar's *commentarii* display—the literal incompleteness of their historical narrative—communicates the same sense of austere power that Cicero observes in their unadorned style. Caesar apparently abandoned his writing coincident with a strategic decision to privilege decisive military defeat of his domestic opponents over the attempts to win them over by means of the persuasion that his *commentarii* constitute and occasionally thematize. His decision to

---

42. Quoting Enrica Malcovati, ed., *M. Tulli Ciceronis, scripta quae manserunt omnia: Fasc. 4. Brutus*, BSGRT (Leipzig: Teubner, 1968). The translation is from Christina Shuttleworth Kraus, "Hair, Hegemony, and Historiography: Caesar's Style and Its Earliest Critics," in *Aspects of the Language of Latin Prose*, ed. Tobias Reinhardt, Michael Lapidge, and J. N. Adams (Oxford: British Academy, 2005), 98.

43. See Kraus for suggestions regarding how Cicero aligns Caesar's style with masculine stereotypes, and for how ancient readers might have connected the *commentarii*'s style and incompleteness to Caesar's authorial persona ("Hair, Hegemony, and Historiography," 109–12 and passim).

stop shaping a self-promoting narrative for public consumption complements the relinquishment of his expectation to rule the republic within an established (if not entirely intact) constitutional framework.[44] Even the literal incompleteness of Caesar's *commentarii*, then, points not to a genuine lack of finish,[45] though Cicero thinks that Caesar may have originally meant for them to be incorporated into more elaborate historiographies (*sed dum voluit alios habere parata, unde sumerent qui vellent scribere historiam*, Brut. 262). It rather signifies that their writer has abandoned the political impulse to which his writings gave voice, choosing instead to achieve his strategic goals by means of military conquest alone. In other words, the formal incompleteness of the work now known as Caesar's *Civil War* is not incidental to—let alone does it detract from—its ultimate ideological import; on the contrary, it is essential to, even constitutive of it.

Caesar's *commentarii* were finally completed by later authors and integrated into histories such as Plutarch's, though some historiographers expressed the same reservations about taking them up that Cicero noted.[46] Others, though, interpreted the distinctive stylistic and ideological features of Caesar's *commentarii* as evidence not of their literary success but of their necessary and anticipated emendation.[47] These developments, though somewhat baffling to connoisseurs of Latin literature, illuminate Mark's peculiar thematic and stylistic features, as well as its early history of interpretation.

Mark occupies a generic position closer to the *commentarii* of Gellius or Caesar than to those of Cicero or Galen. This gospel's well-known rhetorical ruggedness, its episodic nature and frequent lack of discernable order, and its abrupt conclusion were taken by ancient scribes as an invitation to complete and emend, much as some understood analogous

---

44. William Wendell Batstone and Cynthia Damon, *Caesar's Civil War*, OACL (New York: Oxford University Press, 2006), 32, 170–71.

45. Batstone and Damon argue that most of the *commentarii*'s narrative in fact displays a "high state of polish," in the sense of a coherent structure (*Caesar's Civil War*, 31).

46. See, e.g., Hirtius's *Letter to Balbus*, preserved as the preface to book 8 of Caesar's *Gallic Wars*.

47. E.g., Assinius Polio (whose comments are summarized at Suetonius, *Jul.* 56.4) notes that Caesar's accounts are inaccurate and exaggerated, whether deliberately (*consulto*) or through lapse of memory, and posits that *rescripturum et correcturum fuisse*. See Robert A. Kaster, ed., *C. Suetoni Tranquilli: De vita Caesarum libros VIII et De grammaticis et rhetoribus librum*, OCT (Oxford: Oxford University Press, 2016).

features of Caesar's *Civil War*. Both the Markan manuscript tradition and the standard solution to the Synoptic problem make that clear. But not all ancient readers understood Mark as primary *commentarii* or what Gellius would call *annotationes*. The gospel continued to be copied, studied, preached, and commented on independently of its elaboration by Matthew and Luke, and even without the more modest scribal emendations following Mark 16:8—albeit not as frequently as the other New Testament accounts of Jesus.

While Larsen's study is largely persuasive, its conclusion raises a lingering question. Why would ancient Christian scribes and those who employed them go through the trouble of preserving Mark intact if it not only was written as notes for later authors, but so happily fulfilled that purpose in being taken up, emended, and completed by at least two other authors who produced more popular gospels? This question becomes more urgent since many scholars posit that the hypothetical sayings source Q dropped out of existence as an independent textual tradition because Matthew and Luke's subsumption of it rendered Q superfluous. Copying Q may even have been perceived as dangerous, if its lack of narrative contextualization opened Jesus's sayings to unconventional interpretations, or if Q's theology were in some way problematic.[48] Why, then, would scribes continue to copy superfluous Mark, especially since several of the Markan passages not taken up by Matthew and Luke are prone to misunderstanding and controversy?[49]

One answer is that Mark's *commentarii* were supposed to have been based on Peter's preaching, so that they held apostolic authority that made them worth preserving despite their lack of finish and potential for misunderstanding.[50] An alternative—or perhaps complementary—explanation is that Mark was not always perceived as primary *commentarii* akin to Cicero's writings on his consulship or to Galen's on anatomy or perhaps to the sayings collection known as Q, none of which survive. Instead Mark

---

48. John S. Kloppenborg rejects these and related explanations of Q's disappearance on several bases, including that they would make Mark's survival difficult to account for. See Kloppenborg, *Q, the Earliest Gospel: An Introduction to the Original Stories and Sayings of Jesus* (Louisville: Westminster John Knox, 2008), 98–101.

49. E.g., the miracles involving Jesus's saliva (7:31–37 and 8:22–26) were probably viewed as sanctioning magic (Collins, *Mark*, 369, 392).

50. See Papias, frag. 3.17, in *The Apostolic Fathers: Greek Texts and English Translations*, ed. Michael W. Holmes, 3rd ed. (Grand Rapids: Baker Academic, 2007), 738, 740.

constitutes secondary *commentarii*, like the extant writings of Gellius and Caesar. As more carefully composed literary works, rather than hastily written annotations, secondary *commentarii* had a better claim for study and preservation, even though they deploy for aesthetic, ideological, or didactic purposes some of the same formal and stylistic features that primary *commentarii* display, including an ostensible lack of finish. Incidentally, this state of affairs would seem to obtain regardless of whether the secondary *commentarii* in question contain direct testimony (like Caesar's or, perhaps, Mark) or whether they are entirely derivative of other literary sources (like Gellius's). The Second Evangelist employs features of the generic form of *commentarii* or ὑπομνήματα not because he writes rough archival notes for others to incorporate or complete. Mark rather harnesses the generic form's potential for stylistic immediacy (as Caesar more happily managed) and for open-endedness requiring readers to wrestle with polyphonic complexity (as does Gellius's *Attic Nights*, though with less subtlety and success).

Some ancient readers responded to the unfinalizability of Mark's Gospel, its unresolved debates and dialogical provocations regarding resurrection above all, precisely by finishing it. Matthew and Luke emend its equivocal conclusion with guarantees that Jesus really did rise from the dead to restore his faithless disciples. Both offer various redactional solutions to the problems about resurrection that Mark presents elsewhere as well. While this study focuses on Mark itself, rather than constituting a work of reception history, the Second Gospel occupies an originary position in ancient Christian literature, and some early writers in fact viewed Mark as *commentarii* or ὑπομνήματα in the sense of unfinished notes inviting elaboration, emendation, and completion. Critical study of Mark therefore necessitates occasional ventures into the narrative worlds of Matthew, Luke, and other ancient Jesus-believing writers. On this, Larsen is thoroughly persuasive: to the extent that the other evangelists recognized and treated Mark as (primary) ὑπομνήματα, the line demarcating Mark's manuscript tradition from the First and Third Gospels should be seen as far less clear than normally imagined and is perhaps only arbitrarily drawn at all.[51]

In their responses to Mark, Matthew and Luke's (and perhaps John's) elaborate scribal emendations call attention to the provocative questions

---

51. See Larsen, *Gospels before the Book*, 105–7.

the Second Gospel poses about resurrection. Sometimes they introduce material that answers them in illuminating ways; at other times they omit them, with the result that the problems stand in starker relief in the portion of the manuscript tradition normally labeled "the Gospel according to Mark." I occasionally trace such textual developments in the chapters that follow. To the degree that they may be interpreted as shutting down Mark's open-ended incitements, or as sanding away its theological and ideological rough edges, they retrospectively help us to understand the shape, scope, and implications of the provocative questions about resurrection Mark's *commentarii* raise.

I press further forward into the Christian literary tradition Mark helped originate as well. I argue that some of the questions and provisional answers about Jesus's death and resurrection that Mark's apocalyptic narrative presents played a larger role than normally recognized in generating a mythical-theological theme that surfaces in many early Christian writings about Jesus's death and resurrection. I also suggest that Mark's treatment of the disciples' refusal to put faith in resurrection and of their resulting flight from the scene of Jesus's arrest, death, and empty tomb stands near the beginning of a tradition of early debate about acceptable responses to persecution in Jesus's name. Throughout, though, I remain principally interested in the Second Gospel's unfinalized dialogue about faith in and doubt regarding resurrection. I approach later Christian writings as exemplary responses to Mark's *commentarii* (at however many removes) that shed light on its dialogic implications and provocations.

The Paradox of Resurrection in Mark

Mark's treatment of resurrection turns on an intriguing paradox, features of which scholars have misinterpreted, and from which some have mistakenly inferred that the theme of resurrection is not important to this evangelist. Jesus's defeat of death through resurrection is anticipated prophetically and figuratively in several episodes earlier in this gospel, yet Mark cultivates profound ambiguity about Jesus's resurrection within its pages. The risen Christ never appears in Mark. More than that, in every place where resurrection seems to be depicted—others' no less than Jesus's—the Second Gospel introduces uncertainty as to whether or not resurrection took place (ch. 1). Mark goes so far as to include a dialogue between Jesus and the Sadducees featuring the latter party's compelling questions about whether resurrection constitutes a scripturally viable doctrine (ch. 2). On the one hand, Mark's Jesus boldly declares that shameful death in faithful anticipation of God's vindication through resurrection ought to be the destiny not only of himself but of his students as well (ch. 3). On the other, Mark's disciples, and perhaps Jesus, cannot in the end bring themselves to place their trust in God's resurrection power. This lack of faith is integral to Mark's account of Jesus's abandonment to die alone and to Mark's hesitation to demand from readers a trust that Jesus's own disciples are unable to muster (chs. 3–4). These narrative developments inform and complicate resurrection's emergence as the decisive feature of the Markan Son of Man's destiny, with Mark's Christology hinging on an apocalyptic myth the evangelist presents in history-like form. It recounts God's (possible) salvation of Jesus and others from Death's demonic power after Jesus gives himself to it to redeem many (ch. 5). Resurrection, in Mark, turns out to be more an open question than a definitive answer, representing the prospect of hope rather than the certainty of salvation.

This study examines the work—narrative, theological, and ideological—that resurrection performs and falls short of accomplishing in Mark's Gospel. It considers how Jesus's resurrection invites faith but does not guarantee it; how it makes redemption possible but not certain; and how it disrupts expectations of divine condemnation, even if it does not totally overturn them. Mark in its entirety orchestrates an elaborate dialogue between faith and doubt in the face of death, trust and skepticism, conviction and questioning, assurance and fear. I do not claim satisfactorily to resolve Mark's polyphonic and unfinalized thematization of resurrection. In the pages that follow I instead trace its contours, ponder its theological and ideological implications, and situate it within relevant literary-historical and mythological contexts. I also consider how early readers of Mark and participants in the textual and theological traditions Mark's dialogical provocations helped originate responded to the questions regarding resurrection whose centrality to the Second Gospel my reading establishes.

1
Ambiguous Resurrections

Mark's famously open ending suggests a calculated attempt to maintain uncertainty about the possibility of resurrection. It asserts Christ's restoration to life and provides circumstantial evidence of its having taken place (the empty tomb) but offers no sure proof in the form of the risen Jesus's appearances. This chapter explores that ambiguity and locates the Second Gospel's treatment of Jesus's restoration to life within the broader thematic complex of resurrection that Mark's *commentarii* present. Wherever the possibility of resurrection surfaces, the evangelist equivocates. In fact, Mark neglects to guarantee every resurrection it seems to narrate.

Risen Indeed? A Careful Reading of Mark 16:1–8

In discussing Mark's open ending, scholars often fix on the empty tomb and the risen Jesus's promise, reiterated by the young man, to appear to the disciples in Galilee.[1] Mark provides a great deal of narrative information other than these details, though, and this data requires more thorough treatment.[2] In this initial section, I focus on the young man who announces Jesus's resurrection. I identify him with the anonymous disciple from 14:51–52. Since that controversial position is crucial to my

---

1. See Peter N. McLellan, "Specters of Mark: The Second Gospel's Ending and Derrida's Messianicity," *BibInt* 24 (2016): 357–81. For earlier treatments, see, e.g., John Dominic Crossan, "Form for Absence: The Markan Creation of Gospel," *Semeia* 12 (1978): 41–55; Lincoln, "Promise and the Failure"; Norman R. Petersen, "When Is the End Not the End: Literary Reflections on the Ending of Mark's Narrative," *Int* 34 (1980): 151–66.

2. Guy Williams traces the limited range of debate on Mark's final verses. See Williams, "Narrative Space, Angelic Revelation, and the End of Mark's Gospel," *JSNT* 35 (2013): 263–66.

reading of Jesus's resurrection in Mark, I justify it below. But identifying the young man correctly only becomes important because it facilitates a hermeneutically productive understanding of the narrative and symbolic role that he and his message play within Mark's Gospel.

The young man in chapter 16 investigates rather than witnesses. He formulates his proclamation that Jesus returned to life as a series of inferences drawn from the evidence at hand, explaining that Jesus "has risen" (ἠγέρθη) with reference to the tomb's emptiness: "he is not here; behold the place where they laid him" (16:6). The young man neglects to claim a personal encounter with the risen Christ, and his insistence that only in Galilee will anyone see the postmortem Jesus (16:7) underscores this testimonial reticence. He asserts it not on the basis of any special knowledge or revelation, but rather by citing what Jesus had publicly said to his disciples before he died: "Go, tell his disciples and Peter that he goes before you to Galilee; there you will see him, as he told you [καθὼς εἶπεν ὑμῖν]" (16:7). "He goes before you to Galilee" (προάγει ὑμᾶς εἰς τὴν Γαλιλαίαν) is actually attributed to Jesus, with the young man reporting as indirect discourse the master's words to his disciples at the Last Supper: "but after I have risen from the dead, I will go before you to Galilee [προάξω ὑμᾶς εἰς τὴν Γαλιλαίαν]" (14:28). Similarly, the young man's assertion in 16:6 that Jesus "has risen" (ἠγέρθη) recalls "after I have risen [ἐγερθῆναί με]" in 14:28.

Understanding the authority for the young man's claim that Jesus has risen is more important than identifying who or what this young man is, though the two issues interrelate since the only other character in Mark to be identified as "a young man" (νεανίσκος) was presumably present at the Last Supper, when Jesus uttered the words the young man quotes in 16:7. Mark singles out among the disciples who fled the scene of Jesus's arrest on that night a "certain young man who followed him" (νεανίσκος τις συνηκολούθει αὐτῷ, 14:51). His citation of Jesus's words from that scene might suggest that the young man from chapter 16 is this same anonymous disciple, who apparently had followed Jesus from the dinner with his fellow students to nearby Gethsemane, where Jesus was apprehended and whence his disciples fled. Mark describes him as "wrapped [περιβεβλημένος] in a cloak," which he leaves in his would-be captors' hands as he flees in shame (14:51–52). Mark 16:5 describes the young man's attire with the same participle: he is "wrapped [περιβεβλημένον] in a white garment." The reports of a νεανίσκος in 14:52 and 16:5 constitute the only occasions in Mark where the Greek verb περιβάλλω appears, and it appears in the same grammatical form in each.

Given these connections, the two young men are likely the same character.³ In chapter 16, he has put clothes back on, come to the site of Jesus's burial, found the tomb empty, and inferred from that discovery, in the light of Jesus's words at the Last Supper, that his master has risen from the dead, as he said he would. While this interpretation of Mark's closing verses may seem anticlimactic, it turns out to be theologically suggestive. The empty tomb prompts or complements the young man's decision to recall the night of Jesus's violent apprehension from a perspective of faith in resurrection, as opposed to the fear of arrest and execution that characterized his earlier flight.⁴

The anonymous young man may have come to Jesus's tomb to commemorate Jesus's death or honor Jesus's body, as the Marys and Salome do. However, since he so readily infers resurrection from Jesus's empty grave and from his prophecy that he would rise, the young man has more likely arrived to search for evidence of Jesus's restoration. On this reading, he would be retrospectively impressed by how accurately Jesus had predicted his own imminent demise (14:24–25), his followers' desertion (14:26–27), and perhaps even Peter's denial (14:29–31). (Note that the young man refuses Peter the appellation "disciple" in 16:7.) He therefore seeks to learn whether Jesus's accompanying prediction of resurrection (14:28) has been fulfilled as well.⁵ Whether he came searching for evidence, or, like the two Marys and Salome, happened upon it while on a

---

3. Sometimes in dialogue with the so-called Secret Gospel of Mark, which I take to be a forgery, earlier interpreters occasionally elaborate this interpretive suggestion into speculative meditations on the young man's symbolic or even mystical import (see especially Scroggs and Groff, "Baptism in Mark"). See also Albert Vanhoye, "La fuite du jeune homme nu (Mc 14:51–52)," *Bib* 52 (1971): 401–6, esp. 405–6 (on his nudity). For relevant critique, see Francis Neirynck, "La fuite du jeune homme en Mc 14:51–52," *ETL* 55 (1979): 43–66. Vanhoye's study informs my own symbolic interpretation of the young man's clothing below. However, the connections between his two appearances are primarily explicable with reference to how he knows what he says.

On the Secret Gospel of Mark as a forgery, see Peter Jeffery, *The Secret Gospel of Mark Unveiled: Imagined Rituals of Sex, Death, and Madness in a Biblical Forgery* (New Haven: Yale University Press, 2007).

4. The interpretation I propose is similar to but more detailed than that offered by the narratological study of Bas M. F. Van Iersel, "Failed Followers in Mark: Mark 13:12 as a Key for the Identification of the Intended Readers," *CBQ* 58 (1996): 261–62.

5. Gundry notes that Mark stresses Jesus's predictive powers, especially as regards his own death, and he observes the climactic emphasis this theme receives in 16:7 (*Mark*, 993). This coheres with my interpretive suggestion. However, *pace* Gundry,

different mission altogether, he invites these women to draw the same faithful inference from the same data he had confronted: the empty tomb ("behold the place where they laid him"; 16:6) and Jesus's prophecies ("just as he said to you"; 16:7).

Only at this point does it become necessary to address the competing interpretive theory that this young man is an angel. Despite its broad acceptance in scholarship today, including by the two most recent full-scale commentaries in English (Marcus's and Collins's), scholars who adopt this reading seem to be influenced by the finalizations of Mark's *commentarii* the other New Testament gospels provide. By presenting the young man as an angel (or angels), these gospels introduce decisive heavenly testimony about Jesus's resurrection that Mark's more equivocal description of the scene neglects to provide.

The only evidence from Mark's Gospel that might not support equating the young man from 14:51–52 with the one from chapter 16, and would thus invite the alternative interpretation, is the absence of the definite article from 16:5. Potentially, it is not the young man from chapter 14 but "a(nother) young man" who surfaces later in the story. Adela Yarbro Collins places much weight on this possibility in her argument that the young man from chapter 16 is an angel.[6] However, there is a narratological reason for the Greek anaphoric article's absence that has nothing to do with distinguishing 16:5's young man from the character earlier identified with that moniker: Mark is presenting the young man from the women's perspective.

Mark introduces chapter 16 with the women's anxiety about opening the tomb (16:1–3), notes their discovery that the stone has already been rolled away (16:4), and then reports that these women "saw a young man [εἶδον νεανίσκον] sitting toward the right, wrapped in a white garment" (16:5a). Mark goes on to recount their subjective response to the sight ("they were astonished"; 16:5b) and finally reports their terrified flight and silence upon hearing this young man's words (16:8). In narratological terms, Mark's final chapter adopts a modified third-person narrative voice, telling the story from the point of view of the two Marys and Salome, even while formally maintaining the grammatical third person. Far from recognizing the young man, these three women are surprised and confused

---

16:7 does not itself confirm Jesus's prophecy. Only a represented appearance of Jesus to the disciples in Galilee could do that.

6. Collins, *Mark*, 795.

by his presence. From their point of view, it is not "the [already familiar] young man" who appears but rather "a [strange] young man." The absence of the anticipated anaphoric article may give pause to readers expecting Mark rigidly to adhere to Greek grammatical rules (though even on grammatical grounds, the article's anticipation is questionable),[7] but Mark forecloses any puzzlement its absence might occasion by using language to describe this young man in 16:5 that recalls his description in 14:51–52. The evangelist connects the two scenes clearly enough that the reader can recognize the latter young man as the former (many in fact do just that), even while maintaining for aesthetic purposes the modified third-person narrative voice. The anticipated anaphoric article would disrupt this narrative strategy by suddenly shifting to something approximating an omniscient point of view.

Other arguments that the young man from chapter 16 is not the figure from chapter 14 but instead an angel may be dealt with summarily. Commentators sometimes cite the women's terror as evidence that they see an angel, for fear and subsequent reassurance are conventional features of angelophanies in ancient Jewish literature (16:6).[8] However, the women's trepidation begins before they see the young man. Their fearful hesitation to be too closely identified with Jesus reveals itself in the distance they keep from him when he is crucified (15:40–41). This becomes all the more notable if "Mary the mother of James and of Joses" is Jesus's mother (see 6:3), who would then refuse to stand by her own son in his final moments, abandoning him to the scorn of mocking bystanders (15:29–32, 35–36).[9]

---

7. Robertson argues that expectation of the definite article's presence to signal a noun's definiteness constitutes a misunderstanding of Greek. "The article is not the only means of showing that a word is definite.... The word may be either definite or indefinite when the article is absent. The context and history of the phrase in question must decide.... If the word is indefinite ... no article, of course, occurs. But the article is absent in a good many definite phrases as well." Robertson therefore refuses to speak of the article's expectation or omission, preferring the more neutral term "absence." See Archibald T. Robertson, *A Grammar of the Greek New Testament in the Light of Historical Research* (New York: Hodder & Stoughton, 1914), 790–91.

8. Collins, *Mark*, 795–96; Marcus, *Mark 8–16*, 1080; R. T. France, *The Gospel of Mark: A Commentary on the Greek Text*, NIGTC (Grand Rapids: Eerdmans, 2002), 680.

9. Gundry's discussion of the possibility that Mary here is Jesus's mother is persuasive (*Mark*, 977). If one accepts John's dependence on Mark, then the reluctance of Jesus's mother to approach Jesus as he dies is so remarkable as to prompt reme-

The same fear may inform the women's decision to visit Jesus's tomb "early in the morning … the sun just having risen," which allows them to avoid being observed (16:2). In the context of their continuing trepidation in the wake of their master's arrest and execution, the young man's unexpected appearance at Jesus's tomb would more than justify these disciples' terrified shock, which in turn gives rise to his encouraging words (16:5–6). None of this indicates the young man is an angel.

A similar critique may be leveled at the claim that the young man's white clothes make him an angel, since "the motif of white or shining clothing typically characterizes angels and other heavenly beings," with Acts 1:10–11 regularly cited as a parallel.[10] In Mark, the man's clothing may be otherwise accounted for as linking him with the young man from 14:51–52, as noted above. It may also be appropriate to understand his new clothing and demeanor as symbolizing his change in attitude, from agitated fear ("leaving his cloak behind, he fled naked"; 14:52) to established faith ("he was sitting … dressed in a white garment"; 16:5).[11]

The least persuasive interpretive evidence in support of commentators' identification of the young man as an angel is that "in Second Temple Jewish texts it was a widespread convention to speak of angels as 'men' or

---

diation in the Fourth Gospel (19:25–27). Raymond E. Brown views John 19:25–27 as related to traditions of women's attendance at Jesus's execution. See Brown, *The Death of the Messiah: From Gethsemane to the Grave; A Commentary on the Passion Narratives in the Four Gospels*, ABRL (New York: Doubleday, 1994), 2:1014–19. He argues that the new relationship John signals "involves the issue of how Jesus's natural family was related to a family created by discipleship." Thus the episode responds to traditions such as Mark 3:31–35, which involve Jesus distancing himself from his mother in favor of his disciples (Brown, *Death of the Messiah*, 2:1024–25). These traditions are thematized in the distance between Jesus and his mother in Mark 15:40–41. In 15:40, Jesus's mother is not even identified as his parent, but rather as Jesus's siblings' mother (cf. 6:3), and then in 15:41 as just one of several women who followed and provided for Jesus in Galilee. The physical distance between the two when Jesus dies concretizes this interpersonal distance. His mother does not approach him on the cross, even though others do (see 15:35–36). John 19:25–27, in contrast to this thematic development, "brings the natural family (Jesus's mother) into the relationship of discipleship by making her the mother of the beloved disciple who takes her into his own realm of discipleship" (Brown, *Death of the Messiah*, 2:1025).

10. Collins, *Mark*, 795; cf. Marcus, *Mark 8–16*, 1080; France, *Gospel of Mark*, 678–79.

11. Cf. Vanhoye, "La fuite du jeune homme," 404–6.

'young men.'"[12] In all of the examples scholars cite to support interpreting Mark's young man as an angel, such language only appears in contexts explicitly marked in other ways as angelophanies or supernatural divine interventions (e.g., Gen 18–19; Judg 13:3–6; 2 Macc 3:24–30; 10:29–31; 11:8–14; Josephus, *A.J.* 5.277–279). No text that I know understands language analogous to Mark's "a young man dressed in a white garment" as itself sufficient to identify an angelic appearance, with the possible exception of Acts 1:10–11's mention of "two men ... in white raiment" attending Jesus's ascension. These are undeniably angels, despite not being explicitly identified as such in the episode.

Yet here the exception proves the rule. Acts thematizes Jesus's literal movement between earth and heaven, so that attending angels are expected. More significantly, Luke's first volume mentions what appears to be the same two men in its empty-tomb account (Luke 24:4–5) and identifies them as angels there (see 24:23). Even if the identification of the two men as angels remains formally implicit in Acts 1:10–11, contextual considerations require that identification in ways that Mark 16's treatment of the young man does not. In fact, earlier Markan material (14:51–52) points in the same way to the young man's status as a human being, as earlier Lukan material (Luke 24:4, 23) points to the men's status in Acts as angels.

The problem with understanding the young man as an angel in Mark is not simply formal. Mark's narrative neither needs nor, arguably, has imaginative space for an angel at this point. This becomes apparent when one observes that scholars insisting the young man is an angel often assign him the conventional role of interpreting angel, that is, a heavenly being who explains a vision or some sort of future prophecy in an apocalyptic account.[13] As Eugene Boring notes in his discussion of Mark's young man, "events in themselves are mute, and require an interpreting word. The 'interpreting angel' frequently plays this role as a standard feature of apocalyptic literature."[14]

Mute seems a laconic way to characterize the events angels explain in apocalyptic texts such as Daniel or Revelation, which abound in angelic

---

12. Collins, *Mark*, 795.
13. Collins, *Mark*, 796; cf. Marcus, *Mark 8–16*, 1080.
14. M. Eugene Boring, *Mark: A Commentary*, NTL (Louisville: Westminster John Knox, 2006), 444.

interpreters and are cited as parallels.[15] In these books, angels interpret images and occurrences that are transcendently bizarre or hopelessly obscure absent divine instruction—because their symbolism is extravagant, or because they have not yet happened. Jesus's empty tomb is the opposite. His prophecies of his death and resurrection in 14:22–28, not to mention the relevant prophecies about the Son of Man throughout Mark's Gospel (esp. 8:31; 9:31; 10:33–34), have already explained it. The young man acknowledges as much by quoting Jesus when he offers an explanation. To compare the empty tomb to an apocalyptic mystery requiring angelic interpretation misses Mark's point. The empty tomb may be ambiguous, but its meaning is not mysterious, and it is far from mute, in Boring's formulation. In the context of Mark's story, it cries out for interpretation as evidence of Jesus's resurrection. To offer such an interpretation requires no supernatural instruction; it requires only an inferential imagination and, above all, faith.

The other Synoptic evangelists turn the young man into an angel (or angels) as part of their revisionary impulse to finalize Mark's open-ended *commentarii* and answer the questions Jesus's empty tomb poses, to which the Markan young man offers not a definitive resolution but instead a faithful response. What better way to make clear that Jesus's empty tomb proves that God raised him from the dead than by having one angel (Matthew) or more (Luke) point to it and say so? The only superior proof would be an appearance of the risen Christ himself—which the later evangelists likewise provide.

In Mark the story of Jesus's resurrection works differently: the young man, earlier debilitated by fear, now summons the faith required to trust in Jesus's prophecies about resurrection. The female disciples in this scene reject his invitation to join in belief that Jesus rose on the basis of the empty tomb (including the large stone door rolled away) and Jesus's earlier prophecies, and they will not participate in his evangelistic mission. After all, they had come to the tomb to anoint Jesus's dead body, not to encounter signs of their master having risen. Symbolically speaking, they aim to ameliorate death and decay (with incense), rather than to confirm and celebrate its defeat. They cannot bring themselves to view Jesus's tomb as a site of salvation rather than of desolation. Thus, when they resist the young man's call to proclamation and run away in dreadful silence

---

15. E.g., Collins, *Mark*, 796.

(ἐξελθοῦσαι ἔφυγον, 16:8), they ironically emulate his earlier terrified flight from the scene of Jesus's arrest (ἔφυγεν, 14:52) rather than joining him in faithful confession of Jesus's restoration.[16] The young man has come to believe Jesus rose by interpreting the empty tomb against the backdrop of Jesus's prophecies of resurrection. The women, who had "been following Jesus" for some time (15:41), presumably have access to much of the same evidence but will not make that leap of faith.[17]

However, their skepticism is warranted. The evidence of resurrection Mark offers (the empty tomb, the stone rolled back, and Jesus's predictions of his restoration to life) may imply something other than that Jesus rose from the dead. Were any man to predict his death and resurrection—even an exorcist, healer, and miracle worker such as Jesus—and then died and been buried, it would take more than a report of his tomb's emptiness to

---

16. See Vanhoye, "La fuite du jeune homme," 404–5.

17. I remain unconvinced by readings interpreting the behavior of Jesus's followers in 16:8 positively, e.g., the important article of Elizabeth Struthers Malbon: "Fallible Followers: Women and Men in the Gospel of Mark," *Semeia* 28 (1983): 29–48, esp. 44–45. Jesus's skeptical female disciples follow basically the same pattern as his male ones, which I trace in chapter 4: though they observe his crucifixion from a distance, they still fail to accompany the master to death and, in the end, flee the scene of his resurrection in fear.

However, Mark does not present the kind of skepticism Jesus's female disciples display as straightforwardly negative. Moreover, in other Markan passages, female characters represent faith in opposition to doubt, reversing the gendered dichotomy of Mark 16. Consider the mother of the demon-possessed daughter (7:24–30), whose faith in Jesus's power persists even after Jesus's rebuke (7:27–28). Her trust contrasts with the skepticism of the demon-possessed lad's father in 9:14–29, who persists in doubting Jesus's power after hearing an analogous rebuke (9:22–24). As a complement, the hemorrhaging woman's faith (5:34) stands in contrast to Jairus's implicit doubt in the story framing her healing (cf. 5:35). While my study ultimately comes to focus on James, John, and Peter as personally individuated representatives of Jesus's "disciples," the tensions between faith and doubt that Mark explores surface in other episodes as well, including those featuring female characters.

Though they perhaps more often represent faith than doubt in this interpretive complex, *pace* Malbon, I do not view Mark's "women characters [as] 'good' or 'positive' because they are followers or exemplify followership" ("Fallible Followers," 46). Rather, Mark's female characters play a role in the Second Gospel's critical examination of what followership entails for the Markan disciples of Jesus and for Mark's readers. This examination complicates straightforward moral judgments about following Jesus (ultimately, to death in expectation of resurrection; Mark 8:34–9:1) and may imply that in some situations, not following Jesus might be the right option.

compel belief, especially from persons who had observed his death (15:40–41) and burial (15:47). Such a report might be interesting; it might even be provocative. But in the end, it would more readily be explained in other ways than by resurrection, for instance, on the hypothesis that someone, having known Jesus's predictions, removed his body to give the impression that they came true. Only an encounter with the resurrected Jesus himself would constitute probative evidence, rather than merely circumstantial or suggestive evidence, and such encounters are precisely what Mark neglects to offer, even though Jesus-believing writers earlier than Mark (see 1 Cor 15:5–8) and later included them to compel belief in Jesus's resurrection.

Matthew's response to the open-ended conclusion of Mark's *commentarii* suggests that the later evangelist recognized this problem. Matthew recounts the religious leaders and Pilate setting a guard at Jesus's tomb lest his disciples remove the body to sham his resurrection prophecies' fulfillment (27:62–66). After Jesus rises, this evangelist has some of these same leaders bribe the guards to disseminate the story about his disciples' grave robbery anyway (28:11–15). While acknowledging that a proclamation of Jesus's resurrection like Mark's, based on Jesus's prophecies and the empty tomb, will as likely raise questions as resolve them, Matthew thus implies that such inquiries constitute a cynical attempt to deny the truth of Jesus's resurrection.

Not only does Matthew undermine the questions' legitimacy by introducing the story of the guards disseminating rumors that Jesus's body was stolen, but it also confirms that Jesus did rise from the dead.[18]

---

18. Susan E. Schaeffer argues that Matthew introduces the story of the guards into Mark's narrative framework to ensure it provides sound evidence of Jesus's resurrection. See Schaeffer, "The Guard at the Tomb (*Gos. Pet.* 8:28–11:49 and Matt 27:62–66; 28:2–4, 11–16): A Case of Intertextuality?," in *Society of Biblical Literature 1991 Seminar Papers*, SBLSP 30 (Atlanta: Scholars Press, 1991), 499–507. The Gospel of Peter represents a later point on the same interpretive trajectory, revising the Matthean story to make its verification of Jesus's resurrection even tighter.

Ulrich Luz argues that Matthew invented the story of the guards to counter "the rumor that Jesus's body had been stolen by his disciples that circulated among many Jews in his day," citing 28:15 and Justin, *Dial.* 108.2, as support. See Luz, *Matthew 21–28: A Commentary*, trans. James E. Crouch, Hermeneia (Minneapolis: Fortress, 2005), 586. However, it is questionable whether such a rumor circulated before Matthew wrote. Certainly, the citation from Justin constitutes inadequate proof, for it shows literary dependency on the Matthean reference to the rumor itself. Compare Justin, *Dial.* 108.2 and Matt 27:64; 28:13; see Édouard Massaux, *The Apologists and the*

In its finalization of Mark, Matthew transforms the young man announcing Jesus's resurrection into an authoritative angel who descends from heaven like lightning and with earth-quaking power rolls back the stone from the tomb in the Marys' presence (28:1–3).[19] Another change Matt 28:5–7 makes to Mark 16:6–7 clinches the transformation of the Markan young man who infers that Jesus rose from the dead into an angel from heaven authoritatively testifying to it. In Mark, the man concludes his statement to Salome and the Marys with a reference to the master's resurrection prophecy: "just as he told you" (καθὼς εἶπεν ὑμῖν, 16:7; cf. 14:28). In Matthew, on the contrary, the angel's closing words emphasize his own testimony's authority: "Behold, I have told you" (ἰδοὺ εἶπον ὑμῖν, 28:7). Accordingly, just a few verses later, Matthew confirms the angel's testimony by depicting the risen Christ appearing in Galilee, where he commissions his disciples (28:16–20). These emendations obviate the possibility that Mark's *commentarii* leave open, namely, that Jesus's tomb was empty not because Jesus rose but for some other reason—perhaps because someone had removed his corpse.

Luke's transformation of Mark's human figure into angelic ones constitutes a significant agreement with Matthew against Mark. However, it is not implausible that they would independently revise Mark to turn this evangelist's ambiguous messenger into one or, in the case of Luke, two messengers authorized by heaven. Perhaps they each thought that Mark's young man was an authoritative angelic witness and imagined themselves not so much altering as clarifying Mark on that point. Alternatively, the agreement between Matthew and Luke against Mark may amount to evidence for a theory of Markan priority independent of Q, such as the Farrer hypothesis. Matthew may revise Mark by transforming the young man into an authoritative angelic witness of Jesus's resurrection, a revisionary

---

Didache, vol. 3 of *The Influence of the Gospel of Saint Matthew on Christian Literature before Saint Irenaeus*, ed. Arthur J. Bellinzoni, trans. Norman J. Belval and Suzanne Hecht, NGS 5.3 (Leuven: Peeters, 1993), 76–77. Matthew's desire to finalize the equivocal treatment of resurrection Mark's *commentarii* offer sufficiently accounts for the invention and inclusion of the story.

19. Schaeffer notes the oddity of Matthew's decision to have the angels remove the stone only to reveal that the tomb is empty, in contrast to the Gospel of Peter's account, where the angels open the tomb to let Christ out ("Guard at the Tomb," 502–3). Such observations form the basis of her argument regarding an apologetic trajectory running through Matthew and the Gospel of Peter (or, put differently, a trajectory involving increasingly decisive finalization of Mark's open-ended *commentarii*).

tactic consonant with its tendency to resolve the questions about Jesus's empty tomb that Mark's *commentarii* leave open. Luke then expands on Matthew's revision, even while keeping Mark's original in view. It transforms the Markan young man into not one but multiple angels who appear at various points in Luke's account of the risen Jesus, sometimes calling them men, as in Mark (Luke 24:4; Acts 1:10), but also clarifying that they are actually angels (Luke 24:23), as in Matthew.

Since even the author of Matthew's Gospel, the earliest reader of Mark on record, recognized the questions that Mark's empty-tomb account leaves open, some scholars argue that this Markan episode was not meant to guarantee Jesus's resurrection but rather to serve another purpose altogether. Possibilities include distinguishing Jesus from a Greek hero with a cult linked to his grave, or suggesting that Jesus was vindicated from death not by resurrection but by assumption to heaven, as were other divinely favored figures in ancient Mediterranean literature.[20] Such proposals may explain the invention of Jesus's empty tomb in pre-Markan tradition as evidence of a resurrection understood as a translation of his body to heaven.[21] This idea, similar to Romulus's assumption to heaven in Livy's famous account (*Urb. cond.* 1.16), is not altogether incompatible with my

---

20. On the former possibility, see Neill Q. Hamilton, "Resurrection Tradition and the Composition of Mark," *JBL* 84 (1965): 415–21; Helmut Koester, "On Heroes, Tombs, and Early Christianity," in *Flavius Philostratus: Heroikos*, ed. Jennifer K. Berenson Maclean and Ellen Bradshaw Aitken, WGRW 1 (Atlanta: Society of Biblical Literature, 2001), 257–64. On the latter, see Daniel A. Smith, "Revisiting the Empty Tomb: The Post-mortem Vindication of Jesus in Mark and Q," *NovT* 45 (2003): 123–37.

21. Smith understands the two conceptualizations to be distinct and speculates that Mark "used a pre-existing story about the disappearance of Jesus's body from the tomb, and adapted it by adding his characteristic resurrection theology" ("Revisiting the Empty Tomb," 133; see 130–33). This allows Smith to interpret elements of Mark's account against the tradition of heavenly translation, which Mark privileges in his view, even while he acknowledges that not everything Mark includes makes sense in that context. As an example, he argues that Mark's reference to the appearance in Galilee (16:7) should be understood as a heavenly epiphany confirming Jesus's assumption ("Revisiting the Empty Tomb," 130). However, another way of reading Mark 16:7 concludes that the restored Jesus already heads to Galilee (προάγει ὑμᾶς εἰς τὴν Γαλιλαίαν) rather than that he waits in heaven to appear to his disciples there.

Other scholars, too, view heavenly assumption as the appropriate conceptual category for understanding Jesus's resurrection in Mark: e.g., Miller, "Mark's Empty Tomb"; Adela Yarbro Collins, *The Beginning of the Gospel: Probings of Mark in Context* (Minneapolis: Fortress, 1992), 146–48; Collins, *Mark*, 782–94.

interpretation, and the kind of ambiguity Mark features also surfaces in relevant Greco-Roman intertexts.²² Moreover, as argued in this study's introduction, Mark's Gospel is less concerned with defining resurrection precisely than with coming to terms with resurrection's broader corollary, namely, the possibility that one might continue to live, in some personal capacity, even after one has died.

All that having been stipulated, questions remain about the relevancy to Mark's empty-tomb account of Greco-Roman literary traditions depicting divinely favored figures' heavenly translation.²³ A primary motivation for invoking their explanatory potential would seem to be that Jesus's resurrection represents a one-off, rather than a "general collective eschatological moment," with the result that Second Temple Jewish conceptualizations of resurrection are deemed to be marginally relevant.²⁴ However, Jesus's predictions of death and resurrection in Mark usually feature a Danielic background (i.e., the "Son of Man" from Dan 7) and some include explicit quotation of Dan 7 and 12, which thematize resurrection

---

22. E.g., Plutarch, *Rom.* 27 and Livy, *Urb. cond.* 1.16. Miller gestures at the conventionality of such ambiguity in his categorization of "dubious alternative accounts" (Miller, "Mark's Empty Tomb," 773).

23. In addition to the questions discussed in this paragraph, Smith demonstrates that the decisive Markan verb ἠγέρθη, "he has been raised" (16:7), is inconsistent with the kind of assumption narrative to which some features of Mark's empty tomb account might be assimilated ("Revisiting the Empty Tomb," 130). John Granger Cook similarly shows that language normally used to describe heavenly translation is missing from Mark's account. See Cook, *Empty Tomb, Resurrection, Apotheosis*, WUNT 410 (Tübingen: Mohr Siebeck, 2018), 597. In fact, scholars citing assumption traditions as intertextual background often invoke details from other gospels to buttress their relevancy. Miller exemplifies this approach ("Mark's Empty Tomb," 772–74). Some of the most persuasive studies exploring this background explicitly focus on other New Testament accounts of Jesus's resurrection. For instance, Shelly Matthews focuses on Luke 24. See Matthews, "Elijah, Ezekiel, and Romulus: Luke's Flesh and Bones (Luke 24:39) in Light of Ancient Narratives of Ascent, Resurrection, and Apotheosis," in *On Prophets, Warriors, and Kings: Former Prophets through the Eyes of Their Interpreters*, ed. George J. Brooke and Ariel Feldman, BZAW 470 (Berlin: de Gruyter, 2016), 161–82.

24. Miller, "Mark's Empty Tomb," 769–70 n. 19; cf. Matthews, "Elijah, Ezekiel, and Romulus," 167–68. Matthews acknowledges that Greco-Roman sources describing the dead translated into heaven are not necessarily opposed to Jewish sources describing risen bodies ("Elijah, Ezekiel, and Romulus," 170–73). The question becomes one of interpretive emphasis: which intertextual background best informs a reading of the depictions of Jesus's resurrection in Mark and the other gospels.

(e.g., the material encompassing Mark 8:31–9:13, which I will discuss in ch. 3). This suggests that Jesus's resurrection as prophesied and narrated in Mark should be understood in the theological context of Second Temple ideas about collective eschatological resurrection and judgment. In this context, Jesus's solitary resurrection does represent an interpretive problem; however, the solution requires not interpreting Mark's depiction of it in an alternative ideological context, but rather integrating it within the comprehensive story Mark tells.

Within this story, as chapters 3 and 4 will show, Jesus promises his disciples that they will rise from the dead and be vindicated at the rapidly approaching eschatological judgment, provided they follow him to death (see esp. Mark 8:34–9:1). These disciples prominently feature the Twelve, pointing to his community's figurative recapitulation of Israel's twelve tribes. However, they do not believe him and so abandon Jesus to perish alone. Eschatological resurrection admittedly makes little sense in the narrative that develops, and so Mark leaves open the possibility that even Jesus's does not occur; his community's eschatological fate remains even less certain. Jesus's empty tomb in Mark may thus represent an eschatological failure. At best, it constitutes something of a false start that will be remediated in an eschatological future lying beyond the bounds of Mark's narrative world. In this future, the surviving community of faithless disciples Mark features might finally follow Jesus's exhortation to martyrdom and be raised from the dead. The evangelist outlines this possibility in Mark 13, as I will explore in chapter 3.

The Markan Jesus's empty tomb presents problems too sweeping to resolve with reference to a straightforward claim that Jesus indeed transcended death, only not through resurrection per se but rather through the kind of heavenly assumption depicted by Plutarch, Livy, and other Greco-Roman writers, or even in analogous biblical and later Jewish writings (e.g., 2 Kgs 2:11–12 on Elijah's assumption or Philo, *Mos.* 2.288, 291, on Moses's). Mark's sustained equivocation regarding Jesus's resurrection does not permit this interpretive possibility's elimination. In fact, discerning the questions about Jesus's resurrection that Mark raises involves recognizing that Jesus's restoration to life fails to fit neatly within the context of collective eschatological judgment that Mark invokes to explain it. One should come to terms with this problem by exploring both how Mark narrates Jesus's abandonment by his disciples to face execution, burial, and (perhaps) resurrection alone, and also how the Second Gospel thematizes various motifs relevant to death and resurrection throughout (including caverns and escape from them). In so doing it becomes apparent that Mark's empty-tomb account does engage with Greco-Roman literary traditions. A different intertextual context emerges into significance, however, which I will explore in my final chapter.

The Markan empty tomb's potential (or lack thereof) to guarantee Jesus's resurrection does not exhaust its significance, and features of the account in which it figures may have emerged in a conceptual context to which Mark's questions about Jesus's resurrection are not especially relevant. In this pre-Markan context, as well as in later gospels' elaborations of Jesus's resurrection, traditions about heavenly assumption may prove influential. However, with respect to Mark itself, their influence remains marginal. They do not resolve the problem that Mark's empty-tomb account offers only circumstantial and ambiguous evidence of Jesus's restoration to life.

This problem seems to have been recognized by Matthew, who finalizes the Markan *commentarii* in such a way as to resolve the questions Mark's empty-tomb account bequeaths to readers looking to it for definitive evidence of resurrection. Indeed, Matthew's revisionary tactics include introduction of a note about dead saints in Jerusalem emerging from their tombs when Jesus exits his (Matt 27:52–53). This insists, in response to Mark's equivocations, not only that Jesus does rise, but that he rises in the context of collective resurrection. As I will show, in every treatment of restoration to life Mark's Gospel includes, questions surface about what actually has happened and, on occasion, about the occurrence's relationship to eschatological resurrection. Such ambiguity characterizes Mark's development of the resurrection theme.

Figurative versus Literal Resurrections 1: Mark 5

Mark alone of the New Testament gospels contains no indubitable resurrections. In addition to numerous accounts of the risen Christ's appearances to his followers, Luke includes the story of Jesus raising the widow's son at Nain (Luke 7:11–17), John the story of Jesus raising Lazarus (John 11), and Matthew the reference to resurrected holy people emerging from their tombs en masse (Matt 27:52–53). Mark has none of this and, as I will show, carefully narrates those resurrection traditions it does share with the other gospels in such a way as to invite readers to question whether they are stories of resurrection after all, and not instead accounts of lesser forms of physical restoration. The story of Jairus's daughter (Mark 5:21–24a, 35–43;

cf. Matt 9:18–19, 23–26; Luke 8:41–42a, 49–56), which I will discuss in detail below, is the clearest though not the only such example.

Mark's neglect to authorize Jesus's or any other restoration to life constitutes the obverse side of a positive theological claim about one way in which resurrection does function within the Second Gospel. Even if the evangelist will not guarantee that Jesus, or even God, possesses ultimate power over death itself, Mark will employ resurrection as a symbol of the liberation God, through Jesus, offers from the devastating power of evil—in particular, from the power of demons and disease to isolate, immobilize, and waste people. For Mark, Jesus's ministry of exorcism and healing promises much the same deliverance as do his prophecies of the Son of Man's death and resurrection, a correlation I explore in chapter 5. Within the sphere of Jesus's ministry to the living, this promise is fulfilled, but as soon as death enters the picture, questions arise about the extent of the power Jesus exercises over it. These questions come into focus in Mark 5, which contains two episodes of miraculous healing, both of which Mark figures as resurrections (the exorcism of the Gerasene and the hemorrhaging woman's healing), and one actual though ambiguous resurrection (the restoration of Jairus's daughter). In this chapter and elsewhere, resurrection symbolizes spiritual, physical, and social restoration, but Mark stops short of presenting it as something that literally happens.[25]

Mark 5:1–20: Legion

Figurative resurrection is thematically central to the episode involving Legion in chapter 5. A man possessed by demons dwells in isolation

---

25. Scholars sometimes employ the distinction between literal and figurative resurrection in dubious ways to define resurrection narrowly as a somatic concept, instead of understanding it as a broader metaphor that ancient authors employed for various purposes depending on their rhetorical needs—including but not limited to conceptualizing the restoration of life to one who has died (Tappenden, *Resurrection in Paul*, 8–13, 145–46, and passim). I use the terms *literal* and *figurative/symbolic* differently, in their literary-critical sense, to describe and interpret how resurrection is thematized in a work of imaginative literature. The scope of my inquiry is narrow and one to which these terms are appropriate, even necessary. In a sense, Mark's narrative itself inscribes the distinction, by employing resurrection as an obvious metaphor and by neglecting to guarantee the restoration to life of anyone who dies within its pages.

among tombs (5:2–3), chained with corpses, howling and abusing himself (5:4–5). In the symbolic economy the story deploys, Jesus's liberation of the man from oppressive demons constitutes a symbolic resurrection, restoring the man from the realm of death to health and his community.[26]

It is possible to contextualize the story's resurrection symbolism more precisely. Textual problems obscure the exorcism's precise geographical location (5:1), but it takes place somewhere within the Decapolis (see 5:20), a collection of Hellenistic cities in Israel's Transjordan territory.[27] Thus swineherding—hardly a legitimate Jewish practice—features prominently (5:11–13), and the demons are known as λεγιών or "Legion," a Latin loanword referring to a division of several thousand Roman soldiers. The gentile setting leads J. Duncan M. Derrett to interpret the possessed man's activity at the tombs against the backdrop of pagan mourning practices condemned throughout the Hebrew Bible (e.g., Jer 41:4–7; 48:37–39; cf. Isa 65:1–4, which assimilates Israel to pagan nations). His shrieking, self-wounding, and tomb dwelling caricature gentile mourning rituals gone awry.[28] On this reading, Mark's narrative may imply that a horde of unclean spirits has taken advantage of a pagan mourner's vulnerable condition to transform his temporary state of grief into a permanent state of corruption and alienation, both from other people and from God. From a different angle, as the strange detail of his repetitive autolapidation suggests (see 5:5), the life of the possessed man has been reduced to an extended execution by stoning.[29] Always keening and perpetually killing himself, he is all but literally cut off from life and the community of the living. This includes alienation from himself, as the slippage between singular and plural first-person grammatical constructions in 5:9 suggests. Thus the possessed man

---

26. For the possessed man's situation as a living death, see Holly Joan Toensing, "'Living among the Tombs': Society, Mental Illness, and Self-Destruction in Mark 5:1–20," in *This Abled Body: Rethinking Disabilities in Biblical Studies*, ed. Hector Avalos, Sarah J. Melcher, and Jeremy Schipper, SemeiaSt 55 (Atlanta: Society of Biblical Literature, 2007), 137; Jean Starobinski, "Essay in Literary Analysis: Mark 5:1–20," *ER* 23 (1971): 391–92, 397.

27. Marcus, *Mark 1–8*, 341–42.

28. J. Duncan M. Derrett, "Spirit-Possession and the Gerasene Demoniac," *Man* 14 (1979): 287.

29. See René Girard, "Generative Violence and the Extinction of the Social Order," trans. Thomas Wieser, *Salmagundi* 63–64 (1984): 209–10. Girard connects the demon-possessed man's self-stoning with the pigs' later expulsion from a high cliff, another narrative gesture at a ritualistic form of public execution ("Generative Violence," 215–16).

finds a home only among entombed corpses, experiencing a social death, a living demise among the dead.

Mark's depiction of his torment also calls to mind contemporary ancient Mediterranean descriptions of shades suffering in the underworld and associated chthonic monsters. In *Aen.* 6, for instance, Virgil writes of a fortress surrounded by the fiery river Phlegethon and guarded by the fury Tisiphone, from which Aeneas hears the voices of those who experience torture on account of having died with unexpiated sins (see 6.565–572): "groans and fierce beatings sound, / then the rattling of iron and dragged chains" (*gemitus et saeua sonare / uerbera, tum stridor ferri tractaeque catenae*, 6.557–558).[30] Analogous depictions of the underworld appear in Jewish literature (e.g., 2 En. 10). Nicholas Elder sees in Mark's image of the possessed man cutting himself with stones in the tombs an allusion to 1 En. 10.1–6, which describes the fallen angel Azaz'el bound and thrown into a deep hole in the desert to be blanketed by sharp rocks as he awaits the fire of eschatological judgment.[31] Extensive similarities between Greco-Roman traditions about postmortem punishment and those found in the Enochic material may point to direct literary influence, or to the Greco-Roman and Jewish traditions' common reliance on earlier Mesopotamian religious ideas and myths.[32]

There is no need to choose between one or the other as lying in the background of Mark's depiction of the possessed man in chapter 5. However, since the dominant spiritual power in the gentile territory where this exorcism takes place self-identifies with a Latin moniker, Greco-Roman conceptions of death and chthonic monsters may occupy a privileged position in the intertextual matrix.[33] I will explore this interpretive possibility

---

30. Translating R. A. B. Mynors, ed., *P. Vergili Maronis opera*, OCT (Oxford: Oxford University Press, 1969).

31. Nicholas A. Elder, "Of Porcine and Polluted Spirits: Reading the Gerasene Demoniac (Mark 5:1–20) with the Book of Watchers (*1 Enoch* 1–36)," *CBQ* 78 (2016): 441–42.

32. For a starting point, see Thomas F. Glasson, *Greek Influence in Jewish Eschatology; with Special Reference to the Apocalypses and Pseudepigraphs*, BM 1 (London: SPCK, 1961). For a more nuanced, even skeptical view of such connections, see Ekaterina Matusova, "The Post-mortem Divisions of the Dead in 1 Enoch 22:1–13," in *Evil and Death: Conceptions of the Human in Biblical, Early Jewish, Greco-Roman and Egyptian Literature*, ed. Beate Ego and Ulrike Mittmann, DCLS 18 (Berlin: de Gruyter, 2015), 149–77.

33. This might be confirmed by the fact that pigs were conventionally sacrificed to

further in chapter 5, but even at this point one can conclude—regardless of whether one understands the story's imagery against the backdrop of mourning rituals, of dying itself, of postmortem torment, or of all three—that Jesus's restoration of the man to his right mind and to the community of the living constitutes a symbolic resurrection.[34]

It is not merely the man's personal transition from the abode of the dead (5:3) to the sphere of the living (5:15, 19–20) that marks his exorcism as a resurrection. It is also the fact that the evangelist links this rehabilitation to the restoration of Israel, and in particular to the defeat of Israel's enemies, an expectation closely tied up with eschatological resurrection in ancient Jewish literature (e.g., Dan 12:1–3; 2 Bar. 30, 82).[35] Since the demonic horde identifies itself as λεγιών (5:9), a Latin military term (*legio*) transliterated into Greek and referring to a unit of the Roman army, Legion's possession of the man may symbolize Rome's demonically inspired military and political domination of Israel.[36] This possibility finds

---

chthonic divinities in the Greco-Roman world. See Peter Bolt, *Jesus's Defeat of Death: Persuading Mark's Early Readers*, SNTSMS 125 (Cambridge: Cambridge University Press, 2003), 152–53. Ironically, Jesus's destruction of them amounts to a sacrifice that destroys rather than placates dangerous divine beings.

34. See Mark McVann, "Destroying Death: Jesus in Mark and Joseph in 'The Sin Eater,'" in *The Daemonic Imagination: Biblical Text and Secular Story*, ed. Robert Detweiler and William G. Doty, AARSR 60 (Atlanta: Scholars Press, 1990), 125–28; Bolt, *Jesus's Defeat of Death*, 153; J. Duncan M. Derrett, "Legend and Event: The Gerasene Demoniac: An Inquest into History and Liturgical Projection," in *Midrash, Haggadah, and the Character of the Community*, vol. 3 of *Studies in the New Testament* (Leiden: Brill, 1982), 52.

35. See Wright's discussion of the relationship between the two eschatological expectations in the Bible and postbiblical Judaism: N. T. Wright, *The Resurrection of the Son of God*, COQG 3 (Minneapolis: Fortress, 2003), 108–40.

36. For political readings of the passage, see Ched Myers, *Binding the Strong Man: A Political Reading of Mark's Story of Jesus* (Maryknoll, NY: Orbis, 1988), 190–94; Warren Carter, "Cross-Gendered Romans and Mark's Jesus: Legion Enters the Pigs (Mark 5:1–20)," *JBL* 134 (2015): 139–55; and Joshua Garroway, "The Invasion of a Mustard Seed: A Reading of Mark 5.1–20," *JSNT* 32 (2009): 57–75. For discussion of the meaning and connotations of the transliterated Latin term, see Garroway, "Invasion of a Mustard Seed," 60–63.

Christopher B. Zeichmann resists such readings. See Zeichmann, *The Roman Army and the New Testament* (Lanham, MD: Rowman & Littlefield, 2018), 50–58. Zeichmann acknowledges that *legion* was always used with reference to Roman soldiers in Mark's compositional context (*Roman Army*, 55). However, he finds significant the notion that the Decapolis did not hold as prominently anti-Roman senti-

confirmation in the demonic horde's concern that Jesus not drive it from its territory (5:10), whose announcement prompts Jesus to allow the expelled demons to possess a nearby herd of swine. When these pigs rush down a cliff and drown in the sea (5:13), Legion's destruction symbolically forecasts God's eschatological defeat of Israel's current national enemy, Rome, in imagery recalling his defeat of Israel's prototypical enemy, Egypt, whose army was similarly drowned in the Red Sea (see Exod 14:26–15:21).[37]

Mark secondarily associates the episode's figurative resurrection and vanquishment of Israel's foreign enemy with the nation's purification from corrupting pagan influence—a related eschatological expectation in ancient Hebrew literature (e.g., Isa 66:10–17). The episode alludes to Isa 65:4 in particular, for the two by-products of the demons' defeat in Mark 5 (Jesus's removal of the man from corrupt tombs and his elimination of pork from the Gerasenes' diet) correspond to Isaiah's condemnatory assimilation of Israel to its pagan neighbors' unclean cultural practices:[38] "This disobedient and contradictory people …, in tombs [μνήμασιν] and in caves they lie

---

ments as did other parts of Judea (*Roman Army*, 54), that the inhabitants in the story do not celebrate the demonic legion's destruction (*Roman Army*, 53), and that the story's numbers do not support an allusion to Roman military power (i.e., Mark refers to 2,000 pigs when legions contained 5,000–6,000 soldiers; *Roman Army*, 52). Zeichmann is right not to interpret the story as an allegory of the Roman occupation of Gerasa. But he goes too far in reducing the political significance of the Roman military imagery Mark employs: "The pericope understands Roman legions as the most proximate functionaries of government power, and in turn represent the most proximate functionaries of supernatural power [*sic*]. This reading must be nonpolemical, since the Lord had his own legion of angels, as implied in Mark 8:38 and 13:24–27" (*Roman Army*, 56). However, in the cited passages Mark never uses the term *legion* or other imagery associated with the Roman army, as it does in chapter 5. While the story of Legion cannot be reduced to an anti-Roman allegory of Judea's liberation, neither is its attitude toward Roman military power neutral.

Grasping the story's polemical implications is important to understanding its meaning, but I agree with Zeichmann that the passage compares "the demons to the Roman army, not vice versa" (*Roman Army*, 56). Mark remains primarily interested in representing Jesus's defeat of death's demonic power. To this end, it employs imagery associated with the Roman military in chapter 5, where Legion keeps his victim chained among tombs and Jesus liberates him, and in the scene of his death, which features a centurion overseeing Jesus's execution and involved in his entombment.

37. Marcus lays out the parallels (*Mark 1–8*, 349). Derrett also implicitly touches on this dimension of the episode ("Spirit-Possession," 288–89).

38. Joachim Gnilka, *Das Evangelium nach Markus*, EKKNT 2 (Zürich: Neukirchener Verlag, 1978), 1:203–4.

down for sleep, these who eat the meat of pigs" (Isa 65:2, 4 LXX).[39] In driving out Legion from a region of Israel where Judean culture was no longer as dominant as it had been in the past (somewhere in the Decapolis), Jesus symbolically restores Israel's national and religiocultural integrity, figuratively fulfilling eschatological expectations associated with resurrection.

Mark 5:1–20, which features the possessed man's transition from the realm of the dead to the community of the living, in combination with narrative elements that gesture toward Israel's restoration, assimilates the exorcism of Legion to a common Jewish conception of eschatological resurrection. This involves not only the dead returning to life but also the restoration of Israel's communal integrity through the defeat of its national enemies and the expurgation of foreign cultural contaminants. Understood in this way, the episode recalls elaborations of the resurrection theme in the Hebrew Bible that likewise employ restoration to life as a figure of Israel's salvation and renewal. The famous "dry bones" passage from Ezek 37 (cf. 36:16–38) comes to mind, as does the parodic call for repentance in Hos 6:1–3 (which may be important to Mark's predictions of the Son of Man's resurrection).[40] Much like these biblical passages, Mark 5:1–20 invokes imagery associated with resurrection to symbolize the salvation that God (through Jesus) offers, but without making any explicit claim that this salvation actually encompasses the defeat of death. Resurrection is symbolic rather than literal.

Mark 5:24b–34: The Hemorrhaging Woman

The section following the exorcism of Legion exemplifies Mark's tendency to sandwich one episode within another.[41] Literal resurrection is at issue in the framing narrative, the raising of Jairus's daughter—though only in its concluding portion (5:35–43). In fact, Mark's version of the story's

---

39. Quoting Alfred Rahlfs, ed., *Septuaginta* (Stuttgart: Deutsche Bibelgesellschaft, 2006).

40. Harvey K. McArthur argues that the Hosea passage represents the dominant scriptural source of the tradition that Jesus rose "on the third day," preserved in Paul (1 Cor 15:4) and the other Synoptics. See McArthur, "On the Third Day," *NTS* 18 (1971): 81–86. It is not clear, though, whether Mark's refrain that the Son will rise "after three days" (8:31; 9:31; 10:33–34) is consonant with it.

41. See James R. Edwards, "Markan Sandwiches: The Significance of Interpolations in Markan Narratives," *NovT* 31 (1989): 193–216.

introduction, unlike Matthew's, leads the reader to expect merely the girl's healing (5:21–24a; cf. Matt 9:18–19). Jesus finds his journey to her interrupted by an anonymous woman whose situation resembles that of the possessed man in the previous episode. I discuss Jairus's daughter just below. First, I focus on the intercalated episode (Mark 5:24b–34), wherein Mark pursues the same figurative approach to resurrection he took in the preceding pericope.

The woman's ailment, described by Mark as a "flowing of blood" (5:25), appears to be chronic vaginal bleeding—vaginal because the terminology Mark uses (ῥύσις αἵματος, 5:25; πηγὴ τοῦ αἵματος, 5:29) occurs in LXX legislation dealing with genital discharges (Lev 12:4–7; 15:19–31) and chronic because the woman discerns her healing immediately.[42] The woman's disease involved the perpetual loss of vaginal blood, which represented a gradual diminishment of the forces of life and thus the onset of death in the system of priestly logic to which the episode's description of the woman's disease refers (e.g., Lev 17:11, 14).[43] Numbers 5:1–4,

---

42. On the relationship to Leviticus, see Marla J. Selvidge, "Mark 5:25–34 and Leviticus 15:19–20: A Reaction to Restrictive Purity Regulations," *JBL* 103 (1984): 619 n. 3. Charlotte Fonrobert is rightly critical of Selvidge's interpretation, which imagines that Mark critiques a supposedly misogynistic Jewish purity system, but still acknowledges the terminology's probable allusion to Leviticus. See Fonrobert, "The Woman with a Blood-Flow (Mark 5.24–34) Revisited: Menstrual Laws and Jewish Culture in Christian Feminist Hermeneutics," in *Early Christian Interpretation of the Scriptures of Israel: Investigations and Proposals*, ed. Craig A. Evans and James A. Sanders, JSNTSup 148 (Sheffield: Sheffield Academic, 1997), 129–30, esp. n. 24; see also Matthew Thiessen, *Jesus and the Forces of Death: The Gospels' Portrayal of Ritual Impurity within First-Century Judaism* (Grand Rapids: Baker Academic, 2020), 83.

43. There has been extensive debate regarding the presence of this logic, especially as it relates to issues of purity and impurity. Selvidge and, to a lesser degree, Susan Haber view it as significant to the story's meaning. See Selvidge, "Mark 5:25–34 and Leviticus 15:19–20"; Haber, "A Woman's Touch: Feminist Encounters with the Hemorrhaging Woman in Mark 5.24–34," *JSNT* 26 (2003): 171–92. Fonrobert and Mary Rose D'Angelo see it as insignificant, or even absent. See Fonrobert, "Woman with a Blood-Flow"; D'Angelo, "Gender and Power in the Gospel of Mark: The Daughter of Jairus and the Woman with the Flow of Blood," in *Miracles in Jewish and Christian Antiquity: Imagining Truth*, ed. John C. Cavadini, NDST 3 (Notre Dame: University of Notre Dame Press, 1999), 83–109. Amy-Jill Levine denies that the Matthean version of this story either refers to Leviticus or suggests the woman's bleeding was vaginal. See Levine, "Discharging Responsibility: Matthean Jesus, Biblical Law, and Hemorrhaging Woman," in *A Feminist Companion to Matthew*, ed. Amy-Jill Levine, FCNTECW 1 (Sheffield: Sheffield Academic, 2001), 70–87. However, Matt 9:20–22 diverges from

a biblical text requiring that women and men suffering from abnormal genital discharges be expelled from the community, links the ailment with scale disease and death itself (i.e., corpses) as agents of impurity. As Jacob Milgrom observes, "Israel ... restricted impurity solely to those physical conditions involving the loss of vaginal blood and semen, the forces of life, and to scale disease, which visually manifested the approach of death.... All other bodily issues and excrescences were not tabooed."[44] We cannot know how the Jewish community Mark represents in the second half of chapter 5 would have understood this ideology or enforced related praxis. However, the episode's employment of Levitical terminology suggests the evangelist and perhaps the earliest readers had access to an understanding

---

Mark 5:25–34 in many ways and may remove the echo of Leviticus to obviate the Markan Jesus's implicit abrogation of biblical law (Levine, "Discharging Responsibility," 79). (Also compare Mark 7:18–20 and Matt 15:16–18.)

Thiessen argues that Mark 5 assumes a system of purity such as that found in the Bible (*Jesus and the Forces*, 69–122). Comparative analysis shows that the logic found in Leviticus was more widespread in the Greco-Roman world than scholars have recognized (implicitly responding to Levine's critique in "Discharging Responsibility," 82), making it even more likely Mark's readers would have recognized it. Thomas Kazen observes the underlying presence of this logic but is struck by the fact that Mark does not highlight the legal issues as clearly as it does in analogous episodes (see 1:40–45; 7:1–23) or carry them forward into the story of the raising of Jairus's daughter, which expresses no concern about corpse impurity. See Kazen, "Jesus and the Zavah: Implications for Interpreting Mark," in *Purity, Holiness, and Identity in Judaism and Christianity: Essays in Memory of Susan Haber*, ed. Carl S. Ehrlich, Anders Runesson, and Eileen M. Schuller, WUNT 305 (Tübingen: Mohr Siebeck, 2013), 122–23. Kazen concludes that allusions to Leviticus are relevant only to the source material Mark incorporated ("Jesus and the Zavah," 121). Mark itself highlights faith as the central theme.

Kazen also notes that the faith the woman demonstrates is related to faith in resurrection. The woman "becomes not only an example for Jairus, but also a corrective to the women at the resurrection. The latter fear (16:8…) in spite of the exhortation not to (16:6).… The [woman in ch. 5] provides a pattern for [the Markan audience's] own faith, confirming the identity and power of Jesus for anyone believing in his resurrection" (Kazen, "Jesus and the Zavah," 123). Mark's emphasis on faith in resurrection complements rather than supplants the Levitical ideology expressed elsewhere in the story, provided one understands Mark to be fixated on impurity related to death (to be explained below), a concern also relevant to the Legion episode. (Incidentally, Jesus's denial that Jairus's daughter has died explains Mark's lack of concern regarding corpse impurity in that story.)

44. Jacob Milgrom, *Leviticus 1–16: A New Translation with Introduction and Commentary*, AB 3 (New York: Doubleday, 1991), 767.

of the woman's physical condition as a ritually contaminating loss of life.[45] Mark therefore sets up her healing as a figurative resurrection.

Contradictory evidence survives regarding how men or women experiencing abnormal genital effluxes were treated in the Second Temple period. This suggests that different Jewish communities maintained different practices, and the contradiction can be traced to the Pentateuch.[46] Some, apparently privileging the legislation from Num 5:1–4 discussed above, seem to have required those suffering from leprosy, abnormal genital discharge, or contact with corpses to be expelled from the community lest they contaminate it.[47] Others, perhaps because they observed that Lev 15 specifies relatively simple rituals of purification for those who come into contact with the contagious, were less severe.[48] Charlotte Fonfrobert corrects the anti-Jewish assumptions interpreters sometimes smuggle into the text in the form of claims about how this woman's cultic impurity would have led to her harassment.[49] Nonetheless, Susan Haber is still persuasive in her insistence that, though one cannot assume the hemorrhaging woman was shunned as a result of the ailment, let alone oppressed by misogynistic Jewish purity regulations, the passage does seem to thematize social and religious isolation related to her hemorrhaging.[50]

Her sufferance from persistent abnormal genital discharges would have kept her away from the temple. As Matthew Thiessen suggests, twelve years of even this discrete, though significant, exclusion would help explain her desperation in spending everything she possessed on physicians who might ameliorate her condition (Mark 5:26).[51] Beyond that, the woman's discretion in approaching Jesus and her fear in being identified as having done so (5:27, 33) acknowledge her impurity's social and religious

---

45. Thiessen, *Jesus and the Forces*, 83–85; Haber, "Woman's Touch," 181.

46. Haber, "Woman's Touch," 174–79; see also Kazen, "Jesus and the Zavah," 114–20.

47. Josephus's interpretation of the relevant biblical legislation presumes that such people were excluded from the city (*B.J.* 5.227; *A.J.* 3.261).

48. Rabbinic traditions indicate that those suffering from abnormal genital discharges were excluded from the temple but not from the community at large (m. Kelim 1:8; b. Ta'an. 21b; cf. Lev 15:31–33).

49. Scholars often cite D'Angelo, "Gender and Power," but Fonrobert, "Woman with a Blood-Flow" appeared two years earlier, makes much the same point, and is more precisely formulated.

50. Haber, "Woman's Touch," 191–92 and passim.

51. Thiessen, *Jesus and the Forces*, 88–89.

implications: she may or may not be violating quarantine, but she has no business touching a holy man, as she seems to recognize.[52] The episode's climax comes at the point of this woman's surreptitious contact with Jesus. Instead of being somehow infected by her bloody flow, as Lev 15:25–27 imagines, Jesus senses power pouring forth from himself with the result that "immediately, her flow of blood dried up" (Mark 5:29–30).[53]

At this point, Jesus himself seems to assume that the woman's ailment constitutes a social and religious as well as physical condition, requiring acknowledgment of both her healing and purification. He tells her in 5:34 that "your faith has saved you. Go in peace and be well from your plague." The otherwise superfluous second clause probably refers to Lev 15's regulations, which require a public offering after seven days without genital discharge for a person who has suffered from an abnormal efflux to be declared pure (Lev 15:28–30) and fully reintegrated into the community's social and religious life, including access to the temple.[54]

This episode's association of miraculous healing with purification and social reintegration recalls the restoration of the possessed man in the previous story. Not only was the exorcised man freed from unclean spirits and the unclean abode of corpses to be reintegrated within the community of the living, but a herd of impure animals was destroyed in the process. This connection is especially striking insofar as both stories figure the purifying healing as resurrection. The symbolism is clearer in the first, where the man's exorcism involves liberation from tombs, than in the second, which requires reading the healing against an ancient Israelite conception of genital discharges that viewed them as miniature invasions of death into the realm of the living. Yet Mark underscores the second episode's otherwise subtle resurrection symbolism by intercalating it within the story of Jairus's daughter, which features something approximating a resurrection from the dead. In the story of Legion and of the hemorrhaging woman, resurrection emerges as a potent symbol of Jesus's ability to restore, purify, and return to communal life. In reintegrating into their communities those who have been alienated as a result of demonic domination, impurity, and disease, Jesus confronts various encroachments of powers associated with death into the realm of the living, and he resolves problems of isolation so

---

52. Thiessen, *Jesus and the Forces*, 91; Haber, "Woman's Touch," 182–83.

53. Candida Moss probes the implications of this irony. See Moss, "The Man with the Flow of Power: Porous Bodies in Mark 5:25–34," *JBL* 129 (2010): 507–19.

54. Haber, "Woman's Touch," 184–85.

severe that they might reasonably be characterized as social death. In both stories, Jesus restores life, as it were, by rescuing people from situations marked by physical and social devastation symbolically linked to death.

Mark 5:21–24a, 35–43: Jairus's Daughter

The episode following the exorcism of Legion and framing the story of the hemorrhaging woman likewise thematizes resurrection, but here Mark does not relegate it to the realm of the figurative; instead, Mark interrogates the status of the restoration to life it reports, inviting the reader to question whether the account might encompass a literal resurrection rather than describe another symbolic one.[55] In the story of Jairus's daughter, the evangelist's representation of resurrection at first seems to veer toward the literal, but in the end it recoils back toward the symbolic. Jesus initially intends to heal the dying girl (5:22–24), and he appears to restore her to life after she has died because of the delay occasioned by the hemorrhaging woman's interruption (5:35–38). But then, just as he seems to resurrect her (5:40–42), he declares that she never died in the first place (5:39). Mark's reticence to claim that, all appearances to the contrary, Jesus raised this girl from the dead could be taken as undermining an implication of the preceding story of Legion, namely, that in his ministry Jesus anticipates or proleptically exercises God's eschatological authority to raise the dead. Jesus the exorcist and healer resurrects people, *as it were*—by restoring their psychological, spiritual, and even physical integrity, and by reintegrating them into their communities. But his power stops short of literally raising the dead. This is a vital qualification. If Jesus and his ministry only symbolize death's defeat, rather than actualizing it, then faith in Jesus only goes so far. It remains hapless in the face of death.

When the synagogue leader Jairus approaches Jesus and begs him to heal his daughter, he declares she is "at the point of death" (ἐσχάτως ἔχει, 5:23). By using a form of ἔσχατος ("end"), Mark points to the potential

---

55. On this resurrection's ambiguity, see Stephen B. Hatton, "Comic Ambiguity in the Markan Healing Intercalation (Mark 5:21–43)," *Neot* 49 (2015): 105–7. Hatton cites a paper in which I originally argued for the ideas presented here. See Austin Busch, "Resurrection in Mark—or Not?" (paper presented at the Annual Meeting of the Society of Biblical Literature, Boston, 22 November 2008).

eschatological implications of her healing.[56] Jairus's request that Jesus lay his hands on her "in order that she might be saved and live" (ἵνα σωθῇ καὶ ζήσῃ, 5:23) furthers these implications. Apocalyptic eschatological discourse, including that of Mark and Paul, often uses the word σῴζω with reference to God's final salvation of his elect (Mark 8:35; 10:26; 13:13, 20; Rom 5:9, 10; 9:27; 11:26; 1 Cor 3:15; 10:33).[57] Mark's collocation of ἔσχατος ("end") and σῴζω ("save") with ζῶ ("live") thus invites the reader to discern anticipatory eschatological hope in Jairus's prayer for his daughter's salvation. His child is in extremis (Mark 5:23), at death's door, and before Jesus reaches her side her death will be reported (5:35). Though he does not realize it at the time, the synagogue leader's appeal to Jesus amounts to a request that he exercise in the present the resurrection power many expected God to demonstrate at the end of time.[58] After the dramatic interlude of the hemorrhaging woman, this is precisely what Jesus seems to promise and to do.

Mark furthers the episode's figuration of eschatological resurrection in 5:38–40, when Jesus finds a crowd of mourners, whom he promptly "ejects" from the house. The Greek is ἐκβάλλω, Mark's standard term for Jesus's "casting out" of demons (1:39; 3:15, 22, 23; 7:26; 9:18, 28, 38), though it appears in other contexts as well.[59] Here it may evoke Paul's association of resurrection with God's overthrow of death as if it were a demonic power (see Rom 5:12–6:11; 1 Cor 15:20, 24–27, 54–55). This possible critique of mourning as enslavement to death's power aligns with Paul's exhortation in 1 Thess 4:13–14 not to mourn for the dead as do those outside the community of faith who have no hope in resurrection. Believers, according to Paul, have faith that "those who have fallen asleep" (τῶν κοιμωμένων) will rise again with Jesus at his parousia, which makes mourning an inappropriate response to death.[60] This brief narrative makes the same point: mourning capitulates to death's power, denying Jesus's authority over it.

---

56. Ἔσχατος is the Greek adjective the New Testament and other Jewish apocalyptic literature conventionally used to describe the end times, especially in phrases such as ἡ ἔσχατα ἡμέρα (Acts 2:17; 2 Tim 3:1; Jas 5:3; cf. Num 24:14; Jer 23:20). See "ἔσχατος," BAGD, 397–98, esp. definition 2b.

57. See Marcus, *Mark 1–8*, 356–57.

58. Compare John's story of Lazarus's resurrection, esp. 11:23–26.

59. Marcus, *Mark 1–8*, 372.

60. See John R. Donahue and Daniel J. Harrington, *The Gospel of Mark*, SP 2 (Collegeville, MN: Liturgical Press, 2002), 177.

It expresses faithlessness, an attitude directly opposed to the one Jesus requires from Jairus in Mark 5:36, namely, that he confront his daughter's reported death with hope rather than despair.

When people arrive to tell Jairus no longer to bother Jesus, for his daughter has died (5:35), Mark reports that Jesus παρακούει what these people say (5:36). Most understand the verb to mean "overhear."[61] It can also mean "refuse to hear," and does so in all of its LXX appearances; in Matt 18:17, its only other New Testament occurrence; and elsewhere.[62] Refusing to hear makes better sense in the Markan context, for when the people from Jairus's house report his daughter's death and urge him to stop bothering the teacher, Jesus's response indicates not only that he has happened to hear what they say but also that he refuses to acknowledge it. He tells Jairus, "Do not fear; only trust" (μὴ φοβοῦ, μόνον πίστευε, Mark 5:36), and then keeps traveling to his house to restore his daughter.

Mary Ann Beavis convincingly reads the story of Jairus's daughter's resurrection as a rewriting of the story of Jephthah's daughter's sacrifice from Judges, observing that both episodes prominently feature keening.[63] While Jephthah, his daughter, and her companions capitulate to death in bereavement and lamentation even before the girl dies (see Judg 11:34–40), Jesus expels fear and mourning even after Jairus's daughter's apparent demise (see esp. Mark 5:36, 38–40). Jesus's refusal to acknowledge word of her death reverses the behavior of the characters in Judges, who unite in presuming that Jephthah's words promising to kill the girl are as effective in bringing her life to an end as will be the killing itself. Mark's transvaluation of the Jephthah story implicitly critiques the attitude toward death that narrative displays, according to which announcements of death are indisputable and death itself is accepted, even facilitated, by all, as opposed to rejected or resisted by any. This includes God, as the death in question is a human sacrifice to him. In Mark, on the contrary, Jesus and the faith he requires defy death to the end, even after it seems to have won the day.

---

61. Donahue and Harrington, *Gospel of Mark*, 176; Gundry, *Mark*, 272; Collins, *Mark*, 274–75, 284; Robert A. Guelich, *Mark 1–8:26*, WBC 34A (Dallas: Word, 1989), 300; NRSV; etc.

62. Vincent Taylor, *The Gospel according to St. Mark* (London: Macmillan, 1952), 294.

63. Mary Ann Beavis, "The Resurrection of Jephthah's Daughter: Judges 11:34–40 and Mark 5:21–24, 35–43," *CBQ* 72 (2010): 46–62, esp. 56.

1. Ambiguous Resurrections

Upon arrival, Jesus takes with him to the girl's room Peter, James, and John, and they, along with the girl's parents, watch him restore her. Mark reports that Jesus says to her ταλιθα κουμ, an Aramaic phrase the evangelist translates into Greek (τὸ κοράσιον, σοὶ λέγω, ἔγειρε, "little girl, I say to you, arise"; 5:41) before reporting that the girl "was raised" (ἀνέστη, 5:42). Mark uses ἐγείρω and ἀνίστημι for Jesus's resurrection elsewhere (the former in 14:28 and 16:6; the latter in the Son of Man prophecies). If the language used earlier in the story linked the girl's salvation from death with eschatological resurrection, Mark's diction here more closely presages Jesus's restoration to life. That Peter, James, and John alone among the disciples witness her resurrection also links the miracle with Jesus's rising from the dead, for the same three disciples see Jesus in his glorified body in Mark 9:2–8, another episode anticipating Jesus's resurrection, as chapter 3 will show. Early writers often viewed Jesus's resurrection as the opening act of an eschatological drama encompassing death's defeat and a general resurrection (see 1 Cor 15:20–28, 51–57; Rom 5:12–6:11).[64] Thus Mark uses the terms ἐγείρω and ἀνίστημι not only in its various statements forecasting and reporting Jesus's resurrection but also in Jesus's dispute with the Sadducees over eschatological resurrection in Mark 12:18–27, to be discussed in the next chapter. The current episode's evolving terminology, though at its climax anticipating Jesus's resurrection in particular, still affirms the eschatological implications of Jesus's miracle.

In sum, Mark reports Jesus coming to Jairus's daughter when she "is at her end" (ἐσχάτως ἔχει) in order that she "may be saved and live" (σωθῇ καὶ ζήσῃ, 5:23), "casting out" (ἐκβαλὼν) the mourners from the house as if they were demons (5:40), and then evidently raising the girl from the dead: "Little girl, I say to you, arise [ἔγειρε]; and immediately the little girl was raised [ἀνέστη]" (5:41–42). It is hard to imagine how the evangelist could have formulated this brief resurrection narrative to make it bear more theological weight. In theme, diction, and plot it looks forward to Jesus's restoration to life, and forward further to the eschatological resurrection of the dead and the cosmic defeat of death as a demonic power. At the same time, it glances backward at the biblical story of Jephthah's daughter, which features an acceptance of death that Mark subjects to revisionary critique. Jesus's rejection of grieving also gestures at a communal praxis

---

64. See Matt 27:52–53, where the holy dead entombed in Jerusalem exit their graves after Jesus's resurrection.

implied by the story's theological suggestions, complementing a Pauline exhortation with which Mark may have been familiar (1 Thess 4:13–14). Since Jesus raises the dead, mourning is no longer necessary or permitted. In fact, it constitutes mockery of God's power over death (see 5:40, "and they ridiculed him"). In advance of this power's exercise, Jesus forbids fear and demands faith: "do not fear; only trust" (μὴ φοβοῦ, μόνον πίστευε, 5:36). Mark's narrative of Jesus raising Jairus's daughter has implications as sweeping as those Hebrews assigns to Jesus's passion, which occurred "that he might destroy the one having the power of death—that is, the devil—and release all those who by means of fear of death were held in slavery for their whole life" (2:14–15).

Yet Mark complicates this understanding of the story by having Jesus suddenly declare that "the child is not dead but asleep" (οὐκ ἀπέθανεν ἀλλὰ καθεύδει, Mark 5:39). Jesus's denial that the girl is dead is bizarre in narrative terms, since everyone else in the story agrees she has died (5:35, 38). Even more troubling, though, Mark has freighted the story with so much theological weight that it can hardly bear the burden if Jesus himself undermines the resurrection it seems to report. Why would Mark have its hero deny performing a resurrection that those present universally recognize and on which so much depends?[65]

Many readers, ancient and modern, have presumed that Mark would not do such a thing. In his classic formulation of the messianic secrecy motif, Wilhelm Wrede homes in on the command to secrecy in 5:43a as evidence of the motif's clumsy redactional insertion into traditional material.[66] His approach implies an analogous interpretation of Jesus's claim that the girl is sleeping in 5:39. It too represents a lame attempt to conceal something whose hiding no one could reasonably imagine possible (the resurrection of a girl whose funeral had already begun). Mark's Jesus, Wrede's analysis suggests, feebly attempts to deceive when he denies that the girl has died in 5:39—a cover-up he vainly perpetuates in 5:43 by demanding that those present not tell what happened. For Wrede, the Markan Jesus's futile lying evinces anachronistic revision of a traditional story recounting one of his deeds of power. Mark redacted it to overcome the troubling historical fact that Jesus during his ministry was not recog-

---

65. See Fullmer for a brief discussion of puzzlement about this question in commentaries on Mark (*Resurrection in Mark's Literary-Historical Perspective*, 176–77 n. 19).

66. Wilhelm Wrede, *The Messianic Secret*, trans. James C. G. Greig, LTT (Greenwood, SC: Attic Press, 1971), 52–53.

nized as the Messiah early Jesus-believers claimed him to be. Jesus, Mark's narrative insists, kept his identity secret, as well as many remarkable deeds of power that would have indicated his messianic status, though they became known nonetheless (see 1:43–45). The Markan Jesus's denial of the girl's resurrection, part of Mark's broader secrecy motif, represents an awkward literary artifice.

Collins similarly argues that Jesus's supposedly ambiguous wording (5:39) and decision to perform the miracle "away from public view" (5:37, 40, 43) indicate that Mark believes "it is not appropriate that divine power be seen at work" here, though her explanation of the secrecy relates to the exceptional awesomeness of the "mighty deed" of resurrection Jesus accomplishes.[67] Collins's argument articulates a key interpretive presumption that underlies Wrede's interpretation as well, namely, that the story's "narrative rhetoric ... makes clear that the girl is really dead."[68] Collins seems to mean by this that since its coherence evidently demands that the girl has died and risen, her death and resurrection in the story must be self-evident to anyone reading it. Yet this construal is open to question, for its most authoritative character, who performs the supposed resurrection, insists that that the girl is not dead, offers a plausible explanation for her appearing so (namely, that she is in a coma), which is never refuted, and ends his visit by giving mundane advice for her continued care (5:43b). This sequence of events implies not that Jesus obfuscates the true nature of the miracle he performs, but rather that he clarifies it. He has not resurrected Jairus's daughter, but merely helped her mend. In this context, his penultimate words, which command silence about what had happened (5:43a), not to mention the episode's other elements of secrecy (5:37, 40), seem aimed at preventing false rumors about what happened from circulating, rather than signaling that he resurrected her.

Commentators resolve the problem Jesus's disavowal of resurrection introduces by offering nuanced interpretations of his claim that the girl was asleep rather than dead. Gundry and Marcus, for instance, note that sleep commonly functions as a euphemism for death in the LXX (e.g., Ps 87 [88]:5–6; Dan 12:2) and can so function in the New Testament as well (1 Thess 4:13; 5:10). They argue that Mark's Jesus manipulates the com-

---

67. Collins, *Mark*, 285.
68. Collins, *Mark*, 285.

monplace to redefine death as a form of sleep from which God alone can awaken a person.[69] Yet such readings stumble on the fact that that Jesus specifies in 5:39 that the girl is asleep instead of dead (οὐκ ἀπέθανεν ἀλλὰ καθεύδει). Mark opposes rather than metonymically relates the former to the latter.[70]

Attempts such as Gundry's to harmonize Mark's version of the story with Matthew's and Luke's, according to which the girl is indisputably dead, fail to persuade.[71] The passages of Matthew and Luke cited as explanatory parallels (Matt 9:18; Luke 8:42, 49, 52–53) must revise Mark to remove or suppress ambiguity surrounding the girl's death. Gundry's harmonizing impulse fails to come to terms with the most obvious implication of these finalizing emendations, namely, that the later evangelists were sufficiently troubled by the open-ended uncertainty the version Mark's *commentarii* featured so as to resolve it.[72]

Matthew alters Mark's story by having the synagogue leader come to Jesus only after the girl has died, for he asks Jesus to resurrect his daughter (9:18). Consequently, Matthew removes the note that the girl has died and Jesus's refusal to listen to reports of her death, as well as the demand of faith rather than fear from the father. While these alterations do not entirely clarify matters—Matthew's Jesus still claims she is sleeping rather than dead (Matt 9:24), leaving open the possibility that the father was mistaken—they reduce Mark's equivocality by leading the readers to expect Jesus to resurrect the girl from the outset, an expectation Mat-

---

69. Gundry, *Mark*, 273–74; Marcus, *Mark 1–8*, 371; Murray J. Harris, "'The Dead Are Restored to Life': Miracles of Revivication in the Gospels," in *The Miracles of Jesus*, ed. David Wenham and Craig L. Blomberg, GP 6 (Sheffield: JSOT Press, 1986), 306–7.

70. See Guelich, *Mark 1–8*, 301.

71. Gundry, *Mark*, 273–74.

72. Charles W. Hedrick insists on preserving this ambiguity and agrees that "the idea that Mark's story describes Jesus raising a young girl from the dead appears to derive from the influential readings of Matthew and Luke." See Hedrick, "Miracle Stories as Literary Compositions: The Case of Jairus's Daughter," *PRSt* 20 (1993): 230. However, Hedrick's understanding of this ambiguity is qualified. He thinks that it may have been the result of a "careless narrator" ("Miracle Stories," 230 n. 29). He believes that Mark's setting of the account within a "catena of miracle stories" involving "Jesus's mighty (supernatural) deeds" compels the reader to view the story as a resurrection ("Miracle Stories," 221). More fruitful are D'Angelo's brief comments, which connect the ambiguity to that displayed in a closely related story of Philostratus, which I will discuss below ("Gender and Power," 99–100).

thew's story promptly satisfies. In Mark, on the other hand, readers at first see Jesus begged to perform a healing, which only gradually appears to transform into a resurrection, before Jesus finally insists that it is only a healing after all.[73]

This insistence surfaces most clearly in Mark 5:39, but it may arise implicitly as early as 5:36, for here Jesus tells Jairus not to fear and to continue trusting, despite the report that his daughter has died. Jesus's words to Jairus, combined with his refusal to listen to the report of the girl's demise, may suggest that even in death the girl is not beyond his help. However, one might also understand those words retrospectively, in the light of Jesus's claim in 5:39 that the girl was not dead but asleep, to imply that Jairus need not fear because his daughter remains alive. The report he has heard is mistaken; she is not yet beyond Jesus's ability to help.[74] Matthew's reimagining of the episode both presents the girl as having died before her father approaches Jesus and eliminates the later report of her death and Jesus's accompanying demand for faith from her father. The First Gospel thus removes the entire narrative framework supporting ambiguity about the miracle's status in Mark, which reaches its equivocating apex in Jesus's claim of Mark 5:39.

The detail of the flute players' presence in Matt 9:23 may further the revisionary goal of establishing without doubt that the girl is dead. Probing from an ethnomusicological perspective the significance of Matthew's addition of τοὺς αὐλητὰς in its revision of Mark, John Pilch suggests that their presence is meant to signal the girl's soul's safe transition to a disembodied afterlife. Their mention indicates not only mourners' acknowledgement of her death, as in the Markan parallel (Mark 5:38), but also that her soul or spirit has left her body (cf. Luke 8:55) and is being guarded from molesting demons by apotropaic music as it travels to the realm of the dead.[75]

In its Matthean context, in stark contrast to its Markan one, Jesus's claim upon arriving at the synagogue leader's house that the girl is not

---

73. Cf. Everett R. Kalin, "Matthew 9:18–26: An Exercise in Redaction Criticism," *CurTM* 15 (1988): 45–47. Kalin provides an explanation different from (though not incompatible with) mine about why Matthew clarifies the resurrection at the beginning of the story it adopts from Mark.

74. Hedrick explores the ambiguity of 5:36 ("Miracle Stories," 226–27).

75. John J. Pilch, "Flute Players, Death, and Music in the Afterlife (Matthew IX,18–19, 23–26)," *BTB* 37 (2007): 17–18.

dead but sleeping (Matt 9:24) strains credibility to the breaking point. It forces the reader to conclude that Jesus must be lying or mistaken, or else, if an interpretation stressing his dishonesty or incompetence seems implausible, employing sleep as a metaphor for death catachrestically when he claims the girl is not dead but asleep. Of course the girl is dead and Jesus resurrected her! The synagogue leader only went to Jesus after she had already died and in order that he might restore her to life. Her death is a given from the beginning of the story until Jesus's strange words in 9:24, which the mourners and their activities refute. These activities not only confirm that the girl has been dead for some time but also point to her soul's departure from her body. Matthew, however, had to change much (compare Mark 5:23 and Matt 9:18), eliminate even more (all of Mark 5:35–37), and add yet further details (see Matt 9:23) to transform Jesus's claim that the girl is not dead but asleep into a boldly catachrestic metaphor suggesting that for Jesus, death is nothing but sleep, as Paul implies in 1 Thessalonians. The interpretation of Mark 5:39 that Marcus, Gundry, and others propose does apply to Matt 9:24.[76] But one wonders why Matthew would have gone to all this revisionary trouble if the girl's death and resurrection were already clearly on display in Mark.

Luke's revisions of the Markan episode are more surgical than Matthew's and manage to eliminate Mark's ambiguity even more unequivocally. Luke introduces Jairus's daughter by reporting that "she is dying" (ἀπέθνῃσκεν, Luke 8:42). While the formulation retains the vagueness of Mark's "she is at her end" (ἐσχάτως ἔχει, Mark 5:23), it is marginally more explicit, insofar as it uses the Greek word for "die" rather than a periphrasis. Luke also adds to Mark's story a statement specifying that the mourners knew of the girl's death (Luke 8:53, εἰδότες ὅτι ἀπέθανεν), lest the reader imagine they mistakenly assume it (as they in fact do in Mark). Most compellingly, after Jesus tells her to "get up" (ἔγειρε, Luke 8:54) and immediately before "she rose" (ἀνέστη), the Lukan narrator reports that "her spirit returned" (ἐστρέψεν τὸ πνεῦμα αὐτῆς, 8:55), thereby confirming its earlier departure. In analogous contexts, Luke-Acts offers related notices to affirm or deny that a death has occurred (Luke 23:46; Acts 7:59; see also Acts 20:10). To confirm resurrection here, the Third Evangelist substitutes this evidence of life's return for Mark's more modest note of the

---

76. It represents a conventional interpretation of the dominical saying in Matt 9:24. See, e.g., Martin Luther, *Annotationes in aliquot capita Matthaei*, D. Martin Luthers Werke 38 (Weimar: Hermann Böhlau, 1912), 489.

girl's mobility (περιεπάτει, "she walked around"; Mark 5:42). As a complement, Luke retains (in 8:55) the Markan detail of her consumption of food (Mark 5:43), which in its new context serves to anticipate Luke's account of Jesus's resurrection. Like that of Jairus's daughter, Jesus's takes place after the spirit departs from his body (Luke 23:46) and finds confirmation in the risen Christ's eating (24:30, 41–43).

Jesus's disavowal of the girl's demise in Luke 8:52 flies in the face of the verification of her death and resurrection by witnesses and an omniscient narrator. In Luke, even more clearly than in Matthew, Jesus's claim that the girl is not dead but asleep must constitute the kind of logic-straining, catachrestic metaphor Gundry, Marcus, and others believe operates in Mark 5, unless the reader is to assume that Luke's Jesus is lying or mistaken. But Luke, like Matthew, had to make significant alterations to Mark in order to retain the memorable dominical saying of Mark 5:39 while at the same time denying its ability to cast the reported resurrection into doubt.[77] The later Synoptic evangelists make those alterations because they are necessary to obviate the open-ended narrative ambiguity the story displays in Mark's *commentarii*. Matthew and Luke do not confirm that Jesus really raised the girl from the dead in Mark. On the contrary, the later evangelists recognize the ambiguous status of the miracle there reported and work to eliminate Mark's equivocality. Their editorial activity confirms that the girl does not necessarily rise from the dead in Mark's account, rather than affirming that she did.

Additional evidence for the reading I propose may be found in stories of resurrection from the Greco-Roman world that regularly

---

77. That Matthew and Luke each retain the ambiguity-generating dominical saying while eliminating other points of ambiguity may indicate that a version of the girl's restoration to life closer to theirs than to Mark's circulated. The history of the story independent of Mark is obscure, though it could be the same tradition John 4:46–54 includes, which also surfaces in Q (Matt 8:5–; par. Luke 7:1–10). For discussion, see Lawrence M. Wills, *The Quest of the Historical Gospel: Mark, John, and the Origins of the Gospel Genre* (London: Routledge, 1997), 81–82; Fullmer, *Resurrection in Mark's Literary-Historical Perspective*, 173–74. That hypothetical version (or oral performance) would have included Jesus's claim that the girl was not dead but merely asleep as a tongue-in-cheek acknowledgment to auditors or readers, who would have been primed by one or another narrative strategy such as those Matthew and Luke employ to understand that she was in fact dead and would rise. I will offer a different explanation of the other Synoptic evangelists' retention of the dominical saying below.

play on the same sort of uncertainty one finds in the Markan episode about whether the object of resurrection was dead or unconscious. Paul Fullmer traces Mark's representations of resurrection to a Homeric commonplace, carried over with appropriate transposition into Hellenistic novels as well as into Mark. This topos represents a hero's state of unconsciousness as death and a god's restoration of the hero to his or her senses as resurrection.[78] In the works Fullmer discusses, the death in question is always qualified—an experience akin to death or approximating death or, rarely, perhaps even death itself, but never certainly so. The Markan resurrection narrative in chapter 5 is qualified in the same way through the ambiguity that Jesus's denial and related features stress.[79] Judith Perkins, in a study of *Scheintod* ("apparent death") in Greco-Roman literature, argues that Hellenistic novels frequently deploy this literary motif—often with reference to maiden daughters of prominent men—to concretize the theme of social death, or loss of social position and identity. Examples include Challiroe in Chariton (*Chaer.* 1.4.12–9.5), Chariclea in Heliodorus (*Aeth.* 2.1–5), Anthia in Xenophon (*Eph.* 3.6–8), and Leucippe in Achilles Tatius (*Leuc. Clitop.* 3.15.5–7; 5.7.4 [cf. 5.19.1–2]; 7.3–16). Mark's employment of the same commonplace with reference to Jairus's maiden daughter assimilates her story to those juxtaposed to it in chapter 5, which employ related motifs to figure social death and restoration, as argued above.[80]

The kinds of Homeric parallels Fullmer considers are relevant to Jesus's resurrection, and I will discuss them in my study's final chapter, which focuses on Mark's conceptualization of Jesus's redemptive death and restoration to life. With respect to this episode, the most compelling parallels come from Greco-Roman accounts of physicians and itinerant healers. One striking correspondence appears in the *Florida* of the second-

---

78. Fullmer, *Resurrection in Mark's Literary-Historical Perspective*, 99–135, 176–77. A classic example would be Zeus's resurrection of Sarpedon in Homer, *Il.* 5.628–698, which Fullmer discusses (*Resurrection in Mark's Literary-Historical Perspective*, 118–21).

79. Fullmer, *Resurrection in Mark's Literary-Historical Perspective*, 177.

80. Judith Perkins, *Roman Imperial Identities in the Early Christian Era*, RMCS (London: Routledge, 2009), 47–52. The works Perkins cites all explore the struggles elites in the Greek east faced in attempting to understand their evolving social and political situation in the Roman Empire, a struggle perhaps not irrelevant to a local religious leader such as Jairus. The juxtaposed story of Legion may more explicitly reflect on the struggle to maintain one's local identity in a broader imperial context.

century CE writer Apuleius, though the story he recounts appears to have originated in an earlier time. Celsus refers to it as if it were commonly known in the first half of the previous century (*Med.* 2.6.15), and Pliny briefly summarizes it as well (*Nat.* 26.14–15).[81] It concerns the legendary physician Asclepiades recognizing and nurturing subtle signs of life in a patient everyone is convinced had died. Apuleius, Celsus, and Pliny report that Asclepiades interrupts a funeral (like Jesus does in 5:38–40) to insist that the person being interred is alive. According to Apuleius, Asclepiades, like Jesus, forces the mourners to cease their lamentation, brings the man home, and uses drugs to revive his spirit. A later story from Philostratus's *Life of Apollonius* (4.45) similarly shows Apollonius interrupting a funeral for a young woman of a notable family.[82] He proceeds to restore the woman to life by means of his touch and secret words (προσαψάμενος αὐτῆς καί τι ἀφανῶς ἐπειπών, 4.45.1), much like Jesus, who, "having taken the child by hand" (κρατήσας τῆς χειρὸς τοῦ παιδίου), speaks words marked as strange by their Aramaic transliteration (Mark 5:41). Philostratus expresses agnosticism as to whether Apollonius resurrected the girl or simply noticed signs of life everyone else had missed, thereby introducing ambiguity into the story analogous to Mark's (*Vit. Apoll.* 4.45.2).

In all these anecdotes, the healer's refusal of public mourning for the dead precedes the restoration to life, with the mourning crowd mocking the would-be healer in Apuleius as in Mark (*partim etiam inridere medicinam*, *Flor.* 19). In all three, the restoration occurs in private: Apuleius's Asclepiades brings the man home to heal him; Philostratus's Apollonius whispers something secret (*Vit. Apoll.* 45.1); Jesus does both. He restores the girl in the privacy of Jairus's home—even going so far as to eject all but the parents and a handful of his followers—and uses mysterious words. Finally, all three introduce ambiguity about the restoration to life described.[83] In Apuleius, Asclepiades detects faint signs of life but encounters remarkable resistance from people close to the deceased, who are convinced he is

---

81. Johannes van der Vliet, ed., *Lucii Apulei Madaurensis Apologia sive De magia liber et Florida*, BSGRT (Leipzig: Teubner, 1900), 185–88; Frederick Marx, ed., *A. Cornelii Celsi quae svpersunt*, CML 1 (Leipzig: Teubner, 1915), 114; Karl Mayhoff, ed., *C. Plini Secundi naturalis historiae libri XXXVII*, BSGRT (Leipzig: Teubner, 1897), 4:179.

82. Christopher P. Jones, ed., *Philostratus: The Life of Apollonius of Tyana*, 3 vols, LCL (Cambridge: Harvard University Press, 2005), 1:418.

83. For a discussion of typical motifs the Markan story displays vis-à-vis Apuleius, Philostratus, and other parallels, see Collins, *Mark*, 277–79.

dead. The resurrection Philostratus reports at first seems less ambiguous than either Asclepiades's or Jesus's, since the narrator declares from the outset that Apollonius "woke the girl up from seeming death" (ἀφύπνισε τὴν κόρην τοῦ δοκοῦντος θανάτου, *Vit. Apoll.* 4.45.1). Yet Philostratus concludes by explicitly raising the possibility that he resurrected her (εἴτ᾽ ἀπεσβηκυῖαν τὴν ψυχὴν ἀνέθαλψέ τε καὶ ἀνέλαβεν, 4.45.2).

The numerous points of contact between these stories likely constitute evidence of a folktale motif involving a healer who interrupts a funeral to restore a comatose person mistakenly believed dead. Celsus's reference to the story of Asclepiades suggests it was a well-known legend. The later stories about Jesus and Apollonius are probably literary creations shaped with partial reference to it—either imaginative elaborations on genuine historical events or invented fictions composed on the model of the legendary tale.[84] It is also possible that Philostratus knew a version of the story Mark includes, or even Mark itself, and assimilated Apollonius to the Markan Jesus in his *Life*.[85] The exact nature of the literary relationship between these texts is less important than the centrality to them all of ambiguity about whether they recount a healing or a resurrection. If Matthew and Luke were familiar with the general story type of which Apuleius, Philostratus, and Mark all offer specific examples, then that helps to explain their insistence on reducing Mark's ambiguity in their revisions, even while retaining the dominical saying in Mark 5:39: "the child is not dead but asleep" (see Matt 9:24; Luke 8:52). A degree of ambiguity was expected in this kind of tale, and the later evangelists retain it formally in Jesus's memorable saying. At the same time, though, they aim to confirm

---

84. The stories of Elijah's and Elisha's resurrections are also possible models on which Mark may have drawn, as Fullmer points out (*Resurrection in Mark's Literary-Historical Perspective*, 174–81). See esp. 1 Kgs 17:17–24; 2 Kgs 4:31–37.

85. For discussion, see Erkki Koskenniemi, *Apollonios von Tyana in der neutestamentliche Exegese: Forschungsbericht und Weiterführung der Diskussion*, WUNT 61 (Tübingen: Mohr Siebeck, 1994), 189–206. Arguments for Apollonius's dependence on the gospels include Ferdinand Christian Baur, *Apollonius von Tyana und Christus, oder das Verhältniss des Pythagoreismus zum Christentum* (Tübingen: Fues, 1833), and, more recently, Simon Swain, "Defending Hellenism: Philostratus, In Honour of Apollonius," in *Apologetics in the Roman Empire: Pagans, Jews, and Christians*, ed. Mark Edward, Martin Goodman, and Simon Price (Oxford: Oxford University Press, 1999), 157–96, esp. 193–94. Also useful is Andrew Mark Hagstrom, "Philostratus's Apollonius: A Case Study in Apologetics in the Roman Empire" (MA thesis, University of North Carolina at Chapel Hill, 2016).

without doubt Jesus's authority over death, about which Mark equivocates, and so thematically obviate the ambiguity their versions formally retain.

The parallels from Apuleius and Philostratus, not to mention Homer and the Hellenistic novels, bring into focus how special is the pleading required to eliminate the Markan account's pervasive ambiguity about the girl's resurrection. Not only is the episode from Mark ambiguous on its face, but it participates in a literary tradition in which equivocation about resurrection was conventionally expected. Merely by telling the type of story it recounts, Mark leads its readers to anticipate the ambiguity it delivers.

Mark 5 in Its Entirety

I am now in a position to argue for Mark 5 as a thematically coherent unit in which the evangelist's dialogically evolving thematization of resurrection comes into relief, as does that development's characteristic reversion to type at the chapter's end. Resurrection constitutes a symbolic dimension of Jesus's exorcism of the young man driven by a horde of demons from his community to dwell in tombs (5:1–20). The theme receives an oblique nod in the first part of the narrative framing the story of the hemorrhaging woman (5:21–24a): Jairus requests that Jesus save his daughter, who is at death's door, so that she may continue to live (5:23). The hemorrhaging woman's experience interrupts this story, occasioning slippage from the realm of the indirect and figurative into that of the straightforward and literal. This story suggests that the woman's impurity alienates her from her community, somewhat like the possessed man dwelling in unclean tombs. However, according to the Levitical ideology underlying the episode's representation of her impurity, her condition drains away her life force, so as to render her body not only perpetually unclean but corpse-like. As Jacob Milgrom observes in his commentary on Leviticus, "The loss of vaginal blood … meant the diminution of life and, if unchecked, destruction and death…. In the Israelite mind, blood was the archsymbol of life ([Lev] 17:10–14; Deut 12:23…). Its oozing from the body … was certainly the sign of death. In particular, the loss of seed in vaginal blood … was associated with the loss of life."[86] The nature of the woman's disease suggests that her reproductive capacities have turned against her. Her body's ability to

---

86. Milgrom, *Leviticus 1–16*, 767.

bear new life has been somehow perverted so that her womb bears death, for from it her own life perpetually flows.[87] This woman's healing is not literally a resurrection, but, in the light of how the Levitical texts to which Mark alludes conceptualize her ailment, she is a bearer of death. Thus, her restoration, unlike that of the man possessed by Legion, cannot merely be symbolic. It lies somewhere on the threshold between the literal and the figurative, approaching the domain of the former without entering fully into it.

In the second part of the story of Jairus's daughter, symbolic resurrection gives further way to literal resurrection. The account of the girl's healing metamorphizes into a story of revivification. Since she evidently dies during the time Jesus restores the hemorrhaging woman, if Jesus is to restore her, he must raise her from the dead. Yet though Mark opens a door onto literal resurrection here, the evangelist will not walk through it. The narrative disrupts the pattern of intensification by undermining the status of the resurrection it seems to recount. Just before raising Jairus's daughter, Mark's Jesus claims that she has not died after all, but rather fallen into a coma.

Mark 5 at once affirms Jesus's restorative power and suggests it may have a decisive limitation. By words alone can Jesus exorcise a horde of demons and return the young man they drove to the realm of the dead back to the community of the living. Contact with the hem of his garment brings renewed life to a woman who has been hemorrhaging it for years and who has spent all she had on physicians impotent to restore her death-bearing body. Jesus can even restore a girl at the brink of death, one so close to death's door that only he can distinguish between her comatose state and death itself. But Mark 5 will not affirm that Jesus can raise the dead. In chapter 5, as in chapter 16, the narrative voice does not guarantee resurrection as an actual occurrence, though it will more modestly authorize resurrection as a symbolic figuration of Jesus's exorcisms and healings (or, at Mark's close, of at least one disciple's restoration to faithfulness). All these stories in various ways analogize to restoration from death the extraordinary renewal Jesus offers. Jesus's restorative power even approaches resurrection in the authority he exercises over deadly physical ailments. Yet resurrection remains, or at least Mark only endorses it as,

---

87. On the theme of fertility in the intercalated stories, see, e.g., J. Duncan M. Derrett, "Mark's Technique: The Haemorrhaging Woman and Jairus's Daughter," *Bib* 63 (1982): 474–505.

a symbolic dimension of the salvation Jesus offers. The evangelist stops short of affirming that Jesus possesses final authority over death itself.

Figurative versus Literal Resurrection 2: Mark 9:14–29

One finds something similar in Mark 8:27–9:29, particularly in 9:14–29. I will not explore Mark's development of this material in the same level of detail with which I treated Mark 5, for I discuss this section more fully in chapter 3. Here I note only that 9:14–29 serves as the climax of a series of interrelated stories in which the Son of Man's vindication by resurrection from a humiliating death is first prophesied (8:31–32), then presented as a model for Jesus's students to emulate (8:33–9:1), and finally represented proleptically in the transfiguration (9:2–8). Much conflict and confusion about resurrection surfaces in the disciples' minds throughout (8:32–33; 9:5–6, 9–13). In 9:14, Jesus, Peter, James, and John (who also attended the restoration of Jairus's daughter in Mark 5) descend the Mount of Transfiguration to encounter the other disciples attempting to exorcise a demon that has possessed a young boy, which Jesus himself will finally drive out. This story culminates a sequence of episodes thematizing and figuring resurrection and gestures at a literal resurrection, but without guaranteeing that resurrection takes place. Thus, the account of Jesus's exorcism of the deaf-mute demon in chapter 9 raises interpretive problems identical to those in the story of Jairus's daughter in chapter 5.

Formally speaking, this episode constitutes no less a resurrection account than does the earlier one. Though Jesus never claims to resurrect the boy, at the story's climax the Markan narrator notes that anonymous witnesses understood him to have died (9:26) before Jesus, "having taken him by the hand, raised him, and he arose" (κρατήσας τῆς χειρὸς αὐτοῦ ἤγειρεν αὐτόν, καὶ ἀνέστη, 9:27). In Mark 5 also witnesses understand the girl has died and thereby imply that Jesus has resurrected her, though Jesus denies it. Despite these similarities, the latter story is rarely interpreted as a resurrection account.[88] As in the story of Jairus's daughter, commentators dissolve the ambiguity Mark introduces as to whether the restoration it reports constitutes a resurrection—only here, instead of insisting resurrection does take place, they deny it.

---

88. As observed by Hedrick, "Miracle Stories," 221.

Although rarely subject to interpretive inquiry, parallels between this episode and the healing of Jairus's daughter extend well beyond the similar language used to describe the two restorations (compare 9:27, quoted above, and 5:41–42: καὶ κρατήσας τῆς χειρὸς τοῦ παιδίου λέγει ... ἔγειρε. καὶ εὐθὺς ἀνέστη).[89] Mark refers to the boy as "a child" (παῖς, 9:24), but the father claims that his son has suffered "from childhood" (ἐκ παιδιόθεν, 9:21), so he is apparently an older child, like Jairus's twelve-year-old daughter (5:42). Also like Jairus, whose daughter was on the verge of death (5:23), this father asks Jesus for salvation from a demon's repeated attempts to kill his child (ἵνα ἀπολέσῃ αὐτόν, 9:22). Accordingly, Jesus's exchange with the man in 9:22–24 directly recalls Jesus's words to Jairus in 5:36: "Do not fear; only have faith" (μὴ φοβοῦ, μόνον πίστευε). In 9:23, Jesus seizes on the first words of the father's request ("if you are able, have mercy on us and help us"; 9:22) and throws them back in his face: "'If you are able!' All things are possible for the one who has faith" (πάντα δυνατὰ τῷ πιστεύοντι, 9:23). The father replies, "I have faith; help my lack of faith" (πιστεύω· βοήθει μου τῇ ἀπιστίᾳ, 9:24).

The faith Jesus requires from this father is hardly less extreme than that demanded of Jairus after his daughter's death was reported. The man has already recounted in horrific detail how the demon has tortured (9:18) and attempted to kill his son (9:22), with the violent harassment intensifying as he brings the boy into Jesus's presence (9:20). In 9:25–27, Mark narrates the exorcism with the same kind of vivid detail he uses to recount the possession itself. When the demon sees Jesus, it responds to his threatening presence by convulsing the boy (9:20), presumably attempting to kill him yet again. In the process of its expulsion, the demon apparently succeeds in its murderous attempt, for the boy "became like a corpse [νεκρός], so that many said that he died [ἀπέθανεν]" (9:26). Finally, as mentioned above, Mark uses the same theologically resonant verbs to depict Jesus's restoration of this boy as he did his restoration of Jairus's daughter: "Jesus raised [ἤγειρεν] him, and he arose [ἀνέστη]" (9:27; cf. 5:41–42).

Though Jesus himself refutes the testimony of death in 5:39, commentators habitually trust the witnesses over Jesus in chapter 5. Somewhat inexplicably, they distrust the witnesses of chapter 9, whom Jesus never challenges. Collins, for instance, observes similarities between the two

---

89. See figure 27 in Marcus, which compares the two episodes, though without it substantially affecting the interpretive argument (*Mark 8–16*, 662).

episodes relevant to the resurrection theme, but asserts that in chapter 9 "the story does not imply that the boy was actually dead," while in chapter 5 "narrative rhetoric ... makes clear that the girl is really dead" and that Jesus resurrects her.[90] How does one account for such divergent responses to the interrelated stories? Both present a clear pathology culminating in a child's death; both feature witnesses testifying that the child has died; both show Jesus intervening after that declaration to restore the victim; both describe the restoration in identical language, which Mark uses of resurrection throughout the Second Gospel. In the face of these similarities, one encounters a single significant divergence: in the story of Jairus's daughter, Jesus denies that he raises the child, while in chapter 9's story of the exorcism, he issues no denial.[91] Nonetheless, commentators generally agree with Collins that the first recounts Jesus raising a child from the dead but the second does not. In the latter, resurrection functions at the symbolic level alone.[92]

This inconsistency suggests something has gone hermeneutically awry, and its effect has been to mask an important perspective toward resurrection that Mark consistently adopts. With respect to Mark 9, commentators perhaps again interpret Mark from the vantage of Matthew and Luke's revisions (see Matt 17:14–20; Luke 9:37–43a),[93] for the later evangelists eliminate any hints of death and resurrection from the Markan story. They likewise omit Jesus's rebuke of the father's lack of faith, Mark's extended description of the demon's torture of the boy (although discrete elements remain at Matt 17:15 and Luke 9:39, 42; cf. Mark 9:18, 20, 22, 26), and much else besides. In fact, Matthew and Luke's versions of the story are so similar to each other and so distinct from Mark that they constitute an example of Mark-Q overlap troubling for the two-source hypothesis. Luke may follow Matthew's abbreviated revision of Mark, as the Farrer hypothesis would posit, or else the two later Synoptic evangelists may draw on a version of the story different from the one Mark

---

90. Collins, *Mark*, 439, 285.

91. One might also add that in Mark 5 Jesus restores the child in private; here he does so in public (9:25–26).

92. E.g., Marcus, *Mark 8–16*, 664; Gundry, *Mark*, 492.

93. See Hedrick, though he seems to conclude that they are right to do so since Matthew and Luke follow clues to Mark's intent and perhaps even resolve its careless neglect to clarify what should have been made explicit ("Miracle Stories," 221–22, 230).

preserves.⁹⁴ Why they would do either is not easy to explain, given the literary qualities of Mark's vivid narrative. Perhaps they found Mark's version otiose⁹⁵—some unnecessary details too lurid, others too harsh (e.g., Jesus's rebuke of the father). In any case, one cannot assume that the parallel material in Matthew and Luke interprets Mark at all, let alone privilege it as Mark's authoritative interpretation.

My critique of the consensus view of these two "resurrection" stories does not imply that Mark presents the latter episode as a definitive resurrection or the earlier one as a healing instead. On the contrary, both pericopes introduce ambiguity about whether resurrection has occurred. Mark is more consistent in this regard than are Mark's interpreters. In neither episode does the Markan narrator report that the victim has died; in both, death is announced by other characters. Likewise, in neither does the narrator use unambiguous language to describe the victim's restoration. While the words Mark uses in 5:41–42 and 9:27 resemble language employed elsewhere to describe resurrection, they could also refer to waking from sleep or even simply to standing up and thus could point to healing. Similarly, the statement in 9:26 that the boy "became as a corpse" (ἐγένετο ὡσεὶ νεκρός) after the demon convulsed him recalls the father's earlier claim that, as a result of the demon, the boy habitually "becomes rigid" (ξηραίνεται, 9:18). This presents a plausible pathology for the boy's corpse-like appearance, challenging the bystanders' inference that "he died" in 9:26, much as Jesus's insistence that Jairus's daughter lies in a coma (5:39) challenges the mourners' inference that she had passed away.

The equivocality about the recounted restorations that both stories maintain inversely correlates with their demand of faith in the resurrection power of God and his representative Jesus (5:36; 9:23). Each episode presses the possibility that Jesus can and will provide salvation sweeping enough to resolve parents' despair when faced with the possibility of children's untimely deaths (see 5:23, 35; 9:22). Moreover, each goes so far as to have

---

94. For a discussion of the latter possibility, see Gregory E. Sterling, "Jesus as Exorcist: An Analysis of Matthew 17:14–20; Mark 9:14–29; Luke 9:37–43a," *CBQ* 55 (1993): 467–93. I here assume the validity of the two-source hypothesis, though I recognize the difficulty it has accounting for the pattern of Synoptic redaction in this episode and others.

95. On the tendency of compression, see Gerd Theissen, *The Miracle Stories of the Early Christian Tradition*, ed. John Riches, trans. Francis McDonagh (Philadelphia: Fortress, 1983), 175–80, esp. 177.

Jesus command the parent to trust him absolutely in view of this miraculous prospect, even when the power of death seems ascendant (5:36; 9:23). But at the same time each neglects to affirm that the child dies, suggesting that the salvation Jesus offers may be effective only insofar as their predicaments approach but do not amount to the deaths the parents fear. In each story, Mark authorizes Jesus's ability to save up to the point of death. Beyond that, the evangelist leaves the readers to confront Jesus's calls for faith without assurance. In these stories of possible resurrection, Mark's Jesus demands faith that God and his representative can do all things, but the Markan narrative will only guarantee divine power to save within the boundaries of life.

Dialogizing Resurrection Faith

The second father's prayerful confession constitutes an honest response to the existential situation Mark dramatizes: "I have faith; help my lack of faith" (πιστεύω· βοήθει μου τῇ ἀπιστίᾳ, 9:24). The internally dialogic structure of the man's final declaration, which responds to its own faithful confession with a prayer to overcome skepticism, acknowledges a defining feature of faith: for trust to be meaningful, doubt must be allowed to speak. In refusing to resolve uncertainty precisely as it calls for faith, Mark brings this animating tension into sharp focus. The evangelist situates the readers in a precarious interpretive position, inviting them to affirm the intellectual and emotional authenticity of the second father, even while the narrative's authoritative leading character demands dogmatic confession and rigid faith as opposed to honest doubt. Recall that Jesus responds to the father's original request for assistance ("if you are able, have mercy on us and help us!"; 9:22) by throwing his words back in his face: "'If you are able!'; all things are possible for the one who has faith" (τὸ εἰ δύνῃ, πάντα δυνατὰ τῷ πιστεύοντι, 9:23).

Dialogization of faith in resurrection is not unique to Mark 5 and 9. It is prominently on display in Mark's account of Jesus's resurrection itself, which, as I have argued, is not a fait accompli but rather an anonymous character's faithful announcement on the basis of suggestive evidence. In Mark 16, as in Mark 5 and 9, the narrator refuses to guarantee that resurrection has taken place, leaving readers to infer from indirect evidence (the open and empty tomb) and the comments of characters (the young man's announcement and Jesus's prophecies) that Jesus has risen. Moreover, in chapter 16, as in chapters 5 and 9, Mark draws attention to the possibility of persistent unbelief in the face of this situation. The female disciples, when confronted with an invitation to trust in God's power to raise the dead, respond in a way that inverts Jesus's command to Jairus: "do not fear; only have faith" (μὴ φοβοῦ, μόνον πίστευ, 5:36). Instead of repeating the young man's faithful declaration of Jesus's resurrection (16:7), "they said nothing to anyone; for they were afraid" (ἐφοβοῦντο γάρ, 16:8).

In the shadow of the worst kinds of suffering life entails, including deadly political violence, children inexplicably falling sick and dying, and torment at the hands of deadly spiritual powers, Mark's narrative demands that readers trust Jesus for salvation. Yet it also acknowledges that this trust will not necessarily be rewarded. Children (especially in the ancient world) die of sudden illness and inexplicable violence—as did God's Son! Mark presents no clear evidence that God will resolve this horrible catastrophe, even if children at death's door are sometimes saved. In these and analogous situations, Mark demands faith but also recognizes the audacity of that demand. The Second Gospel calls for conviction that God can do anything, including defeat death, but it presents an account of Jesus's ministry that traces possible boundaries protecting death from his divine power. Mark thereby gestures at a pessimistic worldview more familiar from Homer than from the New Testament:

> But death is universal. Even gods
> cannot protect the people that they love,
> when fate and cruel death catch up with them. (*Od.* 3.236–239)[96]

The father's response of "I believe; help my unbelief" articulates this tension between trust and skepticism precisely, dialogizing the confession of faith whose ultimate object is God's power, exercised in Jesus, to defeat death—a power Mark, like Homer, persistently doubts.

---

96. Quoting Homer, *The Odyssey*, trans. Emily R. Wilson (New York: Norton, 2018), 142, with reference to Thomas W. Allen, ed., *Homeri opera*, 2nd ed., 4 vols., OCT (Oxford: Clarendon, 1922).

2
A Dialogue about Resurrection (Mark 12:18–27)

In the previous chapter I invoked a broadly Bakhtinian concept of dialogue[1] to describe the competing representations of and responses to resurrection that Mark's narrative incorporates—some gesturing at literal resurrection from the dead, others restricting it to the realm of the symbolic; some announcing faith in resurrection, others refusing to speak about it or voicing doubt. I also observed the evangelist's neglect to sanction one mode of response at the expense of the other. Mark 12:18–27 involves an actual dialogue about resurrection. Analyzing it will allow for a fuller explanation of the sense in which Mark's *commentarii* constitute a dialogical work of theologically engaged literary art, especially with reference to its treatment of resurrection.

The Questions Debated

The Sadducees propose a scenario that implies the levirate law promulgated in Deut 25 and applied in the story of Tamar (Gen 38), both of which they allude to in Mark 12:19–21, challenges Jesus's belief in eschatological resurrection (ἀνάστασις ἐκ νεκρῶν; see 12:25). If six brothers marry a widow in consecutive attempts to "raise up" (ἐξαναστήσῃ, 12:19) an heir for her deceased husband, their eldest sibling, whose husband will she be at the resurrection (12:20–23)? Since it is impossible for her to be the wife of all seven, there can be no personal resurrection, the Sadducees imply.

---

[1]. I have pursued this approach elsewhere as well (Busch, "Questioning and Conviction," esp. 477–78, 496–98). For the purposes of this chapter's analysis, especially relevant is Bakhtin, *Problems of Dostoevsky's Poetics*, 78–100, with which I engage below.

Hellenistic and rabbinic texts agree that the Sadducees reject resurrection (e.g., Acts 4:1–2; 23:6–8).[2] This may relate to their refusal to accept innovative religious ideas, including belief in angels, supposedly not found in the Torah, which they may have embraced as the only canonical scripture (Josephus, *A.J.* 13.297; Origen, *Cels.* 1.49).[3] For that reason, commentators sometimes understand the Sadducees' scenario to amount to an assertion that faith in resurrection cannot be true because it contradicts the Torah.[4] Since Moses did not anticipate the problem with resurrection they pose, the Torah, which Moses authored, cannot be understood to countenance a belief in resurrection raising that problem.[5]

This interpretation misses the fact that Mark presents the Sadducees as not only refusing to believe in resurrection but also embracing an alternative understanding of life after death, one not linked to a person's eternal survival. In Mark 12:19, Mark's Sadducees conflate in their hypothetical scenario LXX Deut 25:5–6 and Gen 38:8: "If the brother of a certain man dies and leaves behind a wife and he has not left any children ... his brother should take the wife and raise up an offspring for his brother." The phrase "raise up an offspring" (ἐξαναστήσῃ σπέρμα) comes directly

---

2. See also Josephus, *A.J.* 18.16; *B.J.* 2.165; m. Sanh. 10:1, widely understood to condemn beliefs of the Sadducees.

3. Cf. Acts 23:8, though its interpretation is controversial. Acts may suggest that the Sadducees distinguished between angelic and spiritual resurrection and denied both, not that they rejected belief in angels. See Benedict T. Viviano and Justin Taylor, "Sadducees, Angels, and Resurrection (Acts 23:8–9)," *JBL* 111 (1992): 496–98. David Daube and Wright understand Acts to imply the Sadducees denied that the deceased existed in an intermediate disembodied state (i.e., as an angel or spirit). See Daube, "On Acts 23: Sadducees and Angels," *JBL* 109 (1990): 493–97; Wright, *Resurrection*, 131–40. Matthew Thiessen doubts the validity of the Acts report. See Thiessen, "A Buried Pentateuchal Allusion to the Resurrection in Mark 12:25," *CBQ* 76 (2014): 276–77. The Sadducees, like others, believed angels to be celestial bodies. Jesus bases his claim that the risen are like angels in heaven on this common belief. In Mark 12:26, he invokes God's fulfilled promise to Abraham of offspring likened to heavenly stars to convince the Sadducees of the biblical authority of his view (Gen 22:17; 26:4; etc.).

4. Donahue and Harrington, *Gospel of Mark*, 350; Gundry, *Mark*, 702. Even thoughtful treatments of the Sadducees' teaching about the afterlife, such as Viviano and Taylor, Daube, and Wright, tend to frame the issue in terms of what an absolute commitment to the Pentateuch forbids the Sadducees to believe, so that Jesus's opponents become something akin to Torah fundamentalists. See Viviano and Taylor, "Sadducees, Angels, and Resurrection"; Daube, "On Acts 23"; Wright, *Resurrection*, 131–40.

5. Collins, *Mark*, 560.

from Gen 38:8, but it also evokes eschatological resurrection. Paul can use ἐξανίστημι to refer to the eschatological "raising up" or "resurrection from among the dead" (ἐξανάστασις ἐκ νεκρῶν, Phil 3:11). He and other New Testament writers use ἀνίστημι or its nominal form to refer to the resurrection as well (e.g., John 11:24; Rom 6:5; 1 Cor 15:12, 13, 21, 42; 1 Thess 4:16; Heb 6:2; 11:35). In this pericope, Mark uses the word with this meaning multiple times (see 12:23 [perhaps twice] and 25).[6] Mark's Sadducees do not cite Gen 38's example of the levirate law's application merely to show that the Torah rejects eschatological resurrection. More pointedly, as an alternative to Jesus's belief in personal "resurrection from among the dead" (ἀνάστασις ἐκ νεκρῶν, Mark 12:25), the Sadducees hold to a different kind of "raising up" (ἀνάστασις), namely, a "raising up of offspring" (ἐξανάστασις σπέρματος, 12:19). As opposed to revivifying a person's dead body, God resurrects people by "raising up" descendants in whom they continue to live after they themselves die.

Mark 12 not only contrasts Jesus's belief in postmortem continuity of embodied identity with the Sadducees' belief that God provides for life after death by means of familial continuity over generations. As J. Gerald Janzen suggests, it also raises questions about the reasonableness of faith in any kind of divinely overseen life after death whatever.[7] In the scenario the Sadducees invoke, the levirate law *fails* to raise up offspring (οὐκ ἀφῆκαν σπέρμα, 12:22). In fact, Gen 38 features a recurring failure of the levirate law, which the Sadducees' example of a woman being married consecutively to seven brothers who each die without producing an heir extends ad absurdum. In Genesis, Er, Onan, and Shelah in turn fail to produce offspring with Tamar (the first two brothers because of death; the third because his father withholds him). This leads Tamar to the questionable step of seducing her father-in-law, Judah, to produce an heir in whom her deceased husband might live again—a desperate act for which the divinely instituted levirate law certainly did not provide!

The levirate law's insufficiency is not unique to Gen 38's story of Judah's family. As Dvora Weisberg has shown, everywhere the Bible thematizes levirate marriage as a means of providing for family continuity, it registers anxiety about whether the law will be followed, if not resistance to its adherence. This includes the legislation establishing the practice (Deut

---

6. NA[28] brackets as textually suspect its second appearance in 12:23.
7. J. Gerald Janzen, "Resurrection and Hermeneutics: On Exodus 3.6 in Mark 12.26," *JSNT* 7 (1985): 43–58.

25:5–10).⁸ The Genesis text the Sadducees' scenario elaborates remains special, however, in that it assigns God responsibility for the levirate law's failure. By killing Er, Tamar's first husband, for unspecified wickedness before he begets a son, God initiates the crisis in family continuity that levirate marriage must resolve. God does not help matters when he kills Onan, her second, who attempts to avoid impregnating his new wife, for this makes Tamar's father-in-law, Judah, warry to marry her to his third son, Shelah, prompting Tamar to take matters into her own hands and raise up offspring for her original husband outside the levirate framework.

The Sadducees' hypothetical scenario in Mark 12 recalls and exaggerates this failure of the levirate law. As Janzen asks, "If God by the very means divinely provided in the Torah—the Levirate law—cannot or will not raise up children to a dead man (not even after an ideal number of opportunities), on what basis is one entitled to hope that God either will or can raise up that dead man himself—something for which the Mosaic Torah makes no provision at all?" Therefore, the Sadducees "have to be credited with raising a problem which ... dogs that form of religious existence presented within or based upon the biblical tradition ...: What credit can one give to the postulates of faith or the claims of revelation, in the face of the unceasing contradictions in human experience of those postulates and those claims?"⁹ The Markan Sadducees' objections to resurrection are honest and thoughtful. They point to an understanding of life after death that the Torah authorizes as an alternative to Jesus's belief in eschatological resurrection. However, the Sadducees implicitly interrogate their own understanding of postmortem existence as well as Jesus's, elaborating tensions in the scriptural tradition on which they base their teaching. Their hypothetical scenario thus raises questions both about the proper way to understand God's provision of life after death (i.e., as generational continuity or as continuity of embodied personal and social identity) and about God's ability to contend with death by any means at all.

Jesus responds to the former of these questions by suggesting that eschatological resurrection will involve more disjunction with preresurrection embodied life than the Sadducees' reduction of it to continuity of somatic and social identity presumes. Resurrected persons, though remaining themselves in some recognizable sense, will be transformed into

---

8. Dvora E. Weisberg, "The Widow of Our Discontent: Levirate Marriage in the Bible and Ancient Israel," *JSOT* 28 (2004): 405–6.

9. Janzen, "Resurrection and Hermeneutics," 48.

2. A Dialogue about Resurrection (Mark 12:18–27)

angelic beings who will not marry (12:25). Therefore, the kind of familial confusion about which the Sadducees worry will pose no problem.

Mark's description of resurrection existence resembles Paul's. While the similarities could result from a shared religious milieu, if Mark was familiar with Pauline theology or with the Pauline mission, as is increasingly thought,[10] the Second Evangelist may understand the Sadducees' question to present an objection to embodied resurrection related to those the apostle addresses in 1 Cor 15. There is no agreement about what the challenges were, and different people at Corinth probably objected to resurrection on different and even mutually exclusive grounds.[11] I will discuss one interpretive possibility when I analyze the Sadducees' position in more detail below. At this point, though, it is enough to note that Jesus's comparison of resurrected life to angelic existence parallels Paul's argument that the former involves a disjunctive transformation of the body into celestial spirit, on the model of the risen Christ, whom Paul calls a "man from heaven" (ἄνθρωπος ἐξ οὐρανοῦ, 1 Cor 15:42–49).[12] This heavenly man provides an analogue to the Markan's Jesus's "angels in heaven" (ἄγγελοι ἐν τοῖς οὐρανοῖς, Mark 12:25).

The conclusion Mark's Jesus draws from his comparison of risen people to angels—namely, that they will not marry—may stand in tension with the broader ancient Jewish apocalyptic context in which Markan eschatology is normally situated, further supporting a specific connection with Paul. Many contemporary Jewish sources seem to have assumed that mundane personal relationships would resume after the resurrection,[13] but 1 Corinthians urges believers not to marry and, if they are married

---

10. See, e.g., many of the essays in Becker, Engberg-Pedersen, and Mueller, *For and against Pauline Influence on Mark*; and in Wischmeyer, Sim, and Elmer, *Two Authors at the Beginnings of Christianity*. Several of these are cited throughout this volume, including later in this chapter.

11. See Martin, *Corinthian Body*, 104–36.

12. For the possible connection, see Donahue and Harrington, *Gospel of Mark*, 350; Taylor, *Gospel according to St. Mark*, 483. For angelic bodies constituted of πνεῦμα (cf. 1 Cor 15:42–49, which describes risen bodies in the same way), see 1 En. 15.6–7; Tertullian, *Apol.* 22.5.

13. Collins doubts the relevance of many of these sources (which she finds discussed at Str-B, 1:887–90) and the prevalence of belief in postresurrection marital relations they seem to presume (*Mark*, 561). She claims that "the question of the Sadducees is based on a caricature of the belief in resurrection current among Jews in the first century CE" (Collins, *Mark*, 561). But it is not clear why belief in marriage's

already, to live as if they were not (1 Cor 7:25–31). Paul explains the advice with reference to the impending eschatological transformation, which he believes will render such relationships obsolete (1 Cor 7:31b; see also 15:35–54).

Mark's argument is also unusual in that Jewish apocalyptic literature normally presents angels as sexually threatening, not as asexual. Genesis 6:1–4 was widely read as a story of angels mating with human women, including in texts that agree with Mark (and Paul) in presenting resurrected life as angelic (e.g., 1 En. 6–19; see also 15.6–7). Paul himself possibly invokes this popular belief in angelic (hyper)sexuality when he offers "on account of the angels" as one reason why women ought not to prophesy with unveiled heads (1 Cor 11:10), presumably in angels' presence (cf. 1 Cor 13:1–2).[14] Marcus views the conclusion of Jesus's argument in Mark 12 as likewise reflecting a belief in angelic sexuality. He sees the otherwise superfluous assimilation of the resurrected to angels "in the heavens" (Mark 12:25) as indicating their comparison to nonfallen angels, for these alone, as suggested by Gen 6:1–4, resisted mating with human women (see 1 En. 15.3–10).[15] However, it is more likely that 1 Cor 11:8–10 understands angels to have mediated the divine creation of woman from man in Gen 2, just as they mediate the divine institution of the law in Gal 3:19. Women thus reflect God's glory less directly than men (see 1 Cor 11:7) and are appropriately veiled in cultic contexts.[16]

Understood in this way, 1 Cor 11:2–16 complements the passages from 1 Cor 7 and 15 cited above, and the three elucidate Jesus's argument in Mark. Paul and the Corinthians agree that the Christ event dissolves the hierarchically gendered distinction that Gen 2 etiologizes, which underlies both veiling and marriage. Paul expects this dissolution to be consummated at the eschatological resurrection, when human bodies will be recreated in the image of the primal man (see 1 Cor 15:42–49),[17] or perhaps of the originally androgynous "male and female" person from Gen 1:27 (see Gal 3:28). In either case, the first human being would have stood

---

continuance after resurrection should require explicit proof to avoid being labeled a "caricature" of resurrection faith.

14. See Martin, *Corinthian Body*, 229–49.
15. Marcus, *Mark 8–16*, 833–84.
16. Jason David BeDuhn, "'Because of the Angels': Unveiling Paul's Anthropology in 1 Corinthians 11," *JBL* 118 (1999): 308–20.
17. BeDuhn, "Because of the Angels," 318.

among the angels before they mediated God's creation of woman in Gen 2.[18] For Paul, this expected eschatological transformation authorizes marriage's attrition in the present (see 1 Cor 7:25–31), but some Corinthians believed that a wider array of social practices should attest to the abolishment of gendered hierarchies in Christ, including unveiling in cultic settings.[19]

Luke's redaction of the Markan episode clarifies the assumptions about marriage that come into view when Jesus's reference to angels is interpreted against a Pauline background. In revising Mark 12:25, Luke specifies that the eschatologically resurrected will neglect marriage (Luke 20:35) not simply because they will become like angels but because they will become immortal: "they do not marry nor are they given in marriage, for being like angels, they can no longer die" (20:36).[20] Luke's redaction at once eliminates the apparent strangeness of Mark's suggestion that angels are not sexual and makes explicit the logic underlying Jesus's response to his Sadducean interlocutors. Self-perpetuation through procreation (raising up offspring) is irrelevant to the coming age, when the one whose life would thereby be perpetuated has risen from the dead, never to die again. Thus, while Mark's Sadducees expect life after death through the natural procreation of related persons in the context of marriage, Mark's Jesus believes that at the eschaton, the righteous will personally rise to eternal life so that self-perpetuation through procreation will become obsolete.

---

18. For readings that consider Paul's belief in original and eschatological androgyny, see Wayne A. Meeks, "The Image of the Androgyne: Some Uses of a Symbol in Earliest Christianity," *HR* 13 (1974): 165–208; Taylor G. Petrey, "The Resurrection Body," in *The Oxford Handbook of New Testament, Gender, and Sexuality*, ed. Benjamin H. Dunning (New York: Oxford University Press, 2019), 665.

19. For a reconstruction of the unveiled women's position in debate with Paul's, see Shelly Matthews, "A Feminist Analysis of the Veiling Passage (1 Corinthians 11:2–16): Who Really Cares That Paul Was Not a Gender Egalitarian After All?," *LD* (2015): 10–13. Troels Engberg-Pedersen suggests that Paul in 1 Cor 11:11–12 backs away from his resistance to his addressees' position because it coheres with Paul's own "rule of no distinctions." See Engberg-Pedersen, "1 Corinthians 11:16 and the Character of Pauline Exhortation," *JBL* 110 (1991): 683, 688 (cf. Gal 3:28).

20. See Wright, *Resurrection*, 420–22. Luke's alterations may more readily accommodate Paul's anticipation of this eschatological development in present celibacy among believers. See Turid Karlsen Seim, "Children of the Resurrection: Perspectives on Angelic Asceticism in Luke-Acts," in *Asceticism in the New Testament*, ed. Leif E. Vaage and Vincent L. Wimbush (New York: Routledge, 1999), 115–25, esp. 119–20.

Mark's Jesus (like Luke's and perhaps Paul) presumes the purpose of marriage to be procreation. Eschatologically resurrected angelic humans, no longer needing reproduction to ensure immortality, and perhaps no longer sexually differentiated, will abandon the institution.[21]

The Answers Proposed

As mentioned above, the Sadducees pose questions not only about the kind of postmortem existence one might legitimately anticipate but also about God's power to contend with death by any means at all. The latter questions too spring from Gen 38's involvement of God in Judah's scandalous failure to raise up offspring for his son by means of the levirate law. Jesus's words from Mark 12:26, which echo a famous passage from the Torah in which God refers to himself as the three patriarchs' God (see Exod 3:6, 15–16), meet the Sadducees on the terms they have adopted to suggest the following answer. God is not only the one who presided over the generative fiasco in which Judah and his three sons found themselves embroiled; he is also the God of Abraham, Isaac, and Jacob, Judah's three progenitors. In response to Gen 38's implication of the levirate law and God himself in a failure to raise up an heir for Judah's son, which the Sadducees' scenario recalls, the divine appellation from Exod 3 that Jesus quotes thematizes God's involvement in the successful patriarchal generation leading up to Judah and his sons.[22]

Genesis 30:22 reports that God listened to the prayers of Jacob's wife Rachel and "opened her womb," even though she had long been barren. Genesis 29 uses the same phrase of Leah, whose womb was opened so that she bore multiple children, despite her husband's hatred (29:31). Likewise, Gen 25:21 states that when Isaac prayed for his barren wife, Rebekah, God answered his prayer and she conceived Jacob and Esau. Most impressively, God raised up Isaac for Abraham and Sarah when Abraham was one hundred years old (Gen 21:5) and his wife was menopausal (Gen 18:11–13; see also 21:7). Jesus's invocation of God by the names of these patriarchs recalls God's miraculous generative successes that ensured the existence of

---

21. Caroline Vander Stichele, "Like Angels in Heaven: Corporeality, Resurrection, and Gender in Mark 12:18–27," in *Begin with the Body: Corporeality, Religion and Gender*, ed. Jonneke Bekkenkamp and Maaike de Haardt (Leuven: Peeters, 1998), 227–28.

22. Janzen, "Resurrection and Hermeneutics," 51–53.

2. A Dialogue about Resurrection (Mark 12:18–27)

the patriarchal line, which ultimately issued in Judah and his sons. God, all this implies, is willing and able to raise up children through whom parents can continue to live after they die, and he does this not only by the natural means for which the levirate law provides but in more impressive ways as well, including the revitalization of barren bodies.

Mark is not alone to invoke miraculous patriarchal (and matriarchal) generation as evidence of God's power to provide eternal life by raising the dead. The same association surfaces in Romans, where Paul equates faith in the resurrection with Abraham's faith that God would produce for him and Sarah offspring in their old age (Rom 4:16–24). While Paul saw God's revitalization of the couple's aged bodies as a type of Jesus's resurrection, Janzen goes too far in claiming that Mark has in mind this particular understanding of Isaac's miraculous conception and birth when he offers Exod 3:6, 15–16 as a prooftext for resurrection in Mark 12.[23] Nonetheless, the parallel invocation of patriarchal generation to establish God's power to raise the dead buttresses the more expansive interpretation in Mark 12:26 of the reference to the "God of Abraham, Isaac, and Jacob" presented above. That Markan reference not only employs a well-known divine appellation but strategically alludes to a series of patriarchal stories from the Torah understood by some readers (e.g., Paul) to highlight God's miraculous power to raise up offspring even from paternal bodies all but dead.

Just before quoting Exod 3:6, Jesus asks the Sadducees, οὐ διὰ τοῦτο πλανᾶσθε μὴ εἰδότες τὰς γραφὰς μηδὲ τὴν δύναμιν τοῦ θεοῦ (Mark 12:24). Most translators understand this to mean "Are you not therefore wrong because you do not know the scriptures or God's power?"[24] However, the basic meaning of πλανᾶσθαι is to wander or to be led astray (see Mark 13:5–6), and this nuance is crucial:[25] "Are you not therefore led astray because you do not know the scriptures or God's power?" Mark's Jesus suggests that the Sadducees meander ignorantly through the Torah. They wander off on a tangent represented by the anomalous story in Gen 38, which involves not only God's failure to perpetuate the line of generational succession through levirate marriage but also God himself (inadvertently?) almost cutting that line off. The Sadducees are not so much wrong as they are errant, and Jesus directs them back to a more central theme from the

---

23. Janzen, "Resurrection and Hermeneutics," 53–54.
24. E.g., NRSV; NIV; Donahue and Harrington, *Gospel of Mark*, 348.
25. See "πλανάω," BAGD, 821–22, esp. definition 1a.

Torah, namely, the generative power that the God of Abraham, Isaac, and Israel exercises throughout his interactions with the patriarchs and their wives. This divine power, which ensures familial succession even by raising up offspring from withered men and lifeless wombs, is the same power that will raise the dead at the eschaton.

Understood in this way, Mark 12:26 decisively resolves the Sadducees' secondary concern about God's ability to contend with death. It is more difficult, however, to construe Jesus's words as settling their primary question, namely, whether God will provide for personal life after death by extraordinary supernatural intervention (the "resurrection" of the dead) or instead rely on more natural generational continuity (the "raising up" of offspring), as the Torah suggests.[26]

Jesus introduces the Exodus quotation by relating it to the dead's resurrection ("concerning the dead, that they are raised, have you not read in the book of Moses") before invoking God by means of the biblical moniker "God of Abraham, Isaac, and Jacob" (12:26) and declaring that "he is not the God of the dead but of the living" (12:27). This suggests to many that Mark invokes the divine appellation from Exod 3:6, 15–16 as a straightforward prooftext for the eschatological resurrection of the dead. The interpretation follows a line of reasoning such as Craig Evans spells out: "Jesus's hearers, friendly or antagonistic, would all agree that God is a God of the living [Mark 12:27]. If this is true and if God identifies himself also as the 'God of Abraham ..., Isaac, and ... Jacob' [12:26], logic suggests that someday these patriarchs will again be alive. This will take place through the resurrection."[27] However, readers at least since Jerome have found the logic of Jesus's citation less clear than that, for 12:26 and 12:27 in conjunction imply not that the patriarchs are dead and awaiting eschatological resurrection, which is what Jesus's argument requires, but rather that they are (in some sense) still alive.[28] Indeed, this is the interpretive conclusion

---

26. The oppositions (natural vs. supernatural and personal vs. impersonal or collective) are anachronistic and not entirely aligned with the terms of the debate. Although they serve as a useful heuristic for the two positions, Paul troubles them (see n. 47).

27. Craig A. Evans, *Mark 8:27–16:20*, WBC 34B (Nashville: Nelson, 2001), 256; see also Morna Dorothy Hooker, *The Gospel according to Saint Mark*, BNTC (Peabody, MA: Hendrickson, 1991), 285.

28. Jerome writes in book 3 of his *Commentary on Matthew* (referring to 22:31–32, the Matthean parallel) that Jesus, "in order to prove the truth of resurrection, could have used many other examples that were much more clear" and later speculates that

2. A Dialogue about Resurrection (Mark 12:18–27)

4 Maccabees draws from the very same trigenerational divine appellation in a similar rhetorical context: "but as many as take thought of piety from the whole heart, these alone are able to overcome the passions of the flesh, believing that they do not die to God [θεῷ οὐκ ἀποθνῄσκουσιν], as our patriarchs Abraham, Isaac, and Jacob do not, but rather live to God [ζῶσιν τῷ θεῷ]" (4 Macc 7:18–19; see also 16:25). While scholars sometimes co-opt 4 Maccabees in support of Mark's use of Exod 3:6, 15–16 as a prooftext for resurrection, this book clearly understands immortality as something akin to a soul that surviving the body after its death (4 Macc 13:15; 18:23), rather than as the eschatological resurrection of dead bodies.[29]

Jesus, "for the sake of proving the eternity of souls, lays down the example from Moses [Exod 3:6] ... so that, when he will have proved that souls continue after death (for it could not come about that [God] would be the God of those who in no way remained in existence), as a consequence, the resurrection of bodies will be maintained, which have done good or evil along with the souls." See Émile Bonnard, ed., *Saint Jérôme, Commentaire sur S. Matthieu: Texte Latin, introduction, traduction et notes*, 2 vols., SC 242, 259 (Paris: Cerf, 1977). According to Jerome, if the Exodus passage establishes anything about postmortem existence, it is the immortality of souls, with resurrection a secondary inference.

Bradley R. Trick critiques Evans's interpretation for its lack of logical rigor. See Trick, "Death, Covenants, and the Proof of Resurrection in Mark 12:18–27," *NovT* 49 (2007): 246 n. 36. Some modern scholars propose constructions of Jesus's perplexing interpretive argument more complicated than the one Evans lays out, claiming, for instance, that Jesus was using a typical rabbinic mode of grammatical exegesis by playing on the present tense of Exod 3:4 in order to argue for immortality. See E. Earle Ellis, "Jesus, the Sadducees and Qumran," *NTS* 10 (1964): 274–79. Alternatively, François Dreyfus argues that Jesus's use of this text to prove resurrection parallels other ancient uses of it to invoke God as a protector in the present based on the commitments he made to the patriarchs in the past. See Dreyfus, "L'argument scripturaire de Jésus en faveur de la résurrection des morts (Marc, Xii, 26–27)," *RB* 66 (1959): 224. Dennis Nineham cites as a parallel a rabbinic interpretation of Deut 11:9 as proof of resurrection "on the grounds that God there promised the three patriarchs to give the land *to them*" (emphasis original). See Nineham, *The Gospel of St. Mark*, PNTC (Hammondsworth: Penguin, 1969), 321. These last two arguments have more recently been developed by Trick, "Death, Covenants, and the Proof." For a discussion of a range of understandings of Jesus's employment of the Exodus passage, see David B. Sloan, "God of Abraham, God of the Living: Jesus's Use of Exodus 3:6 in Mark 12:26–27," *WTJ* 74 (2012): 85–98.

29. F. Gerald Downing observes analogous parallels between Mark and Philo's understandings of Exod 3:6, both of which, he believes, draw conclusions from the text about something approximating immortality of the soul: "Relatedness to God constitutes a life that death cannot disrupt." See Downing, "The Resurrection of the

Perusing the relevant scholarship, one encounters claims that though Mark's exegesis in support of resurrection may not be persuasive or even intelligible to us, the Second Evangelist was playing by accepted hermeneutical rules of his day.[30] But the problems with the Markan Jesus's interpretive argument cannot be dismissed as modern impositions on an ancient text. Jesus's argument troubles not merely because it fails to provide clear exegetical support for eschatological resurrection. More seriously, the text Jesus cites and the evident logic of his citation actually point to the view of postmortem existence for which the Sadducees have been arguing, namely, that people rise again naturally and collectively in their offspring. The God of Abraham, Isaac, and Jacob is not a God of the dead but of the living. Therefore, Abraham, Isaac, and Jacob are not dead but alive. That conclusion makes perfect sense from the Sadducees' perspective: the patriarchs continue to live in their line of descendants, whose perpetuation the levirate law facilitates. Beyond that, Jesus's careful introduction of Exod 3:6, 15–16 as a prooftext demands its properly contextualized interpretation (Mark 12:26), especially in the light of his earlier critique of the Sadducees for themselves wandering lost through Scripture (12:24). Such an interpretation requires reading the Torah in a way that supports the Sadducees' understanding of life after death as generational continuity rather than Jesus's belief in eschatological resurrection.[31]

Dead: Jesus and Philo," *JSNT* 5 (1982): 45. For Wright, the parallels between Mark, Philo, and 4 Maccabees buttress the argument that the saying in Mark points to the continued existence of the patriarchs in some sort of intermediate state awaiting resurrection (*Resurrection*, 424–25).

30. E.g., Gundry, *Mark*, 704. Some scholars take issue with this argument, claiming that Jesus's exegesis violates rather than upholds the conventions invoked to explain it. See Dan M. Cohn-Sherbok, "Jesus's Defence of the Resurrection of the Dead," *JSNT* 4 (1981): 64–73; John P. Meier, "The Debate on the Resurrection of the Dead: An Incident from the Ministry of the Historical Jesus?," *JSNT* 22 (2000): 11–12. Meier notes that no argument from the Talmud uses Exod 3:6 to prove the resurrection; it is not until the medieval Midrash HaGadol that one finds such a use of Exod 3:6 (in a variant reading).

31. Although dated, see H. Wheeler Robinson, *Corporate Personality in Ancient Israel*, rev. ed. (Philadelphia: Fortress, 1980), 25–28. See also Otto Schwankl, *Die Sadduzäerfrage (Mk 12, 18–27 Parr): Eine exegetisch-theologische Studie zur Auferstehungserwartung*, BBB 66 (Frankfurt am Main: Athenäum, 1987), 154. For an argument about ancient Israelite belief in the afterlife that integrates this interpretation of the Pentateuch, see Herbert Chanan Brichto, "Kin, Cult, Land and Afterlife—A Biblical Complex," *HUCA* 44 (1973): 1–54. Brichto elaborates his reading of the Pen-

When God expels Adam and Eve from Eden (Gen 3:24), he immediately compensates them for their loss of eternal life by helping them conceive a child: "Adam knew Eve his wife and having conceived she bore Cain and said, 'I have gotten a man through God'" (Gen 4:1 LXX). Genesis thereby introduces human generation as an alternative to the source of presumably everlasting life human beings forfeited after having been ejected from Eden and denied access to its tree of life.[32] This association of procreation with immortality explains why, when Rachel later begs Jacob to raise up an offspring in her womb, she says, "Give me children; if not, I will die" (Gen 30:1 LXX). Robert Alter sees her words as evidence of "impulsivity," "impetuousness," and "simmering frustration," but this is a case where his focus on literary dynamics, as opposed to religious background, leads to a less than satisfactory reading of the text. [33] Rachel may be frustrated but for good reason. Without children her life will end in the same way Eve's would have had she not given birth. Outside Eden, offspring represent the only form of immortality the Torah offers.[34]

One finds a related assimilation of eternal life to the generation of offspring in the Abraham cycle. There God makes a covenant with Abraham and proceeds to call it eternal (διαθήκην αἰώνιον) because it involves Abraham's "offspring" (σπέρμα) as well as himself: "I will establish my covenant between myself and you and your offspring after you, including their descendants, for an eternal covenant, to be the God of you and your offspring after you. And I will give to you and your offspring after you the land" (Gen 17:7-8 LXX). Abraham can transcend his personal life's temporal limitations and participate in an everlasting covenant with the eternal God because that covenant involves Abraham's descendants as well as himself. The interrelationship, even identity, of these two parties helps explain why God constantly (and confusingly) shifts back and

---

tateuch, which focuses on generational and geographical continuity, with reference to biblical writings about Sheol. According to ancient Israelite religion, "The condition of the dead in this afterlife is, in a vague but significant way, connected with proper burial upon the ancestral land and with the continuation on that land of the dead's proper progeny" (Brichto, "Kin, Cult, Land," 23).

32. See, e.g., Ziony Zevit, *What Really Happened in the Garden of Eden?* (New Haven: Yale University Press, 2013), 227–36.

33. Robert Alter, *Genesis: Translation and Commentary* (New York: Norton, 1996), 158.

34. As Janzen observes in response to a similar comment Alter elsewhere makes on Gen 30:1 ("Resurrection and Hermeneutics," 58 n. 13).

forth between addressing Abraham and Abraham's offspring as the recipients of the promised land (see, e.g., Gen 12:1–3 and 7; 13:14–15 and 17; etc.), which Abraham himself never owns (unless one counts the tomb he purchases in Gen 23).[35] He will only possess that land through his descendants' receipt of it.

This helps explain Exod 3:15–16, which Jesus quotes in Mark 12:26. In Exod 3, God tells Moses to assemble the elders of Israel and to say to them, "The God of your fathers, the God of Abraham and the God of Isaac and the God of Jacob has sent me to you.... I will lead you up out of the ill usage of the Egyptians into the land of the Canaanites" (Exod 3:15–17 LXX). God remains faithful to the eternal covenant he made with Abraham and the other patriarchs by delivering the patriarchs' descendants from Egypt and leading (as it will turn out) the patriarchs' descendants' descendants (see Num 14:22–23) into the land he had promised to Abraham and the patriarchs themselves. He identifies himself as the God of Abraham, Isaac, and Jacob in his dealings with their descendants in Moses's time and later because, as the Torah understands it, the patriarchs live on impersonally in these descendants.[36]

One cannot underestimate the significance of this point for Mark 12. In its original literary context, the divine invocation that Jesus claims to prove God capable of raising the dead actually thematizes the continuing existence of Abraham, Isaac, and Jacob in their σπέρμα, their descendants in Moses's own generation and subsequent to him. That coheres not with Jesus's view of personal embodied resurrection but with the impersonal, collective view the Sadducees put forth. Moreover, it is Mark's Jesus him-

---

35. Abraham's tomb is important to Brichto's speculative construal of an ancient Israelite belief system regarding the afterlife, according to which the ancestor lives on by means of his descendants insofar as the descendants cultivate his tomb on the land he inhabited while alive (Brichto, "Kin, Cult, Land").

36. My analysis of the passage and the logic of Jesus's exegesis complements Trick, who understands Jesus to be making the point that in order for God to honor his covenants with the patriarchs, the patriarchs must be alive ("Death, Covenants, and the Proof"). That, Trick argues, is one of the reasons Jesus denies that the covenant of marriage continues after death (see also Rom 7:1–3; 1 Cor 7:39). According to Trick, Jesus's response to the Sadducees' invocation of the levirate law suggests that covenants such as marriage, which the levirate law relies on, will not last beyond death (Mark 12:25; see Trick, "Death, Covenants, and the Proof," 243). Since God keeps his covenants with the patriarchs even after they die (12:26, in context), death must be reversed by resurrection.

2. A Dialogue about Resurrection (Mark 12:18–27)

self who emphasizes the importance of the appellation's scriptural context (12:26), and it is Jesus who critiques the Sadducees' own irresponsible use of Scripture (12:24). Jesus underscores how out of place is their fixation on the failure of divinely sanctioned levirate marriage to provide for familial continuity featured in the idiosyncratic patriarchal narrative of Gen 38. He recalls for them in response the broader story of generational continuity implicit in Exod 3's divine appellation. Jesus's citation of the Torah itself points to the dominant theme of the patriarchs' divinely overseen generational successes. His inference from it that God provides for personal immortality by raising the dead, rather than collective immortality by raising up offspring, constitutes an interpretation no less errantly idiosyncratic than he claims the Sadducees' fixation on Gen 38 to be.

From Debate to Dialogism

The Markan passage's rhetorical context appears to require Jesus in 12:24–27 both to repudiate the Sadducees' implicit doubt in God's ability to overcome death through any means at all and to endorse Jesus's own position that God wills to do this through resurrecting persons from the dead. However, when Jesus's invocation of the Torah is examined with the attention to context that Jesus demands, it succeeds only in the former. While resolving the skepticism about God's power to overcome death implicit in the scriptural scenario the Sadducees posit, Jesus perpetuates questions about whether the eschatological resurrection he anticipates is part of God's plan to preserve God's people—shockingly so, since resurrection is central to his own prophetic destiny (8:31; 9:31; 10:33–34; 14:28).

Something similar occurs in Jesus's argument from Mark's version of the Beelzebul controversy, which I have elsewhere interpreted from a Bakhtinian perspective as internally dialogized double-voiced discourse.[37] Mark 3:22–30 seems to require Jesus to refute the Jerusalem scribes' accusation that he performs exorcisms under the authority of Satan. However, Mark's rhetoric subverts that expectation, so that Jesus's argument comes to support the scribes' point of view at least as well as his own. Jesus employs the symbol of a house in 3:25 to signify the continuing integrity of Satan's realm, whose violation would imply that he participates in a demonic civil conflict threatening that realm's stability: "if a house be divided against

---

37. Busch, "Questioning and Conviction."

itself, that house cannot stand. And if Satan rise up against himself, and be divided, he cannot stand, but hath an end" (3:25–26 KJV). In Mark 3:27, however, Jesus himself figures the violated autonomy of Satan's realm precisely as a house broken into and unable to stand. Thus, according to the logic laid out in verse 25, Jesus's exorcistic activity comports with the scribes' accusation: Jesus may be a party in the kind of demonic civil conflict that would mean the end of Satan's dominion, the fall of his house.[38]

Treating discrete exchanges between Jesus and other religious leaders in Mark as dialogical in a Bakhtinian sense does not represent an innovative interpretive tactic. It aligns with recent trends in the study of ancient Jewish religious debate, especially as represented in the Talmud.[39] For readers concerned about arbitrarily designating Markan controversies as other than straightforwardly disputative, my analyses of Mark 3:22–30 and 12:18–27 suggest a method of identification. Clear rhetorical signals pointing to Jesus's argument turning against itself so that it comes to support his opponents' position should be present to authorize interpretation of a particular discursive exchange as genuinely dialogic, rather than as straightforward debate. Such markers would include contradictory employment of the same motif within a single controversy (e.g., "house," in 3:22–30), leading to tension or even incoherence in Jesus's argument, were it to be construed as merely oppositional.[40] They would also include Jesus's situation of a prooftext in its scriptural context, even when that context supports the position against which he supposedly argues. I will mention other rhetorical signals relevant to Mark 12 presently, in addition to considering more carefully the interpretive implications of this broadly

---

38. Busch, "Questioning and Conviction," 482–84.

39. Most notably, Daniel Boyarin, *Socrates and the Fat Rabbis* (Chicago: University of Chicago Press, 2009). Boyarin argues that the Talmud constitutes a dialogue between disjunctive discursive fields, especially the serious and the comedic (drawing on Bakhtin's interest in Menippean satire and the carnivalesque). For a critique of Boyarin's approach and an alternative application of Bakhtinian categories, see Barry Scott Wimpfheimer, "The Dialogical Talmud: Daniel Boyarin and Rabbinics," *JQR* 101 (2011): 245–54, esp. 254. Moshe Simon-Shoshan presents a dialogic approach to religious dispute in the Talmud more closely aligned with the way in which I understand Bakhtinian dialogue to operate in the Markan Jesus's debates with competing religious authorities. See Simon-Shoshan, "Talmud as Novel: Dialogic Discourse and the Feminine Voice in the Babylonian Talmud," *PT* 40 (2019): 105–34.

40. That is not the only such marker in Mark 3:22–30; for fuller treatment, see Busch, "Questioning and Conviction," 478–86.

2. A Dialogue about Resurrection (Mark 12:18-27)

Bakhtinian approach for understanding Mark's thematization of resurrection. At this point, it is sufficient to reiterate that Jesus's invocation of Exodus does not resolve a debate about resurrection; it rather embodies a dialogue, settling some questions while leaving others open. Jesus's exegetical argument implicitly acknowledges that resurrection's skeptics have valid points. Mark 12:18-27 complements the analysis of Mark 5, 9, and 16 presented in the previous chapter. When it comes to resurrection, Mark insists on ambiguity. The Second Gospel always equivocates, authorizing alternative understandings of resurrection, even when rhetorical context would seem to demand straightforward affirmation of Jesus's view.

Connections between Mark 12:18-27 and Pauline writings suggest a plausible context in which to situate this dialogue regarding resurrection, for similar debates occurred among believers who looked to Paul as an authoritative teacher. Above I mentioned 1 Cor 7, 11, and 15 as possible interpretive background. Even more apposite are two interrelated second-century texts featuring or attributed to Paul. These assign to Paul's opponents (Demas and Hermogenes in the Acts of Paul and Thecla; Hymenaeus and Philetus in 2 Timothy) a view of resurrection identical to the Sadducean belief Mark articulates in chapter 12:

> καὶ ἡμεῖς σε διδάξομεν, ἣν λέγει οὗτος ἀνάστασιν γενέσθαι, ὅτι ἤδη γέγονεν ἐφ' οἷς ἔχομεν τέκνοις.
> And we [Demas and Hermogenes] will teach you concerning what this man [Paul] says is resurrection [or perhaps, "what this man calls the resurrection to come about"], that it has already come about in the children we have. (Acts Paul Thecl. 14) [41]

> They [Hymenaeus and Philetus] have deviated from the truth, saying that the resurrection has already come about [ἀνάστασιν ἤδη γεγονέναι]. (2 Tim 2:18)

Also relevant is 1 Tim 2:13-15, on Eve's salvation through childbirth as a model for all women (σωθήσεται δὲ διὰ τῆς τεκνογονίας, v. 15), since it seems to presume that procreation was the mode of eternal life God provided for Adam and Eve after their expulsion from Eden.

---

41. Translating Richard Lipsius, ed., *Acta Apostolorum apocrypha post Constantinum Tischendorf* (Leipzig: Mendelssohn, 1891), 1:245.

All these texts are later than Mark, but the dispute to which they allude likely dates to an earlier period. According to 1 Cor 15, resurrection was controversial among believers in Pauline churches as early as the mid-50s, and some scholars identify the Corinthian denial of resurrection (1 Cor 15:12) with the position attributed to Paul's opponents in 2 Tim 2:18, though they rarely bring to bear Acts of Paul and Thecla in attempting to reconstruct it.[42] This is not to say that opponents to Paul's teaching about resurrection necessarily privileged procreation over eschatological renewal as God's preferred means for ensuring life after death. However, the former belief may have been more widespread among first- and second-generation Jesus-believers than New Testament scholars have recognized, and it may have been a factor in generating the confusion about resurrection, or "raising up," that Paul's argument in 1 Cor 15 attempts to resolve.

The reframing of resurrection (ἀνάστασις ἐκ νεκρῶν, Mark 12:25) as procreation (ἐξαναστήσῃ σπέρμα, 12:19) that the Sadducees propose may understandably be assimilated to a denial of life after death, and 1 Cor 15 in fact goes back and forth between characterizing the Corinthians as objecting to resurrection (e.g., 15:12) and as lacking belief in personal eternal life as a more general proposition (e.g., 15:19).[43] In this interpretive context,

---

42. See, e.g., Ernst Käsemann, "On the Subject of Primitive Christian Apocalyptic," in *New Testament Questions of Today*, trans. William J. Montague (Philadelphia: Fortress, 1969), 125–26. Anthony C. Thiselton discusses interpretations of 1 Cor 15:12 privileging 2 Tim 2:17–18 as explanatory background. See Thiselton, *The First Epistle to the Corinthians: A Commentary on the Greek Text*, NIGTC (Grand Rapids: Eerdmans, 2000), 1173–74.

Scholars often interpret 2 Tim 2:18, like the denial of resurrection to which Paul responds in 1 Cor 15, under the theological rubric of "realized eschatology." Richard Bauckham holds to such an understanding, despite his appreciation of the verse's link with the Acts of Paul. See Bauckham, "*The Acts of Paul* as a Sequel to Acts," in *The Book of Acts in Its Ancient Literary Setting*, ed. Bruce W. Winter and Andrew D. Clarke, vol. 1 of *The Book of Acts in Its First Century Setting* (Grand Rapids: Eerdmans, 1993), 116–30. Bauckham believes that Acts Paul 14 presents a tendentious interpretation of 2 Tim 2:18 "occasioned by its author's desire to situate the [epistle's] teaching in the context of the story of Paul and Thecla," where resurrection is associated with procreation ("*Acts of Paul*," 128). However, Matthijs den Dulk more persuasively suggests that the Acts of Paul elaborates a theological concept of resurrection as procreation with which the author of the Pastoral Epistles also engages. See den Dulk, "I Permit No Woman to Teach Except for Thecla: The Curious Case of the Pastoral Epistles and the *Acts of Paul* Reconsidered," *NovT* 54 (2012): 176–203, esp. 198–200.

43. Later Christian writers assimilate to the Sadducees Christians skeptical about

2. A Dialogue about Resurrection (Mark 12:18-27)

Mark 12:18-27 would reflect not only debate between Sadducees and Jesus about the compatibility of belief in eschatological resurrection with the levirate law. More urgently, it would reflect a theological dispute in Pauline churches among those who believed that "resurrection ... has already come about in our children" (Acts Paul Thecl. 14; cf. 2 Tim 2:18) and those who expected persons to rise from the dead as corporeally transformed celestial beings at the end of time.[44] Mark, evidently favoring an understanding of resurrection like Paul's in 1 Cor 15, also acknowledges the persuasive potential of the alternative view on display in Mark 12. This view, after all, comports with the Torah, and many Jesus-believers might have held it, especially those committed to following the Jewish law. Thus, even as Mark 12 rejects doubt in God's power to defeat death as springing from errant focus on an idiosyncratic pentateuchal passage, it also admits that understanding resurrection as procreation might be more consistent with Scripture than Jesus's (and Paul's) belief in a personal restoration to life at the eschaton.

The dialogue of Mark 12 confirms what we know from Paul and other early writings of Jesus-believers: faith in resurrection was not a settled matter in the earliest church but a hotly debated topic.[45] Different parties understood resurrection, and life after death more generally, in different

---

resurrection (e.g., Tertullian, *Res.* 36). Although that assimilation may be based on this pericope and purely rhetorical, it is also conceivable that the connections ran deeper.

44. In much the same way, Jesus's debate with the Pharisees and scribes from Jerusalem about traditions of the elders (Mark 7:1-23) may reflect disputes between Paul and other Jesus-believing missionaries urging gentile believers to observe Jewish customs from the Torah. See Kasper Bro Larsen, "Mark 7:1-13: A Pauline Halakah?," in Becker, Engberg-Pedersen, and Mueller, *For and Against Pauline Influence on Mark*, 175-76.

Debates about resurrection in Pauline communities may have intersected with those disputes and also with debates about veiling and the role women should play in the church. As argued above, in 1 Corinthians, belief in eschatological resurrection seems to correlate with a willingness to relax gendered hierarchies and to question the value of the primary relationship stabilizing them (i.e., marriage), though not all parties agreed on the appropriate extent of that relaxation. The Pastoral Epistles (esp. 1 Tim 2:11-15) and Acts of Paul and Thecla (esp. §14), on the contrary, invoke "salvation" or "resurrection" through procreation to stabilize gendered hierarchies, especially within the context of marriage.

45. Outi Lehtipuu, *Debates over the Resurrection of the Dead: Constructing Early Christian Identity* (Oxford: Oxford University Press, 2015), esp. 67-108. One implication of my study is that these debates' participants were not uniformly acrimonious or uncompromising, and that scholars have sometimes wrongly privileged dispute over

ways, and some voiced doubt about God's power to resolve the problem of death in any satisfactory way at all. Mark represents a debate like this in chapter 12, and it includes textual signals suggesting that it remains unresolved, such as situating a prooftext for resurrection in a scriptural context that supports the Sadducees' position rather than Jesus's. It may be that Matthew's recognition of that problem led him to omit the prooftext's contextualizing introduction, counter to the tendency the First Gospel elsewhere displays to expand rather than reduce scriptural evidence supporting Jesus's controversial positions or actions (compare Mark 2:23–28 and Matt 12:1–8; Mark 3:1–12 and Matt 12:9–21). Mark also has Jesus tell the Sadducees that they are "much in error" (πολὺ πλανᾶσθε, 12:27), which, in context, should be read as a confirmation that they are not entirely wrong. Matthew and Luke evidently recognized this, for they each emend Mark's *commentarii* to provide a finalizing rejection of the Sadducean position and affirmation of Jesus's. Luke replaces "much in error" with the scribes' explicit approval of Jesus's arguments (Luke 20:39), while Matthew does the same with a statement about the persuasiveness of Jesus's argument amazing the crowds (Matt 22:33). Mark, though, is not so quick to present the understanding of ἀνάστασις Jesus holds as unimpeachable at the expense of the Sadducees' view. Jesus's debate partners (perhaps as a cipher for Paul's) offer serious challenges to faith in resurrection that were not unknown among early believers. The evangelist carefully situates these concerns within a dialogue that allows for reflection not only on the mode of life people might enjoy after death but also on questions about whether God can guarantee any life after death at all. Mark's Jesus affirms the latter against the Sadducees' implicit skepticism, even as his response to the Sadducees leaves the former question open.

In Bakhtin's formulation, the complex idea about resurrection that Mark explores in 12:18–27 reveals itself to be "inter-individual and inter-subjective—the realm of its existence is not individual consciousness but dialogic communion *between* consciousnesses. The idea is a *live event*, played out at the point of dialogic meeting between two or several consciousnesses.... The idea wants to be heard, understood, and 'answered' by other voices from other positions." The "truth" of this idea is "unified," but it cannot be finalized. The kind of idea Bakhtin has in mind "cannot in

---

dialogue as the appropriate conceptual model for understanding controversies about resurrection and afterlife in early Christian literature.

2. A Dialogue about Resurrection (Mark 12:18–27)

principle be fitted into the bounds of a single consciousness," for it is "by its very nature *full of event potential* and born at a point of contact among various consciousnesses."[46] Mark is not professing a totalizing theology of life after death, here or anywhere else. The evangelist rather orchestrates a coherent but polyphonic dialogue about it—literally so, in chapter 12, but also in the passages considered in the previous chapter, where dialogue or dialogism operates as an ideological and perhaps aesthetic principle.[47]

Mark does not exhort or instruct readers about what they must believe regarding Jesus's claim that God will raise those of his own who have died. To do so would be to skew its dialogic *commentarii* toward a different generic and ideological mode, something approaching Socratic dialogue, according to which a single consciousness (i.e., Jesus's) fully understands an idea about which his disputants (the Sadducees, the scribes, the disciples, etc.) are ignorant or obviously mistaken and thus receive imperious instruction.[48] That is not what occurs in Jesus's dialogue with the Sadducees. In chapter 12 (and elsewhere) Mark models an approach to resurrection according to which multiple and competing responses find articulation and remain valid. Mark may go so far as to suggest that resurrection can only be understood at the intersection of opposing views, poised between faith and skepticism, trust and fear, innovation and tradition. Certainly, the dialogic strategies Mark adopts in chapter 12 are peculiarly appropriate for communicating the troubling mystery of Jesus's unguaranteed promise that God will defeat death supernaturally by raising the dead.

In every place where Mark's Gospel thematizes resurrection, one finds the same thing: expressions of conviction alongside a willingness to ponder questions, including skepticism regarding whether God's king-

---

46. Bakhtin, *Problems of Dostoevsky's Poetics*, 88, 81, emphasis original.

47. Paul would approach this problem differently. At times he refutes or even delegitimizes the skepticism of those posing questions. First Corinthians 15 exemplifies this approach. However, Paul can also synthesize opposing perspectives on resurrection, yet another strategy for incorporating alternate points of view. Caroline E. Johnson Hodge highlights how Paul combines imagery of procreative generation to describe the communal inclusion of gentiles among Abraham's descendants with discourse about the gentiles' glorification at the eschatological resurrection (Rom 8:29–30). See Hodge, *If Sons, Then Heirs: A Study of Kinship and Ethnicity in the Letters of Paul* (Oxford: Oxford University Press, 2007), 109–16.

48. On philosophical monologism as pedagogical dialogue, see Bakhtin, *Problems of Dostoevsky's Poetics*, 81.

dom really can overcome death's relentless reign. Mark's Jesus finally finds himself affected by the skeptical voices about resurrection that resonate throughout the Second Gospel. At the moment he fulfills his role as the Son of Man by suffering and dying on the cross, he cries out with words expressing not trust that God will raise him but doubt in God's salvation: "My God, my God, why have you forsaken me?" (15:34). A straightforward reading of the Markan Jesus's last words holds that as the moment of his demise finally approaches, his initial faith in his own resurrection (see 8:31; 9:31; 10:34; 14:28) gives way to fear that God will not raise him from the dead after all. Jesus's question expresses the same skepticism about his father God's willingness to save his son that other fathers in Mark voice when they doubt God's ability or will to save their children from death (see 5:35–36; 9:23–24). Far from silencing cries of fear and doubt in favor of Jesus's dogmatically authoritative faith, Mark, in its depiction of Jesus's death on the cross, places an expression of faltering faith on the lips of Jesus himself.

I will have more to say about Mark 15:34 in the final chapter of my study, where I suggest that his prayer of dereliction, somewhat like the father's prayer in 9:24, reveals itself to be internally dialogized. At this point, suffice it to conclude that Jesus's dying declaration shows that skeptical questions about resurrection—including doubt regarding any form of personal life after death at all—were posed not only by voices conventionally situated at the canon's fringes or beyond its borders (e.g., anonymous members of Paul's Corinthian congregation, whose views must be reconstructed; obscure "opponents" of that apostle, such as those referred to in the Pastoral Epistles; Thomasine Christians; and so on). Such questions were posed from the dead center of the New Testament. They lie at the heart of the earliest gospel, and perhaps in the consciousness of its protagonist Jesus. This situation confirms, with Karen King and others, that distinctions between center and margin, orthodoxy and heterodoxy, unity and schism are only tendentiously drawn and of minimal value in describing the varieties of ancient Christian religious experience, which include sustained skepticism and clear-cut unbelief.[49]

---

49. Karen L. King, "Which Early Christianity?," in *The Oxford Handbook of Early Christian Studies*, ed. Susan Ashbrook and David G. Hunter (New York: Oxford University Press, 2018), 66–84.

3
Jesus's Demand for Faith and the Disciples' Doubt

At the same time as Mark's Gospel allows for voices skeptical about resurrection to sound, the evangelist amplifies voices that not only call for resurrection faith but demand willing death on its basis and threaten with eschatological condemnation those who refuse. This imperative becomes explicit in Jesus's mandate that his disciples emulate the prophesied destiny of the Son of Man, which involves betrayal, suffering, and death in anticipation of imminent resurrection (see 8:31; 9:31; 10:33-34). The expectation that Jesus's students will join him in embracing the Son of Man's prophesied fate first surfaces in 8:31-9:1, where Jesus requires those who would follow to "take up their cross" (8:34) in anticipation of resurrection life (8:35-37).[1] Jesus elaborates his requirement that disciples follow him to crucifixion in the hope of resurrection at various points throughout

---

1. Jesus's requirement that his disciples embrace the fate he prophesies for himself as Son of Man relates to Dan 7, where the figure at least in part symbolizes God's holy people Israel. According to John J. Collins, the "collective interpretation" became not without reason "the standard [critical] view [of the Son of Man in Dan 7] by the end of the nineteenth century." See Collins, *Daniel: A Commentary on the Book of Daniel*, Hermeneia (Minneapolis: Fortress, 1993), 308-9 (esp. n. 285); see also Delbert Burkett, *The Son of Man Debate: A History and Evaluation*, SNTNMS 107 (Cambridge: Cambridge University Press, 2000), 35-37. The arguments for this interpretation are compelling. See especially Morna Dorthy Hooker, *The Son of Man in Mark: A Study of the Background of the Term "Son of Man" and Its Use in St. Mark's Gospel* (London: SPCK, 1967), 11-32; Maurice Casey, *The Solution to the "Son of Man" Problem*, LNTS 343 (London: Bloomsbury, 2009), 82-91.

Scholars occasionally acknowledge that the corporate dimension of the Son of Man informs Mark's treatment of the figure. See, e.g., Hooker, *Son of Man in Mark*, 156-59, on Mark 13, and especially Jane Schaberg, "Daniel 7, 12 and the New Testament Passion-Resurrection Predictions," *NTS* 31 (1985): 215-17. On the historical Jesus's (speculated) use of "Son of Man" for Israel, whose destiny of suffering and vin-

Mark's *commentarii*. Yet Mark always circumscribes Jesus's discourse to indicate a particular application to his students within the Second Gospel, rather than a broader application to later believers including Mark's readers—a distinction scholars do not always observe, though its significance is crucial. The imperative of 8:34, and the succeeding material in chapter 9, provides a conceptual framework for understanding Mark's depiction of Jesus's students throughout the passion narrative. Mark ultimately portrays Peter, James, and John, alongside the others, refusing to follow the Son of Man to suffering, death, and resurrection, with that refusal reflecting their lack of trust in God's willingness or ability to save by resurrection those who die in his service. Mark will not require the readers, who presumably understand themselves to be disciples of Jesus in a different sense, to exercise the faith that Jesus's original disciples fail to demonstrate within its pages.

The Disciples' Skepticism about Resurrection in Mark 8:27–9:29

Mark 8:31–9:1: Rebuking Resurrection

After the Markan Jesus's first prediction of the Son of Man's suffering, death, and resurrection (8:31), the evangelist reports that Peter immediately "began to rebuke" (ἤρξατο ἐπιτιμᾶν) his master (8:32), prompting a rebuke from Jesus (ἐπετίμησεν) in return: "Get behind me, Satan, for you do not have in mind the things of God but human things" (8:33). Commentators often soften Jesus's reproach, insisting that he neither really calls Peter Satan nor implies the disciple is under the devil's influence. Collins, for instance, argues that "Satan" here signifies "the role of adversary or opponent, the basic meaning of the Hebrew equivalent," so that in resisting Jesus's death, Peter is merely "taking a role similar to the one that Satan usually plays."[2] Marcus makes a more complex argument: supposed parallelism between this episode and the preceding two-staged cure of a blind man (8:22–26) "suggests that Peter ... must pass through an intermediate stage of partial sight, partial blindness before arriving at the full insight symbolized by the cured blind man's final condition." Satan has momen-

---

dication the evangelists saw concretized in Jesus's fate, see Francis J. Moloney, "Constructing Jesus and the Son of Man," *CBQ* 75 (2013): 730–38.

2. Collins, *Mark*, 407.

tarily deluded Peter, but Jesus recalls him to discipleship in 8:33, with his restoration confirmed in 16:7.[3]

Symbolic interpretation of the blind men whose sight Jesus restores as figures of Peter and the other disciples' restoration surfaces frequently in scholarship. However, it usually depends on a more positive interpretation of 16:7 than that verse's laconic reference to the risen Jesus going to Galilee before "his disciples and Peter" sustains.[4] In contrast to Marcus, Collins, and others, I believe that an adequate interpretation not only of this passage but also of the Markan passion narrative demands giving full weight to Jesus's condemnation of Peter as under satanic influence or even possession. I pursue such an interpretation in the next section of this chapter as well as in chapter 4.

Complementing the tendency to moderate Jesus's censure of Peter as Satan, scholars sometimes claim that this disciple "clearly ... does not understand Jesus's divinely appointed death" and that this motivates his "rebuke of Jesus's passion prediction."[5] Adam Winn's study generally constitutes a voice of dissent from the impulse to see Mark as unduly focused on Jesus's suffering and death. With respect to 8:27–9:1, however, it relies on an assumption that Jesus's death constitutes the episode's main interpretive question. Peter's problem becomes, in Winn's reading, not the kind of open satanic hostility to Jesus's mission that the master calls out; instead, it is inability to fathom why his beloved master must die.[6] Winn's claim about Peter's motives relates to a common strand of interpretation holding that Peter rebukes Jesus because the disciple understands him to be redefining the messianic mission as one of suffering rather than of eschatological victory.[7] But this whole approach seems dubious when one

---

3. Marcus, *Mark 8–16*, 608, 614–15, 1086.

4. See, e.g., Elliott J. Johnson, "Mark VIII. 22–26: The Blind Man from Bethsaida," *NTS* 25 (1979): 370–83, esp. 383; Ernest Best, *Following Jesus: Discipleship in the Gospel of Mark*, JSNTSup 4 (Sheffield: JSOT Press, 1981), 134–37; Gabi Markusse, *Salvation in the Gospel of Mark: The Death of Jesus and the Path of Discipleship*, Kindle ed. (Eugene, OR: Wipf & Stock, 2018), ch. 3. For resistance to this line of interpretation, see Terence V. Smith, *Petrine Controversies in Early Christianity: Attitudes towards Peter in Christian Writings of the First Two Centuries*, WUNT 15 (Tübingen: Mohr Siebeck, 1985), 169–70; Winn, *Purpose of Mark's Gospel*, 117.

5. Winn, *Purpose of Mark's Gospel*, 120.

6. Winn denies that his reading of the scene detracts from his study's focus on Jesus's power and glory (*Purpose of Mark's Gospel*, 120–21).

7. Nineham, *Gospel of St. Mark*, 226; Collins, *Mark*, 407.

attends to the fact that Jesus predicts in 8:31 not only the Son of Man's suffering and death but also—and climactically—his restoration to life. There is no "clear" reason to presume that Peter's rebuke of Jesus in 8:32 focuses on his "divinely appointed death" at all, let alone to conclude that it results from inability to understand how that death fits into God's confusing messianic plan.

A hypothesis that Peter lacks faith in God's willingness and ability to save Jesus from death by resurrecting him explains the textual data better—especially Jesus's subsequent elaboration of the Petrine rebuke into an accusation that this disciple has set his mind "not on the things of God, but rather on human things" (οὐ ... τὰ τοῦ θεοῦ ἀλλὰ τὰ τῶν ἀνθρώπων, 8:33). Coming on the heels of a prophecy of resurrection just three days after death, this apothegm implies that Peter has not expanded his mind to comprehend God's miraculous power, which stands outside the realm of human potential in its capacity to save from death even one who has died. Thus when Peter in Mark 10:23-31 doubts the possibility of God's salvation in another context (if not the blessed rich, then "who can be saved?"; 10:26), Jesus responds with a parallel aphorism that reprimands this disciple's lack of faith in God's extraordinary ability to rescue: "it is impossible for human beings, but not for God" (παρὰ ἀνθρώποις ἀδύνατον, ἀλλ' οὐ παρὰ θεῷ, 10:27).[8] As a complement, in Mark 4:35-41 the disciples lack faith in Jesus's willingness to rescue them from death in a storm: "Does it not matter to you that we're perishing?" (4:38). In responding "Why are you afraid; do you not yet have faith?" (4:40), Jesus does not so much rebuke their misunderstanding of a mysterious divine plan involving deadly danger at sea as he reproaches their refusal to trust God to save them from the death that threatens. In 8:33, Jesus's reprimand of satanic Peter's lack of attention to "the things of God" is harsher than either of these rebukes. After all, the disciple had not merely questioned Jesus about God's willingness or ability to save but had rebuked his proclamation of such salvation as the Son of Man's destiny (8:32). Thematically, however, all three episodes interrelate, and 10:27 resembles 8:33 in wording as well. The passages combine to signal Peter and the disciples' persistent lack of trust in God's power, realized in Jesus, to rescue people beyond evident hope of

---

8. Mark 10:23-31, like 8:34-9:1, defines following Jesus in such a way as to anticipate Peter's future failure. While Peter has no problem leaving behind all to follow Jesus (10:28-29; cf. 1:16-18), he will deny Jesus when faced with the possibility of persecution (see 10:30, μετὰ διωγμῶν), which Mark immediately elaborates (10:33-34).

salvation—including those who have died. Peter's satanic resistance to the Son of Man's prophesied resurrection three days after his death manifests this faithlessness by opposing head-on the mission of Jesus, which is to be fulfilled in the Son's death issuing in resurrection.[9]

Understood in this way, 8:33 finds its complement in Mark's subsequent paragraph, where Jesus doubles down on his prophecy of the Son of Man's death and resurrection to require that dying and rising become the paradigm for his students as well. In response to Peter's rebuke for proclaiming that the Son of Man will suffer, die, and immediately rise again, Jesus announces that this fate belongs to all present who would follow him (8:34–9:1). To save their lives, Jesus's students must lose them (8:35) in crucifixion with their master: "If someone wants to follow me, let him deny himself and take up his cross and follow me" (8:34). This deadly imperative becomes intelligible against the backdrop of the faith in resurrection that Jesus articulated just a few verses earlier in his prophecy of the Son of Man's destiny (8:31) and with reference to the following verses' meditation on resurrection life (8:35–37). It constitutes a provocative rejoinder to Peter's reproach in 8:32. Instead of rebuking Jesus for proclaiming his faith that God will resurrect the executed Son of Man, Jesus's disciples must exercise their own faith by dying with him in anticipation of resurrection.

Mark 9:2–13: Skeptical Perplexity

This hypothesis concerning 8:31–9:1 finds support in the episodes that follow. The transfiguration (9:2–13) features Peter again fixated on Jesus's prophecy of resurrection (9:9–10), though here he seems to have put opposition to one side. The account anticipates the Son's resurrection—Jesus stands alongside two possibly resurrected figures from Israel's history—as well as his attainment of the eschatological authority prophesied in Mark 8:38, whose imminent fulfillment 9:1 underscores.[10] In the next episode,

---

9. Scholarship on Mark's negative portrayal of the disciples is extensive. I will not review it but rather refer to specific works that touch on aspects of my interpretation as I lay it out. In general terms, my understanding of the disciples' failure of faith in this chapter and the next is more specific than most other scholarly accounts (e.g., Winn, *Purpose of Mark's Gospel*, 139–50), in that I identify exactly what they fail to believe in Mark's narrative, in contrast to what Mark's Jesus trusts.

10. Boobyer, "St. Mark and the Transfiguration," esp. 25–26; Howard Clark Kee elaborates the insight. See Kee, "The Transfiguration in Mark: Epiphany or Apocalyptic Vision?,"

God's voice identifies as messianic ruler ("my son" in 9:7; cf. Ps 2:7–8, on Israel's anointed king) a shining Jesus (Mark 9:3) who resembles the eschatologically resurrected ones prophesied in Dan 12:2–3: φανοῦσιν ὡς φωστῆρες τοῦ οὐρανου ("they will shine like the luminaries of heaven," OG) or ἐκλάμψουσιν ὡς ἡ λαμπρότης τοῦ στερεώματος ("they will glow like the splendor of the firmament," Theod.).[11] Daniel invites readers to link the prophecy of resurrection from 12:3 with the vision of the Son of Man elevated to rule from 7:13–14, which Jesus had quoted a few verses earlier (Mark 8:38), and Second Temple Jewish writings in fact connect the two (e.g., 1 En. 108.10–15).[12] Mark's Jesus may himself refer to both in 9:9, when he commands that Peter, James, and John "tell no one what they

---

in *Understanding the Sacred Text: Essays in Honor of Morton S. Enslin on the Hebrew Bible and Christian Beginnings*, ed. John Reumann (Valley Forge, PA: Judson, 1972), 137–52. Some argue that the transfiguration is a misplaced resurrection account. For a description of the debate, see Clare K. Rothschild, *Baptist Traditions and Q*, WUNT 190 (Tübingen: Mohr Siebeck, 2005), 142–48. Regardless, in its current context the episode anticipates Jesus's resurrection glory. See Candida Moss, "The Transfiguration: An Exercise in Markan Accommodation," *BibInt* 12 (2004): 71–73.

Moses and Elijah may be not resurrected but heavenly figures returning to earth, whence they were translated instead of dying. (For Moses's assumption, see, e.g., Philo, *Mos.* 2.288; for Elijah's, 2 Kgs 2:11–12.) Accordingly, Delbert Burkett argues that this scene previews Jesus apotheosized subsequent to his resurrection, not the risen Christ per se. See Burkett, "The Transfiguration of Jesus (Mark 9:2–8): Epiphany or Apotheosis?," *JBL* 138 (2019): 413–32, esp. 424. However, it is not clear that Mark believes Moses was translated to heaven like Elijah (see Deut 34:6–7). Moreover, Mark's conflation of Elijah with John the Baptist, who has been decapitated and entombed (Mark 6:27–29), may point to eschatological resurrection as the proper context for understanding John/Elijah's appearance in chapter 9 (see Rothschild, *Baptist Traditions and Q*, 148–54).

Determining whether or not Moses and Elijah are resurrected, or otherwise defining the precise terms of immortal life this scene imagines, remains less important than recognizing its thematic relevancy to Jesus's prophesied restoration to life, the subject of the disciples' inquiry on its heels (9:9–12) and of Peter's doubt in the previous episode. On this, see Margaret E. Thrall, "Elijah and Moses in Mark's Account of the Transfiguration," *NTS* 16 (1970): 310–12.

11. Kee, "Transfiguration in Mark," 140–1.

12. Marcus, *Mark 8–16*, 752. On linking the prophecy of resurrection from Dan 12:2–3 with the vision of the Son of Man elevated to rule from 7:13–14, see Schaberg, "Daniel 7, 12 and the New Testament," 211–12; Hooker, *Son of Man in Mark*, 142. Compare the references to "books" of judgment in Dan 7:10; 12:1, discussed in Collins, *Daniel*, 391.

have seen until the Son of Man [see Dan 7:13–14] rises from the dead" (ἐκ νεκρῶν ἀναστῇ; cf. Dan 12:2, ἀναστήσονται, OG).[13]

In this context, and in light of Jesus's earlier statements about the Son of Man's resurrection "after three days" (8:31) and eschatological reign (8:38–9:1), Peter, James, and John apparently infer from their vision of the transfigured Jesus alongside possibly resurrected figures from Israel's past that Jesus, the Son of Man from Dan 7, will rise from the dead at the eschatological consummation. The general resurrection Dan 12 prophesied is near; it will occur just a few days after Jesus's death, if it has not already begun with the risen Moses and Elijah's appearance at the transfigured Jesus's side. In this rapidly developing eschatological scenario, the three disciples presume that the Son of Man's execution and resurrection will involve Jesus's immediate assumption of regnant authority over the cosmos (see Mark 8:38). Their confusion about the master's reference to "resurrection from the dead" (συζητοῦντες τί ἐστιν τὸ ἐκ νεκρῶν ἀναστῆναι, 9:10) emerges from the extremely compact eschatological sequence Jesus's statements seem to presume. Peter, James, and John thus formulate a question regarding how that scenario's unfolding rapidity could accommodate the prophesied ministry of Elijah redivivus, which some strains of Jewish apocalyptic thought imagined would occur before the eschatological consummation (9:11).[14]

While their muddled inquiry asks how the resurrection Jesus has prophesied fits into an anticipated eschatological timetable, it also metonymizes several unarticulated questions relevant to the Second Gospel's development of the resurrection theme. What did Jesus mean when he proclaimed a few verses earlier that not only will the Son of Man die and rise again, but so must Jesus's followers? Is he presuming a conventional scenario of general resurrection and divine judgment in which Jesus and his disciples will participate, such as one finds in Dan 7 and 12? If so, how can the extreme urgency of the faith he expresses (in a resurrection after just a few days; 8:31; see also 9:1) and whose fulfillment Jesus's transfiguration straightaway anticipates accommodate unfulfilled eschatological expectations such as Elijah returning before the final judgment?[15] With

---

13. On the relevance of both Danielic intertexts, see Kee, "Transfiguration in Mark," 142–43.

14. See Gundry, *Mark*, 484.

15. Such questions may have resonated with Mark's readers, who might have begun to view as misguided the extreme eschatological urgency that characterized

questions such as these unresolved, how can the disciples embrace Jesus's suggestion that God will immediately resurrect them if they die with him (8:34–38)? In what exactly are they being asked to trust by following the Son of Man to death in expectation of restoration to life? Their confusion (9:10) and articulated question (9:11) indicate that while they may not oppose the faith in resurrection Jesus professes and demands, as Peter did in the previous chapter, they still interrogate it from a position of bewilderment, if not of outright skepticism.

The terms of their inquiry suggest that these three, like Peter before, are not concerned with "the things of God but with human things" (8:33). Peter, James, and John do not fix their attention on the prophecies and commands about death and resurrection that Jesus had uttered in the previous episode, despite God's directive that they attend to their master's teaching (9:7). They rather focus on tangentially relevant scribal traditions about Elijah, to which they inappropriately attempt to assimilate Jesus's teaching (9:11). Their fixation on the scribes' teaching that Elijah must return before the resurrection and final judgment, presumably occasioned by that prophet's presence at the side of an already exalted Jesus, prompts their inquiry into the timing of the resurrection of the Son of Man that Jesus has been prophesying.[16] The question "why [ὅτι] the scribes say that Elijah must come first" (9:11) suggests knowledge of an interpretation of Mal 4:5–6 that held the eschatological Elijah would "make peace in the world" in anticipation of God's eschatological reign (m. Ed. 8:7).[17] The meaning of Jesus's response in Mark 9:12–13 comes

---

some preaching of early Jesus-believers. Other New Testament authors wrestle with the problem of eschatological delay (e.g., 2 Pet 3:7–9). See Richard Bauckham, "The Delay of the Parousia," *TynBul* 31 (1980): 3–36.

16. On ancient apocalyptic-eschatological interpretations of Malachi's expectation of Elijah's return, see Markus Öhler, "The Expectation of Elijah and the Presence of the Kingdom of God," *JBL* 118 (1999): 461–64. On the association of Elijah with eschatological restoration and resurrection—originating in but not limited to reflection on Mal 4:5–6—see Albert L. A. Hogterp, "Belief in Resurrection and Its Religious Settings in Qumran and the New Testament," in *Echoes from the Caves: Qumran and the New Testament*, ed. Florentino García Martínez, STDJ 85 (Leiden: Brill, 2009), 312–13, 315–16.

17. Quoting Moses H. Segal, trans., 'Eduyyoth, in *The Babylonian Talmud: Seder Nezikin*, ed. Isidore Epstein (London: Soncino, 1935), 4:50. On Mark's predilection for ὅτι (or ὅ τι) to introduce a direct question, see BDF §300.2, which includes discussion of this passage.

3. Jesus's Demand for Faith and the Disciples' Doubt

into focus as a decisive rejection of the traditional interpretation of the Malachi passage the disciples invoke.

This interpretation expansively construes a statement found, with minor variations, in Mal 4:5–6 MT and LXX: "Behold, before the coming [πρὶν ἐλθεῖν] of the magnificent and glorious day of the Lord, I will send you Elijah the Tishbite, who will restore the heart of a father to his child and of a man to his neighbor [ὃς ἀποκαταστήσει καρδίαν πατρὸς πρὸς υἱὸν καὶ καρδίαν ἀνθρώπου πρὸς τὸν πλησίον αὐτοῦ]." Mark's Jesus at once echoes the Malachi passage and challenges its interpretation when he asks in response: "Is it really the case that Elijah, when he comes first, restores all things [ἐλθὼν πρῶτον ἀποκαθιστάνει πάντα]? How then has it been written concerning the Son of Man that he is to suffer many things [πολλὰ πάθῃ] and be set at naught?"[18] (Mark 9:12). Jesus's question implies he does not accept a scenario according to which the coming Elijah brings about a restoration of the created order in anticipation of eschatological consummation. If Elijah were to "restore all things" before the eschaton, then no setting would remain in which the Son of Man might "suffer many things," including the contemptuous death (ἐξουδενηθῇ, 9:12b; see also 8:31) from which Jesus had just prophesied that God would resurrect him (9:9).[19] Jesus's rhetorical question about the prophecy from Mal 4:6 and his implicit equation of Malachi's Elijah with John the Baptist (see Mark 9:13) combine to reinterpret that Malachi passage. Jesus's understanding of the scripture accommodates its prophecy of Elijah's eschatological mission to his own expectation of the Son of Man's suffering, death, and immediate resurrection in the near future.

Jesus insists that Elijah already "has come [ἐλήλυθεν] and they did to him whatever they desired [ὅσα ἤθελον], as it is written about him" (9:13). This has given interpreters much trouble. The first clause

---

18. I adopt Joel Marcus's translation from "Mark 9,11–13: 'As It Has Been Written,'" *ZNW* 80 (2009): 46–48; see also Marcus, *Mark 8–16*, 644–45. Marcus persuasively develops an argument about the passage's grammar that Julius Wellhausen proposed in the early twentieth century.

19. Marcus understands 9:11–13 to pose and resolve this problem ("Mark 9,11–13," 48, 55–58). I agree but differ as to the answer Mark suggests.

Rabbinic writings note resistance on the part of some to a standard view that the eschatological Elijah's return would involve cosmic restoration, referring to the opinions of several rabbis who believe Elijah will return to settle discrete social and legal disputes, before landing authoritatively on the more expansive interpretation of Mal 4:6 (m. Ed. 8:7).

refers to Herod's killing of John the Baptist in Mark 6, but there is no biblical prophecy of the eschatological Elijah falling victim to the sort of violence that ended John's life. Scholars offer ingenious exegetical explanations. Some infer a reference to Elijah's suffering at the hands of Ahab and Jezebel in 1 Kgs 19:1-3 as a pattern for the eschatological Elijah (John the Baptist) to follow.[20] Others hypothesize apocalyptic traditions no longer extant, which might also lie behind Rev 11:6-7's prophecy of the killing of two eschatological witnesses, similarly likened to Moses and Elijah (cf. 1 Kgs 17:1; 18:1).[21] Others still apply to the eschatological Elijah a "pervasive scriptural motif" involving prophets being rejected, threatened, and killed.[22] Marcus argues that Mark simply assimilates eschatological Elijah's mission to the role of suffering he assigns to the Messiah. If, according to Mark's understanding of Scripture, "the Son of Man is to be a suffering Messiah, and Elijah is to be the Messiah's forerunner, then it stands to reason that Elijah himself must be a suffering figure."[23]

As this brief survey suggests, scholars tend to conclude that "as it is written about [Elijah]" (9:13) refers not to Mal 4:6 but to some other scriptural passage, motif, or pattern that may or may not have anything directly to do with Elijah at all. This seems untenable, for both Mark 9:12 (Ἠλίας μὲν ἐλθὼν πρῶτον ἀποκαθιστάνει πάντα) and 9:13 (Ἠλίας ἐλήλυθεν) obviously allude to Mal 4:5-6's references to that prophet (Ἠλίαν τὸν Θεσβίτην πρὶν

---

20. Austin Farrer points to 1 Kgs 19:10, 14. See Farrer, *St. Matthew and St. Mark*, ECLectures 1953-54 (Westminster: Dacre, 1954), 5; cf. Nineham, *Gospel of St. Mark*, 241; Gundry, *Mark*, 465. This possibility seems attractive in light of Mark's persistent association of John with Elijah, including in 6:14-29. See Christine E. Joynes, "A Question of Identity: 'Who Do People Say That I Am?' Elijah, John the Baptist and Jesus in Mark's Gospel," in *Understanding, Studying and Reading: New Testament Essays in Honour of John Ashton*, ed. Christopher Rowland and Crispin H. T. Fletcher-Louis, JSNTSup 153 (Sheffield: Sheffield Academic, 1998), 20-23.

21. Nineham, *Gospel of St. Mark*, 241.

22. Collins, *Mark*, 432.

23. Marcus, *Mark 8-16*, 650-51. Here he develops the line of reasoning he originally presented in "Mark 9,11-13." Compare Enrique Nardoni, *La transfiguración de Jésus y el diálogo sobre Elías segun el Evangelio de San Marcos*, TED 2 (Buenos Aires: Editora Patria Grande, 1977), 216-23. Nardoni argues that parallels between John's and Jesus's sufferings point to the central role in God's plan of obedience to death. Death ultimately gives way to the glorious eternal life attested by the transfigured Jesus and Elijah/John's appearance at his side.

ἐλθεῖν ... ὃς ἀποκαταστήσει). When Jesus goes on to say later in the verse that "they did to him whatever they desired [ὅσα ἤθελον], as it was written about him," the writing in question is none other than Mal 4:6. This finds confirmation in a careful reading of Mark 6:14–29, which 9:13 echoes.

The traditional interpretation of Mal 4:6 construes the verse more expansively than the biblical passage's circumspect language about the future Elijah's mission easily accommodates. Malachi 4:6 LXX says of Elijah only that "he will restore the heart of a father to his child and the heart of a man to his neighbor." This turns out to anticipate and encapsulate Mark's narrative of John the Baptist's death (Mark 6:14–29), whom Mark has introduced as Elijah redivivus from the very beginning of the gospel (1:6; cf. 2 Kgs 1:8). Mark invokes this episode in the final words of 9:13 ("they did to him whatever they desired [ὅσα ἤθελον]"), for Herod, tetrarch of Galilee and Perea, had John killed precisely to satisfy his daughter's desire: "Ask me whatever you desire [ὃ ἐὰν θέλῃς], and I will grant it to you.... I desire [θέλω] ... the head of John the Baptist on a platter" (6:22, 25). Herod also wanted to please the neighbors whom he had invited to the banquet—identified as leading men of his region (τοῖς πρώτοις τῆς Γαλιλαίας, 6:21)—for whose sake he "did not desire [οὐκ ἠθέλησεν]" to refuse his child's request and ruin the party (6:26). The echo of this episode in 9:13 (ὅσα ἤθελον) and the references to Mal 4:6 in Mark 9:12–13 suggest that by killing John to please his daughter and his Galilean neighbors, Herod fulfills Malachi's prophecy that the eschatological Elijah "will restore the heart of a father to his child and of a man to his neighbors" (4:6).[24] Malachi's prophesied Elijah has come as John the Baptist; in dying, he has performed the prophesied reconciliations. By overseeing the situation in which all collectively did to the eschatological Elijah "whatever they desired" (Mark 9:13), Herod shows himself to be the father whose heart Elijah would turn to his child and the man whose heart he would turn to his neighbors (Mal 4:6).

According to Jesus's construal of the prophecy, the Son of Man's suffering, death, and vindication through resurrection need not wait for Elijah's eschatological advent in fulfillment of Mal 4:6. Elijah has already returned

---

24. Cf. Caryn A. Reeder, "Malachi 3:24 and the Eschatological Restoration of the 'Family,'" *CBQ* 69 (2007): 695–709. Reeder explores the implications of the familial language Malachi employs and considers how it might have been understood by ancient readers. They would have been primed to see the verse as a prophecy of familial rather than cosmic restoration, although understanding family variously.

in the figure of John and fulfilled that scripture's prophecies. Moreover, he has done so by proactively emulating the Son of Man's destiny, just as Jesus requires his students to emulate it on his heels. John the Baptist suffers persecution and arrest for his prophetic witness; he is executed and entombed, presumably in hope of resurrection (Mark 6:29). Insofar as Mark assimilates John to Elijah, the appearance of the latter beside the transfigured Jesus in 9:4 may even imply that John has already risen from the dead.[25] Mark will not guarantee this, of course, and the vague notice of Moses and Elijah "having appeared" to Peter, James, and John (ὤφθη αὐτοῖς), whatever precisely it reports (a vision? heavenly visitation? the eschatological resurrection's commencement?), should be understood as another of the ambiguous resurrections Mark's *commentarii* feature.

Jesus's statement about Elijah fails to resolve the three disciples' confused doubt about the Son of Man's prophesied resurrection, as their continued misunderstandings attest. In his defense, the disciples formulate an idiosyncratic question about eschatology based on acknowledged human wisdom whose accuracy Jesus challenges. As N. T. Wright observes, "faced with the question about resurrection," they seem to have been desperately "casting about for some fixed points."[26] In fact, their question could be subject to the same rebuke Jesus earlier issued to the scribes for preoccupying themselves with human traditions at the expense of divine commands (7:8). The disciples do not ask Jesus directly about his claims regarding the Son of Man's imminent resurrection, which they cannot or will not grasp, either here or earlier. Instead, they ill-advisedly try to situate them on a traditional eschatological timetable whose accuracy Jesus does not accept. He corrects them on that discrete point, but their confusion and doubt about resurrection grow rather than recede.

It will later become apparent that when Jesus speaks of the Son rising just a few days after his execution (Mark 8:31), his words refer not to eschatological resurrection and final judgment, but rather to God's immediate vindication of the Son of Man from death's power. However, at this point in Mark, it is not clear whether the disciples themselves, should they choose to follow Jesus to crucifixion, are promised an immediate experience of resurrection at his side or will have to await eschatological resurrection at some later point (see, for instance, the murdered witnesses

---

25. Rothschild, *Baptist Traditions*, 148–54; cf. Thrall, "Elijah and Moses," 310–12, which connects the transfiguration with Mark 16's account of Jesus's resurrection.

26. Wright, *Resurrection*, 415.

of Rev 6:9–11). It could even be argued that distinguishing between immediate (Jesus's) and eschatological (general) resurrection at all makes no sense at this juncture of Mark's narrative, for that distinction may only come into existence because Jesus dies not with his community of followers but rather on their behalf (see Mark 10:45). Since the disciples resist dying and rising with their master according to Jesus's plan (8:31, 34–37), as the gospel approaches its conclusion, the eschatological consummation Mark's Jesus originally anticipates in conjunction with their communal resurrection (see 8:31, 38–9:1) recedes into the more distant future. This offers his original disciples additional opportunities to emulate the Son of Man's destiny before final judgment, a possibility I will explore in my treatment of chapter 13 below.[27]

Mark 9:14–29: Total Faithlessness

If Mark's narrative in 9:2–13 moves away from rejection of the resurrection faith that Jesus's prophecy exemplifies in 8:31 and toward a confused interrogation of that prophecy's eschatological implications, then 9:14–29

---

27. Compare the interpretation of Matt 10:23 in Albert Schweitzer, *The Quest of the Historical Jesus: A Critical Study of Its Progress from Reimarus to Wrede*, trans. William Montgomery, 2nd ed. (London: Black, 1911), 358–64, 389–93. When the disciples return from their mission, which Jesus had expected to be fulfilled by the eschatological consummation, he comes to understand that "his death must at last compel the Coming of the Kingdom" and accordingly sets his face toward Jerusalem (Schweitzer, *Quest of the Historical Jesus*, 390). This approach to the historical Jesus's evolving eschatological consciousness sheds light on my argument about Mark.

Mark presumes Jesus originally expected the communal eschatological resurrection of the dead in the immediate wake of his and his disciples' executions in Jerusalem. "Son of Man" from his prophecies of death and resurrection (esp. 8:31; 9:31; 10:33–34) may have a communal meaning (see n. 1 above), referring not only to Jesus himself but to his assembled community. Anticipating all of their executions would not be hard, given John the Baptist's fate. Moreover, "after three days" might mean "after a few" or "several" days (see McKnight, *Jesus and His Death*, 233–35), vaguely insisting on the eschaton's rapid consummation after their executions. However, Jesus increasingly doubts whether this eschatological expectation will be fulfilled, for his disciples show sustained resistance to his teaching about the Son of Man's fate. Since they will not join him in death, he begins to adjust his eschatological views, introducing a distinction between his own immediate death and resurrection in the person of the Son of Man, with the disciples' to follow later, when they are executed in a subsequent period of eschatological travail (see Mark 13:9–13).

returns to thematize resurrection faith's rejection. At the beginning of this account, Jesus rebukes his disciples' lack of faith ("faithless generation"; γενεὰ ἄπιστος, 9:19) when he finds them unable to exorcise a possessed boy. The reproach logically relates to Jesus's demand that the possessed lad's father demonstrate faith in God's ability to save his son from devastating spiritual enemies (9:21–23, esp. v. 23: πάντα δυνατὰ τῷ πιστεύοντι). These enemies would seem to include death itself, for the demon-beset boy's symptoms involve muteness and rigidity (9:17–18), anticipating death's onset. Moreover, as discussed in chapter 1, the story's dramatic climax may recount a resurrection: "And having screamed and convulsed him many times, [the spirit] came out. And [the boy] was like a corpse [νεκρός], so that many said that he died [ἀπέθανεν]. But Jesus, having taken him by the hand, lifted him up and he rose [ἤγειρεν αὐτόν, καὶ ἀνέστη]" (Mark 9:26–27).

The father demonstrates imperfect faith in Jesus's ability to save his son from destructive demonic power or even death itself: "I have faith; help my lack of faith" (πιστεύω· βοήθει μου τῇ ἀπιστίᾳ, 9:24). This contrasts with the total faithlessness of the disciples, who are unable to mediate the divine salvation from a deadly demon that this boy needs, despite Jesus's earlier authorization of them to do just that (3:14–15). In fact, unlike the father, whose faith in God's power is limited but still leads him to God's representative for help in his desperation, the disciples evidently never even think to ask God for assistance once they find themselves unable to cast out the demon in Jesus's absence. When they inquire of Jesus why their exorcistic attempt has fallen short, he again draws attention to their total failure of faith in the divine power he just exercised, which may overcome death itself: "this kind can come out in no other way unless through prayer" (9:29).[28] That is to say, though it is beyond their ability and comprehension, God can defeat the deadly demonic power that attempted to destroy this boy and perhaps finally did take his life. The disciples, accordingly, must turn to and trust in God's power over death—here and when they go with Jesus to Jerusalem for their own executions in expectation of resurrection, as commanded at the end of chapter 8.

---

28. Failure to understand this irony helps account for the addition of "and fasting" in some manuscripts of Mark and in the Matthean parallel (17:21). It turns the rebuke of the disciples' faithlessness into instruction about how to confront especially malicious demons.

3. Jesus's Demand for Faith and the Disciples' Doubt

***

Material in the pericope featuring Peter's rebuke of Jesus (8:27–9:1) and in the two following episodes (9:2–13 and 14–29) helps to interpret Jesus's prophecy of the Son of Man's resurrection in chapter 8. That prophecy implies a requirement that not only Jesus (8:31) but also his followers (8:34–37) put such comprehensive trust in God's power to raise the dead that they be willing to face execution in anticipation of resurrection. Peter's rebuke of Jesus's initial prediction of the Son of Man's death and resurrection reflects doubt directed at Jesus's willingness to trust God in the face of death. This disciple's initial incredulity soon evolves into skepticism about whether the resurrection faith Jesus professes coheres with a traditional understanding of eschatological resurrection. Even if it can be made to square, 9:14–29 finally suggests that the disciples as a group will still hesitate to dispose of their lives on the basis of trust in God's power to save them from death. They do not put stock in God's willingness or ability even to rescue a boy possessed by a life-threatening demon. How much less will they trust God to save Jesus or themselves by resurrection from the dead?

Jesus's Demand in 8:31–9:1

Earlier I raised the possibility that the opposition to Jesus's death and resurrection Peter demonstrates in 8:32 points to his own demonic possession. Here I elaborate that understanding of Peter's resistance and integrate it within a sustained discussion of Jesus's demand that his disciples follow him to death and resurrection in 8:31–9:1, which includes a threat of eschatological condemnation to those who refuse to obey.

Henry Swete goes too far in dismissing any hint that Jesus's rebuke of Peter in 8:33 incorporates a positive call to follow Jesus, as it is sometimes construed.²⁹ However, it is hard to argue with his basic assessment of the Greek: "ὑπάγειν is not = ἐλθεῖν (v. 34); it implies removal, not approach, and ὀπίσω μου in this connexion represents defeat and banishment from the sight of the conqueror, not a closer attachment to the company of the Master; cf. [LXX] Ps ... xlix. (l.) 17, Isa. xxxviii. 17."³⁰ Some scholars there-

---

29. E.g., Marcus, *Mark 8–16*, 614–15.
30. Henry Barclay Swete, *The Gospel according to St. Mark: The Greek Text with Introduction, Notes and Indices*, 3rd ed. (London: Macmillan, 1913), 181. Robyn J.

fore advocate the possibility that Peter operates as an agent of Satan when he reproaches Jesus a verse earlier.[31] The possibility persuades because Jesus's identification of Peter as Satan closely follows Peter's confession that Jesus is the Christ (Mark 8:29), though editions and translations (such as the UBS and NRSV) that introduce a section break between 8:30 and 8:31 obscure the link. Mark indicates no change in setting between Peter's two exchanges with Jesus in 8:29–33, however, and Jesus's rebuke in 8:33 follows his previous rebuke of Peter and the other disciples in response to Peter's confession of Jesus as the Christ (ἐπετίμησεν αὐτοῖς, 8:30). Since that reproach incorporates a command of silence, scholars as early as Wrede have linked 8:30 with Jesus's silencing of demons who confess his identity elsewhere in Mark.[32] Parallels between previous accounts of Jesus muzzling such demons (1:24–25, 34; 3:11–12; etc.) and Jesus's command of silence and rebuke of Peter as Satan in 8:27–33 press the possibility that Peter's initial "confession" (8:29) signals satanic influence, if not outright possession. Thus Jesus immediately reproaches Peter and his fellow disciples, only to see a Satan-possessed disciple respond with faithless hostility in 8:32, leading to Jesus's attempted exorcism in the subsequent verse.

Mark's *commentarii* do not demand this reading. The Second Gospel's stories of Jesus's demonic confrontations normally proceed from exclamations of Jesus's identity directly to demons' silencing and exorcism, but in this episode a prophecy that the Son of Man will suffer, die, and rise intervenes (8:31). Moreover, Mark neglects to note that the demon possessing Peter flees at Jesus's words—the standard climax in parallel accounts. These anomalies make it significant that Jesus follows his identification of Peter as Satan with ὕπαγε ὀπίσω μου. In its Markan context, the phrase requires that Satan, whom Jesus discerns influencing Peter, get behind Jesus in the

---

Whitaker fails to persuade that the word lacks any negative connotations because her argument does not sufficiently attend to context. See Whitaker, "Rebuke or Recall? Rethinking the Role of Peter in Mark's Gospel," *CBQ* 75 (2013): 672–73. However, the parallel Whitaker observes at Mark 10:21 is significant and confirms ambiguity in Jesus's words that I will explore.

31. B. A. E. Osborne, "Peter: Stumbling-Block and Satan," *NovT* 15 (1973): 187–90; Smith, *Petrine Controversies*, 167–69; Donald Juel, *A Master of Surprise: Mark Interpreted* (Minneapolis: Fortress, 1994), 73–75; Kim E. Dewey, "Peter's Curse and Cursed Peter (Mark 14:53–54, 66–72)," in *The Passion in Mark: Studies on Mark 14–16*, ed. Werner H. Kelber and John R. Donahue (Philadelphia: Fortress, 1976), 111.

32. Wrede, *Messianic Secret*, 118.

3. Jesus's Demand for Faith and the Disciples' Doubt

sense of getting out of his way or sight, as Swete shows.[33] However, Mark's diction also recalls Jesus's initial invitation that Peter and Andrew "come behind" to "follow him" as disciples (δεῦτε ὀπίσω μου ... ἠκολούθησαν αὐτῷ, 1:17–18; see also v. 20). This echo is amplified when Jesus goes onto say, "if anyone wants to follow behind me [ὀπίσω μου ἀκολουθεῖν], let him deny himself and take up his cross and follow me [ἀκολουθείτω μοι]" (8:34). The recollection of Jesus's original command to follow makes it possible that his rebuke of Peter as Satan in 8:33 involves an urgent demand that Peter return to following Jesus. Moreover, at the beginning of the next episode, Mark writes that Jesus παραλαμβάνει ("takes to himself") Peter, which could also suggest earlier rapprochement. At this point in Mark, the meaning and result of Jesus's rebuke of satanic Peter remains uncertain.

Though ambiguity must be stipulated, readings placing much weight on the reprimand's positive connotations fail to convince. Rhetorically, the repetition of "behind me" (ὀπίσω μου) in 8:33 and 34 does not transform Jesus's rebuke into an invitation to follow but rather contrasts the two possibilities. Unless Peter gets behind the master by following the Son of Man to his prophesied death in expectation of resurrection (8:34–37), he will get behind Jesus by being forcibly excluded from the Son's eschatological presence (8:38–9:1).[34] The ambiguity of the portrayal of Peter in 8:27–33 lies in the fact that he has not yet made his final choice—though *choice* is a questionable word, since Peter acts under the devil's influence. In any case, it remains unclear at this point whether Peter will emulate Jesus's faith in God's willingness and ability to save from death, as Jesus requires him to do in 8:34–37, or continue opposing that faith by refusing to die with Jesus in expectation of resurrection. Satanic intervention (8:32–33) has undermined his initial decision to follow (see 1:17–18), and Peter must heed

---

33. Also see "ὀπίσω," BAGD, 716, esp. definition 1a; Matthew Black and Géza Vermès, *An Aramaic Approach to the Gospels and Acts*, 3rd ed. (Oxford: Clarendon, 1967), 218; C. H. Dodd, "Review of *Theologisches Wörterbuch zum Neuen Testament*," *JTS* 5 (1954): 244–45.

34. Paul Middleton, "Christology, Martyrdom, and Vindication in the Gospel of Mark and the Apocalypse: Two New Testament Views," in *Mark, Manuscripts, and Monotheism: Essays in Honor of Larry W. Hurtado*, ed. Chris Keith and Dieter T. Roth, LNTS 528 (London: Bloomsbury, 2015), 219–37. Observation of this connotative contrast resolves the problem Dodd articulates of the strange intrusion of μου into Jesus's otherwise perspicuous order that Peter withdraw ("Review of *Theologisches Wörterbuch zum Neuen Testament*").

Jesus's warning to get back on track (8:34) or else suffer the eschatological consequences (8:38–9:1).

The distinction between Peter's getting behind Jesus as a rebuked demon (8:33) and following behind him as a faithful disciple (8:34) opens a series of dichotomies Jesus addresses to all the disciples in the presence of the crowd, culminating in the threat of 8:38. According to the first, one either saves one's life to lose it in the end, or else one loses one's life (see 8:34) and thereby genuinely saves it (8:35).[35] The second dichotomy emphasizes what is at stake in understanding the true way to save one's life (i.e., by being crucified with Jesus in anticipation of resurrection; see vv. 33–34): without life, even possession of the entire world would have no value, for one would not be alive to enjoy it (8:36–37).[36] Mark 8:38 offers a related warning: when the Son of Man's glory is finally revealed, he will reject rather than sponsor those whose lives, by their very preservation, demonstrate shame in Jesus and rejection of his command to die and rise with him. The circumstantial clause from 8:38 ("in this generation [τῇ γενεᾷ ταύτῃ]") clarifies the temporal horizon of all three dichotomies:[37] Jesus expects his current disciples to stand behind him by demonstrating, in communion with the Son of Man (see 8:31), denial of the self so extreme as to culminate in execution on Jesus's heels (8:34). If they choose to preserve their lives instead, they will forgo the resurrection he offers (8:35–37) and lose all standing with him at the eschatological judgment in God's coming kingdom (8:38).

Interpreters sometimes fix on the implications in 9:1 for how urgently Jesus or Mark thought the eschaton impended:[38] "there are some standing here who will not taste death until they see the kingdom of God having come with power." These are pertinent, for the disciples' subsequent inquiries in 9:11–12 elaborate a related question, although they rely on an interpretation of Mal 4:5–6 that Mark's Jesus rejects. Yet in its immediate

---

35. Mark in 8:35 shifts between mundane life (cf. 3:4, which uses the same noun and verbs to oppose "taking" and "saving" a life) and resurrection. For discussion, see Van Iersel, "Gospel according to St. Mark," 25. However, since Mark is more interested in the general possibility of eternal life than in a particular understanding of resurrection, the ambiguity of the Greek noun ψυχή ("soul"?) may be significant.

36. Pudussery, "Discipleship," 89.

37. See Friedrich Büchsel for the fundamentally temporal meaning of γενεά in New Testament idiom ("γενεά," TDNT 1:662–65, esp. 663).

38. Rudolf Bultmann, *The History of the Synoptic Tradition*, rev. ed., trans. John Marsh (Oxford: Blackwell, 1968), 121; Collins, *Mark*, 413.

3. Jesus's Demand for Faith and the Disciples' Doubt

context, 9:1 does not primarily stress the imminence of the Son of Man's final judgment or even speak to its timing. Rather, it points to the state in which Jesus fears the Son will find his disciples when he encounters them in his role as regent of God's cosmic kingdom—namely, with lives preserved rather than given up to be miraculously restored. Jesus addresses not so much how long his students are expected to live (i.e., only until the rapidly approaching eschatological consummation) as their choice to preserve life at all, rather than to suffer execution with him in emulation of his faith in resurrection (8:34–35). Mark 9:1 proleptically condemns those disciples present who will remain alive to experience the Son's judgment, whenever it comes. Any disciples whom Jesus publicly addresses in this section of Mark's narrative and who subsequently refuse his call to follow him to crucifixion will be liable to eschatological condemnation (see 8:38) in the course of the life they thereby foolishly prolong (8:36–37). This is the case regardless of whether it be by only a few days (if Jesus's prophecy of resurrection "after three days" is understood, at this point in Mark, to anticipate eschatological resurrection on the heels of his execution, as suggested earlier) or somewhat longer.[39] As will become clear, Peter, whose resistance Jesus has characterized as satanic, finds himself in especial jeopardy in this regard.

Attention to how Mark's passion narrative elaborates the imagery Jesus here employs supports this interpretation. The gastronomic formulation in Mark 9:1 ("taste death")—a Semitic idiom that stands out as odd in Greek[40]—anticipates the imagery of consumption the evangelist will use in the Last Supper scene, where Jesus metaphorically serves his disciples his body (14:22–25). When Jesus feeds them bread and wine symbolizing his broken body and his shed blood, he no longer expects that they will die with him (though perhaps he hopes it), for he suggests that he will die not with but for many (14:24). When the disciples go with Jesus to the Mount of Olives in the subsequent episode, the master more clearly anticipates

---

39. The possibility of interpreting ἕως ἂν ἴδωσιν in 9:1 conditionally, on analogy with πρίν ἂν + subjunctive in Attic, sharpens this interpretation of the verse, implying that some are so committed to mundane life that they will desperately cling to it unless divine intervention takes it from them. On the conditional interpretation, see Pudussery, "Discipleship," 128; on πρίν ἂν + subjunctive in Attic, see Herbert Weir Smyth and Gordon M. Messing, *Greek Grammar* (Cambridge: Harvard University Press, 1956), §2433; cf. BDF §383.

40. See Collins, *Mark*, 413; Marcus, *Mark 8–16*, 621.

their desertion (14:26–27), and imagery of consumption surfaces yet again to function in a similar way. As Jesus struggles in Gethsemane against his own desire to avoid drinking "the cup" of death that God is serving (14:32–42, esp. vv. 36, 39), Peter, James, and John keep falling asleep instead of watching with him in prayerful expectation of arrest. Finally, just before Jesus expires on the cross, abandoned by his disciples, a random bystander gives him a drink of spoiled wine (15:36), clinching the symbolic association between his lone execution and the tasting of death mentioned in 9:1. Returning to that verse, some disciples standing in Jesus's presence when he utters its words indeed "will not taste death until they see that the kingdom of God has come with power." All of them potentially fall into that category, for they all shamefully avoid execution at his side. Through flight, denial, or even betrayal, they save their lives, leaving Jesus to taste death and rise again alone, and leaving themselves exposed to the eschatological condemnation he threatens.

The Scope of Jesus's Demand

Mark 8:34–9:1 is often thought to be a collection of originally independent sayings the evangelist assembled after 8:31–33 because of their thematic correspondence to Jesus's discussion of the Son's destined death and resurrection. Interpreters usually read them with primary reference to later believers, including Mark's readers, rather than to Jesus's disciples in Mark's narrative.[41] The disparate origins of the various apothegms helps explain this approach. Some of the sayings Mark includes in 8:34–37 appear in a different context in the double tradition (see Matt 10:33, 38–39; par. Luke 12:9; 14:26–27; 17:33) as well as in John 12:25. This suggests they circulated as independent logia, possibly finding earlier employment in homiletic contexts urging faithfulness to Christ in the face of anticipated harassment.[42] However, it remains important to distinguish the meaning

---

41. Marcus, *Mark 8–16*, 623–25; Collins, *Mark*, 407–8.

42. For discussion of the sayings' interrelationships, see Francis Neirynck, "Saving/Losing One's Life: Luke 17,33 (Q?) and Mark 8,35," in *Von Jesus zum Christus: Christologische Studien: Festgabe für Paul Hoffmann zum 65. Geburtstag*, ed. Rudolf Hoppe and Ulrich Busse, BZNW 93 (Berlin: de Gruyter, 1998), 295–318. Bultmann too remains influential (*History of the Synoptic Tradition*, 82–83). See also Roskam, *Purpose of the Gospel of Mark*, 36–46; John Dominic Crossan, *In Fragments: The Aphorisms of Jesus* (San Francisco: Harper & Row), 166–68; Boring, *Mark*, 243.

3. Jesus's Demand for Faith and the Disciples' Doubt

of Jesus's words in their Markan context, which requires identification of the characters to whom Mark's Jesus speaks and of those characters' situation within Mark's unfolding narrative. From this interpretive angle, one should not uncritically assimilate Jesus's addressees to Mark's readers or to any other first-generation Jesus-believers, even if all would understand themselves to be disciples of Jesus in one sense or another.

Some interpreters, even while claiming to focus on narrative context, assume Jesus speaks in 8:34–9:1 to Mark's readers, rather than to the characters who hear his words in Mark's narrative world. This assumption already influences the interpretations of Mark 9:1 mentioned above as highlighting the verse's supposed assurance to Mark's readers about the eschaton's immanence at the expense of Jesus's warning to the disciples he has just addressed, lest they fail to die with him.[43] It can lead to other questionable interpretations as well. For example, in a section of her essay on Mark 8:34 that focuses on narrative context, Joanna Dewey argues that Mark refers to the cross as a specific instrument of Roman execution instead of as a metaphor for "human suffering in general," a more common interpretation.[44] On this point, Dewey is persuasive, as is her critique of interpretations that leverage Mark 8:34–37's encouragement of present suffering in the hope of "reward … in the age to come" to suppress marginalized persons.[45] However, despite this professed focus on narrative context, Dewey does not carefully contextualize within Mark's narrative discourse Jesus's demand that Peter and his fellow students join Jesus in crucifixion. Instead, she proposes a generalization analogous to the one her earlier analysis of Mark 8:34's reference to the cross eschewed, interpreting it as a symbol not of "human suffering" but rather of "political persecution." As the slippage between the gospel's "disciples" and its "audiences" in the following quote suggests, Dewey conflates imaginary

---

43. See Marcus, *Mark 8–16*, 630.

44. Joanna Dewey, "'Let Them Renounce Themselves and Take Up Their Cross': A Feminist Reading of Mark 8:34 in Mark's Social and Narrative World," *BTB* 34 (2004): 101–2. The relevant section begins on 100: "Mark 8:34 in Its Social and Narrative Context." Dewey announces her intent "to read Mark 8:34 in the contexts of both Markan narrative and first-century culture."

For the cross as a symbol of suffering in the sense of generalized exposure to ridicule associated with a Christian identity, see Gundry, *Mark*, 435–36. For interpretation of Mark from that perspective, with attention to competing readings, see Pudussery, "Discipleship," 99–105.

45. Dewey, "Let Them Renounce," 98.

characters whom Jesus addresses within Mark's narrative (the disciples) with flesh-and-blood readers of Mark: "In Mk 8:34 and following, the narrative attempts to prepare the disciples—and the Gospel's audiences—for ... persecution and to encourage faithfulness in the face of it."[46]

While Dewey's reading is more sensitive to the cross's plausible metaphorical implications than is the traditional interpretation she critiques, her approach's problems become clear in the light of James Phelan's complication of the influential model of narrative communication that Seymour Chatman proposed in the late 1970s.[47] Phelan argues that authors (actual and implied) employ variable resources in communicating with audiences (actual and authorial/implied) through the production of narrative texts. These resources include narrator and narratee (or narrative voice and implied auditor/reader), on which Chatman focused, but also "characters ... who sometimes function as tellers" when they speak to other characters in the course of a narrative. Phelan suggests that heuristically useful models of narrative communication ought to make these characters "explicitly present" as narrators,[48] because narrative discourse is not necessarily monologic, even when it features an authoritative character given to didactic discourse, such as the Markan Jesus.

This suggestion is analogous to the one made in the previous chapter about Mark's dialogic discourse: one cannot assume that statements the Markan Jesus utters are more authoritative than those of his opponents, or that they perfectly align with the narrator's or implied author's views on the subject about which Jesus speaks. Authors such as Mark employ diverse channels of both argumentation and narrative communication. The latter include the third-person narrative voice, of course, but also characters Phelan calls "tellers" in the above quote, whose statements, questions, commands, ejaculations, and the like incidentally provide crucial narrative information. Such channels work synergistically, or even dialogically, to constitute the narrative, although individual voices or utterances can be displaced from the narrative to make on their own a different sense irrelevant to the role they play in its construction.[49]

---

46. Dewey, "Let Them Renounce," 102–3.

47. James Phelan, "Authors, Resources, Audiences: Toward a Rhetorical Poetics of Narrative," *Style* 52 (2018): 2–3.

48. Phelan, "Authors, Resources, Audiences," 3.

49. Phelan, "Authors, Resources, Audiences," 3–10.

This theory of narrative communication helps explain what has gone awry in Dewey's analysis of 8:34, which conflates the authoritative voice of Mark's lead character, Jesus, with the narrative voice, so that Jesus's attempt "to prepare the disciples ... for ... persecution" becomes indistinguishable, in the rhetoric she adopts, from "the narrative attempt[ing] to prepare the Gospel's audience" for the same thing. As Phelan shows, though, the narrator's voice cannot necessarily be assimilated to even an authoritative character such as Jesus. The two function as independent narrative resources the author synergistically employs. The implied reader understands the narrative by grasping not the identity of narrator and character/teller, so that Jesus's commands to his disciples become the narrative's exhortations to the audience, but rather their synergy or complementarity.

Dewey resists interpretations of 8:34 that encourage suffering by arguing that properly read, the verse constitutes a more limited exhortation that the audience "remain faithful to Jesus and the rule of God in face of persecution, even execution, by political authorities."[50] However, its interpretive scope should be constrained further still: in the context of Mark's narrative of Jesus and his disciples, 8:34 exhorts only those disciples Jesus addresses, not the audience at all. As situated in Mark, this dominical saying functions synergistically with the narrative voice to constitute a proleptic reference to the specific political execution of Jesus, the protagonist crucified by Rome at the end of Mark's Gospel. This character's execution was prophesied in detail just a few verses earlier (8:31) and will be predicted again and again in increasingly vivid terms as the gospel proceeds to narrate it (9:31; 10:33-34; 14:17-27). By calling his own students to "take up the cross and follow" in 8:34, the Markan Jesus requires these characters to be crucified alongside himself in hopes of resurrection within Mark's narrative world. The teller Jesus's discourse works in tandem

---

50. Dewey, "Let Them Renounce," 103. For other readings of Mark that stress the relevance of the fear or even experience of communal persecution to the evangelist's community, see Van Iersel, "Gospel according to St. Mark"; Van Iersel, "Failed Followers in Mark"; Incigneri, *Gospel to the Romans*; Roskam, *Purpose of the Gospel of Mark*. Some are skeptical that Christians were persecuted this early in history. See, e.g., Candida Moss, *The Myth of Persecution: How Early Christians Invented a Story of Martyrdom* (New York: HarperOne, 2013); Brent D. Shaw, "The Myth of the Neronian Persecution," *JRS* 105 (2015): 73-100. However, it is widely acknowledged that Mark's Gospel, especially in chapter 13, reflects its original auditors' fear of persecution (see Marcus, *Mark 1-8*, 28-29; Collins, *Mark*, 96-102; etc.), even if that fear exceeded the reality of the first-century threat.

with the narrator to advance the Markan narrative by setting up the master's prophesied execution as a test of faith that his students will fail when, at the narrative's climax, they flee from Jesus's side rather than following him to arrest, execution, and possibly resurrection.[51]

At this point, it may be possible to rehabilitate Dewey's interpretation. The synergy between Jesus's warning to the disciples and the narrator's discourse to the narratee is admittedly complex. The character Jesus uses the indefinite pronoun τις, "anyone," when addressing his students in front of the crowd in 8:34. In this the narratee (and thus the implied reader) could potentially discern an oblique self-reflection. In other words, the character Jesus's demand to his disciples may have implications for the audience "overhearing" that demand, if its members think of themselves as disciples of Jesus in a less literal sense than the Markan characters who go by that title. Such auditors, if a situation involving deadly political harassment were to arise, might feel obliged to treat the Markan Jesus's words to these characters as if they were binding on themselves, as Dewey imagines. Michal Beth Dinkler reminds us that it is important to posit a variety of historically situated reading profiles when speculating about how ancient audiences might have responded to a given biblical text.[52] My ultimate point, then, is not to dismiss Dewey's interpretive construal as illegitimate but rather to insist on a more careful investigation of Mark's narrative context than she offers to determine whether the synergy between the Markan narrator and the words of Mark's character Jesus easily accommodates or actively resists such a response from Mark's audience.

While I remain suspicious of the former, Elizabeth Struthers Malbon pursues the possibility vigorously. Her approach to Mark thus resembles Dewey's, though it is more theoretically rigorous in that it acknowledges the kind of narrative complication Phelan tries to model. Malbon does not assume but rather argues with reference to Mark's rhetoric that the

---

51. Robert C. Tannehill interprets 8:34–35 in a way similar to my reading, though his is not as detailed or as pessimistic. See Tannehill, "Reading It Whole: The Function of Mark 8:34–35 in Mark's Story," in *The Shape of the Gospel: New Testament Essays* (Eugene, OR: Cascade, 2007), 189–99, esp. 194–97. David P. Seccombe also anticipates this interpretation, though its methodological framework is historical rather than literary. See Seccombe, "Take Up Your Cross," in *God Who Is Rich in Mercy: Essays Presented to Dr. D. B. Knox*, ed. Peter Thomas O'Brien and David Gilbert Peterson (Grand Rapids: Baker Books, 1986), 145–48.

52. Michal Beth Dinkler, "Reading the Potentials of Jesus's 'Triumphal Entry' (Luke 19:28–40)," *RevExp* 112 (2015): 535–41.

Second Gospel imaginatively situates its implied audience in the position of the disciples and crowds to whom Jesus speaks in 8:34 and elsewhere. Investigating the Second Gospel's various statements about the disciples and crowds, Malbon argues that the two groups complement each other in Mark, with the "extension of both the invitation and demand of followership from the disciples to the crowd set[ting] up its further extension—to the hearers/readers."[53]

Mark's accounts of Jesus addressing the disciples do not differ measurably from those focused on Jesus's words to the crowds, Malbon finds. In fact, Mark's Jesus sometimes addresses them all together (as in 8:34) and sometimes even seems to refer to both groups under a common rubric: "The Markan Jesus addresses the disciples, but the words he employs, many and all, are open-ended. The disciples are surely among the many for whom Jesus gives his life [10:45; 14:24]; the crowd is also among the many; but the many embraces as well the hearers/readers of the Markan narrative."[54] Malbon believes that the Second Gospel's rhetorical impulse to generalize or even universalize the addressees of Jesus's discourse effectively blurs the boundaries of Mark's narrative world and the world of the audience. As a result, readers are always justified in imagining themselves among the "many" of 10:45, the "anyone" of 8:34, and in other references to groups of disciples and/or the assembled throng that Jesus addresses.[55]

Malbon's careful analysis of Mark's Gospel is frequently insightful, and I agree with her interpretation of certain passages (esp. 13:37, to be discussed below). However, her totalizing conclusion raises questions. Are the Markan Jesus's words to the disciples and crowds "many *and all* ... open-ended" in the sense of "embrac[ing] ... the hearers/readers of the Markan narrative"? With respect to 8:34–9:1, the evangelist includes rhetorical signposts that seem to deny their status as exhortations addressed at Mark's readers to remain faithful to death in the face of political harassment. The conditional relative clause opening Jesus's initial threat of eschatological judgment, though it employs an indefinite construction, explicitly narrows the audience Jesus addresses to exclude people of subsequent generations: "whoever is ashamed [ὃς γὰρ ἐὰν ἐπαισχυνθῇ] of me and of my words in this generation [ἐν τῇ γενεᾷ ταύτῃ]" (8:38). This would

---

53. Elizabeth Struthers Malbon, "Disciples/Crowds/Whoever: Markan Characters and Readers," *NovT* 28 (1986): 124.
54. Malbon, "Disciples/Crowds/Whoever," 126.
55. Malbon, "Disciples/Crowds/Whoever," 126.

eliminate Mark's readers, based on a standard dating of the Second Gospel. The next verse further limits the scope of the eschatological warning's application, this time spatially as well as temporally, to "some standing right here" (τινες ὧδε τῶν ἑστηκότων, 9:1).[56]

Mark's double circumscription of Jesus's addressees, both temporally and spatially, suggests that the master's decision to speak to his students in front of a crowd specially summoned to hear his words does not universalize the call to die with the Son of Man and the accompanying warnings about failure to do so in 8:34–9:1, *pace* Malbon and others.[57] The invocation of the crowd rather solemnizes Jesus's admonition to the characters identified as disciples by publicizing it: "having summoned the crowd with his disciples, he said to them" (προσκαλεσάμενος τὸν ὄχλον σὺν τοῖς μαθηταῖς αὐτοῦ εἶπεν αὐτοῖς, 8:34a). There is no need for αὐτοῖς, the verb of speech's indirect object, to refer both to τὸν ὄχλον and to τοῖς μαθηταῖς. It could refer to Jesus's disciples alone, who are the pronoun's immediate antecedent. Moreover, the Greek word προσκαλέω regularly functions in the middle-passive as a legal term meaning "summon" or even "summon to a hearing" (e.g., Acts 5:40), and it is often used of summoning witnesses

---

56. The abrupt transition between 8:38 and 9:1 follows a convention of biblical narrative by reiterating a verb of speech without a change of speaker to indicate the addressees' silence—in this case registering the disciples' stupefied shock at Jesus's words. For brief discussion of the convention, see Robert Alter, *The David Story: A Translation with Commentary of 1 and 2 Samuel* (New York: Norton, 1999), 297. Jesus responds to their mute surprise by insisting on his warning's urgency: some standing here will fail to die with him (9:1), and thus will experience the threatened eschatological judgment without benefit of the Son's patronage (8:38).

Interpreters usually view 9:1 as conciliatory encouragement (i.e., the eschaton is coming, even if it is delayed) rather than as a warning complementing 8:38. This view is unpersuasive. Etienne Trocmé identifies synonymous parallelism between 8:38 and 9:1 in support of the alternative interpretation. See Trocmé, "Marc 9,1: Prédiction ou réprimande," *SE* 2 (1964): 259–65. Winn's (positive) assessment of the consensus view (articulated, e.g., at Pudussery, "Discipleship," 128–29, 140, though with reservation) is telling in its tautology: "Trocmé's interpretation [of 9:1] has found few followers because the text seems to function as an encouragement to Mark's readers—an encouragement that was needed after Jesus's ominous words in … 8:34–38" (Winn, *Purpose of Mark's Gospel*, 52 n. 21).

57. Malbon, "Disciples/Crowds/Whoever," 109–10; cf. Collins, *Mark*, 407, and, more emphatically, Marcus, *Mark 8–16*, 624.

and others to court (compare, e.g., Plato, *Leg.* 936e).⁵⁸ Thus, the crowd constitutes not so much Jesus's addressees as witnesses of the warning to his students in a formalized public context.⁵⁹ Mark's inclusion of both parties invites not a universalizing but a narrow interpretive application of Jesus's words. The Markan Jesus speaks exclusively to the Markan characters identified as "disciples" in 8:34–9:1, with the urgent significance of his warning underscored by the presence of witnesses he summons to hear its terms.

The only other Markan use of προσκαλέω with reference to a crowd has the same connotation. After Pharisees and scribes from Jerusalem challenge Jesus's students' neglect of lustrations demanded by the elders' traditions (7:1–5), Jesus begins to rebuke the religious leaders for their willingness to privilege human tradition over divine commandment (7:6–13). Following this rebuke, Mark notes that Jesus "summoned the crowd" (προσκαλεσάμενος τὸν ὄχλον, 7:14),⁶⁰ as in 8:34. Before it as public witnesses he makes a denunciatory exclamation undermining these religious leaders' critique of own his community's praxis: "All of you hear me and understand" (7:14–15). In this passage, one is tempted to translate ἀκούσατέ μου πάντες καὶ σύνετε, Jesus's opening tag, as "Oyez! Oyez!" or "Hear ye, hear ye!"

---

58. MGS, s.v. "προσκαλέω," esp. definition 2; see also Marcus, *Mark 8–16*, 615, although emphasizing the word's military connotations.

59. Ernest Best draws an analogous distinction between the crowd and the disciples. He argues that Mark distinguishes between the two as "the religious" and "the group from which those who will be religious are called." See Best, "The Role of the Disciples in Mark," *NTS* 23 (1977): 390–93. Best's interpretation of 8:34 is structurally similar to mine, though formulated in terms that exceed the narrative context of 8:34–9:1 and ignore its limitation of the logion's applicative scope to the Markan Jesus's students. He takes 8:34 as teaching generally addressed to followers of Jesus (especially believers in Mark's community) but designed to give outsiders or the uncommitted a sense of what following Jesus entails (Best, *Following Jesus*, 30–31).

60. Many manuscripts include πάλιν, while some have πάντα and others nothing. Editors tend to see πάλιν as the more difficult reading, with a better claim to originality (so NA²⁸) because the crowd had not been mentioned since 6:45. However, a scribe may have introduced it (perhaps as a replacement for πάντα) to emphasize Jesus's broad popularity over against the Jewish religious leaders opposing him. The previous episode, while not mentioning a crowd, focuses on Jesus's celebrity as a healer (6:53–56). By having Jesus call the crowd again or back, a later scribe (or conceivably Mark) would imply that the throng constitutes a friendly witness to his caustic denunciation of the religious leaders. From this angle, the word's omission, which removes emphasis on the crowd's implicit support for Jesus, could represent the harder reading.

This episode too suggests that the Markan Jesus's public declaration before a summoned crowd does not signal that discourse's universal application, including to Mark's readers, but instead emphasizes his condemnation of the scribes' and Pharisees' traditional distinctions by formally publicizing it. Notably, the evangelist includes a subsequent scene wherein related teaching important to Mark's readers surfaces; however, this takes place not in public before the throng, but in private, and involves the master's instruction of his disciples alone. Only in this setting, isolated from the crowd, does Jesus draw out and explain for the benefit of Mark's readers the implications of the theological principle on which his public rebuke of the Pharisees and scribes is based. Here, the narrator overtly intervenes to specify the application of the character Jesus's teaching to an issue Mark's audience likely faced after the time of Jesus's narrated ministry: controversial alimentary praxis occasioned by the presence of gentiles in Jesus-believing communities (see Acts 10–11; Gal 2:11–14). That is the significance of the phrase καθαρίζων πάντα τὰ βρώματα ("so making all foods clean"; 7:19b), which constitutes the narrator's interpretive commentary addressed to the implied reader, parenthetically embedded within the Markan Jesus's extended discourse to his disciples (7:17–23).[61]

In 8:34, Mark's note that Jesus summons the crowd "with" or "alongside the disciples" (σὺν τοῖς μαθηταῖς) is not sufficient to authorize the direct relevance to Mark's implied readers of Jesus's commands that the disciples face with him crucifixion in hope of resurrection. The crowd's presence does not obviate the Markan Jesus's claim in 8:38–9:1 to be speaking only to people of his time and in his proximity—that is, within the narrative world of Mark's Gospel. Similarly, the Markan Jesus's use of indefinite pronouns does not universalize his exhortation so that it encompasses even Mark's audience. One finds nothing in this section like the overt signal 7:19 offers to Mark's readers about the implications of Jesus's teaching for situations especially relevant to them. Nor does one find an invocation of the reader such as in 13:14, which I will discuss presently. One instead finds much the opposite: joint statements limiting the applicative scope of the Markan Jesus's commands, in terms of both time and place, so that Mark's readers stand outside their region of pertinence.

---

61. For a range of interpretation of this phrase, taken by Origen, John Chrysostom, and almost all modern scholars as the author or narrator's explanatory gloss of Jesus's words in 7:18–19, see Collins, *Mark*, 341 n. q and 354 n. 121.

Mark on occasion addresses the readers more-or-less directly through the character Jesus's public declarations to the disciples and/or the crowd, as Malbon argues. I will discuss an example of this below. There are also times when the Markan narrative voice intervenes to signal the direct application to Mark's readers of words the character Jesus speaks to the disciples in private settings, as in 7:19. At other times, on the contrary, the Markan narrative signals the urgent application of particular words Jesus speaks to the disciples as characters, even going so far as to exclude Mark's implied audience from Jesus's addressees. Careful investigation is required before drawing conclusions about any narrativized dominical saying's broader applicative scope. Even if one can imagine ancient readers of Mark applying it straightforwardly to their own circumstances, Mark's narrative might resist rather than accommodate that application. Within the context of Mark's discourse, such sayings, addressed by the teller Jesus to other characters in the narrative, function as resources of narrative communication and should primarily be interpreted in terms of how they synergize with related resources to advance the author's story. Interpreters concerned with narrative context should exercise caution in taking them as exhortations directed at the audience, unless the narrator licenses such an application. They should exercise especial care if the narrative circumscribes a dominical saying's addressees in a way that would seem to exclude readers from its applicative reach. And, I would add, they should be very careful indeed when those words would otherwise call for readers willingly to suffer violent death in the hope of an unguaranteed resurrection, especially insofar as Christ-followers today continue to be threatened by political violence.[62] From this vantage, choosing the proper theory of reading involves ethical considerations as well as hermeneutical ones.

Mark 13, the Disciples' Second Chance to Die and Rise with Jesus, and the Readers' Flight

The subsequent episode picks up the reference to "those standing here" from 9:1 to emphasize the urgency of Jesus's words, at the same time continuing to delimit their relevancy to the Markan disciples alone. At the transfiguration, three of the disciples who were in fact standing before

---

62. Consider the bomb detonated during a 2016 Easter service in Lahore, Pakistan, killing approximately seventy-five people and wounding hundreds more. See Adam Taylor, "An Easter Sunday Suicide Bombing Shows Plight of Pakistan's Christians," *Washington Post*, March 28, 2016, https://tinyurl.com/SBL4532a.

Jesus when he warned them of the judgment they were liable to incur proleptically witness his eschatological elevation to authority and hear God's voice draw attention to what he had just said: "this is my son; listen to him" (9:7).[63] This amounts to a supplementary warning addressed to these characters in particular lest they fail to die with Jesus and forgo the Son of Man's patronage when he comes in glory. Peter, James, and John all catch a glimpse of his authority (9:2-9), which will be fully revealed to them sooner than they think (see 9:1) since Elijah, the eschatological forerunner, has already come and gone (9:10-13). Related to their supplementary foretaste of Jesus's glory, these three come to emblematize the disciples' collective failure to follow Jesus to death and resurrection in Mark's passion narrative, leaving them vulnerable to the vindicated Son of Man's eschatological disavowal (8:38). In 14:32-42 the same trio's sleep emblematizes the Markan disciples' apathy in the face of Jesus's warnings to stay awake and watch with him as he prepares in prayer to die, with hopes of rising again. Moreover, the Second Evangelist underscores through narrative irony the absence of these three disciples from the scene of Jesus's death and (possible) resurrection, as I will show in the next chapter.

Mark's Jesus addresses the Olivet discourse in chapter 13 to the same disciples, with Andrew mentioned also, perhaps as a gesture that Jesus's words here apply to the other Markan students in much the same way as to these three representatives. Like Mark 8:34-9:1, this block of dominical

---

63. Ancient Christian and modern biblical scholars have discerned a relationship between 9:1 and the transfiguration. See David Wenham and A. D. A. Moses, "'There Are Some Standing Here...': Did They Become the 'Reputed Pillars' of the Jerusalem Church? Some Reflections on Mark 9:1, Galatians 2:9 and the Transfiguration," *NovT* 36 (1994): 146-63, esp. 148-51. While I do not accept their argument precisely as formulated, Wenham and Moses show that Mark 9:1 may refer to Peter, James, and John, insofar as they immediately see Jesus transfigured, proleptically fulfilling the prophecy of 9:1.

On the transfiguration as anticipating eschatological judgment, see Thomas R. Hatina, "Who Will See 'The Kingdom of God Coming with Power' in Mark 9,1—Protagonists or Antagonists?," *Bib* 86 (2005): 20-34, esp. 22, including n. 6. Hatina does not connect the divine voice's command (Mark 9:7) to Jesus's call to follow him to death and resurrection, or to his warning of eschatological condemnation for those that fail to do so (8:34-9:1). A connection is more often asserted between 9:7 and Jesus's Son of Man prophecy in 8:31. See, e.g., Charles Edwin Carlston, "Transfiguration and Resurrection," *JBL* 80 (1961): 240; cf. Collins, *Mark*, 426, though she secondarily notes that the voice confirms the "prophecies and admonitions of Jesus," referring to all of 8:34-9:1.

teaching anticipates the disciples' failure to die and rise with Jesus in the Markan passion narrative. At the same time, though, it vividly imagines a time that exceeds Mark's narrative bounds, in which these disciples may experience supplemental opportunities to succeed at the endeavor they will fail to accomplish within Mark's Gospel itself. This extratextual future incorporates the experiences of Mark's readers as well as those of the disciples, for which reason Mark's rhetoric in the Olivet discourse is related to but more hermeneutically capacious than that of 8:34–9:1.

The anticipation of the disciples' failure reveals itself most clearly in the parable of the returning master, with which Jesus ends the discourse (13:32–37). That parable hinges on an order to "keep watch" (γρηγορῇ, 13:34 and passim), which will find an echo in Jesus's command that Peter, James, and John "keep watch" as he prays in Gethsemane (γρηγορεῖτε, 14:34).[64] Jesus cautions these three (with Andrew) to keep watch for the coming hour (ὥρη, 13:32–33), lest the master come home and "find you sleeping" (εὕρῃ ὑμᾶς καθεύδοντας, 13:36). In chapter 14, as Jesus prepares for his impending death, "the hour has come" (ἦλθεν ἡ ὥρα, 14:41) and Jesus "finds sleeping" (εὑρίσκει ... καθεύδοντας) Peter, James, and John, the first of whom he signals out for a pointed rebuke: "Can't you watch for a single hour?" (μίαν ὥραν γρηγορῆσαι, 14:37).

As the Markan passion narrative advances, the disciples fail to participate in the Son's death and resurrection at the precise moments when the parable of the returning master demands their preparation for the anticipated homecoming:[65] "evening [ὀψέ], or midnight, or at the cockcrow [ἀλεκτοροφωνίας], or in the morning [πρωΐ]" (13:35). The Passover meal occurs in the evening (ὀψίας, 14:17), when Jesus predicts his death and warns all the disciples lest they abandon him. The Gethsemane scene discussed above occurs in the middle of the night, as implied by the narrative's chronological sequencing and Mark's statement that "their eyes were heavy" (14:40). Peter's denial of Jesus occurs at cockcrow (ἀλέκτωρ ἐφώνησεν, 14:72; see also 14:30). Finally, it is in the morning (πρωΐ, 15:1)

---

64. Werner H. Kelber, "Hour of the Son of Man and the Temptation of the Disciples (Mark 14.32–42)," in *The Passion in Mark: Studies on Mark 14–16*, ed. Werner H. Kelber and John R. Donahue (Philadelphia: Fortress, 1976), 48–49; cf. Timothy J. Geddert, *Watchwords: Mark 13 in Markan Eschatology*, JSNTSup 26 (Sheffield: JSOT Press, 1989), 90–94.

65. See Robert H. Lightfoot, *The Gospel Message of St. Mark* (Oxford: Clarendon, 1950), 50, elaborated by Geddert, *Watchwords*, 94–111, whose analysis is excellent.

when Jesus is delivered to Pilate for crucifixion, as well as when his resurrection is revealed and his female disciples flee instead of proclaiming it (λίαν πρωΐ, 16:2). From this interpretive angle, the parabolic master's homecoming points to the passion and resurrection of the Son of Man, in which the Markan disciples (especially Peter, James, and John, as the next chapter will show) all fail to participate, and which most will not even observe, despite that parable's command to watch.

These points of contact do not stand on their own; they culminate an elaborate pattern of parallels between chapter 13's Olivet discourse and Mark 14–16, more of which I will discuss presently.[66] However, recognition of this intratextual relationship does not exhaust the hermeneutical potential of Mark 13. The sermon rhetorically suggests that some of Jesus's words apply directly to the readers in addition to (or even instead of) the characters Peter, James, John, and Andrew (with the last perhaps standing in for all the remaining Markan disciples).[67] For example, "all" are invited to fulfill the concluding parable's command to watch: "what I say to you [ὑμῖν] I say to all [πᾶσιν]: keep watch" (13:37). Mark's Jesus here distinguishes between ὑμῖν, the disciples to whom he speaks, and πᾶσιν, a universal audience that would include Mark's readers/hearers, as Malbon argues.[68] The command to "watch" would thus apply to both the characters Jesus addresses the parable and to the audience reading it in the Second Gospel. What watching means for each party is not necessarily the same, though, given their different situations vis-à-vis the Son of Man's passion and the future eschatological afflictions that will culminate in the Son's parousia (see 13:6–8, 14–23), one allegorical meaning of the master's homecoming. Not only in 13:37 but elsewhere in the Olivet discourse as well, the evangelist provides signposts that indicate when and how Jesus's exhortations pertain to the implied reader, and when and how they apply

---

66. See Dean B. Deppe, "Charting the Future or a Perspective on the Present? The Paraenetic Purpose of Mark 13," *CTJ* 41 (2006): 89–101.

67. On the Markan Olivet discourse's multiple levels of reference, see Dale C. Allison, *Constructing Jesus: Memory, Imagination, and History* (Grand Rapids: Baker Academic, 2010), 60–61; Peter Bolt, "Mark 13: An Apocalyptic Precursor to the Passion Narrative," *RTR* 54 (1995): 10–32; Deppe, "Charting the Future," 95–97; Geddert, *Watchwords*, 107–11.

68. Malbon, "Disciples/Crowds/Whoever," 126, although this is often observed; cf. Collins, *Mark*, 619.

in a direct way only to the characters he addresses (and perhaps the larger group of characters known as the disciples).

Earlier in chapter 13, Jesus prophetically exhorts his followers to suffer betrayal, trial, and execution in the hope of final salvation (13:9–13). All this is to occur in a time of eschatological tribulation, as suggested by the preceding section's references to false messiahs, wars and reports of them, and other transnational calamities that constitute "the beginnings of birth pains" (13:6–8). Its eschatological horizon is expansive, but the section of Jesus's Olivet discourse that 13:6–8 introduces narrowly addresses those characters present to hear Jesus speak, namely, Peter, James, John, and Andrew. Note that Mark's Jesus begins the exhortation to martyrdom encompassing 13:9–13 by declaring βλέπετε δὲ ὑμεῖς ἑαυτοὺς ("and as for you, you all watch out for yourselves"; 13:9). Marcus rightly observes that the verse's "pileup of references to the addressees" is "awkward," to say the least, which probably explains why many manuscripts omit them. Marcus conjectures that the repeated "emphasis on 'you [all]' ... underline[s] the relevance for [Mark's] community of the prophecies in 13:9–13," but this fails to convince.[69] After all, the evangelist adopts the opposite procedure in emphasizing the relevance of Jesus's prophecies to Mark's implied readers at the conclusion of the parable of the returning master (13:37). There the Markan Jesus's "you all" (ὑμῖν) refers to the characters listening to him in distinction from a broader audience encompassing Mark's community (πᾶσιν, "everyone"), as Marcus acknowledges.[70] Moreover, at the beginning of the subsequent section of the Olivet discourse (13:14–23), precisely when Mark's Jesus turns from exhorting martyrdom to authorizing flight from persecution, the narrator intervenes to invoke the reader as the one to whom these new exhortations apply (ὁ ἀναγινώσκων νοείτω, 13:14).[71] The Markan Jesus's "pileup of references" to his addressees in 13:9, by contrast, stresses the relevance of the earlier section's prophetic

---

69. Marcus, *Mark 8–16*, 882.

70. Marcus, *Mark 8–16*, 922.

71. Most interpretations associate the parenthetical reference to the reader—either individual readers/auditors or the person reading to the audience—only with the supposedly esoteric Danielic phrase. See, e.g., Ernest Best, "The Gospel of Mark: Who Is the Reader?," *IBS* 11 (1989): 124–32; see Collins, *Mark*, 597–98, for discussion. I connect it more broadly to the entire section it introduces, contrasting this section's relevance to the reading community with the previous section's relevance to the characters Jesus emphatically addresses in Mark 13:9.

commands to the disciples as characters Jesus actually addresses within Mark's narrative world.

Against a calamitous eschatological horizon spreading out beyond Mark's pages (13:6–8), Mark's Jesus therefore situates exhortations to martyrdom specifically addressed to Peter, James, John, and Andrew (13:9–13), much as the exhortations to crucifixion with the Son of Man in 8:34–9:1 address Peter and the other Markan disciples alone, although Jesus issues them in the presence of the crowd. In this section, Mark's Jesus seems to be imagining the possibility that his disciples may manage to obey his directives to die and rise in his footsteps in a later time of eschatological travail, even if they will fail to do so in his narrated passion and resurrection. In the terms suggested by the parable of the returning master, they may still succeed in watching in the context of an eschatological future exceeding Mark's narrative, even though they fall asleep within the passion narrative itself. In fact, 13:9–13 anticipates the latter eventuality as well the former possibility, for its rhetoric not only anticipates general eschatological travails involving the disciples' martyrdoms but also foreshadows the Son of Man prophecies' (8:31; 9:31; 10:33–34) fulfillment in Mark's account of Jesus abandoned by his disciples to die and possibly rise alone.[72]

The prediction of the Son's suffering and death in 10:33–34 provides a useful lens through which to discern that frame of reference. In chapter 13 Jesus prophesies that his disciples will be "given over to councils" (παραδώσουσιν ... εἰς συνέδρια, 13:9). This echoes the earlier prophecy that the Son of Man "will be given over [παραδοθήσεται] to the chief priests and the scribes" (10:33), key constituencies of "the council" (τὸ συνέδριον) in Jerusalem that tries Jesus after his arrest, from which his disciples fled (14:55; 15:1). A few verses later, Jesus prophesies that his disciples will be "given over ... to death" (παραδώσει ... εἰς θάνατον) and "put to death"

---

72. Various scholars comment on the hermeneutical capaciousness of the prophetic discourse in Mark 13, recognizing its joint (or at least ambiguous) references to Mark's passion narrative and to eschatological events (or to events fulfilled beyond the narrative confines of Mark's Gospel). Geddert believes these parallels present the eschatology of Mark 13 as "highly infused with Mark's passion theology" (*Watchwords*, 106). Deppe infers from such parallels the evangelist's insistence that the readers interpret Jesus's apocalyptic discourse as practical guidance for situations analogous to those the disciples face in the passion narrative ("Charting the Future," 95–97). Bolt sees the correspondence as requiring a redirection of the disciples' attention, from apocalyptic signs to their own activity in the mission Jesus pioneered ("Mark 13," 26–32).

(θανατώσουσιν αὐτούς, 13:12). This also recalls the prediction about the Son of Man in 10:33-34, where the chief priests and scribes "will condemn him to death" (κατακρινοῦσιν αὐτὸν θανάτῳ, 10:33) and Romans "will kill him" (10:34; cf. 14:53-15:39). More specifically, Jesus predicts that his disciples will be "flayed" in 13:9, evoking the earlier prophecy that enemies will "scourge" the Son of Man (10:34), fulfilled in 15:15.

The prophecies of 13:9-13 (with those of 10:33-34) find fulfillment in Mark's passion narrative, but, ironically, not in the experiences of Peter, James, John, or Andrew, to whom they are directed, or any of Jesus's other disciples. These all flee from the scene of the Son of Man's arrest precisely to avoid participating in the prophecies' consummation, leaving the master to fulfill them by suffering, dying, and rising alone.[73] Even Jesus's female disciples only watch him die from a distance (15:40-41) and join the others in fearful flight when confronted with the empty tomb (16:8). Mark never loses sight of the disciples' failure within the narrative, not even in 13:9-13, where the evangelist gestures at the possibility of their successful martyrdoms beyond its bounds.

Unsurprisingly, in the light of Mark's treatment of the resurrection theme, Mark 13 will not explicitly prophesy resurrection as martyrdom's eschatological terminus for Jesus's disciples, even outside the boundaries of the Second Gospel's narrative. Mark 13:13's reference to the salvation of those who stand until the end possibly hints at it. So does the Olivet discourse's later predictions of eschatological tribulations culminating in a promise of the Son's advent (see 13:14-27). The regnant Son of Man, Mark's Jesus says, "will collect his chosen ones from the four winds, from a corner of the earth to a corner of heaven" (ἐκ τῶν τεσσάρων ἀνέμων ἀπ' ἄκρου γῆς ἕως ἄκρου οὐρανοῦ, 13:26-27). These verses not only quote Dan 7:13-14 but also recall the resurrection depicted in Dan 12:2-3 (OG), which describes the dead to be raised in terms similar to those the Bible uses of scattered exiles, as "the ones who sleep in the expanse of the earth

---

73. Points of ironic contact between the prophesied experiences of Jesus's followers in chapter 13 and those of Jesus alone, abandoned by those followers, multiply when comparative analysis moves beyond 13:9-13 and 10:33-34 to connect other sections of the Olivet discourse to the different Son of Man prophecies and the particularities of their fulfillment in Jesus's narrated passion. For example, Mark's Jesus predicts a darkening of the sun that his followers will see in advance of the Son's parousia (13:24-25); such a darkening occurs just before Jesus expires (15:33). See Allison, *Constructing Jesus*, 60, for other parallels.

[ἐν τῷ πλάτει τῆς γῆς]" (cf. Isa 43:6-7; Zech 2:6 [LXX 2:10]).[74] The eschatological gathering of Jesus's followers scattered throughout the earth (Mark 13:14-18) in conjunction with the vindicated Son of Man's reign (13:24-27) may therefore include the resurrected Markan disciples resting within it after having been martyred (13:9-13), though the reference to resurrection remains oblique.[75]

The reference to the "desolating sacrilege" (τὸ βδέλυγμα τῆς ἐρημώσεως), upon whose establishment Mark understands Jesus's words to authorize flight in 13:14 (τότε οἱ ἐν τῇ Ἰουδαίᾳ φευγέτωσαν εἰς τὰ ὄρη), alludes, again via Daniel, to the desecration of the temple by Antiochus IV Epiphanes as part of his policy forcing Judeans to hellenize. That policy involved persecuting those who retained allegiance to their religious beliefs and traditions (see Dan 9:27; 11:31-35; 1 Macc 1:54-64), with historical accounts featuring the faithful's flight to the mountains (e.g., 1 Macc 2:7-34). This background informs Jesus's command in Mark 13:14 and the entire section it introduces (13:14-23). The Second Evangelist understands Jesus's reference to the Danielic "desolating sacrilege" and his accompanying command to flee as prophesying an analogous experience of harassment and evasion that will encompass the readers in particular, for they are explicitly invoked in 13:14. This invocation stands in contrast with 13:9, which rhetorically limits to the Markan disciples alone the previous section's exhortations to martyrdom. Mark 13:14 thus complements the rhetorical development in 8:34-9:1. There the evangelist circumscribed Jesus's original demand that followers emulate his execution in anticipation of resurrection to ensure that it applied only to those disciples present to hear him speak and not to Mark's future readers. In 13:14, Mark authorizes the

---

74. As Collins notes, this prophecy "alludes to the motif of the gathering of all the exiles of Israel from the nations" (*Mark*, 615). Also relevant is that the martyred disciples are executed in various geographical locales, as they are killed while preaching the gospel to the nations (Mark 13:10).

75. Marcus views Mark 13:27 as imagining the same sort of eschatological gathering as 1 Thess 4:15-17, involving both the living and the risen dead (*Mark 8-16*, 905). Also compare Schweitzer's comments on the relationship of resurrection to the conviction that God will protect the scattered remnant until the restoration of Israel's sovereignty. See Albert Schweitzer, *The Mysticism of Paul the Apostle*, trans. William Montgomery (New York: Holt, 1931), 75-90. The idea of resurrection is a subsequent and logical development of faith in national restoration, with Daniel as a crucial transitional text. The conflated references to scattering and resurrection thus make theological/ideological as well as literary sense.

future readers' flight, in juxtaposition to the previous section's dominical exhortations to martyrdom in the face of eschatological persecution, which are addressed to the disciples in particular (13:9–13). Interpretation of Mark 13:14 often turns on speculation about what historical event the evangelist might have had in mind, if any;[76] however, recognizing the overt application to Mark's reading audience of the prophetic command to flee, in contrast to the earlier exhortations to martyrdom directed at the characters of the disciples, is just as important.

In the narrative discourse of Mark's Gospel, the character Jesus repeatedly commands his disciples as characters to follow him to crucifixion and resurrection from the dead. Mark foreshadows their failure to do so by representing them responding with faithlessness and confusion to Jesus's directives, prophetic warnings, and prefigurations of his death and resurrection at various points in the narrative. Related to this impending disaster, the eschaton seems to recede into a more distant future transcending Mark's narrative bounds as the Second Gospel progresses to the passion narrative, when the disciples decisively refuse to heed Jesus's commands and leave Jesus to die (and possibly rise) alone. Accordingly, in chapter 13, Mark's Jesus, as he continues to issue prophecies that emphasize his students' failure to follow within the narrated world of the gospel, countenances the possibility that these same characters might set themselves aright in a future exceeding that narrative. Since the eschaton will not after all be consummated in the Son of Man's (solitary, as it turns out) death and resurrection, the Markan Jesus urges his disciples to remain alert (see 13:32, 37) for supplemental chances to emulate his death (13:9–13) in an eschatological period of global calamities exceeding the geographical and temporal limits of Mark's story (see 13:6–8). In terms of the parable of the returning master (13:33–37), the disciples will fail to keep watch in the

---

76. I interpret the reference in Mark 13:14 to the "desolating sacrilege" as a vivid recollection of Antiochus IV Epiphanes's program of harassment of Judeans for their faithfulness to Yahweh. Mark invites the readers to view this as a model for the persecution they evidently fear. It may secondarily gesture at Roman forces' prolonged siege of Jerusalem and defilement of the temple in 70 CE (cf. 13:2), or at a specific political event associated with that development. For discussion of the range of interpretive possibilities, see Marcus, *Mark 8–16*, 890–91. On the association of the phrase with the Roman destruction of the temple, see Incigneri, *Gospel to the Romans*, 126–33 (esp. 130–33). If this approach is persuasive, the desolating sacrilege would amount to a specific historical correlative in Mark's original readers' time to Antiochus's sacrilege (cf. Dan 9:26–27; 11:31–35), in addition to alluding to the broader program of harassment.

passion narrative but may manage to succeed in doing so during the time of eschatological travail.

Mark's readers live in this same extranarrative era. Like the Markan disciples, they too must be on guard, for Jesus explicitly addresses his words at the parable's conclusion "to all" (13:37). However, for these readers, Jesus prophetically authorizes flight from persecution (13:14–23), with the Markan narrator overtly intervening to specify that application of Jesus's discourse (13:14). They are commanded to look for opportunity to flee, while Mark's narrative will condemn the disciples' flight as refusal of Jesus's command to die at his side in hopes of resurrection with him.

This interpretive complex points to the Second Evangelist's reticence to encourage readers to suffer execution by proffering resurrection as a consolation for their deaths. Mark's narrative rhetorically limits the applicative scope of Jesus's prophetic commands to die in anticipation of resurrection, which primarily function as narrative resources the author employs to advance the story Mark tells. They anticipate the narrated crucifixion and resurrection of Mark's Jesus and establish a test of faith that his disciples all fail when they leave Jesus to face arrest, trial, execution, and (possibly) resurrection on his own. Mark employs various rhetorical tactics to affirm that dominical exhortations to suffer execution in hope of resurrection, such as those in 8:34–9:1, are not directly addressed to the implied audience, even when the evangelist imagines them possibly implemented in a future lying beyond the Second Gospel's narrative horizon, as in 13:9–13. As a complement, Mark includes a notice specifying that readers ought to flee rather than to endure persecution and death in hope of resurrection during that period of eschatological travail (13:14). For readers alone, such flight constitutes something other than faithless failure.

With respect to the Markan disciples, by contrast, the Second Evangelist always leaves this crucial fact in focus: when given the opportunity to follow Jesus's commands to die with him, they refuse to put their trust in his prophecies of resurrection. The Second Gospel maintains this focus on their refusal to trust even when Jesus anticipates that they may reform and follow him to death and resurrection in a period exceeding the bounds of the story Mark tells. Thus Mark 13:9–13, even as it exhorts the disciples to die in the eschatological future, ironically anticipates Jesus's solitary martyrdom, abandoned by his disciples, in Mark's passion narrative. Moreover, the Second Gospel's Jesus prescinds from predicting resurrection for them. In contrast to his clear prophecy of the regathering of refugees from persecution, Jesus's Olivet discourse provides only vague hints of (13:13) or figurative gestures at (13:27) the resurrection of the eschatologically martyred disciples, leaving questions open about whether faithful death will ever issue in divine restoration to life.

Mark and Martyrdom

This analysis complements and possibly contextualizes standard historical-critical conclusions about Mark 8:34. Parallels to Mark 8:34 in Q (see Matt 10:33, 38–39; par. Luke 14:27; 17:33) and John (12:25) suggest that dominical sayings such as those Mark includes in 8:34–37 were commonly employed in early preaching to exhort believers to endure unto death social and political harassment they may have faced and certainly feared.[77] Perhaps resisting this trend, Mark's *commentarii* use these traditional logia as narrative resources, contextualizing Jesus's sayings about dying and rising with him in 8:31–9:1 so that they do not address the experiences of the audience but only anticipate those of the disciples as characters.[78] In Mark's narrative discourse, Jesus's words urge his disciples

---

77. See n. 42 for scholarship on the historical-critical background.

78. My reading supplements Roskam, who does not carefully enough consider how Mark's editorial emphases relate to the evangelist's integration of the material into a broader narrative context (*Purpose of the Gospel of Mark*, 36–46). I find especially unpersuasive Roskam's insistence that Mark's phrase ἕνεκεν ἐμοῦ καὶ τοῦ εὐαγγελίου (8:35), instead of the simple ἕνεκεν ἐμοῦ, "was certainly motivated by his intention to ensure that the saying should be applicable not only to the audience of Jesus, but also to his own contemporaries. Strictly speaking, after Jesus's death, dying for his sake is no longer a real option; dying for his message, however, is" (*Purpose of the Gospel of Mark*, 45). (Pudussery makes basically the same argument about καὶ τοὺς ἐμοὺς λόγους in Mark 8:38; such interpretations are common ["Discipleship," 121].)

However, one can die "for the sake" of a person who does not live, just as one can die for the sake of an ideal. Whether Jesus lives or dies is irrelevant to the loyalty one dying for his sake demonstrates. Similarly, the reference to "the gospel" in Mark 8:35 makes better sense in the narrative context I have been fleshing out than as a gesture toward readers' social context. In 1:14–15, immediately after John is arrested, Jesus begins to proclaim the same message of repentance as John the Baptist (see 1:4), which Mark twice identifies as τὸ εὐαγγέλιον. In saying ἕνεκεν ἐμοῦ καὶ τοῦ εὐαγγελίου, Mark's Jesus insists that those who proclaim what he and John proclaim (as the Twelve are called to do; see 3:14) will likely face execution like he and John. Far from pointing to a time after Jesus's death, the reference recalls that John, a preacher of τὸ εὐαγγέλιον even before Jesus, has already been killed for the gospel's sake.

as characters to die and rise with him, and they draw attention to these disciples' skepticism about, struggle to understand, and failure to obey Jesus's exhortations. Jesus's words perhaps secondarily gesture at these characters' ultimate success in an eschatological future that exceeds Mark's narrative bounds, though that future is neither clear nor guaranteed, especially as it pertains to resurrection.[79] The Second Evangelist employs various rhetorical tactics to insist on this limited application, which those same sayings' contextualizations in the double tradition do not feature.[80] Mark carefully forecloses interpretations that would find in Jesus's words a general exhortation to martyrdom in anticipation of resurrection that applies to readers as well as characters.

As Paul Middleton and Candida Moss have shown, Mark 8:34 and related material in the Second Gospel were commonly interpreted by ancient Christians as a universal call to martyrdom.[81] Clearly, then, what I have described as this evangelist's attempt to delimit the applicative scope of Jesus's teaching about violent death in anticipation of resurrection was not entirely successful. However, as Dinkler reminds us, it is important to

---

79. As mentioned above, Jesus's demand may be indirectly relevant to Mark's readers. Readers confronted by Mark's words about the implications of apostasy (8:38) in the face of execution (8:34) might recommit themselves to faithful discipleship, especially because of the resurrection life promised to the faithful (8:35–37). Or they might wonder whether the unguaranteed offer of eternal life issued to Jesus's original disciples provides sufficient grounds for a confession that could lead to execution, especially since Jesus's original followers seem not to have trusted it themselves. Other responses are plausible as well (see, e.g., Tannehill, "Reading It Whole," 197).

80. For example, Matt 10:38–39 (cf. Mark 8:34) comes in a sermon Jesus addresses to the Twelve (see Matt 10:5), but that has a clearer general application throughout, including with respect to martyrdom (e.g., compare Matt 10:32–33 and Mark 8:38–9:1). Luke 14:27 (cf. Mark 8:34) comes in a sermon addressed not to Jesus's disciples but to crowds (see Luke 14:25). Although not directly relevant to the double tradition, Luke also eliminates in its revision the rhetorical features of Mark 8:38–9:1 identified above as circumscribing the relevance of Jesus's directives. Emendations in 9:23 (adding "daily" to Mark's "take up his cross" and having Jesus speak to all present, as opposed to his disciples in the presence of the crowd) suggest an attempt both to universalize and transform into metaphor Jesus's command in Mark 8:34 that his original disciples be crucified with him.

81. Paul Middleton, *Radical Martyrdom and Cosmic Conflict in Early Christianity*, LNTS 307 (London: T&T Clark, 2006), 135–36, 146–56; Candida Moss, *The Other Christs: Imitating Jesus in Ancient Christian Ideologies of Martyrdom* (New York: Oxford University Press, 2010), 28–33.

3. Jesus's Demand for Faith and the Disciples' Doubt

posit a variety of historically situated reading profiles when speculating about how ancient audiences might have responded to a given biblical text.[82] Some ancient Christians did limit the application of evangelical teaching about persecution and martyrdom in ways analogous to those my reading of Mark proposes. A little more than a century after Mark wrote, Tertullian introduces careful distinctions between the gospels' teaching about persecution that he believes applies only to Jesus's original disciples (e.g., the command to flee in Matt 10:23, discussed at *Fug.* 6.1-2) and teaching applicable to readers in later generations as well (e.g., statements about followers suffering betrayal and death in Matt 10:21, discussed at *Scorp.* 9.3).

Tertullian bases these distinctions on theological conviction rather than on careful rhetorical analysis, and he would not have agreed with my understanding of 8:34-9:1 and the related Markan passages treated in this chapter. However, his writings still testify to early debates about the question I hypothesize Mark attempts to answer and with whose response some ancient believers would have agreed. The early church commonly debated whether Jesus's exhortations that disciples suffer execution in emulation of him bore directly on later believers, as, say, the writings of Cyprian and the controversies in which this bishop of Carthage was embroiled attest.[83] Even when these dominical commands were understood to apply to all Christians, it remained controversial what precisely they required or merely encouraged (i.e., confession, even if resulting in death), what they allowed in some cases or prohibited in all (i.e., flight), and whether or under what conditions what they forbade might be forgiven (i.e., apostasy and betrayal of one's fellow disciples). Mark may be participating in such controversies about persecution and martyrdom as they first began to emerge by narrativizing teaching attributed to Jesus so as to resist voices requiring any and every believer to persevere to death in faithful expectation of resurrection life. One can only speculate about why the author of

---

82. Dinkler, "Reading the Potentials," 535-41.
83. On Cyprian's controversial flight to avoid persecution, see, e.g., Cyprian, *Ep.* 8; 9; 20, as analyzed in Henneke Gülzow, *Cyprian und Novatian: Der Briefwechsel zwischen den Gemeinden in Rom und Karthago zur Zeit der Verfolgung des Kaisers Decius*, BHT 48 (Tübingen: Mohr, 1975), 20-51, 58-67; see also Hugo Montgomery, "The Bishop Who Fled: Responsibility and Honour in Saint Cyprian," StPatr 21 (1989): 264-67. For discussion of Cyprian's response to the Decian persecution and the theological and pastoral controversies it raised, including the possibility of forgiveness for the lapsed, see Michael M. Sage, *Cyprian*, PMS 1 (Cambridge: Philadelphia Patristic Foundation, 1975), 165-265.

Mark's *commentarii* would have done this, but the broader interpretation of the Second Gospel I propose suggests a possibility: this evangelist, like certain members of Paul's Corinthian congregation and others associated with the apostle, was not convinced that resurrection defeats death. Mark attempts to frame Jesus's teaching and commands about resurrection so that they will not persuade readers to go to death willingly, in anticipation of a resurrection the evangelist found implausible.

The anticipation of the disciples' refusal to participate in the Markan Jesus's crucifixion and resurrection by dying and rising at his side in Mark 8:34–9:1 affirms that the Second Gospel always presents resurrection as an object of interrogation. Mark's reticence to universalize Jesus's command to follow him to death in expectation of resurrection also dovetails with the *commentarii*'s tendency to present resurrection as subject to inquiry rather than as a settled matter. The Second Gospel prescinds from establishing all characters' resurrections, including Jesus's (ch. 1). Mark acknowledges that the resurrection faith Jesus exemplifies and demands does not align closely with the Torah (ch. 2). Mark further recognizes that Jesus's understanding of resurrection does not neatly cohere with standard eschatological expectations, for which reason (in part) the Markan Jesus's original disciples fail to grasp their master's teaching about it and refuse to follow relevant directives (ch. 3). Considering all this equivocation, confusion, and doubt about resurrection, how could Mark require readers to embrace violent death in anticipation of it—on the threat of eschatological judgment, no less? The answer is that Mark will not, even if some ancient Christian preachers and writers would.

4
Faithlessness Condemned or Redeemed?

This chapter continues my exploration of the disciples' doubt about Jesus's claims regarding the Son of Man's resurrection by considering their faithless abandonment of Jesus to die and rise without them in Mark's passion narrative. While the study's first two chapters showed that Mark dialogizes resurrection faith, this one pursues the argument of chapter 3 to show that the Second Evangelist orchestrates a complementary dialogue about doubt. Mark's passion narrative invites readers to infer that the fleeing disciples' lack of trust in God's power over death leaves them exposed to eschatological condemnation. At the same time, it implies distinctions between the kinds of doubt different disciples display, which complicate such judgments.

I gestured earlier at the mechanism of the eschatological second chance by which Mark might have imagined some of the disciples' final salvation to remain viable, despite their failures to obey Jesus's commands to follow him to death and resurrection within the gospel narrative's confines. In this chapter I elaborate that possibility and consider it from various angles of approach. Though it may encompass James, John, and some of the others, including the Marys and Salome, whom chapter 1 discussed, it would not appear relevant to Peter. He already receives multiple chances to be crucified and rise with Jesus within Mark's passion narrative, and Peter's condemnation seems assured when his behavior is evaluated according to criteria Mark 8:34–9:1 establishes. Yet Mark's development of Peter's trajectory nonetheless manages to leverage the possibility that even this disciple will be saved. Chapter 5, which returns to a focus on Jesus's resurrection, fleshes out the understanding of Jesus's possible redemption of Peter presented in skeletal form here. It points to a thematically unified reading of Mark's Gospel, according to which Mark persistently dialogizes faith in resurrection and suggests that even diabolical doubt such as Peter's may be capable of redemption.

Peter's Failure

Since Jesus's call that his disciples take up their crosses and follow him in Mark 8:34 requires them to share in the execution that he had predicted for the Son of Man (8:31), that demand provides a lens through which to examine their behavior in Mark's account of Jesus's crucifixion. Faced with the possibility of arrest and execution at his side, the disciples all flee rather than joining him on the cross (ἔφυγον πάντες, 14:50)—except for Peter, who continues to follow Jesus from a distance (ἀπὸ μακρόθεν ἠκολούθησεν,14:54), only to issue public denials and curse his master in the end (14:66–72). As I discussed in chapter 1, after Jesus's arrest, the two Marys and Salome also remain to observe his execution and burial "from a distance" (ἀπὸ μακρόθεν, 15:40–41; cf. 15:47), as Peter's following is described.[1] However, since Mark concludes with their fearful flight from Jesus's empty tomb (ἔφυγον) and refusal to speak (16:8), the Second Evangelist more closely assimilates the female disciples to the absconding others rather than to apostate Peter. Of course, Judas betrays Jesus (14:10–11, 43–45), exemplifying a different kind of failure altogether, which I will discuss in passing below.

Since Jesus's instruction about losing life to save it in 8:35–37 envisages all his disciples' inclusion in the postmortem resurrection that Jesus anticipates for the Son of Man, their refusal to die with him finds a complement in their absence or fearful flight from Jesus's empty tomb. These developments relate to the evangelist's neglect to certify or represent any encounter at all of the disciples with the risen Christ.[2] Moreover, even if

---

1. Since these women are identified as followers of Jesus in the very next verse (αἳ ... ἠκολούθουν αὐτῷ), like Peter in 14:54, in Mark following Jesus from a distance seems to signal an attempt to straddle the master's demand for dangerous association with himself as a condemned criminal and the disciples' own desire for self-preservation (cf. 8:34–37).

2. The other gospels rectify Mark on one or another of these points, either omitting the male disciples' abandonment of Jesus (Luke), insisting on their presence at the empty tomb with the women (John), or describing the risen Christ's appearances to the Eleven (Matthew) and especially to Peter (John). On the implications for Peter's rehabilitation of Mark's lack of Jesus's resurrection appearances, see Smith, *Petrine Controversies*, 183–84.

readers presume the risen Jesus somehow does manage to find the disciples and Peter in Galilee beyond the pages of Mark's Gospel (despite the Marys and Salome's refusal to relay the memorandum about this meeting; 16:7–8; see 14:28), in the light of Mark 8, they are not justified in expecting that encounter to be a happy one. Jesus had warned that the Son of Man would be ashamed of those who refused solidarity with him in death and resurrection (see 8:34–38) and had gone on to emphasize the urgency of his warning for his addressees (9:1). This warning implies that the vindicated Jesus's meeting with the ruined disciples, were it to take place, would entail condemnatory reproach anticipating or enacting divine judgment, rather than forgiveness and reconciliation.

Of all the disciples, Peter stands in clearest jeopardy of the condemnation Mark 8:38 threatens. For this character, unwillingness to put faith in God's resurrection power veers into satanic opposition to Jesus (8:31–32). Although Jesus issues an exorcistic rebuke of Peter (8:33), Mark neglects to specify whether it results in the devil's departure. This omission becomes notable since Mark later depicts Peter subverting the demand Jesus makes in 8:34–37: he will deny his master to save his own life, instead of denying himself and losing his life to regain it with Jesus (14:66–72; see 8:34–37). Peter's failure exceeds the other disciples' (save Judas's betrayal). While they flee—either from Jesus's arrest to save themselves (14:50–52) or from his tomb after being commanded to proclaim the executed criminal's resurrection (16:7–8)—Peter repudiates (14:68, 70) and curses Jesus (14:71). Mark's reference to Peter in 16:7 ("the disciples and Peter") denies Peter the designation of "disciple" that Peter himself had renounced.[3] The young man speaking these words both acknowledges Peter's denial of Jesus and anticipates the disavowal Peter will face from the Son of Man, according to 8:38.

Mark makes it clear that Peter's refusal of solidarity with Jesus constitutes a failure to obey his master's call to follow him to crucifixion and resurrection from 8:34. Though Jesus predicts at the Last Supper that his disciples will "fall away" (σκανδαλισθήσεσθε) and "scatter"

---

3. Smith, *Petrine Controversies*, 184. Paul Middleton similarly traces the Markan disciples' trajectory of failure. See Middleton, "Suffering and the Creation of Christian Identity in the Gospel of Mark," in *T&T Clark Handbook to Social Identity in the New Testament*, ed. J. Brian Tucker and Coleman A. Stohl (London: Bloomsbury, 2016), 183–87. However, he does not adequately distinguish Peter's apostasy from the others' flight.

(διασκορπισθήσονται, 14:27), he prophesies of Peter in particular that "on this night ... you will deny [ἀπαρνήσῃ] me three times" (14:30).[4] Peter responds to Jesus's prophetic warning in language that continues to recall Jesus's earlier demand that anyone present desiring to follow him must "deny himself" (ἀπαρνησάσθω ἑαυτὸν) and "take up his cross" (8:34) in solidarity with the Son's divinely necessitated suffering and death (δεῖ ... ἀποκτανθῆναι, 8:31). "Even if I must die with you," Peter says, "I will not deny you" (ἐὰν δέῃ με συναποθανεῖν σοι, οὐ μή σε ἀπαρνήσομαι, 14:31). In addition to looking backward to 8:34–9:1, Peter's diction also anticipates the climactic scene of his triple denial of Jesus (ἠρνήσατο, 14:68; ἠρνεῖτο, 14:70; see also 14:71), which amounts to a decisive, even subversive, rejection of 8:34's demand of self-denial leading to death.

Mark never specifies Peter's motives for refusing to admit association with Jesus. It might seem reasonable to presume he was driven by the desire to preserve life and reputation against which Jesus had warned his disciples in 8:34–38. However, careful consideration of the scene of Peter's denials suggests that these are not the most prominent forces impelling the disciple to disavow his master. Peter initially follows Jesus to the high priest's residence (14:53–54), in contrast to the others (the Marys and Salome temporarily excepted) who flee in fear—one in literally naked panic, as he leaves behind his garment in his arrestor's hand (14:50–52). This naked young man constitutes a would-be follower urgently concerned to preserve his life, and he emblematizes all the fleeing disciples in Mark.[5] Their alarm is reasonable, as Mark describes the scene: since there had initially been some violence on the part of Jesus's disciples when guards arrived to apprehend him (14:47), had any students been taken into custody with Jesus, they would have been in no less serious criminal jeopardy than was their master. However, Mark's Peter, in contrast to the others, does not flee in fear; instead, he keeps following the master after Jesus's arrest right into the high priest's courtyard, albeit from a distance (14:54). This indicates an initially successful attempt to overcome the fear and shame arising from dangerous association with an arrested criminal. Even if "from a distance" (ἀπὸ μακρόθεν) hints at the collapse that follows,

---

4. I take Peter's denial and the disciples' prophesied flight not as faits accomplis but as possibilities against which they are warned. Compare Mark 14:38, referring, as Luke discerns (Luke 22:31, 40), to Peter's denial.

5. Harry Fleddermann, "The Flight of a Naked Young Man (Mark 14:50-51)," *CBQ* 41 (1979): 412–18, esp. 417.

Mark's narrative at first vindicates Peter's objection to Jesus's prediction of 14:27: "even if all desert you, I will not" (14:29).

This distinction between Peter's and the other disciples' behavior in the immediate wake of Jesus's arrest finds corroboration in Jesus's use of the word σκανδαλίζω in his prediction that the disciples will "fall away" (14:27). Mark's Jesus employs the same word in an earlier passage that elucidates Peter's divergence from the others. In chapter 4, Jesus discusses the second type of soil (i.e., disciples, hearers and teachers of "the word") in the interpretation of the parable of the sower he privately issues to his students (see 4:10). He says of those whom the rocky soil represents (cf. 4:5–6) that "once affliction has arisen, or persecution [διωγμοῦ]…, they will immediately fall away" (εὐθὺς σκανδαλίζονται, 4:17). The echo of this verse in 14:27 implies that those who immediately flee upon Jesus's arrest fall away under the motivation of a desire to avoid persecution at the hands of the authorities.

Scholars occasionally observe this connection, which clarifies the motives of the fleeing disciples.[6] They usually include Peter among those whose behavior 4:17 anticipates and 14:27 prophesies, sometimes offering a supposed pun between Simon Peter's name (Πέτρος) and the πετρώδης ("rocky ground"; 4:5–6) as support for the interpretation.[7] However, the significance of this pun seems questionable since Mark, unlike Matthew, never draws attention to the etymology of Peter's nickname. Moreover, Peter does not neatly fit into the category of "rocky soil" from Mark 4, which encompasses those who "immediately fall away [σκανδαλίζονται]" when faced with persecution (4:17). Peter claims in chapter 14 that even if others "fall away [σκανδαλισθήσονται]," he will not (14:29). He proves himself right, for he keeps "following" Jesus into hostile territory after having been faced with the threat of persecution implicit in his master's arrest (ἠκολούθησεν, 14:54).

Mark first employs the verb ἀκολουθέω in its account of Peter's initial decision (with Andrew) to leave his nets and become Jesus's disciple (ἠκολούθησαν, 1:18). Peter recalls this decision in chapter 10 (ἡμεῖς ἀφήκαμεν πάντα καὶ ἠκολουθήκαμέν σοι, 10:28), where Jesus affirms his resolve and encourages those who abandon all and follow him to with-

---

6. Mary Ann Tolbert explores this interpretive dimension. See Tolbert, *Sowing the Gospel: Mark's World in Literary-Historical Perspective* (Minneapolis: Fortress, 1989), 145, 151–61 (and passim).

7. Tolbert, *Sowing the Gospel*, 145.

stand persecution (διωγμοί) in hope of eternal life (10:29–30). Jesus here proleptically fortifies the firmness of purpose Peter will show in 14:54. The verb ἀκολουθεῖν also features in Mark 8:34, which demands of Jesus's disciples that they deny themselves and follow him to execution. This echo too suggests that in following Jesus to the high priest's palace, where the parties whom Jesus had prophesied would reject the Son of Man a few verses earlier have assembled (8:31; cf. 14:53), Peter makes a positive decision aligned with his commitment to Jesus. He chooses to obey Jesus's injunction to follow the Son of Man to persecution, condemnation, and execution in expectation of resurrection, thereby distinguishing himself from the scattering disciples (14:50–52), assimilated to seed unable to put down root in rocky soil (4:16–17). The idea that Mark links Peter's behavior to that same section of the parable of the sower fails to convince. However, a genuine connection between Peter's actions and this parable will emerge from more careful consideration of the interpretive questions Mark's *commentarii* raise about his denial and curse of the master.

After Mark's initially positive portrayal of Peter in the moments following Jesus's arrest, especially in comparison with the fleeing disciples, how might one account for the sudden and total collapse of faithfulness that 14:66–72 recounts? Does Peter simply stay a step ahead of the fearful shame of being associated with an apprehended criminal until it finally catches up with him in the high priest's courtyard? Why, then, does his faithfulness dissolve not merely into flight, like the others', but into dishonest denials and finally a curse of his master? The answers to these questions are far from clear, especially since Peter's resolve does not break under the pressure of an interrogation like Jesus's, but rather upon being asked informally—by a young female slave (ἡ παιδίσκη, 14:66, 69) alongside some random bystanders (14:70)—whether he had been with Jesus. In the course of his formal questioning, Jesus at first remains silent (14:60–61) and then basically affirms his identity as Son of Man, with no attempt at misdirection, evasion, or retraction—not even when he begins to be tortured (14:65)![8] Peter, in contrast, though he might have

---

8. If John used Mark's passion narrative or traditions like it, then it is significant that John identifies Peter as the disciple who wounded the high priest's slave during Jesus's arrest (18:10; cf. Mark 14:47). As a complement, John identifies the bystander who questions Peter before his third denial as this slave's relative, who had been present at Peter's assault and recognizes him (John 18:26). In John, Peter denies association with Jesus because of fear to be identified as the man who had attacked a member of

4. Faithlessness Condemned or Redeemed?

commanded the slave to mind her own business, instead evades, lies, and curses his master to avoid the possibility that he might participate in the Son of Man's destiny.

This behavior appears very strange indeed when the reader considers that Peter has been carefully prepared for questions about his association with Jesus. Jesus recently had issued two prophetic warnings (14:30, 38) lest this disciple fail to do what Jesus earlier required in 8:34. The former echoes that command while at the same time anticipating the precise moment in which Peter will find himself when he is tempted to disobey it: "in this night, before the rooster crows twice, you will deny me three times" (14:30). Yet despite this prophetic preparation for the moment of testing, Peter declares he cannot even grasp what the slave who questions him in the high priest's courtyard is talking about: "I don't know, nor do I understand, what you're saying" (14:68). Granting that her initial accusation might have caught Peter off guard, he still receives additional chances to recover (14:69, 70b). The cock crowing upon his first denial (14:68) should bring to Peter's mind Jesus's recent prophetic warning while there is still time to heed it.[9] But instead of correcting his error, he twice repeats

---

the high priest's household. The Fourth Gospel therefore explains the Markan Peter's rapid transition from courage to denial by suggesting that reckless bravery first leads him to resist Jesus's arrest before it prompts him to follow Jesus to the high priest's palace (see 18:15), where he finds himself in danger of being identified as the man who had mutilated a member of Jesus's arresting party. Accordingly, John eliminates Peter's curse of Jesus (see 18:27), leaving his denials to amount to a refusal to place himself at the scene of his crime.

9. The textual tradition makes it difficult to determine how many reminders Peter receives. Some manuscripts eliminate the reference to the double crowing in Jesus's prophecy (Mark 14:30) and/or locate "twice" at different points in the verse, and/or eliminate the reference to the first crowing in 14:68, and/or eliminate the notice that the cock crows "a second time" in 14:72. The simplest explanation for this variation may be not Mark's desire to harmonize the account of Peter's denial with Jesus's prophecy, as sometimes proposed. Instead, early discomfort with Mark's insistence that Peter continues to deny and even curse Jesus after the prophecy of two crowings (14:30)—with the first coming in time to have reminded him of that warning (14:68) while there was still opportunity to heed it before the second (14:72)—may have troubled early readers. A scribal tendency to remediate Peter's portrayal by altering the original prophecy or adjusting the narrated crowings became compounded by the impulse to harmonize Mark to the other gospels, which likewise suggested solutions. See Bruce M. Metzger, *A Textual Commentary on the Greek New Testament: A Companion Volume to the United Bible Societies' Greek New Testament*, 3rd ed.

the denial and finally curses his master to prove he has nothing to do with Jesus (14:70–71).

It would be wrong to claim that Peter's behavior in Mark remains impervious to psychological explanation. Choking under pressure is common enough; sports history offers illuminating examples (e.g., Barcelona in the 2018 and 2019 Champions League competitions). The reference to Peter following Jesus only "at a distance" (14:54) possibly anticipates the fragility of his faithfulness, which in the end cannot withstand even the modest pressure of the slave's questioning. This reading might be bolstered if one were to press the all who flee in 14:50 to include Peter, in which case he would already have capitulated to cowardice before temporarily recovering and then succumbing to fear yet again in the high priest's courtyard. But even granting this possibility, there remains something enigmatic about his rapid progression from initial flight, to following his master into danger, to not only denying but also cursing Jesus.

Mark's narrative progression from Petrine loyalty to apostasy is complemented by a perplexing detail in the evangelist's account of these denials. What does Peter mean by claiming not to understand the slave's accusation (14:68)—a strange declaration the other gospels omit in their finalizing revisions of the scene? Commentators have had difficulty making sense of it.[10] Some interpretive construals seem to point toward his gross hypocrisy; others speculate it amounts to fearful deflection.[11] However, if taken as a meaningful description of Peter's mental state, rather than hypocritical mendacity or an inconsequential utterance of panic, this confession of bewilderment yields important interpretive insight. It suggests a genuine link between Peter's behavior in the passion narrative and the hermeneutically programmatic parable of the sower, in lieu of the spurious connection between Peter and the seed sown in rocky soil considered above. In this same parable, the seed chocked by thorns (4:7), which figures disciples overcome by "the deceitfulness of wealth" (ἡ ἀπάτη τοῦ πλούτου, 4:19), likely anticipates Judas's betrayal of Jesus for money (14:10–11, 43–45). One must therefore consider the possibility that the parable's lone

---

(London: United Bible Societies, 1975), 96–97; John W. Wenham, "How Many Cock-Crowings? The Problem of Harmonistic Text-Variants," *NTS* 25 (1979): 523–25.

    10. Even grammatically it has problems (Brown, *Death of the Messiah*, 1:600).

    11. For an example of the former, see Geoff R. Webb, *Mark at the Threshold: Applying Bakhtinian Categories to Murkan Characterisation*, BibInt 95 (Leiden: Brill, 2008), 208–10. For the latter, see Collins, *Mark*, 708; Marcus, *Mark 8–16*, 1019.

remaining report (4:4) and interpretation (4:15) of seed fruitlessly sown corresponds to the lone remaining disciple's failure of his master in the passion narrative, namely, Peter denying and cursing Jesus.

Jesus interprets the parable of the sower's description of birds consuming seed sown on the path (4:4) as an allegory of satanic activity among hearers of the word: "Immediately Satan comes and takes away the word sown in them" (4:15). In the scene of his denial, Peter is unwary and reeling because Satan interferes. He steals from Peter's mind the prophetic words Jesus had imparted so that he forgets his master's warnings from a few hours before (14:30, 38), as well as his earlier command that Peter deny himself and be crucified with Jesus (8:34). Luke seems to pick up this interpretive possibility in his revision. The Lukan Jesus's warning to Peter of temptation specifically mentions Satan (22:31; cf. Mark 14:38), before assuring Peter that the devil will fail to destroy his faith (Luke 22:32).[12] Luke goes on to link Jesus's gaze to Peter's penitent weeping after his final denial, with Jesus's regard explicitly prompting the disciple's sudden recollection of his master's warning (ὑπεμνήσθη ... τοῦ ῥήματος, 22:61). Luke's optimistic revision thus affirms that when Mark's Peter initially says to the slave "I do not know, nor do I understand, what you're saying" (Mark 14:68; cf. Luke 22:60), he speaks straightforwardly. Peter is under Satan's influence and cannot grasp the implications of the slave girl's inquiry. He has been made to forget the exhortations and prophetic warnings that should have prepared him for her questions and is left vulnerable to the fear and shame one might plausibly experience upon being linked with an arrested criminal. Those feelings drive Peter to act in desperate confusion to save his life. Mark's vivid detail of the rooster crowing may ominously refer to this satanic influence by echoing the relevant section of the earlier parable, which allegorizes Satan to a bird eating seed thrown on the path, as if feed for domesticated fowl (Mark 4:4, 15).[13]

While this interpretation is subtle, Mark has sufficiently prepared the reader to observe Peter's manipulation by Satan in the scene of his denials.

---

12. On Luke's understanding of this scene vis-à-vis inherited traditions, see Marc Rastoin, "Simon-Pierre entre Jésus et Satan: la théologie Lucanienne à l'oeuvre en Lc 22,31–32," *Bib* 89 (2008): 153–72, esp. 168–72.

13. Satanic manipulation also informs Peter's curse of Jesus in Mark 14:71, which, according to Paul, would indicate the absence of God's Spirit and the presence of an evil one. See Jouette M. Bassler, "1 Cor 12:3: Curse and Confession in Context," *JBL* 101 (1982): 415–18.

Mark's Jesus suggests that Satan played a role in Peter's earlier confession of Jesus as the Christ (8:29–30, interpreted in the previous chapter). Mark further indicates that Satan prompted the disciple to rebuke Jesus after his master uttered the first prophecy of the Son of Man's death and resurrection (8:31–32). This prompts Jesus in return to rebuke Satan operating within Peter before ordering Peter and the others to deny themselves and die with him (8:33–34). Mark 14:37–38 contains another prophetic warning to Peter, signaling his vulnerability to satanic influence. Here, Jesus mentions Peter by name when he issues a caution about the testing (πειρασμὸν) the disciples are soon to undergo. The warning recalls the satanic temptation Jesus underwent at the initiation of his ministry (πειραζόμενος ὑπὸ τοῦ σατανᾶ, 1:13), just before Jesus and his disciples began to terrify demons throughout Galilee and beyond (1:23–28, 34; 3:11, 15, 22; and passim). This recollection primes the reader to interpret Peter's denials and curse of Jesus in the high priest's courtyard as a moment of successful satanic testing, reversing Satan's evident setback in 1:12–13.[14] No longer are Satan and his demons in flight from Jesus and his crew; instead, the disciples flee, abandoning Jesus to die alone at Satan's hands, and Peter too seems to be on his heels from Satan's blows.

This interpretation of the Markan scene of Peter's denial situates in an appropriate literary-historical context the modern critical intuition that Mark's portrayal of Peter is psychologically complex.[15] In Greco-Roman literature, such characterization often involves divine beings manipulating characters to perform horrendous deeds that on first glance seem to

---

14. See Marcus, *Mark 8–16*, 979; cf. Karl Georg Kuhn, "New Light on Temptation, Sin, and Flesh in the New Testament," in *The Scrolls and the New Testament*, ed. Krister Stendhal (New York: Harper, 1957), 94–113, esp. 94–95. Jesus's temptation immediately precedes the Galilee ministry, which features Jesus's exorcistic prowess. It would seem to have been successfully endured and amounted to a significant satanic setback. However, Mark will not explicitly affirm this, and other interpretations are possible (see Mark 3:22). On Jesus's open-ended temptation as an ambiguous defeat of Satan, see Susan R. Garrett, *The Temptations of Jesus in Mark's Gospel* (Grand Rapids: Eerdmans, 1998), 55–60. Jesus's possible resurrection constitutes another ambiguous defeat of Satan, as chapter 5 will argue. Thus, none of Jesus's direct confrontations with Satan (see also 1:12–13; 8:33) are decisively resolved.

15. Originally, Erich Auerbach, though scholars have widely taken up his judgment (cf. Marcus, *Mark 8–16*, 1023, on the account's "great psychological depth"). See Auerbach, *Mimesis: The Representation of Reality in Western Literature*, trans. Willard R. Trask (Princeton: Princeton University Press, 1953), 40–46.

stand in tension with their established attitudinal or behavioral inclinations but on deeper analysis realize them in extreme ways. Greek tragedy provides the most obvious examples—Sophocles's Ajax or Euripides's Herakles in the eponymous tragedies.[16] Peter in Mark 14 is no tragic hero, yet it remains significant that within Greco-Roman literature, characters who behave in extreme ways they come to regret conventionally act under the influence of malevolent divinities, whose presence may be represented literally (see Sophocles, *Aj.* 1–133; Euripides, *Herc. fur.* 816–1038) or symbolically (compare the ominous *extispicium* of Seneca, *Oed.* 299–383—an elaborate analogue to the portentous rooster's crows in Mark 14:66–72).[17] This is especially the case for characters such as Euripides's Herakles or Mark's Peter, who display hostility toward familiars that is shockingly transgressive and whose tragic implications these characters tearfully grasp only after emerging from a fog of malevolent divine control (see 14:72). The idea that Mark portrays Peter as subject to satanic manipulation or even possession allows for a coherent construal of the evangelist's representation of this character that acknowledges the aesthetic power of Mark's portrayal within its Greco-Roman literary-historical context.

Though Peter never again appears within Mark, the evangelist gestures at his story's denouement by including a final, ironic notice of his failure to "take up the cross and follow" Jesus. The scene of Jesus's trial before Pilate (15:1–21), which immediately follows Peter's denials and curse of Jesus, culminates in a brief statement regarding the Roman soldiers leading Jesus to be crucified: "they compelled a certain passer-by from Cyrene, Simon the father of Alexander and Rufus, as he was coming from the field, to take up his cross" (ἵνα ἄρῃ τὸν σταυρὸν αὐτοῦ, 15:21). Why does Mark so carefully identify this conscripted passer-by? Commentators usually answer the question historically. The evangelist includes the detail of his cross carrying because it had happened, and Mark names Simon's sons, presumably familiar to his audience, to identify their father.[18] Scholars sometimes sup-

---

16. Turnus from the *Aeneid* also comes to mind, as does Oedipus from Seneca's drama. Ruth Scodel warns against modern psychological interpretations of tragic characters, which tend to elide the role ancient Greek (and Roman) literature assigns to divine beings as the motivating factor of bizarre behavior. See Scodel, *An Introduction to Greek Tragedy* (Cambridge: Cambridge University Press, 2010), 26–27.

17. See Austin Busch, "*Versane Natura Est*? Natural and Linguistic Instability in the *Extispicium* and Self-Blinding of Seneca's *Oedipus*," *CJ* 102 (2007): 225–67.

18. For discussion and citation of relevant scholarship, see Collins, *Mark*, 734, 736.

port this construal with reference to extratextual evidence of questionable relevance, for example, a first-century CE family tomb in the Kidron Valley, in which ossuaries inscribed with the name Alexander were found.[19] Richard Bauckham pushes this historicizing tendency to its extreme, treating the reference as the guarantor of the reliability of Mark's entire crucifixion account: "There does not seem to be a good reason available other than that Mark is appealing to Simon's eyewitness testimony, known in the early Christian movement not from his own firsthand account but through his sons."[20] Bauckham's claim that his explanation is the only "good reason available" for the verse's inclusion exaggerates, for several scholars have pursued a different line of interpretation. If followed a step further than they have taken it, it offers a more compelling explanation of the verse.

There exists an often-observed thematic connection between Simon's carrying of Jesus's cross (ἄρῃ τὸν σταυρὸν, 15:21) and the cross carrying that Jesus demands of disciples who would follow him (ἀράτω τὸν σταυρὸν, 8:34).[21] In order ironically to underscore that Peter's denial amounts to a total rejection of Jesus's command from 8:34, Mark invents (or perhaps inventively names) a replacement for him, a random passer-by who unwittingly fulfills the responsibility Peter has abdicated. Simon of Cyrene literally takes up Jesus's cross as Simon Peter had been commanded but refused to do by denying Jesus rather than himself.[22] Simon Peter, having renounced his status as Jesus's disciple, has been supplanted by his namesake, Simon of Cyrene.

---

19. Collins, *Mark*, 736; Marcus, *Mark 8–16*, 1041; Gerd Theissen, *The Gospels in Context: Social and Political History in the Synoptic Tradition*, trans. Linda M. Maloney (Minneapolis: Fortress, 1991), 176–77. Gundry raises additional possibilities: Simon or his sons might have been among the Cyrenians mentioned in Acts who opposed Stephen (6:9) or who founded the church in Antioch (11:19–20), or Rufus may be the one mentioned in Rom 16:13 (*Mark*, 953–54).

20. Richard Bauckham, *Jesus and the Eyewitnesses: The Gospels as Eyewitness Testimony* (Grand Rapids: Eerdmans, 2006), 52, anticipated by Johannes Schreiber, who traces elements of the passion narrative to Simon's testimony. See Schreiber, *Theologie des Vertrauens: Eine redaktionsgeschichtliche Untersuchung des Markusevangeliums* (Hamburg: Furche-Verlag, 1967), 32–33, 62–66.

21. Klemens Stock, *Boten aus dem Mit-Ihm-Sein: Das Verhältnis zwischen Jesus und den Zwölf nach Markus*, AnBib 70 (Rome: Biblical Institute Press, 1975), 169; Marcus, *Mark 8–16*, 1048; etc.

22. See Smith, *Petrine Controversies*, 168–69; Austin Farrer, *A Study in St. Mark* (New York: Oxford University Press, 1952), 316; etc.

Mark's naming of Simon's sons invites complementary interpretation sensitive to the names' thematic function. One could be no more Hellenic (Alexander); the other is obviously Latin (Rufus). Taken together, they emphasize not the familiarity of Simon and his family to Mark's readers but the foreignness of this North African pilgrim to Jerusalem. Stephanie Crowder, sensitive to the symbolic significance of Simon (in the Lukan writings especially), argues that his identification as "a distant foreigner and a socially displaced person coming in from the country … represents the extent to which the Gospel must be told … and lays the groundwork for going beyond Jerusalem."[23] From a certain angle, as Crowder acknowledges, Simon's conscripted cross carrying represents an antithetical perversion of the voluntary discipleship Luke idealizes.[24] But from another, as her analysis also suggests, his and his son's naming invites the reader to view Simon the Cyrenian carrying Jesus's cross as one of the ironic reversals of insider and outsider positions characteristic of Mark's treatment of the disciples[25] and presaging the controversial inclusion of gentiles in the early church, which Acts goes on to depict. Simon Peter, the Markan Jesus's first follower and fellow Judean, has denied and abandoned his master, thereby relinquishing his position as disciple; another Simon, a stranger from as far away as Cyrene in North Africa (even his children have foreign names!), at the last minute steps up to accomplish what Simon Peter neglected to do.

Mark's final reference to Peter also reflects his failure of discipleship. In the gospel's penultimate verse, the anonymous young man says to the women having come to anoint Jesus, "Go, tell to his disciples and Peter that he will go before you to Galilee, where you all will see him, just as he said" (16:7). Despite Mark's omission of the risen Jesus's appearances and his notice that the women neglected to deliver the young man's message, interpreters still take the reference to Peter as an allusion to Jesus's special appearance to this disciple, which one reads about in Luke 24:34;

---

23. Stephanie R. Buckhanon Crowder, *Simon of Cyrene: A Case of Roman Conscription*, StBibLit 46 (New York: Lang, 2002), 54–55. Her exploration of the symbolic significance of his naming in Luke-Acts is different from mine, but likewise based on a comparison of Simon of Cyrene's literary role with his namesake's.

24. Crowder, *Simon of Cyrene*, 31–37, 54.

25. See Joel Marcus, "Mark 4:10–12 and Marcan Epistemology," *JBL* 103 (1984): 559–60, 569–70, and passim.

1 Cor 15:5; John 21; and elsewhere.[26] This presumption lays the foundation for an optimistic interpretation of Mark's conclusion, such as the one Robert Stein offers in his widely used textbook on the Synoptic problem: 16:7 presents "an affectionate and forgiving promise of a reunion of the disciples and Peter with Jesus."[27] Some, Stein included, go further by arguing that Mark originally included an account of this reconciliation but that the ending was accidentally lost.[28] A positive assessment of the young man's final reference to Peter frequently works in tandem with speculation about Mark's supposedly lost ending, for the assessment goes beyond anything the extant Second Gospel itself contains. Interpretations such as Stein's assume on the basis of the young man's identification of Peter as one of those to whom the risen Christ might appear both that Mark knew reports of his encounter with the risen Christ and that the evangelist (and his readers) would have understood the meeting to guarantee Peter's forgiveness and rehabilitation.

The first assumption is sound. Reports of Jesus's postmortem appearances to Peter are widely attested in early Jesus-believing literature. An increasing tendency to view Mark as dependent on Paul, whose own report of a Petrine appearance predates Mark's Gospel (1 Cor 15:5), renders claims of the evangelist's ignorance about them otiose. The legitimacy of the second assumption is more difficult to assess because of the limited information about what Peter's encounter with Christ was thought to have entailed in the earliest literature. As Geoffrey Lampe observes,

> The fact that he was forgiven and recommissioned has to be reconstructed from meager fragments of tradition concerning an appearance of the risen Christ to Peter (an event of which we have only the bare mention [1 Cor 15:5; Lk 24:34; cf. Ignatius, *Smyrn*. 3.2]) ... or inferred from the secondary *post eventum* prophecy in which Luke, using the missionary vocabulary of the early Church, makes Christ speak of Peter's "conversion" [Lk 22:32; cf. ... 17:4; Acts 3:19; 9:35; 11:21; 14:15] and

---

26. Collins, *Mark*, 797; Marcus, *Mark 8–16*, 1086. See Smith, *Petrine Controversies*, 183–84 n. 173 for further citations of this view.

27. Robert H. Stein, *Studying the Synoptic Gospels: Origin and Interpretation*, 2nd ed. (Grand Rapids: Baker Academic, 2001), 71.

28. Robert H. Stein, "The Ending of Mark," *BBR* 18 (2008): 79–98; Wright, *Resurrection*, 616–31. See also Nicholas P. Lunn, *The Original Ending of Mark: A New Case for the Authenticity of Mark 16:9–20* (Eugene, OR: Pickwick, 2014).

from later reflections upon Peter's career embodied in the "appendix" to the Fourth Gospel.[29]

Although one finds multiple reports of the risen Christ's appearance to Peter in earliest Jesus-believing literature that take the form of agonistic references and allusions to it—Mark 16:7 may constitute one of them—one finds little discussion of the shape that encounter took, especially in the tradition's primary stages. Later writers such as Luke and John insist it authorized Peter's leadership and witness, even while implicitly acknowledging that neither was uncontested (see John 20:1–10; 21:15–23). Luke links a reference to Christ's special appearance to Peter (24:33–34) with a dominical statement insisting on the apostate disciple's future rehabilitation and authority (see 22:31–32). However, later presentations such as this ought not determine one's evaluation of how Mark understands whether the encounter occurred or, if it did, what it entailed.

Stein himself articulates a useful method for interpreting Mark's vague reference to this possible meeting that avoids reliance on later accounts. Mark neglects to contextualize its extant conclusion within the traditions of the risen Jesus's appearances to the disciples presented elsewhere in ancient Jesus-believing literature (in Stein's view, through an accident of manuscript transmission). Though this "makes it ... difficult to understand the meaning of Mark 16:1–8, we nevertheless possess Mark 1:1–15:47, and this provides us with a context for understanding."[30] Intratextual connections between 16:1–8 and earlier material in the Second Gospel can provide an interpretive basis for interpreting what Mark says about Peter in 16:7. They can ground hypotheses about how Mark expects the readers to understand Peter's possible encounter with Christ, or even speculation about the shape of a supposedly lost ending that featured such a meeting. They can also provide a starting point for exploring how certain other extant traditions of the risen Jesus's reunion with Peter might have intersected with and aimed to finalize Mark's open-ended *commentarii*.

Stein's requirement of contextualizing interpretation refuses on methodological grounds the presumption that 16:7–8 expects the risen Christ's

---

29. Geoffrey W. H. Lampe, "St Peter's Denial and the Treatment of the *Lapsi*," in *The Heritage of the Early Church: Essays in Honor of Georges Vasilievich Florovsky on the Occasion of His Eightieth Birthday*, ed. David Neiman and Margaret A. Schatkin, OrChrAn 195 (Rome: Pont. Institutum Studiorum Orientalium, 1973), 113–14.

30. Stein, "Ending of Mark," 95.

appearance to Peter and the disciples, let alone that it anticipates a positive encounter. The Marys and Salome fail to pass on the young man's message to these men. One can eliminate the possibility that this disrupts Jesus's planned encounter with the disciples only by minimizing the bleakness of their response to the news of Jesus's resurrection,[31] as frightening and shameful rather than the climactic culmination of "the good news of Jesus" that Mark has been recounting from the start (1:1). As I argued in chapter 1, a straightforward construal of their behavior holds that it expresses disbelief in the young man's proclamation of Jesus's resurrection. Having come to the tomb in the dim morning light, probably to avoid being observed tending to an executed criminal's corpse (16:1-2), they are shocked by this man's presence and message, and they fearfully refuse to participate in what may be a dangerous plot to sham Jesus's resurrection. Accordingly, Mark's statement about their abscondence (ἔφυγον, 16:8) assimilates the Marys and Salome to the disciples whose fearful flight (ἔφυγον, 14:50) the second type of soil in the parable of the sower anticipated (4:5-6, 16-17). Their refusal to proclaim the word of Jesus's resurrection that the young man repeats from Jesus's prophecy (see 16:7 and 14:28) may secondarily recall the stealing away of the word in the account of the first type of soil from that parable (4:4, 15). This would more distantly link them with Peter, from whom Jesus's prophetic word has been stolen in a different way. Mark's notice that they followed and observed Jesus "from a distance" after his arrest (15:40-41) also links them with Peter (see 14:54), as mentioned in chapter 1. Mark's final verses thus frame the female disciples' flight and refusal to evangelize as failures analogous to those of the other disciples and Peter in Mark's passion narrative. Against the backdrop of Mark's passion narrative, chapter 16 does not so much point to the rehabilitation of Peter or any of Jesus's other disciples as it confirms the faithlessness of all.

However, Mark's closing verses are complex and difficult to interpret. First of all, anticipation that Christ will manage to meet up with Peter and the others is not an unreasonable response to what Mark writes, for Jesus's Galilee encounter with them does not depend on the Marys' and Salome's delivery of the message they were given. Mark specifies that Jesus had earlier told the disciples he would go before them there after his resurrection (14:28). The language that 16:7 shares with 14:28 suggests the young man of chapter 16—presumably the same one who fled naked at Jesus's

---

31. For an attempt to do this, see Wright, *Resurrection*, 621–22.

arrest (14:51–52)—recalled and believed Jesus's prophecy of a postresurrection appearance in Galilee upon his own encounter with Jesus's empty tomb. The renewal of the young man's clothing may symbolize his personal transformation from the fearful shame of naked flight to the faithful proclamation of Jesus and his message. No longer wrapped in the σινδών ("linen cloth") that he had discarded in panic (14:51), which evokes the "linen shroud" wrapping Jesus's dead body (σινδόνι, 15:46), this young man now wears a στολὴν λευκὴν ("white robe") as he announces Jesus's resurrection (16:5).[32] His new clothing harks back to the foretaste of resurrection glory that Jesus already granted to Peter, James, and John when they were amazed by their master's outfit "shining extremely white" (στίλβοντα λευκὰ λίαν) at the transfiguration (9:3; cf. 9:9–10). That episode features a divine voice demanding attention to Jesus's words (9:7) about the Son of Man's death and resurrection (see 8:31–9:1). The young man retrospectively pays this attention, recounting to the women almost verbatim what Jesus said in 14:28. Like this young man, then, the other disciples, including Peter, might come to remember and trust Jesus's prophecy of the Son's resurrection, even if Mark's final note of the Marys' and Salome's fearful silence casts a shadow of doubt over that prospect.[33]

Thus, while Mark's ending will not guarantee the risen Christ's encounter with Peter and the others in Galilee, it makes room for its possibility. It is something else entirely, though, to expect that meeting to involve forgiveness and reconciliation—especially for Peter. In its Markan context, far from promising "an affectionate and forgiving … reunion" with Jesus, as Stein would have it, 16:7 confirms Peter's apostasy. Mark's anonymous young man, either having learned of Peter's denials or recalling and trusting Jesus's prophecy about them (14:30), as he does Jesus's prophecies of resurrection, omits Peter from the disciples' roles when he repeats Jesus's prediction in 16:7.[34]

Mark invites the reader to understand Peter's denial as an apostatic rejection of Jesus and his directives from 8:34–37, and Mark further

---

32. Scroggs and Groff offer an analogous interpretation of his nakedness and reclothing, as does Vanhoye (see Scroggs and Groff, "Baptism in Mark"; Vanhoye, "La fuite du jeune homme," 404–6).

33. For a different attempt to balance the optimistic and pessimistic components of Mark's final verses, see Lincoln, "Promise and Failure."

34. See Smith, *Petrine Controversies*, 184. Compare chapter 1's argument about the young man's knowledge of Jesus's words from 14:28.

makes clear what the consequence for this lack of loyalty will be. The prediction of eschatological condemnation from 8:38–9:1 finds an echo in 16:7's reference to Peter and the disciples "seeing" the risen Christ in Galilee (ὄψεσθε). In 8:38, Mark's Jesus threatened that the Son of Man would disavow the one who demonstrates shame in him. Using a Greek verb of sight related to the verb of observation in 16:7, Jesus went on to promise that some of the disciples there present "would see" that judgment occur (ἴδωσιν, 9:1), if they chose to preserve life rather than to deny themselves and die alongside Jesus in hope of resurrection (see 8:34–37). Lest the reader miss the relevance of this prophecy to Peter's self-preserving denial of his master, at the moment of Jesus's confession, to which Peter's denial is negatively juxtaposed, Mark again refers to the eschatologically condemned "seeing" the Son of Man vindicated and empowered to judge (ὄψεσθε, 14:62). If Peter does manage "to see" the risen Son of man in Galilee, then, this pattern of intratextual allusions suggests that he will witness the Son condemning rather than forgiving him, along with the Son's other enemies.

Admittedly, the interrelated Son of Man prophecies of 8:38 and 14:62 seem to point primarily toward the eschaton. But for Mark, that frame of reference is not fixed, as the interpretation of Mark 13 presented in chapter 3 demonstrates. The hermeneutically capacious Olivet discourse's prophecies, including its reference to the Son of Man's appearance, anticipate not only eschatological events exceeding the temporal confines of Mark's narrative but also developments in the passion narrative. Thus, the Markan Jesus's prediction of the elect scattered in the face of persecution and regathered upon the Son of Man's glorious advent (13:26–27) may look forward to the resurrection of his disciples martyred in a time exceeding Mark's narrative bounds, as well as to the regathering of fugitives at the final judgment, as shown in the previous chapter. But it may at the same time anticipate the regathering of the Markan Jesus's fleeing disciples in Galilee, where the resurrected Son of Man will appear to judge them.

Jesus's resurrection would by definition vindicate his death, but this vindication is not widely acknowledged at Mark's close. It becomes clear on retrospect that only at the eschatological consummation will all those condemned for their treatment of the Son of Man—both demonic and human, perhaps including satanic Peter and Jesus's other disciples—actually *see* the living Son displayed to the world, as the three apocalyptic sayings anticipate: ἴδωσιν, 9:1; ὄψονται, 13:26; ὄψεσθε,

14:62.³⁵ This comes to define the relationship between Jesus's resurrection "after three days" and his final advent: the Son of Man's (possible) vindication in Mark's narrative versus that vindication's revelation and universal acknowledgment in an eschatological future exceeding Mark's narrative. However, this distinction may not explain but result from the disciples' abandoning Jesus to die and rise alone, if that development delays an eschatological consummation that would otherwise have taken place at the resurrection of the Son of Man with his community a few days after their deaths.

In any case, the young man in 16:6–7 attempts to publicize Jesus's resurrection from a scandalous death discretely to the failed disciples even before the Son of Man's vindication is broadly recognized at his parousia. If that attempt succeeds, these few at least "will see him just as he said" in Galilee (αὐτὸν ὄψεσθε, καθὼς εἶπεν ὑμῖν, 16:7).³⁶ The risen Christ's possible meeting with the scattered disciples (14:27–28) would thus anticipate or even begin to enact the regnant Son of Man's eschatological regathering (13:26–27) and his revelation as cosmic ruler and judge (8:38–9:1). If the risen and vindicated Son of Man manages to meet up with his scattered disciples in Galilee, then, he will likely adopt an approach toward them analogous to the one Jesus had predicted the Son would take at the eschaton. He will judge them according to the criterion Jesus had solemnly publicized, namely, willingness to die with the master in faithful anticipation of God's resurrection (8:31–9:1).

I argued in the previous chapter that Mark mitigates intimations of the disciples' condemnation by having Jesus prophesy for them future opportunities to testify in Jesus's name and be executed in anticipation of resurrection (13:9–13). In the time of eschatological travail, they may compensate for their craven abandonment of Jesus to die and rise alone within the passion narrative. But note Mark's emphasis on the multiple

---

35. The "powers of the heavens" from 13:24–25 are the subject of the verb of seeing in 13:26, an apparent reference to Jesus's demonic enemies, given the ancient tendency to view stars as spiritual beings. On this see Dale C. Allison, "The Magi's Angel," in *Studies in Matthew: Interpretation Past and Present* (Grand Rapids: Baker Academic, 2005), 17–41.

36. Bolt resists an eschatological reading of the chapter by arguing that the discourse's prophecies are all fulfilled in Mark's narrative of Jesus's death and resurrection ("Mark 13"). From this interpretive perspective, one might likewise read 8:38–9:1 as assurance of the failed disciples' condemnation by the Son upon his resurrection, which the final reference to Peter in 16:7 would anticipate.

opportunities Peter is already given to offer testimony about Jesus within this narrative. He receives three chances to do so, with divine omens interspersed (the rooster's crows) to recall Jesus's prophetic warnings lest he fail. Peter wastes all these opportunities to bear witness to Christ under the influence of the Holy Spirit, whose guidance the Olivet discourse promises (13:11). Instead, he denies and curses Christ under the competing influence of Satan.[37] If Mark 16:7 expects the risen Christ's appearance to Peter at Galilee, then Stein is right that "Mark 1:1–15:47 ... provides us with a context for understanding" how Mark envisions it. However, Stein's optimistic interpretation of 16:7's reference fails to convince. Against the backdrop of 1:1–15:47, Mark 16:7 anticipates Jesus's condemnation of Peter.

This is not to say that Mark forecloses the possibility of Peter's redemption. The Second Gospel's final reference to Peter, though far from the "affectionate and forgiving promise of a reunion" Stein finds, at least equivocates. This equivocation relates to Satan's manipulation of Peter into faithlessness, which would call into question the appropriateness of his eschatological condemnation. James, John, Andrew, and even the Marys and Salome, who refuse to testify to Jesus's resurrection, might all repent of their cravenness and recommit themselves to faithful confession under the Holy Spirit's guidance (13:11). Peter, on the contrary, has been driven to deny and curse Jesus by this Spirit's antithesis, the unclean spirit. His rehabilitation requires not merely forgiveness, reconciliation, and the second chance at faithfulness Jesus seems to hold out to his disciples in the Olivet discourse (see 13:9–11). It requires deliverance from the devil.

Jesus has a strong record of saving the demon-possessed in Mark's Gospel. That may explain the internally dialogical equivocation in Mark's final reference to apostate Peter in 16:7, which encompasses Peter's liability to condemnation as a result of denial but remains sufficiently vague that his redemption is possible. This more optimistic possibility appears increasingly likely insofar as Mark presents Jesus's passion as the climax of

---

37. Markusse connects the disciples' failure of witness to the absence of the Spirit (which she believes 1:8 promises only upon Jesus's death) and to 13:11's promise of the Spirit's support of future witness (*Salvation in Mark*). Without spiritual support, all believers will fail to obey, as did Jesus's disciples. However, the Holy Spirit's testimonial guidance (13:11) ought to be conceptually opposed not to the Spirit's inaccessibility, but rather to the presence of an unholy spirit inspiring not confession but apostasy, as Peter's experience demonstrates.

his ministry of exorcism, as I will argue in the next chapter. Jesus's death and resurrection may deliver Peter from demonic enslavement so that he will be able to make the kind of Spirit-inspired confession in the face of execution that 13:11–13 prophetically urges from him and the other disciples in a future exceeding Mark's story. The extant accounts of Peter's martyrdom, which frequently refer to the Markan demand that Jesus's disciples follow him to death, imaginatively elaborate this redemptive possibility (e.g., Mart. Pet. 6).[38]

My final chapter will consider the prospect of Peter's redemption more carefully. At this point, though, the situation of the disciple appears quite grim. Based on clear criteria Mark's Jesus publicly establishes (8:34–9:1), Peter's eschatological salvation is in jeopardy and may already be forfeit. James, John, and the others have also demonstrated fearful shame to be identified with the executed Jesus, and something similar holds for the Marys and Salome, as I have argued. Though the disloyalty of none of these is as perverse as Peter's (let alone Judas's) and their forgiveness and

---

38. Lipsius, *Acta Apostolorum apocrypha*, 7–8. If Mark was written in Rome, and in the wake of Nero's persecution of Christians, in which Peter himself possibly died, this might explain the centrality of both the requirement to die with Jesus and Peter's choice to apostatize rather than to face death. See especially Timothy David Barnes, "'Another Shall Gird Thee': Probative Evidence for the Death of Peter," in *Peter in Early Christianity*, ed. Helen K. Bond and Larry W. Hurtado (Grand Rapids: Eerdmans, 2015), 76–95. (For discussion of Mark's setting, see n. 62 below.) If Peter had recently taken the opportunity of martyrdom offered in Mark 13:11–13, the evangelist might have felt free to explore the implications of his apostasy without fear of endangering his reputation. As subtle as the gestures toward Peter's rehabilitation are in Mark, readers would probably discern them if they knew that Peter had recently been executed. For relevant discussion, see Helen K. Bond, "Was Peter behind Mark's Gospel?," in Bond and Hurtado, *Peter in Early Christianity*, 50–54.

It is also possible that the Second Evangelist was not troubled by the possibility of damaging Peter's reputation, e.g., if he was a Paulinist concerned to defend the gospel Paul had preached from continuing attacks sponsored by the Jerusalem church. See, e.g., David C. Sim, "The Family of Jesus and the Disciples of Jesus in Paul and Mark: Taking Sides in the Early Church's Factional Dispute," in Wischmeyer, Sim, and Elmer, *Two Authors at the Beginnings of Christianity*, 73–99; see also n. 57 below. For a different account of the relationship between Paul and Mark's representation of Peter, which is in my view overly congenial and optimistic in its assessment of the latter, see Finn Damgaard, "Persecution and Denial—Paradigmatic Apostolic Portrayals in Paul and Mark," in Becker, Engberg-Pedersen, and Mueller, *For and Against Pauline Influence on Mark*, 295–315.

rehabilitation somewhat more likely, at Mark's close they too remain at risk of the condemnation 8:38–9:1 promises.

The Failures of James and John

A less extensive textual complex characterizes the situation of James and John in the Markan passion narrative. It also emphasizes their refusal to suffer, die, and rise with Jesus. However, in the end, Mark's treatment of these two disciples is more optimistic than its treatment of Peter, pointing to a distinction between faithlessness that issues in apostasy and fearful doubt that results in flight, especially from persecution.

Mark's portrayal of Peter's faithlessness emerges from Jesus's first prophecy of the Son of Man's death and resurrection in 8:31. Mark's presentation of James and John as ruined disciples begins in earnest on the heels of Jesus's third such prophecy, in 10:33–34. Zebedee's sons demand of Jesus that he "grant us to sit, one at your right hand and at one your left [εἷς σου ἐκ δεξιῶν καὶ εἷς ἐξ ἀριστερῶν], in your glory" (10:37). Their request looks back to the prediction Jesus has just issued that the Son of Man will suffer, die, and rise from the dead in Jerusalem, where Judah's kings traditionally reigned and where Jesus is now leading his followers (10:32). It also recalls 8:38–9:1, Jesus's first prophecy of the Son coming in glory, proleptically glimpsed in the transfiguration (9:2–8) and now anticipated in his approach to Jerusalem.

Scholars usually link James and John's request of Jesus to his prophetic announcement of the Son of Man's suffering and death, rather than to his prediction of resurrection, much as they do Peter's rebuke of Jesus in Mark 8:32. Collins is typical in claiming that James and John's request to share in Jesus's coming glory "creates a jarring contrast with the prediction of Jesus's suffering and death in vv. 33–34 and constitutes the climactic example of the disciples' misunderstanding of (or refusal to accept) Jesus's revelation ... that the messiah must suffer."[39] Yet 10:33–34 culminates in the Son rising from the dead, and since James and John request to share in Jesus's eschatological glory, one ought to connect their request to the final element of the prophecy rather than emphasize its divergence from that prophecy's earlier section. The idea of the Son's suffering and death is not unrelated to Jesus's subsequent conversation with James and John

---

39. Collins, *Mark*, 495.

(10:35–40), or to Jesus's address to the others in its wake (10:41–45). Collins's comment rightly points out that James and John fail to attend to the whole of Jesus's prophecy. But still, the prediction of miraculous resurrection after three days drastically limits the scope of the previous prediction of suffering, and it is what prompts these disciples' request.

Granting the resurrection prophecy the weight it deserves leads to the conclusion that the sons of Zebedee do not misunderstand Jesus's statement about the Son's suffering, nor do they refuse to accept it. They merely focus on the final and most amazing part of what Jesus prophesies, namely, that the Son will rise from the dead a few days after he is killed, to which their request to reign at his side constitutes not a befuddled or recalcitrant non sequitur but a reasonable, if self-interested, response. While Jesus's reaction to their appeal insists on the integration of suffering and glory, servitude and power, it does not "flatly refuse" what the sons of Zebedee ask.[40] On the contrary, it tells them how to attain their goal, namely, through self-sacrificial service (10:42–44) culminating in the giving of their lives in anticipation of resurrection glory and eschatological authority, as the Son of Man exemplifies (10:33–34, 45). As David Seeley and Matthew Thiessen both show, Mark's Jesus participates in a popular philosophical discourse that imagined the ideal king as one who combined governance with willingness to serve his subjects with generous beneficence, up to and including giving his life on their behalf.[41] That tradition, which Mark evokes and polemically employs against Roman imperial rule (see 10:42), combines ideas of regal authority and service, rather than opposing one to the other.

James and John's request presumes that the Son of Man's impending death and resurrection in the Holy City will usher in the eschatological consummation and the Son's cosmic reign, which Jesus has previously predicted (8:38–9:1). Their appeal to reign at his side therefore relates to confusion regarding the eschatological timetable analogous to that underlying Peter's question about Elijah in 9:9–11. Yet incomprehension about the precise eschatological time frame of Jesus's resurrection prophecies constitutes not James and John's only mistake, nor their most serious one. Their request also evinces a failure to grasp that the res-

---

40. *Pace* Collins, *Mark*, 498.
41. David Seeley, "Rulership and Service in Mark 10:41–45," *NovT* 35 (1993): 234–50; Matthew Thiessen, "The Many for One or One for the Many? Reading Mark 10:45 in the Roman Empire," *HTR* 109 (2016): 447–66.

urrection glory the Son of Man will enjoy is not his to distribute but God's. It depends on radical trust in God's sovereignty. That is why Jesus speaks in 8:38 of the Son coming "in his father's glory," recalling the one like a son of man ruling at the pleasure of the "Ancient of Days" from Dan 7:13–14.[42] In Mark 10, Jesus uses a divine passive construction to resolve James and John's confusion by indicating that the omniscient God chooses who will rule alongside him as the Son of Man at the eschatological consummation: "to sit at my right hand or left is not mine to grant, but it belongs to those for whom it has been prepared" (10:40).[43] Their suggestion that Jesus presume upon God's prerogative by distributing this authority on his own rather than deferring to God's ordained will (10:37) furthers the impertinence of their already manipulative request (10:35). Jesus confronts their audacity head-on: "You don't know what you ask" (10:38a), a milder version of the rebuke issued to Peter in 8:33 ("you have in mind not the things of God but of human beings"). He then directs their attention to the requirement that they suffer and die at his side in order to attain the dominion they seek: "Are you able to drink the cup that I drink or be baptized with the baptism with which I am baptized?" (δύνασθε πιεῖν τὸ ποτήριον ὃ ἐγὼ πίνω ἢ τὸ βάπτισμα ὃ ἐγὼ βαπτίζομαι βαπτισθῆναι, 10:38b). When James and John claim that they are, Jesus exhorts them to fulfill that claim, repeating his references to the cup and to baptism (10:39).[44] Instead of bargaining with Jesus to guarantee receipt of glory he could not grant even if he wanted, they must put their lives at God's disposal (as Jesus will do in accepting his own cup in 14:36) in the trust that God will save and elevate them to the positions of glory they seek (see 8:34–37).

---

42. Cf. Mark 12:35–37, where Jesus quotes Ps 110:1 to argue that God enthrones the Christ.

43. See Beniamin Pascut, "The So-Called 'Passivum Divinum' in Mark's Gospel," *NovT* 54 (2012): 330–31. Comparison of Mark 8:38 and Luke 9:26 is informative. In Luke's revision, the coming Son, the Father, and the angels all possess their own glory; in Mark, only the Father has glory, in which the Son shares.

44. The futures in 10:39 are usually taken as prophetic statements pointing beyond Mark's Gospel. I will explore this interpretative dimension presently, but here I take them as jussive futures (see Smyth and Messing, *Greek Grammar*, §1917; BDF, §362). They function in a way analogous to the future copulas in 10:43 and 44, which likewise have an imperatival force. This interpretation seems to make the best sense of the sayings in their immediate context, in which they urge the characters James and John to suffer and die with Jesus within Mark's Gospel.

That Jesus at this juncture uses figurative language to describe suffering and death at his side demands attention. Mark's Jesus earlier spoke of the Son of Man's fate in vivid detail (8:31; 9:31; 10:33-34), and he was blunt in his exhortation that his disciples follow him to death (8:34). In chapter 8, Mark affirms that Jesus "spoke … openly [παρρησίᾳ … ἐλάλει]" about his death and resurrection (8:32), in contrast to his tendency to speak in parables (ἐν παραβολαῖς λαλεῖν, 12:1; cf. 3:23; 4:2, 11). That tendency reasserts itself in 10:38-39, though the subject remains the same as in 8:31-34. The Markan Jesus articulates an identical symbolic configuration twice within the span of two verses: "Are you able to drink of the cup that I drink or to be baptized with the baptism with which I am baptized?" (10:38-39). Βαπτίζω ("immerse"), the intensive form of βάπτω ("dip"), is used in ancient Greek of sinking (e.g., drowning, being shipwrecked, mired in quicksand or mud, etc.).[45] It constitutes a comprehensible metaphor of anxious suffering. Libanius, for instance, can use the verb to speak of "sorrow sinking the soul" (λύπη βαπτίζουσα μὲν τὴν ψυχήν, Or. 18.286).[46] Similarly, the cup (τὸ ποτήριον) is a common image for affliction in the Bible, sometimes for that associated with God's displeasure (e.g., Ps 75:8 LXX; Isa 51:17 LXX; etc.).[47] The metaphor appears throughout the passion narrative. Jesus himself uses it just before his arrest, when he prays that God might "take this cup [τὸ ποτήριον] from me" (Mark 14:36). It surfaces in a related context at Jesus's Passover meal with his disciples, where it symbolizes his blood, soon to be shed as an anthropophagic sacrifice for many (14:23-24).[48] Finally, related imagery appears as Jesus dies on the cross, where he at one point is sarcastically offered a luxurious drink of wine mixed with myrrh (15:23) and at another vinegar, or spoiled wine, on a sponge (15:36). Jesus's use of this gastronomic metaphor in chapter 10, where he urges James and John to suffer and die with him in anticipation of resurrection, anticipates all these scenes from the passion narrative. Of course, it also recalls Mark's use of the phrase "taste death" (γεύσωνται

---

45. Albrecht Oepke, "βάπτω, βαπτίζω," *TDNT* 1:529-46, esp. 530.

46. Quoting Richard Foerster, ed., *Libanii opera*, vol. 2, BSGRT (Leipzig: Teubner, 1904).

47. Marcus, *Mark 8-16*, 747; Collins, *Mark*, 496.

48. See Patrick Henry Reardon, "The Cross, Sacraments and Martyrdom: An Investigation of Mark 10:35-45," *SVTQ* 36 (1992): 103-15; cf. Marcus, *Mark 8-16*, 754, where Marcus observes the "sacramental" sense of Jesus's metaphors.

θανάτου, 9:1) in 8:34–9:1 to warn the disciples about the eschatological consequences of avoiding death at his side.

James and John's initial fixation on glory, and Jesus's oddly figural response to it in 10:38–39, foreshadows their failure to suffer and die with Jesus in the passion narrative. In 10:40, Mark's Jesus repeats the terms of James and John's request (10:37), but with notable adjustments: "to sit at my right hand or my left is not mine to grant; it is rather for those for whom it has been prepared." The omission of "in your glory," combined with the addition of "but for whom it has been prepared," sets the stage for a darkly ironic moment later in Mark. During Jesus's crucifixion, James and John do not occupy the positions at the master's sides; instead two bandits are crucified with Jesus in public humiliation, "one at his right hand and one at his left" (ἕνα ἐκ δεξιῶν καὶ ἕνα ἐξ εὐωνύμων αὐτοῦ, 15:27).[49] Having slept instead of keeping watch with Jesus while he prepares to drink his cup (14:32–42), and having abandoned him (see 14:50) before he is offered wine and vinegar on the cross (15:23, 36), James and John, according to the logic of 10:42–45, will forgo their share of Jesus's ensuing resurrection glory. Mark 10:40 turns James and John's manipulative request for eschatological authority on its head: since not they but others "for whom it has been prepared" find themselves at Jesus's right and left side as he dies on the cross, James and John will not find themselves in positions of eschatological preeminence they seek.

Jesus's exchange with James and John in 10:35–40 resembles his exchange with Peter in 14:29–31, which itself harks back to 8:34–9:1. Peter insists he will die alongside Jesus rather than scatter with the others at Jesus's arrest (14:29; cf. 14:27). Jesus responds by warning Peter that he will deny him (14:30), which he does (14:66–72). This sets the stage for Simon of Cyrene in 15:21 to take up, in ironic literalness, the cross that Simon Peter abdicates by apostatizing. Analogously, in their exchange with Jesus in 10:35–40, James and John seek to occupy glorious positions at Jesus's sides (10:37), affirming they will suffer and die with him in anticipation

---

49. This detail is frequently observed. See, e.g., John Muddiman, "The Glory of Jesus, Mark 10:37," in *The Glory of Christ in the New Testament: Studies in Christology in Memory of George Bradford Caird*, ed. Lincoln D. Hurst and N. T. Wright (Oxford: Clarendon, 1987), 51–58; Frank J. Matera, *The Kingship of Jesus: Composition Theology in Mark 15*, SBLDS 66 (Chico, CA: Scholars Press, 1982), 171–72 n. 8; Dale C. Allison, "Anticipating the Passion: The Literary Reach of Matthew 26:47–27:56," *CBQ* 56 (1994): 710–11.

of this divinely granted eschatological authority (10:38–39a; cf. 10:32–34). But in 15:27, the positions at his right and left hand, redefined in 10:40 as places of servile suffering prerequisite to the glory James and John seek, stand abandoned by these fugitive disciples. Mark again introduces new characters who fill in ironic literalness the roles Jesus's disciples refuse. The notices about Simon of Cyrene and the crucified bandits recall the master's earlier exchanges with his students so as to emphasize their scandalous absence from the scene of his death.

In spite of Jesus's repeated exhortations that Peter, James, John, and the others join him in placing their lives in God's hands, they refuse to follow him to death in expectation of resurrection and eschatological glory. They do not trust God to raise them from the dead and so choose to preserve mundane life, even though Jesus warned against this decision in 8:34–9:1. Jesus's abandonment is concretized in his cry of dereliction, a quotation of Ps 22 depicting an experience of profound spiritual isolation: "My God, my God, why have you forsaken me?" (15:34). While the theological implications of this cry have frequently been probed, no less significant is the subjective despair to which Jesus gives voice. He dies abandoned by his disciples, whom he had earlier identified as his "mother and brothers" (3:33–34). Instead of going to the cross with his family of students accompanying him, he is followed by a stranger; instead of being executed with his brothers, he is killed alongside criminals. Even the women who remain to watch keep their distance from him (15:40), including perhaps Jesus's actual mother (cf. 6:3). While previously they had all attended to him in Galilee (15:41), now cruel bystanders take the place they abandon and mockingly offer him drink (15:23, 36). Accordingly, the Markan Jesus's quotation of the psalm expresses a feeling of desolation so overwhelming that it affects his sense of the presence of God, the father (see Mark 1:11; 9:7; 14:36) whom Jesus must trust to raise his son from the dead. It suggests doubt on Jesus's part about whether God will save him after all from death's power.[50] Jesus's faith in God's resurrection power may itself be undermined by his disciples' faithlessness.

From this angle, the Markan Jesus's acceptance of the Son of Man's destiny is itself challenged by his disciples' doubt; from another, it constitutes a miracle of vicarious redemption, according to which the faithless

---

50. Gérard Rossé, *The Cry of Jesus on the Cross: A Biblical and Theological Study*, trans. Stephen Wentworth Arndt (New York: Paulist, 1987), 64.

disciples are saved by the faith of Jesus (cf. Gal 2:16, 20). I will discuss the latter possibility more systematically in the next chapter, but 10:38–40 already gestures at its relevance to the situation of James and John—more clearly, it turns out, than does Mark's treatment of Peter. I have been taking the verbs in 10:39 as jussive futures, since "you will be baptized" and "you will drink" figure the servile suffering and death Jesus exhorts his followers to share with him in 8:34 and elsewhere. However, in contrast to the earlier verse, 10:39 expresses the demand using ambiguous future indicatives rather than aorist imperatives, and employing hermeneutically capacious metaphors for Jesus's death rather than referring prosaically to his crucifixion. These rhetorical tactics have a purpose supplementing the reiteration of Jesus's command in terms anticipating James and John's failure to obey it in the passion narrative. They point to a time in the future that exceeds the temporal confines of Mark's story, much as does 13:9–13's anticipation of the disciples' martyrdoms.

While no strong case can be made for John's historical martyrdom independent of Mark 10:39, according to Acts, James is the first of the Twelve who is martyred (12:1–2), with his absence from the so-called Jerusalem pillars Paul names in Gal 2:9 possibly confirming the report.[51] The historical figure corresponding to Mark's character James would thus avail himself of the second chance to die with Jesus that Mark 13:9–13 offers the disciples outside Mark's narrative. In this way, he might metaphorically drink from Jesus's cup and share in his baptism, as Jesus prophesies. Perhaps more importantly, though, the emphatically repeated imagery of baptism and cup evokes the initiation and eucharistic rituals that Mark's implied audience would have regularly practiced and whose supposed origins Mark recounts.[52] Distinct features of Jesus's exhortations in 10:38–40, even when their imperatival force is granted, anticipate a future exceeding Mark's narrative confines and spilling into readers' own social situation—one involving well-known religious rituals practiced in early congregations and some of the historical disciples' martyrdoms as well.

---

51. See Richard I. Pervo, *Acts: A Commentary*, Hermeneia (Minneapolis: Fortress, 2009), 303 n. 22. On John's historical martyrdom, see François-Marie Braun, *Jean le théologien et son évangile dans l'église ancienne*, vol. 1 of *Jean le théologien*, EBib (Paris: Gabalda, 1959), 375–88.

52. Mark 1:1–11, Jesus's baptism; Mark 14:22–25, his final meal, which includes ceremonial language used in eucharistic celebrations (see 1 Cor 11:23–26).

This passage is hermeneutically capacious in a way similar to the Olivet discourse of chapter 13.

When Jesus declares in 10:39 that James and John will drink his cup, he anticipates, among the other cups the passion narrative features, the Passover meal that Mark's Gospel recounts (14:23). That passage recalls the episode under investigation not only in its reference to the cup from which James, John, and the others drink but also in Jesus's declaration that he pours out his blood "on behalf of many" as he serves it (ὑπὲρ πολλῶν, 14:24). The phrase picks up on Jesus's instruction to the disciples in the passage from chapter 10, when he urges them to embrace "service" (διακονῆσαι) like the Son of Man's and goes on to define it as "giving his life as a ransom for many" (ἀντὶ πολλῶν, 10:45).[53] By presenting this final meal that Jesus shares with his disciples as a metaphor for his death on others' behalf, Mark 14:22–25 stands in thematic continuity with early liturgical practices. Mark in fact echoes the language Paul reports as conventionally employed during early eucharistic celebrations (see 1 Cor 11:23–26).[54] Even in its intratextual anticipation of the Markan Last Supper, then, Mark 10:38–39 still points outside Mark's narrative discourse and toward the liturgical life of the early Jesus-believing congregations.

A similar case can be made about Mark's reference to baptism, a ritual especially important to Mark's story of Jesus. In contrast to all other gospels, Mark introduces its protagonist at John's baptism (1:1–11). For Mark, this initiates Jesus's identity as God's Son. The narrative conceit mirrors an early understanding of baptism as initiating Jesus-believers into a new life with God.[55] Comparison with Paul again proves instructive. The apos-

---

53. As frequently observed (e.g., Collins, *Mark*, 503, 657). The Greek verb for "serve" used in 10:45 can refer to table service. See Hermann Beyer, "διανοέω, διακονία, διάκονος," *TDNT* 2:82; cf. Acts 6:2, διακονεῖν τραπέζαις. It seems not to have been a dead metaphor but to have been used by Mark and other New Testament authors with that concrete image in view.

54. For the relationship between Paul (or traditions similar to those Paul recounts) and Mark, see Elizabeth V. Dowling, "'Do This in Remembrance': Last Supper Traditions in Paul and Mark," in Wischmeyer, Sim, and Elmer, *Two Authors at the Beginnings of Christianity*, 221–41; Jesper Tang Nielsen, "The Cross on the Way to Mark," in Becker, Engberg-Pedersen, and Mueller, *For and Against Pauline Influence on Mark*, 293.

55. See the classic treatment in George Raymond Beasley-Murray, *Baptism in the New Testament* (Grand Rapids: Eerdmans, 1962), 45–67, esp. 62–67. According to James D. G. Dunn, Paul's understanding of baptism as into Jesus's death (see Rom

tle associates baptism with Jesus's death and resurrection in Rom 6:3–6 (see also Col 2:12), where he understands immersion in water to recapitulate Jesus's execution and entombment. Baptized believers' emergence from the water thus symbolizes their participation in Christ's "newness of life" (καινότητι ζωῆς περιπατήσωμεν, 6:4) and expectation of eschatological resurrection (6:5). In conjunction with their symbolic partaking in Jesus's death and resurrection, they receive new identities that assimilate them to Christ as God's children (Gal 3:26–28), much as Jesus does in Mark 1:9–11.[56] Mark's figuration of James and John's call to suffer, die, and rise with Christ as a call to experience "baptism" in 10:38–39 draws on and reinforces baptism's significance among Pauline and perhaps other early Jesus-believing communities as a ritual identifying the believer with Christ in death and resurrection.

Against this background, Jesus's insistence in Mark 10:39 that James and John drink Jesus's cup and experience Jesus's baptism has interpretive implications standing in dialogical tension with those explored above. James and John indeed refuse to share the master's cup in the figurative sense of suffering and dying at his side within Mark's narrative confines; but they will drink from Jesus's cup at the Last Supper (14:23), and that meal, as Mark recounts it, reflects the eucharistic ceremony in which James and John will likewise take part as leaders in the early church. Similarly, although these two disciples decline to join Jesus in metaphorical baptism

---

6:3–6) constitutes a traditional recollection of Jesus himself "having taken up and adapted [John] the Baptist's metaphor and applied it to his own death" in historical situations similar to the dialogue between Jesus and the sons of Zebedee analyzed here. See Dunn, *The Theology of Paul the Apostle* (Grand Rapids: Eerdmans, 2006), 452. However, it is more likely that the evangelist imaginatively employed baptism as a symbol for Jesus's suffering and death under the influence of Pauline theology. See William Loader, "The Concept of Faith in Paul and Mark," in Wischmeyer, Sim, and Elmer, *Two Authors at the Beginnings of Christianity*, 456–57; Nielsen, "Cross on the Way," 287–89. For analysis of how baptism relates to death and resurrection in Paul's writing, see Tappenden, *Resurrection in Paul*, 137–46.

56. See again Beasley-Murray, *Baptism in the New Testament*, 126–51. Although even older, Albert Schweitzer's treatment of these themes in *Mysticism of Paul the Apostle* remains provocative. For a study of the Markan passage exploring this connection from a perspective informed by Stoic physics, see Gitte Buch-Hansaen, "The Politics of Beginnings—Cosmology, Christology and Covenant: Gospel Openings Reconsidered in the Light of Paul's Peneumatology," in Becker, Engberg-Pedersen, and Mueller, *For and Against Pauline Influence on Mark*, 213–42.

4. Faithlessness Condemned or Redeemed?   169

by dying and rising alongside him in Mark itself, they will still participate in the baptismal rite assimilating early believers to the dying and rising Christ (presumably as baptizers, if not as baptizands themselves). Finally, James may emulate Jesus's actual suffering and death outside the confines of Mark's passion narrative, for Acts 12:1–2 plausibly reports his execution by King Herod in something like the context Mark 13:9–13 anticipates. Against the interpretive horizon opened by Mark's clear allusions to early rituals and historical developments with which readers would presumably have been familiar, 10:39 suggests that James and John's failure of faith, disastrous though it be, does not obviate their status as disciples. Despite their refusal to die and rise with Jesus in Mark, as emphasized by the presence of bandits crucified in the positions James and John affirmed they would occupy but in the end abandon, Jesus dies and rises for them, among many others (10:45; 14:24). These disciples will avail themselves of his vicarious death and resurrection by participating in the rituals understood symbolically to recapitulate them. For James, moreover, symbolic assimilation may give way to actual imitation, for this disciple seems to have been martyred in a future exceeding Mark's narrative, just as the Olivet discourse encourages (13:9–13). To use somewhat anachronistic language that reflects theological controversies emerging in Mark's wake, 10:39 indicates that James and John, though fleeing arrest instead of suffering martyrdom, will not experience excommunication and its attendant eschatological condemnation but instead remain within the community of believers and even become future martyrs.

While they demonstrate fear of death rather than faith in resurrection, James, John, and the other disciples who abandon Jesus to die and rise alone do not go so far as to deny or curse their master, as does satanic Peter, let alone sell him out, like Judas. They flee from the scene of his arrest, and later from the empty tomb, rather than apostatize. Mark anticipates this important difference in faithlessness in its representation of different types of soil in the paradigmatic parable of the sower, as discussed above. Some soil (Peter) is rendered fruitless by satanic activity affecting God's prophetic word (4:4, 15). Other soil (Judas) supports thorny weeds hostile to good growth as a result of a desire for wealth (4:7, 18–19). Yet a different kind of soil (James and John, as well as the others) does support vegetation, though its growth be weakened as a result of fear of persecution (4:5–6, 16–17). In this interpretive light, it seems significant that Jesus's Olivet discourse not only requires from interrogated disciples the Spirit-inspired confession that Peter fails to issue (13:9–13), and not only reproaches internecine betrayal such as Judas's (13:12), but also authorizes the decision to flee in the face of persecution (13:14–16). The evangelist rhetorically flags that authorization as directly relevant to the gospel's readers, rather than to the Markan Jesus's disciples, as argued in the previous chapter, but it nonetheless suggests a more lenient attitude toward flight than toward denial and betrayal. The former alone remains compatible with discipleship. Complementing that distinction, Mark's anticipation of James and John's flight from death with Jesus in 10:35–40 (see 15:27) hints at their future faithfulness in a world exceeding Mark's narrative, while no such intimations surface in the related passage anticipating Peter's denial (8:34–9:1).

Mark's Olivet discourse also introduces an intriguing connection between Jesus's words in 13:14–16 and the one fleeing disciple whose rehabilitation seems assured in the passion narrative itself, namely, the anonymous young man of 14:51–52 and 16:5-7. His flight involves a panicked relinquishment of clothing to facilitate escape from pursuers (14:52), which analogizes him to the one urged to flee in 13:16, where Jesus commands the fugitive to abandon his outer garment: "let him not turn back in order to get a coat." Peter's denials and curse of Jesus, let alone Judas's betrayal of the master, constitute obscene perversions of Jesus's directives in chapters 8 and 10, as I have shown. The young man's escape similarly recalls Jesus's authorization of his future followers' flight in the hermeneutically capacious chapter 13, possibly confirming that the other Markan disciples' frightened abscondence remains assimilable to the requirements of following Jesus.

Flight for Mark's disciples, either from the scene of his arrest or from that of the empty tomb, is hardly ideal; in the imagery of the parable of the sower, it constitutes meager fruit indeed. However, it does represent at least shabby growth, opening the possibility of better harvests to come, as the young man demonstrates. These various intratextual allusions shore up Mark's intertextual suggestions that the historical figures corresponding to the characters James and John will find a place in the early church, despite their flight from Jesus's arrest and absence from his execution and empty tomb within the passion narrative. Indeed, for James this may involve belatedly obeying Jesus's directive to die with him in anticipation of resurrection, precisely as 13:9–13 exhorts.

Mark's Exploration of Faith's Failure

As mentioned, Mark provides no such reassuring indications for Peter in the narrative complex dramatizing his failure to follow. Far from suggesting that he will participate in the future life of the church, this gospel's closing reference to him segregates Peter from the community of disciples in a way rhetorically analogous to excommunication ("the disciples and Peter"; 16:7). Peter's perversion of Jesus's demand to deny himself and be crucified with the master may not be as bad as Judas's betrayal, but it remains worse than the other disciples' panicked breakaway from the scene of Jesus's arrest, let alone the women's frightened flight from the empty tomb. Categories that are perhaps anachronistic but heuristically useful nonetheless clarify this difference. Peter not merely flees from possible persecution but actively apostatizes. As a result, Mark anticipates his meeting with the risen Jesus to take the form of a condemnatory encounter involving the Son of Man's shameful denial in return.

Intimations of Peter's redemption are not absent from Mark; I have already begun to outline them. But Mark offers no confidence that Peter will be saved. If Mark's Gospel originated in Pauline circles or was composed in engagement with Paul's letters, this distinction could polemically reflect Paul's occasional tension with the original apostles or their representatives, on the one hand, and his serious public conflict with Peter, on the other (see Gal 1–2).[57] Thus, while Peter, James, John, and the others all fail to follow Jesus's directives and example, the Markan Peter's failure in particular calls into question his status as a disciple of Christ. As a complement, Mark refuses to certify that any of Jesus's original disciples met the risen Christ in the wake of his purported resurrection but singles out Peter (16:7). This could serve, if not to cast doubt on their apostolic credentials (especially Peter's), at least to suggest their testimony about the risen Jesus is no more authoritative than Paul's own, a concern Paul's letters occasionally attest (see 1 Cor 15:5–8; Gal 1:15–24).

Mark's treatment of resurrection, including its representation of Peter and the other disciples' refusal to die with their master in faithful anticipation of it, can also be explained from another interpretative perspective. Mark's sustained meditation on resurrection contains complementary theological impulses. The first, explored in chapters 1–2, presses unre-

---

57. See Sim, "Family of Jesus"; Michael D. Goulder, *St. Paul versus St. Peter: A Tale of Two Missions* (Louisville: Westminster John Knox, 1995), 16–23; Anne Vig Skoven, "Mark as Allegorical Rewriting of Paul," in Becker, Engberg-Pedersen, and Mueller, *For and Against Pauline Influence on Mark*, 13–27. Skoven develops an allegorical reading of Mark 2:13–17 proposed by the nineteenth-century New Testament scholar Gustaf Volkmar as a polemical recasting of the events Paul recounts in Gal 2:11–21.

solved, even indissoluble questions about God's power over death. Mark features faithful characters but gives prominent voice to those who have difficulty trusting in resurrection, such as the fathers of dying children (Mark 5:21–23a, 35–43; 9:14–29). Mark's narrative itself leaves open the possibility that there is no resurrection of the dead or any other form of supernatural eternal life, not even for Jesus himself. Resurrection remains a possible but not a necessary conclusion to draw from the evidence and arguments Mark presents, whose ambiguity Mark underscores. Mark's closing verses capture that interpretive dynamic precisely: though the young man believes Jesus rose, the two Marys and Salome apparently do not and refuse to proclaim it.

At the same time, though, Mark's Jesus demands faith in resurrection. He requires it not only from parents of dead or dying children but, above all, from his students themselves. Despite the questions about resurrection that Mark's narrative neglects to resolve, Mark's Jesus nonetheless calls on these to join him in a torturous and humiliating execution—all in expectation of a resurrection Mark will not warrant. The Second Gospel constitutes a literary context in which resurrection faith is never guaranteed but compelled nonetheless. Mark's character Jesus requires and exemplifies obedient trust in God that issues in willingness to die in hope of salvation, but Mark's discursive framework raises questions about whether such faith is well-founded. Moreover, as Mark draws to its close, not only does the disciples' willingness to trust in God's power to save them from death fail, but even Jesus's own faith that God will resurrect him seems to falter. The master's final words express doubt rather than trust that his father will rescue him after he dies (15:34).

In a literary work exploring faith in resurrection and that faith's limitations and failure, the Second Evangelist reasonably distinguishes between different types of faithlessness, different ways in which faith fails to take hold. Some doubt is more forgivable than other, as this chapter's interpretation of James, John, and Peter in the passion narrative indicates. Or perhaps more precisely, different kinds of doubt are amenable to different modes of remediation. It is one thing to question God's salvation while dying in his service, as Jesus does in 15:34. Such existential confusion and despair is all but unavoidable. It is also what the parents of dead and dying children experience in Mark, and in part explains the Marys' and Salome's response upon encountering Jesus's empty tomb after having witnessed his execution and interment. Death, especially when one examines it up close (as all these characters do, in one way or another), seems to be precisely a dead-end. It is difficult or impossible to force oneself to view it otherwise from that vantage, despite what Jesus says or shows.

It is something different, though, to succumb to panic because one cravenly privileges an instinctive desire to preserve one's life over a reasoned decision to risk it in God's service. Mark's Gospel condemns this sort of doubt, which James and John in particular demonstrate, as do all of Jesus's disciples save Peter and Judas. This includes the female disciples, to the extent that fear to proclaim the resurrection of an executed criminal motivates their silent flight from Jesus's empty tomb, not to mention the distance they keep from him during his crucifixion. However, in the final analysis it too may be amenable to forgiveness and remediation, as the rehabilitation and reclothing of the young man who fled naked as well as the prophetic gestures at James and John's participation in the early church suggest. After all, the urge to flee is common, even universal, and Mark will legitimize it as the reader's acceptable response to persecution (13:14).

It something different still, though, to adopt a cynical demeanor toward God's ability or willingness to save from death, so that one is not just content to flee but denies allegiance to Christ or even curses Christ to prove disdain of him. Someone like Peter, who adopts such a diabolical attitude toward God's power over death by flaunting faithlessness in this way, has moved beyond the realm of pardon into the territory of unforgivable sin (see Mark 3:29, to be discussed presently). However, such a one may still be redeemed from Satan's captivity, as I have already suggested and will explain more fully in my final chapter.

In drawing such distinctions, Mark stands near the beginning of a trajectory of ancient Christian interpretive reflection on the role faith in God's power over death ought to play in the actions of believers confronted with the possibility of arrest, interrogation, and execution.[58] This tradition finalizes Mark's *commentarii* in a way different from the other gospels' emendatory revisions. Or rather, in its own lack of finalization, it continually reformulates and relitigates from different interpretive perspectives the questions Mark poses about the theological and ideological implications of the disciples' failures to die with Jesus in anticipation of resurrection. Martyrdom like the Markan Jesus's faithful death was usually treated as

---

58. For a reading of Mark as a pastoral response to issues such as these, see E. A. Russell, "The Gospel of Mark: Pastoral Response to a Life or Death Situation? Some Reflections," *IBS* 7 (1985): 206–22. For a brief survey of related interpretations, see Paul Middleton, "Suffering and the Creation," 180–83.

an ideal, even if it entailed faith-challenging anxiety.[59] Early Christians normally found apostasy such as the Markan Peter's unacceptable, and scholars have argued that Mark's presentation of Peter intentionally assimilates that character to an apostate believer.[60] Self-serving betrayal of one's brethren to the authorities, such as Judas's betrayal of Jesus for money, was entirely beyond the pale. But ancient Christians vigorously debated the permissibility of flight to avoid persecution—the decision James, John, and most of the other disciples make, and about which the Second Gospel seems more ambivalent.[61] Mark's reflection on both faith in and doubt about resurrection, especially as figured in Jesus's execution and possible resurrection and the disciples' failures to die and rise with him, may instantiate early Christian theological debate about appropriate responses to persecution, which was never resolved.

This is not to presume that Mark's community faced persecution. The interpretation merely recognizes that anxiety about it represents a clear theme throughout Mark, whether or not such fear was founded in ancient social or political realities.[62] Given that Mark's community of auditors pre-

---

59. Mark is sometimes taken as the archetypical martyrdom account, standing as a vital source of that literary tradition (Moss, *Other Christs*, 33; Middleton, *Radical Martyrdom*, 135–36, 146–56).

60. Esp. Lampe, "St Peter's Denial"; cf. J. Duncan M. Derrett, "Cursing Jesus (I Cor. Xii. 3): The Jews as Religious 'Persecutors,'" *NTS* 21 (1975): 544–54. Derrett's speculation about the interrogation of "Christians" within the synagogue is not persuasive.

61. Peter of Alexandria, Athanasius, Lactantius, and others maintained a similar distinction between believers who flee to avoid arrest (legitimate) and those who apostatize (prohibited, as was cooperating with the authorities to facilitate the arrest of fellow believers). See, e.g., Jan Leemans, "The Idea of Flight from Persecution in the Alexandrian Tradition from Clement to Athanasius," in *Origeniana Octava: Origen and the Alexandrian Tradition*, ed. Lorenzo Perrone, BETL 164 (Leuven: Peeters, 2004), 901–10; Oliver Nicholson, "Flight from Persecution as Imitation of Christ: Lactantius's Divine Institutes IV. 18, 1–2," *JTS* 40 (1989): 48–65. Other ancient writers resisted this view (esp. Tertullian, *De fuga in persecutione*). That Cyprian's decision to flee Carthage during the Decian persecution forty years after Tertullian wrote was so controversial indicates that Tertullian's rejection of flight's legitimacy was not anomalous, as does the fact that so many early Christian writers felt obliged to defend flight's legitimacy over so long a time. For scholarship on the Cyprianic controversies related to this issue, see ch. 3 n. 83.

62. This fear may relate to Nero's purported persecution of Christians in Rome in 64 CE (Tacitus, *Ann.* 15.44), if Mark's traditional association with the city is correct. In

sumably claimed fealty to a supposedly resurrected man who had been executed by Roman imperial authorities, such anxiety, concretized in the experience of the Marys and Salome at the empty tomb, is understandable. While Mark's contextualization of Jesus's exhortations to martyrdom may obstruct readers' straightforward application of them to their own social situation, as argued in chapter 3, the evangelist still understands those commands, deployed as narrative resources in the context of Mark's developing story, to be relevant to the implied reader's fears. Mark's narrative of Jesus's martyrdom, Peter's apostasy, and the other disciples' flight (let alone Judas's betrayal) explores different ways to respond to anticipated harassment and suggests that some responses are better than others. Instead of a mandate to die with Jesus in expectation of eschatological resurrection, or any other form of eternal life, Mark offers a somber meditation on the varied experiences of Jesus and his disciples as they confront the fear of death. It surveys a range of responses (from heroic faith to tragic doubt) and of their possible consequences (from resurrection to damnation). While Mark's open-ended exploration of questions about resurrection obviates dogmatism, it does not precipitate a collapse into agnosticism. Mark leaves the reader with neither facile exhortations to faithfulness nor

---

support of that setting, see Winn, *Purpose of Mark's Gospel*, 76–83; Incigneri, *Gospel to the Romans*, esp. chs. 4–5. However, Shaw argues that Tacitus's account of the Neronian persecution is mistaken ("Myth of the Neronian Persecution").

My reading does not depend on a particular historical contextualization of Mark's Gospel. Locating Mark in an historically verifiable context of first-century persecution, or even believing persecution of Christians to have been anything other than rare in the first century, is less important to understanding Mark's treatment of the theme than is the plausibility that Mark and/or the readers were concerned with it. It is easy to imagine that a community claiming to follow Jesus, who had himself been executed as a criminal by Rome, might worry that it, too, could be subject to arrest, trial, and execution. Precisely such a fear animates the author of Revelation, even though this writer only identifies a single believer among the several churches he addresses who had ever lost his life in connection with testimony about Jesus (Rev 2:13).

Even independent of the compelling response to Shaw's argument by Christopher P. Jones, I remain persuaded by a number of readings of Mark holding that *fear* or *anxiety* about Roman persecution was an important element of the experience of Mark's community of readers. See Jones, "The Historicity of the Neronian Persecution: A Response to Brent Shaw," *NTS* 63 (2017): 146–52. See also especially Roskam, *Purpose of the Gospel of Mark*; Winn, *Purpose of Mark's Gospel*; Incigneri, *Gospel to the Romans*; Middleton, "Suffering and the Creation." Also worthy of note are Pudussery, "Discipleship"; and Van Iersel, "Gospel according to St. Mark."

paralyzing theological indecision. In fact, it explicitly authorizes the reader to flee, even though it seems to present martyrdom as an ideal. The Second Evangelist therefore offers thoughtful, even practical consideration of how the faith in resurrection that Jesus demands bears on the actual experience of death, including what and whether to believe and how to behave in situations wherein following Jesus could itself threaten one's life.

5
A Ransom for Many

Mark acknowledges that not all followers of Jesus will be convinced of resurrection. Even Jesus's original disciples, when faced with the possibility of execution at their master's side, rejected the ideal Jesus laid out of dying with him in faithful anticipation of eternal life. However, Mark still calls for faith in resurrection and exemplifies it as well—especially in the young man who believes Jesus rose (16:5–7). Mark opens for readers the possibility of flight and will not go so far as to demand that they follow Jesus to death in expectation of resurrection. The evangelist may view the flight of Jesus's students depicted within the narrative as forgivable, even as assimilable to the requirements of discipleship. But the Second Gospel's representation of Jesus's teaching nonetheless entails a conception of loyal service unto death that requires resurrection faith for coherence. This remains the case whether or not the faithful ideal is ever fully realized in Mark's Gospel, even by Jesus, who may himself, at the moment he dies, doubt God will raise him (15:34). Therefore, while a sound interpretation of Mark will recognize the ample space this gospel leaves open for doubtful questions about resurrection, it must also come to terms with the significance of that in which Mark invites faith.

Of particular importance in this regard is the role Jesus's crucifixion and resurrection play in God's plan to redeem many from death (see esp. 10:45). Their redemptive role constitutes not only a vital element of Christian dogma but also an important feature of Mark's narrative, which concentrates on the disciples' failure to die and rise with their master. Abandoned by his followers, Jesus dies alone while his fugitive disciples continue to live. This narrative dynamic may have given original impulse to theological reflection on Christ's atoning death and resurrection, so that the idea of Jesus dying for others only emerges as a theologoumenon secondarily; primarily, it would have been a feature of how Jesus's death was traditionally recounted. Mark's *commentarii*, then, would elaborate a narrative of Jesus's disciples leaving their master to die (and possibly rise) without them and connect it to a sequence of legends from Jesus's ministry—especially his exorcisms—so as to suggest a theological understanding of the Son of Man's death and resurrection. This understanding finds inchoate articulation in discrete christological statements scattered throughout Mark (esp. 10:45 and 14:24, though 3:27 is also important).[1] In order to grasp their import, one must triangulate them with Mark's narrative of Jesus's death and resurrection, on the one side, and with its development of literary and mythological motifs gesturing at these events' broader significance, on the other. That triangulation is the focus of this final chapter of my study.

Two theologically resonant verses in Mark address how Jesus saves people by dying. One makes little sense unless the reader keeps resurrection in view (10:45). The other figures Jesus's death as a single sacrifice for many people (14:24) and does not require resurrection for coherence.[2] In fact, it may make more sense if resurrection is ignored, for a sacrifice's efficaciousness necessarily relates in some measure to the sacrificer's permanent separation from the object of value devoted to the god through destruction.[3] That object's immediate restoration to the one who sacri-

---

1. See J. Christopher Edwards, *The Ransom Logion in Mark and Matthew: Its Reception and Its Significance for the Study of the Gospels*, WUNT 327 (Tübingen: Mohr Siebeck, 2012) for the tradition history of the christological statement of 10:45.

2. On 14:24 as imagining sacrifice, see Adela Yarbro Collins, "Finding Meaning in the Death of Jesus," *JR* 78 (1998): 175–96.

3. This is not the place for detailed discussion of sacrifice in the ancient Mediterranean religious imagination. However, the gift theory provides a useful conceptual model, as formulated by Edward Burnett Tylor in *Primitive Culture: Researches into the Development of Mythology, Philosophy, Religion, Language, Art, and Custom*, 4th ed. (London: Murray, 1920), 2:375–93 (originally published in 1871). The theory was later complicated by Henri Hubert and Marcel Mauss, *Sacrifice, Its Nature and Function*, trans. W. D. Halls (Chicago: University of Chicago Press, 1964); see also Mauss, *The Gift: Forms and Functions of Exchange in Archaic Societies*, trans. Ian Cunnison (London: Cohen & West, 1966); and, more recently (and distantly), F. S. Naiden, *Smoke Signals for the Gods: Ancient Greek Sacrifice from the Archaic through Roman Periods* (Oxford: Oxford University Press, 2013). The sacrifice must genuinely be given to the deity to be effective: it must be devoted through destruction, aesthetically arranged (e.g., Homer, *Od.* 3.437–438), and with the best parts of the meat left for the gods (e.g., *Od.* 3.455–463; or the use of Heb. *ḥēleb*, the suet offered to God [Lev. 3:3], as a term meaning "the best" [see Gen 45:18; Milgrom, *Leviticus 1–16*, 207]).

ficed it potentially undermines the sacrifice's logic and utility. From this interpretive angle, the possibility that Jesus immediately regains by resurrection the lifeblood he sheds on the cross to propitiate God's just wrath at many raises questions as to whether Jesus effectively sacrificed it at all or perhaps about whether God accepted the sacrifice he offered.[4] These questions become urgent given the possibility of divine condemnation for Peter and the other disciples. Their rapprochement with God's representative the Son of Man is plausible but far from assured as Mark draws to a close, especially Peter's. The problem may be not their exclusion from "the many" for whom Christ died, but rather that God, whose absence Jesus senses as he expires (15:34), will not accept his son's sacrifice on behalf of any. Jesus's resurrection would clinch God's rejection of his son's self-devotion through destruction, with the women's refusal to acknowledge it as good news furthering that bleak possibility. From one interpretive angle at least, the passion narrative of Mark's *commentarii* leaves the atoning efficacy of Jesus's death as open to interrogation as it does Jesus's restoration to life.

Later I will argue that Mark 14:24–25 complements rather than challenges a theological understanding of Jesus's death and resurrection as effectively redemptive. In this emerging interpretive context, 15:34 becomes something more than Jesus's final question about whether God wills his sacrificial death or about God's willingness or ability to rescue him from death's power. However, Mark 10:45 remains the more illuminating passage for understanding Mark's redemption theology. This verse's conceptualization of Jesus's death as λύτρον ἀντὶ πολλῶν, "a ransom for many," lays the foundation for an interpretation of Jesus's crucifixion and resurrection that positions the passion narrative theologically as well as structurally at the climax of Mark's *commentarii* about Jesus.

"A Ransom for Many"

Mark 10:45's proper interpretive context has occasioned extensive debate. Some believe it presents Jesus's death as "an expiation or propitiation to God for offenses that 'the many' have committed," in the manner of sin offerings

---

4. As Naiden shows, it is possible for the deity to reject the sacrifice (*Smoke Signals*, 131–82). Indeed, discrete features of Mark's narrative point to this possibility; e.g., compare Mark 15:33 and texts discussed at *Smoke Signals*, 139.

from Lev 4.[5] Often scholars assimilate Jesus's words to the depiction of the Isaianic servant (Isa 53:10-12), or infer a connection between Jesus and the Maccabean martyrs whose deaths atone for Israel's sins.[6] Others, in contrast, view it as a ransom payment to Death, Satan, or analogous hypostasized evils.[7] From a rigorously monotheistic perspective, the possibilities interrelate, since God created death and Satan to administer his justice.[8] Satan tests people to determine their righteousness, at God's direction (e.g., Job 1-2). Death represents the divinely appointed outcome of the Bible's paradigmatic example of Satan's uncovering of human sin, namely, the serpent's temptation of Adam and Eve in the garden (Gen 2-3), as popularly interpreted in Hellenistic Judaism. Granting this complicating theological stipulation, within the context of Mark's narrative, understanding 10:45 as referring to a ransom payment to Satan, Death, or some other evil power proves more sensible than does understanding it with reference to divine wrath's assuagement, or to a vicarious satisfaction of God's requirement of justice.[9]

---

5. Adela Yarbro Collins, "Mark's Interpretation of the Death of Jesus," *JBL* 128 (2009): 548.

6. For examples of the former, see R. T. France, "The Servant of the Lord in the Teaching of Jesus," *TynBul* 19 (1968): 26-52; Rikki E. Watts, "Jesus's Death, Isaiah 53, and Mark 10:45: A Crux Revisited," in *Jesus and the Suffering Servant: Isaiah 53 and Christian Origins*, ed. W. H. Bellinger and William Reuben Farmer (Harrisburg, PA: Trinity Press International, 1998), 125-51. For an example of the later, see C. K. Barrett, "The Background of Mark 10:45," in *New Testament Essays: Studies in Memory of Thomas Walter Manson, 1893-1958*, ed. A. J. B. Higgins (Manchester: Manchester University Press, 1959), 1-18, esp. 11-15. Barrett tendentiously translates 4 Macc 6:29 to assimilate it to Mark 10:45 ("Background of Mark 10:45," 12). Moreover, the *comparanda* specify that the martyrs' deaths are aimed at satisfying God (e.g., 4 Macc 17:22), while in the Markan context, Jesus dying as a "ransom for many" more obviously suggests a satisfaction of Satan or demonic forces, as argued below.

7. Anton Fridrichsen, "The Conflict of Jesus with the Unclean Spirits," in *Exegetical Writings: A Selection*, trans. Chrys C. Caragounis and Tord Fornberg, WUNT 76 (Tübingen: Mohr Siebeck, 1994), 71-83; cf. Frederick W. Danker, "The Demonic Secret in Mark: A Reexamination of the Cry of Dereliction (15:34)," *ZNW* 61 (1970): 48-69, though without detailed discussion of 10:45.

8. Gustaf Aulén, *Christus Victor: An Historical Study of the Three Main Types of the Idea of Atonement*, trans. A. G. Hebert (New York: MacMillan, 1956), e.g., 59.

9. See Sharyn Dowd and Elizabeth Struthers Malbon, "The Significance of Jesus's Death in Mark: Narrative Context and Authorial Audience," *JBL* 125 (2006): 271-97, esp. 279-85. Collins's rebuttal fails to persuade, although she rightly resists their apparent refusal of this understanding of Jesus's death anywhere in Mark, including at the Last Supper ("Mark's Interpretation," esp. 545-50).

Interpreters who understand God as one subject of the exchange 10:45 announces sometimes privilege a quasi-technical definition of λύτρον, inferred from the word's use in various LXX passages, instead of construing the term with primary reference to its Markan context. While a purported allusion to Isa 53 (with which Mark 10:45, however, shares almost no language in common) bolsters the decision to read the ransom logion with more careful attention to its possible Old Testament background than to the surrounding narrative, this interpretive approach still features a basic problem. In the Markan pericope within which it appears, *ransom* picks up on the language of hostile dominance and enforced submission from the description of gentile rulers just a few verses earlier (10:42). Against this characterization (or caricature) of Roman imperial rule, Jesus contrasts voluntary submission and servitude leading to eschatological prominence and ultimately to the many's liberation from oppressive masters. The Son of Man giving his life as a "ransom for many" emblematizes this service and effects this deliverance (10:43–45).[10]

Mark's Jesus distinguishes voluntary servitude from coercive political power. While rulers in gentile (i.e., Roman) realms of authority depend on structures of domination to preserve their prominence (10:42), leaders in God's realm achieve prominence by submitting to others as slaves and serving with the aim of achieving others' freedom (10:45).[11] The Markan Son of Man epitomizes this strategy of advancement by offering his life as a ransom payment in return for the liberation of many people enslaved to captors, all the while trusting in God to free him from death (see 10:34). He identifies with the servile humiliation of many and, in serving them himself, purchases their freedom with his life.[12] The divergent concep-

---

10. See Myers, *Binding the Strong Man*, 279; Dowd and Malbon, "Significance of Jesus's Death," 281–82.

11. Mark here participates in a Greco-Roman popular philosophical discourse that defines ideal kingship as benefitting one's subjects, even at great personal expense (up to the ruler's life). See Seeley, "Rulership and Service" and Thiessen, "Many for One." This discourse was employed to praise and blame rulers in the classical and Hellenistic worlds, and Mark may polemically subvert a strand of it popular in imperial Rome that conceived of the ruler as so beneficial that his subjects would be willing to die for him (Thiessen, "Many for One," 456–63).

12. See Hooker, who interprets 10:45 in the context of Jesus's liberating ministry (*Son of Man in Mark*, 144–45). Hooker argues that "God's acts of deliverance … both at the Exodus and at the long-awaited Return from Exile" inform the verse, and she offers biblical references where the same Greek terminology appears (of the exodus,

tions of authority and power thematized in 10:41–45 come into conflict in Mark's passion narrative. That section features figures of gentile authority (Pontius Pilate and the centurion) exercising dominance coercively, by ordering and overseeing Jesus's unjust execution, and the figure of divine authority (the Son of Man) submitting to death at their hands in expectation of God's resurrection. Jesus does this on behalf of many—in particular, his community of disciples, who all flee to preserve their own lives and freedom while Jesus alone confronts the authorities who crucify him (cf. 14:23–27).

Against the rhetorical and ideological background of the Markan episode it caps, 10:45 can only with difficulty be interpreted to characterize God as a despotic slaveholder, the ultimate enforcer of the oppressive social order Jesus critiques in 10:42–45, who demands a life in return for releasing his captives.[13] This, however, is the implication of readings holding that the Son of Man gives his life as a payment to God in exchange for God's release of those he holds in bondage or coercive obligation. Beyond that, gentile rulers administer the structures of domination and enslavement that ultimately require the Son of Man's life in exchange for captives' freedom (10:42), and gentile rulers actively torture and kill the Son (see 10:33–34). The implication that God is behind this hostile violence, while not impossible to maintain,[14] remains problematic insofar as the passion narrative itself opposes these gentile authorities to God's representative Jesus, whose actions model the proper exercise of authority in God's kingdom, according to 10:42–45. It becomes more awkward still since the Bible's central narrative is an account of God liberating his people from enslavement to gentile rulers (namely, the Egyptian pharaoh in Exodus), which Mark echoes in passages that develop the redemption theme.

If one is to infer a spiritual dimension of 10:45's ransom logion, then demonic authorities more likely constitute the unidentified party receiving

---

see Exod 6:6; Deut 7:8; 9:26; Isa 43:1; Mic 6:4; of return from exile, see Isa 52:3; 62:12; Jer 15:21; 31:11; Mic 4:10).

13. Another reason for this view's difficulty is that traditional Hellenistic discourse about kingship often idealizes the ruler as benefitting his subjects by analogizing him to the kind and beneficent Zeus (Seeley, "Rulership and Service," 236, 243–44). The idea of God as a coercive slaveholder does not fit within the discursive tradition in which Mark participates.

14. Compare Hab 1 on God's use of Babylon to punish Judah by bringing its people into captivity.

the Son's life as a ransom. These are frequently associated with gentile or pagan gods in ancient Jesus-believing literature, and are also understood to lie behind the foreign nations and rulers dominating Judea (see 1 Cor 10:20-22; Justin, *1 Apol.* 5, 64; Rev 12:1-14:13; 17; and passim). In this more-or-less dualistic model of atonement, the Son gives himself over not to God but to these demonic forces when he submits to the related gentile authorities' decision regarding his life (10:33). God subsequently intervenes to free the Son from their power by raising him from the dead, as 10:34 anticipates. Thus, God is the one who liberates the Son from his voluntary servitude to hostile spiritual powers by overturning their destruction of him; God is not the one who receives the Son's life as a ransom payment prompting his release of others from slavery.

The possible implication in 10:45 that Jesus's death frees many from enslavement to foreign and demonic powers, perhaps including Death itself as an hypostasized enemy (see 1 Cor 15:26),[15] becomes even more compelling when the verse is interpreted within the broader context of Jesus's ministry, which it culminates. The episode within which the ransom logion surfaces begins with a statement that Jesus and his disciples start journeying toward Jerusalem for his passion (10:32-34), with two pericopes intervening before Jesus's entry into the city where he will die at the beginning of chapter 11. Those episodes (Mark 10:46-11:10) occur as Jesus approaches Jerusalem from its proximate northeast, where Jericho, Bethphage, and Bethany were located.[16] The Second Evangelist thereby

---

15. On Death as a personification, see also 1 Cor 15:54-55. For Paul's personification of Sin and Death in Rom 5-7, see Joseph R. Dodson, *The "Powers" of Personification: Rhetorical Purpose in the Book of Wisdom and the Letter to the Romans*, BZNW 161 (Berlin: de Gruyter, 2008), 119-39. Whether Paul conceived of them as personal demonic powers remains debated, but he at least presented them as such for rhetorical effect. For a statement of the problem, see Bultmann, *Theology of the New Testament*, 1:244-45.

16. Mark 10:1 indicates that Jesus begins his journey southward from Galilee at that point (see Collins, *Mark*, 457 n. a). As observed in the study of Markan geography by Willi Marxsen: "Chapter 10 is then in the nature of a transition, as vss. 46ff. also indicate." See Marxsen, *Mark the Evangelist: Studies on the Redaction History of the Gospel*, trans. James Boyce et al. (Nashville: Abingdon, 1969), 75. I view Mark 10:32-45 as the transition's pivot point: it first identifies Jerusalem—the destination of the journey (10:32) on which Jesus and his followers have already embarked (10:1) but will only later complete (11:11)—as the site of Jesus's death and resurrection (10:33-34, 45).

marks the pericope comprising 10:32–45 as the end of Jesus's ministry in Galilee, well north of Jerusalem, where he has for the most part been since his baptism. It initiates his journey to Jerusalem, which Jesus approaches in the subsequent episodes, arriving in 11:11.

This ministry in Galilee prominently features Jesus's confrontations with Satan and other demons. Just after his baptism, Jesus experiences testing at Satan's hands in the wilderness (1:12–13). When he surfaces in Galilee to begin his ministry, his first miracle is an exorcism (1:23–28). Demonic confrontations continue throughout, both explicit (1:32–34; 3:11–12, 15; 5:1–20; 6:7–13; 7:24–30; 8:32–33; 9:14–29, 38–41) and implicit (e.g., 4:35–41).[17] The most dramatic of these links the demons Jesus vanquishes to the Roman authorities who later destroy him (the story of Legion, in ch. 5). Jesus's exorcistic prowess in Galilee soon raises questions among Jerusalem leaders regarding his authority (see 3:22), which prompts him to interpret his exorcisms as the violent liberation of people from Satan's custody (3:22–30). Jesus speaks of himself "in parables" (3:23) as a robber who ties up the "strong man" before stealing his property (3:27), which is to say, as an exorcist who frees people from Satan's dominion by overpowering the demons who have possessed them.[18]

The transition Mark effects at the end of chapter 10 is not only geographical (from Galilee to Jerusalem) and stylistic (from episodic to more sustained narration); it is also theological, highlighting Jesus's evolving liberative tactics. When he speaks of the Son of Man giving his life as a ransom for many, Jesus envisions a strategic transition corresponding to the end of his exorcistic ministry in Galilee and his return to the environs of Jerusalem, where he will again confront Satan (see 1:12–13)—this time in the guise of the Roman authorities working in tandem with his domestic enemies in the city, who have already challenged his opposition to Satan (3:22). Jesus's goal remains the same as in Galilee, namely, to free people from demonic power (see 3:27). The difference is that now he will achieve the liberation of many at once, by paying the ransom of his life to their demonic captors (10:45), rather than by violently defeating individual demons or groups of them that enslave one hapless person or another, as he has been doing throughout his ministry.

---

17. For Jesus's calming of the storm as an exorcism, see Collins, *Mark*, 261.

18. Busch, "Questioning and Conviction," 484–85. On the theological implications of 3:27, see Fridrichsen, "Conflict of Jesus," 127.

In what follows, I develop this understanding of Jesus's redemptive death by exploring intratextual links between Mark's depiction of Jesus's crucifixion and resurrection and Jesus's exorcisms, especially that of Legion, which is echoed in the passion narrative's account of Jesus's dying cry. I then situate Mark's story of Jesus's confrontation with satanic powers in a Greco-Roman literary-mythological context. Finally, I show that the interpretation of Jesus's death and resurrection that emerges may be illuminated by, and itself shed light on, later ancient Christian writings that elaborate a related mythological understanding of Jesus's redemptive work. Mark, I argue, stands in closer continuity with these writings than normally imagined, in terms of both theology and intertextual strategy.

The Centurion and Legion: Mark 15:39 and 5:1–20

The interpretive insight that Jesus through his passion and resurrection continues his exorcistic activity by other means finds confirmation in links between Mark 15:33–16:8 and Mark's account of Jesus's most impressive exorcism, that of Legion in 5:1–20. The moniker of the demonic horde Jesus destroys bears similarities to that of the Roman soldier overseeing Jesus's death in Mark 15. The evangelist identifies both with Latin loanwords referring to units in the Roman army (λεγιών, 5:9, 15; κεντυρίων, 15:39, 44–45). *Centurio* designates an officer in charge of a *centuria*, traditionally a grouping of one hundred soldiers, and *legio* designates an even larger military grouping. In Mark 5, the demons' name imaginatively assimilates the satanic forces opposing God and his kingdom through the occupation of their victim to Rome's military and political occupation of the Levant.[19] Mark's presentation of the centurion administering Jesus's execution amounts to an analogous act of imaginative assimilation—this time moving in the other direction, from Roman military forces to Satan and his demons.

During his ministry in Galilee and the Decapolis, only demons hostile to Jesus publicly announce his divine heritage, and they do so against Jesus's will (see 3:11–12; 5:7; see also 1:24–25, 34). During his interrogation and execution in Jerusalem, the high priest and the centurion publicly refer to Jesus as God's "son" (14:61; 15:39). Exceptions prove the rule that only Jesus's enemies openly proclaim his divine identity in Mark, for on the rare occasions when God's voice refers to Jesus as his son (1:11; 9:7),

---

19. For further discussion and engagement with scholarship, see ch. 1, esp. n. 36.

context always stresses privacy—if not secrecy—and only Jesus himself or at most his closest followers hear God's words.[20] Frederick Danker infers from Mark's assimilation of the high priest's public declaration to demons' earlier confessions that this priest and the Sanhedrin he represents are "in league" not merely with Rome but "with demonic forces" when they go on to recommend Jesus's execution to Pilate (14:63–64; 15:1).[21] By implication, the same would hold for the Roman authorities to whom Mark's Jesus is given over for execution—especially the centurion who, upon seeing Jesus die, issues a proclamation similar to the high priest's in 14:61 and to those of demons earlier: "truly this man was son of God" (ἀληθῶς οὗτος ὁ ἄνθρωπος υἱὸς θεοῦ ἦν, 15:39).[22] Jesus's enemies in Jerusalem make what amount to public demonic announcements as they destroy him.

Scholars often interpret the centurion's "confession" positively, linking it to the divine declarations of Jesus's sonship in 1:11 and 9:7 as a proto-Christian confession bearing witness to Jesus's redemptive death.[23] However, given the centurion's association with Legion, the words of the Roman officer as he oversees Jesus's execution more meaningfully recall the possessed man's declaration in 5:7: "what do I have to do with you,

---

20. See, e.g., Edward P. Dixon, "Descending Spirit and Descending Gods: A 'Greek' Interpretation of the Spirit's 'Descent as a Dove' in Mark 1:10," *JBL* 128 (2009): 776–77. Matthew's editorial alterations retrospectively clarify the private nature of the Markan Jesus's visionary experience upon baptism by pushing it into the public sphere (compare Matt 3:17 and Mark 1:11).

21. Danker, "Demonic Secret," 62. Marcus agrees (*Mark 8–16*, 1016).

22. As Danker apparently fails to recognize, leading him to identify Jesus rather than the centurion with the demon ("Demonic Secret," 67–69).

23. Much commentary on 15:39 assimilates it to the tradition represented by its Matthean and Lukan revisions, which alter Mark to make the centurion's confession benign—with Luke removing its demonic resonances (see 23:47) and Matthew recontextualizing it. Gundry, for example, draws on Howard M. Jackson to argue that the centurion's declaration is predicated on his observation that "the wind of the Spirit, exhaled when in his last breath Jesus let loose a loud shout, rent that veil [of the temple] in two." See Gundry, *Mark*, 950; Jackson, "The Death of Jesus in Mark and the Miracle from the Cross," *NTS* 33 (1987): 16–37, esp. 28. However, while Matthew specifies that the centurion and those with him ἰδόντες τὸν σεισμὸν καὶ τὰ γενόμενα ἐφοβήθησαν σφόδρα immediately before declaring Jesus "son of God" (27:54), Mark's centurion faces Jesus (παρεστηκὼς ἐξ ἐναντίας αὐτοῦ) and sees only how he dies (ἰδὼν ... ὅτι οὕτως ἐξέπνευσεν, 15:39). He has no visual access to the rending of the temple curtain in 15:38, undermining the interpretation's relevance to Mark. (Gundry seems to recognize this problem later; cf. *Mark*, 970.)

Jesus son of the most high God [υἱὲ τοῦ θεοῦ τοῦ ὑψίστου]?" It is not merely that each verse uses the relatively rare (in Mark) moniker "son of God" for Jesus. More specifically, as Whitney Shiner observes, "Every time that such phrases appear as predicate nominatives, Mark uses the article (1.11; 3.11; 9.7; 14.61).... In contrast, there are only two [other] times when the article is omitted before υἱός used as a title. In both these cases υἱός appears as an appositive to the name Jesus ... (1.1; 5.7)."[24] Though Shiner fails to acknowledge it, υἱὸς θεοῦ in 1:1 is textually suspect, leaving the distinctive moniker "son of God" to appear without an article indubitably at Mark 15:39 and 5:7 alone.[25] This grammatical anomaly, which might imply that Jesus is "a son of God" rather than "the Son of God" (in some sense divine, like angels and unclean spirits, but not God's unique representative), increases the likelihood of the centurion's declaration in 15:39 recalling Legion's panicked exclamation in 5:7.[26]

The likelihood further increases when one recognizes that this centurion, upon Jesus's death, cooperates with Pilate and Joseph of Arimathea to entomb the son of God in a cave (15:42–46), much as Legion keeps its victim chained among tombs. Scholars habitually assimilate the Markan Jesus's burial to other evangelists' treatment of the same material as an

---

24. Whitney T. Shiner, "The Ambiguous Pronouncement of the Centurion and the Shrouding of Meaning in Mark," *JSNT* 22 (2000): 6.

25. Collins and Marcus both omit υἱὸς θεοῦ in 1:1 (Collins, *Mark*, 130 n. a; Marcus, *Mark 1–8*, 141). NA[28] brackets it. Tae Hun Kim excludes Mark 5:7 from consideration because the phrase is vocative and thus has no article. See Kim, "The Anarthrous Υἱὸς Θεοῦ in Mark 15,39 and the Roman Imperial Cult," *Bib* 79 (1998): 224 n. 11. However, Mark's decision to place the entire phrase in the vocative (Ἰησοῦ υἱὲ τοῦ θεοῦ τοῦ ὑψίστου), instead of shifting υἱὲ to the nominative with article (cf. Rev 11:17, 16:7), is potentially significant, especially considering what the anarthrous phrase "son of God" could imply. Moreover, Mark virtually marks the phrase as anarthrous by omitting the particle ὦ, which can take the place of the definite article for vocatives and is expected in the sort of adjuration the demons make in this verse. See Georg B. Winer, *A Treatise on the Grammar of New Testament Greek: Regarded as a Sure Basis for New Testament Exegesis*, trans. William F. Moulton, 9th ed. (Edinburgh: T&T Clark, 1892), 228–29.

26. Michael Peppard observes the connection, reading Mark's placement of "Son of God" in the centurion's mouth, with its Roman imperial ideological overtones, as an example of "colonial mimicry. Roman power, concentrated in the figure of its military, is at once both the challenge to and the legitimation of Jesus's divine sonship." See Peppard, *The Son of God in the Roman World: Divine Sonship in Its Social and Political Context* (Oxford: Oxford University Press, 2011), 130–31.

act of Joseph's generosity (see Matt 27:57–60). Yet in Mark, Jesus's interment instead constitutes the final stage of his unjust destruction at the hands of hostile enemies. His tomb is his corpse's prison, not his body's resting place.

Mark identifies Joseph, who prompts Jesus's burial, as a "respected member of the council" (15:43) that conspired to condemn him (see 14:55) and that unanimously recommended that Pilate execute him (πάντες κατέκριναν αὐτὸν ἔνοχον εἶναι θανάτου, 14:64; cf. 15:1). Joseph confirms this association when he works with the Roman authorities, including the centurion, to bury Jesus after killing him. Mark says nothing about Joseph that obviates his connection with the council that turned Jesus over to the Romans for crucifixion. Therefore, the other gospels must first remediate the reproachful association before establishing a sympathetic interpretation of Joseph's participation in Jesus's burial. Matthew (27:57) and John (19:38) declare Joseph to have been a disciple of Jesus (closeted, in John's account). Luke more modestly affirms that though he belonged to the council, Joseph was "good and just ... and had not assented to their decision and deeds" (Luke 23:50–51).[27] Mark has none of this, nor does its brief note that Joseph "was awaiting the kingdom of God" mitigate his responsibility for participation in Jesus's unjust execution (Mark 15:43). It rather underscores the hypocritical piety his concern about the disposal of Jesus's corpse displays.

Mark connects Joseph's request of Jesus's corpse from Pilate and the centurion to the Sabbath's approach (15:42–43). Joseph is so concerned about God's judgment (see 15:43) that he cannot countenance the polluting exposure of Jesus's crucified corpse for more than a single day—let alone a Sabbath!—evidently because he fears that God will condemn Israel for thereby defiling the land.[28] Yet Joseph has just participated in the trial of an innocent man that relied on demonstrably false testimony (14:57–60), and then supported Jesus's execution on the basis of the high priest's dubious and hysterical accusation of blasphemy (14:61–64). It is hard to envisage a more apt example, to paraphrase Jesus's earlier words, of setting

---

27. Brown, *Death of the Messiah*, 2:1213–16. Luke agrees with Mark that Joseph was not a disciple and acknowledges that Jesus was buried by enemies (Acts 13:27–29). Its more complex treatment develops subtle Markan cues (e.g., Joseph's boldness in approaching Pilate) to present him as a less than wholehearted enemy.

28. On Joseph's probable motivation, see Brown, *Death of the Messiah*, 2:1216. It may have been based on Deut 21:22–23.

aside God's commandments for the sake of establishing pious-seeming human traditions (7:8–9). Indeed, one can imagine Jesus using the scenario of a leader ordering an unjust execution and then making sure the defiling corpse is not left too long exposed as an example of the "many similar things" (7:13) that religious authorities "from Jerusalem" (see 7:1) hypocritically teach and do.

Mark characterizes the high priest, the only other individuated member of the Sanhedrin, as similarly implicated in hypocritical piety. As he leverages false testimony to pressure Jesus into a statement he preemptively declares blasphemous (14:55–64), the high priest tears his clothes (14:63). This could amount to "an extravagant display of mourning," as E. P. Sanders sees it,[29] but Leviticus, the biblical book on whose statutes the priest relies in calling for Jesus's death on a blasphemy charge (Lev 24:10–16, 23), forbids the act to the high priest (at 21:10). Mark's depiction of the priest has little claim to historical accuracy. Sanders more plausibly reconstructs his motivations and involvement in Jesus's execution with reference to John 11:50.[30] The point I make is literary rather than historical, touching on Mark's characterization of the Sanhedrin's activities. The Second Gospel represents everything the Jerusalem council does as demonstrating the same diabolical hypocrisy with which Jesus had previously charged its constituents (scribes from Jerusalem; Mark 3:22–30; 7:1–13). While the other New Testament evangelists alter Mark to differentiate Joseph from the Sanhedrin, Mark assimilates him to the hypocritical high priest and closely associates him with the council that unanimously recommended Jesus's unjust execution. When Joseph continues to collaborate with the Romans in disposing of Jesus's corpse, he maintains his status as a representative of that council and perpetuates its hypocrisy.

The cooperation of Joseph, Pilate, and the centurion in entombing Jesus links them all back to Legion, the demonic horde whose possession of the Gerasene man resulted in his imprisonment among rock-hewn tombs (5:3–4), the gospels' presumed mode of interment (see Mark

---

29. E. P. Sanders, *The Historical Figure of Jesus* (London: Penguin, 1993), 272.

30. "He did not act because of theological disagreement, but because of his principal moral and political responsibility: to preserve the peace and to prevent riot and bloodshed" potentially caused by "trouble-makers" like Jesus, "especially during festivals" such as the Passover (Sanders, *Historical Figure of Jesus*, 273, 269). During such times the city was full and "Roman troops would put down [riots] with great loss of life" (Sanders, *Historical Figure of Jesus*, 272).

15:46; Matt 23:28-29; 27:51-53; John 11:38).[31] When Jesus drew the possessed man out of those tombs (Mark 5:6), in the process destroying the unclean spirits controlling him (5:7-13), he attributed the man's salvation to God (5:19). Similarly, God will not leave Jesus entombed among the dead under the power of the demonic enemies to whom he gave his life as "a ransom for many" (10:45). The empty tomb in Mark implies that God quickly saves Jesus from death, just as Jesus predicted (8:31; 9:31; 10:34; 14:28). This connection between the two sepulchral liberations evinces a tactical advance on the part of Jesus the exorcist in Mark. Earlier he destroyed many demons to free one life (λεγιὼν ὄνομά μοι, ὅτι πολλοί ἐσμεν, 5:9); now he offers his own life under the centurion's watch to achieve the freedom of many from demons' power (δοῦναι τὴν ψυχὴν αὐτοῦ λύτρον ἀντὶ πολλῶν, 10:45).

Against the interpretive backdrop these intratextual connections offer, a multifaceted interpretation of Jesus's final moments in Mark comes into view. Upon observing Jesus die, the demonic powers to whom he gives his life cry in giddy, even disbelieving victory over the divine representative who has so easily fallen into their hands: "Really? This was [one of] God's son[s]?!" (ἀληθῶς οὗτος ὁ ἄνθρωπος υἱὸς θεοῦ ἦν, 15:39).[32] The centurion, who speaks a version of Legion's declaration (see 5:7), has already been assimilated to the demonic horde by his Latin military title. The echo of 5:7 therefore functions ironically, reversing the terrified despair of that demonic horde. Complementing this ironic echo, Jesus's dying screams recall the horrified shrieks of Legion (and other demons; see 1:26; etc.) when Jesus expels them: Legion "cried with a great voice" (κράξας φωνῇ μεγάλῃ, 5:7). On the cross, "Jesus called out with a great voice" (ἐβόησεν ... φωνῇ μεγάλῃ, 15:34), and "letting loose a great voice [ἀφεὶς φωνὴν μεγάλην], Jesus breathed his last" (15:37).

The centurion's participation with the Sanhedrin and Pilate in entombing Jesus in a cave recalls with similar irony Legion's entombment of the Gerasene man. Jesus liberates the man from a living death overseen by Legion in chapter 5. In chapter 16, Jesus himself requires liberation from the death and interment the centurion has overseen. Jesus's cry of dereliction in 15:34 suggests that as he dies, he no longer remains confident

---

31. For discussion of contemporary burial practices, see Rachel Hachili, *Jewish Funerary Customs, Practices and Rites in the Second Temple Period*, JSJSup 94 (Leiden: Brill, 2005).

32. Cf. Juel, *Master of Surprise*, 74 n. 7.

that God will rescue him. Comparison with another exorcism/resurrection from earlier in Mark clarifies that implication: just as the father of the child possessed by a deadly demon struggled to trust God for salvation issuing in resurrection (Mark 9:21–27), so Jesus struggles on the cross to trust God will defeat the demons and death claiming him. Like the earlier episode's father, Jesus does not seem able to overcome his doubt regarding whether God will save his Son.

Admittedly, this interpretive framework for understanding Jesus's death and burial remains implicit. The crucial role demons play in Mark's passion narrative emerges only through a careful reading of the *commentarii* in the light of the theologically capacious claim in Mark 10:45 regarding Jesus's death as a ransom, and in dialogue with Mark 5. However, comparing the Second Gospel's treatment of Jesus's execution and interment to its analogous treatment of Jesus's resurrection confirms the interpretation's plausibility. As Mark neglects to represent or guarantee God's salvation of Jesus from death, so it offers no assurance of that death's emancipatory efficacy. Mark neither represents the ransom payment's reception by demonic Death nor signals the liberation of many from it. Accordingly, Matthew revises and finalizes Mark's *commentarii* on precisely those points, in addition to certifying Jesus's resurrection.

Matthew guarantees the liberating exchange that Mark's representation of Jesus's crucifixion and burial leaves implicit. At the moment Jesus dies, "the tombs were opened and many bodies of sleeping holy people were raised" (Matt 27:52). Michael Licona has argued that this passage constitutes eschatological "'special effects'—a mythic notice meant to accentuate an event of cosmic, even divine significance."[33] His hermeneutical insight does not go far enough, for the passage not merely accentuates but depicts and explains in mythical terms the redemptive significance of Jesus's death. By representing "many [πολλὰ] bodies" being freed from death at the precise moment Jesus dies (27:52), Matthew establishes that Jesus has attained that for which he paid his life as a ransom "in exchange for many [πολλῶν]" (Matt 20:28). That these revivified persons remain in their tombs only to emerge once the angel rolls away the stone from Jesus's own (see 27:53) has a complementary theological explanation. At the

---

33. Danny Akin et al., "A Roundtable Discussion with Michael Licona on *The Resurrection of Jesus: A New Historiographical Approach*," *STR* 3 (2012): 74; see also Michael R. Licona, *The Resurrection of Jesus: A New Historiographical Approach* (Downers Grove, IL: InterVarsity, 2010), 548–53.

same time as Matthew mythologically narrativizes the ransom theology it derives from Mark, the First Gospel also affirms an emerging conception of Jesus as "the firstborn of the dead" (ὁ πρωτότοκος τῶν νεκρῶν, Rev 1:5; Col 1:18). Matthew insists that Jesus's resurrection is the prototype of the eschatological resurrection (see 1 Cor 15:23), perhaps in response to the possibility Mark's empty-tomb account neglects to obviate, namely, that Jesus was solitarily translated to heaven rather than resurrected in a communal, eschatological context.[34]

Mark's neglect to guarantee that Jesus by his own death redeems any from Death's power frees the Second Evangelist from having to negotiate the mythological-theological complications that confound readers of Matthew, as controversies surrounding Matt 27:52–53 testify. Perhaps such avoidance constitutes yet another reason Mark prefers open-ended implication over finalizing certification when treating Jesus's death and restoration to life. Still, it remains important that Mark's narrative at least implies that Jesus's death ransoms many human thralls from hostile spiritual powers and from Death's fearful reign. In what follows, I explain how Mark's innovative emphasis on Jesus's empty tomb (or, as the evangelist understands it, the grave cave from which Jesus escapes) elaborates a well-known mythical paradigm to press this possibility, even if not guarantee it.

Legion and Polyphemus: Mark 5:1–20; 16:1–8; and *Odyssey* 9

While one could read Mark against any number of Greco-Roman literary backdrops (for example, the Hellenistic novel), Homeric epic remains especially important in this regard because of its status as authoritative

---

34. W. D. Davies and Dale C. Allison view the reference to Jesus's resurrection in 27:53 as a scribal interpolation bringing Matthew's account into line with the view that Jesus was the "firstborn of the dead." See Davies and Allison, *A Critical and Exegetical Commentary on the Gospel according to Saint Matthew*, ICC (Edinburgh: T&T Clark, 1988), 3:634–35. See also Kenneth L. Waters, "Matthew 27:52–53 as Apocalyptic Apostrophe: Temporal-Spatial Collapse in the Gospel of Matthew," *JBL* 122 (2003): 489–515. Waters argues that the notice is an apocalyptic-eschatological prophecy awkwardly inserted for similar theological purposes. My interpretation complements these, though I would stress that Matthew imposes dogmatic order on Mark's open-ended *commentarii*. For Matthew, Mark here is unacceptably equivocal about both Jesus's resurrection and the redemptive efficacy of his death.

On the distinction between heavenly translation and collective eschatological resurrection, see Matthews, "Elijah, Ezekiel, and Romulus," 176–77.

scripture in the ancient Mediterranean world.³⁵ Since Mark is a competent Greek writer, it is all but impossible to deny his familiarity with Homer. Greek literacy was acquired through progressively advanced rhetorical engagements with Homeric epic, which represented the core of the informal Hellenistic curriculum, according to Teresa Morgan's study of literacy in the Hellenistic world.³⁶ It comes as no surprise, then, as Dennis MacDonald and others have argued, that Mark occasionally draws on and recasts Homeric epic in a manner consistent with ancient literary practices.³⁷ The expansive scope of MacDonald's work detracts from its persuasive power, but it plausibly shows that Mark on two separate occasions (the Legion episode from ch. 5 and the empty tomb from ch. 16) engages with the Cyclopeia (*Od.* 9), perhaps the most famous classical myth of a hero's battle with a monster.³⁸ MacDonald has further demonstrated that these

---

35. See Austin Busch, "Gnostic Biblical and Second Sophistic Homeric Interpretation," *ZAC* 22 (2018): 195–217, esp. 196–97 and the scholarship there discussed. For readings of Mark against the background of Hellenistic novels, see Tolbert, *Sowing the Gospel*; Fulmer, *Resurrection in Mark's Literary-Historical Perspective*.

36. Teresa Morgan, *Literate Education in the Hellenistic and Roman Worlds*, CCS (Cambridge: Cambridge University Press, 1998), 67–73 and passim. Plausible familiarity is one reason to question the relevancy of the Greco-Roman literary tradition of heavenly assumption to Mark's depiction of Jesus's resurrection (discussed in ch. 1). The understanding of heavenly translation those texts exemplify may have influenced Mark through a shared religious milieu, but the kind of detailed parallels Miller explores (for instance) seem to presume more direct intertextual engagement with literary traditions Mark is not likely to have known (see Miller, "Mark's Empty Tomb," 772–74).

37. In addition to the examples discussed below, see Dennis R. MacDonald, *The Homeric Epics and the Gospel of Mark* (New Haven: Yale University Press, 2000), 111–19. MacDonald persuasively compares the foot-washing from *Od.* 19 to Mark 14:1–9 (cf. Mark 13:33–37). This allusive parallel is elaborated in Austin Busch, "New Testament Narrative and Greco-Roman Literature," in *The Oxford Handbook of Biblical Narrative*, ed. Danna Nolan Fewell (New York: Oxford University Press, 2015), 68–70. Others have posited different connections between Mark and Homer, e.g., Dixon, "Descending Spirit," 765–77, on Mark 1:12.

38. See MacDonald, *Homeric Epics*, 67–76; Dennis R. MacDonald, *The Gospels and Homer: Imitations of Greek Epic in Mark and Luke-Acts* (Lanham, MD: Rowman & Littlefield, 2015), 198–204, 213–21. In a different version of the argument presented below, I have compared Mark's engagement with the Cyclopeia to a similar pattern of echoes from Philostratus's *Life of Apollonius*. See Austin Busch, "Scriptural Revision in Mark's Gospel and Philostratus's *Life of Apollonius*," in *Classical Greek Models of the Gospels and Acts: Studies in Mimesis Criticism*, ed. Mark G. Bilby, Michael Kochenash,

allusions were recognized by ancient readers of Mark.[39] Below I summarize some of the most significant parallels MacDonald observes, supplemented with insights and analysis of my own, in order to show how this intertextual matrix elaborates the explanation I have offered of Jesus's redemptive death and victorious resurrection. Jesus gives his life to liberate people held prisoner by demons and Death, and then is saved from their clutches when God raises him from the dead.

(1) In both *Od.* 9 and Mark 5, a sea voyage brings the hero and his companions to a monstrous savage (*Od.* 9.105–107; Mark 5:1), whose violent unsociability is figured both by his anthropophagy and his dwelling not in humane community but rather "in caves" (ἐν σπέσσι, *Od.* 9.114, 182, etc.; ἐν τοῖς μνήμασιν, Mark 5:2, 3, etc.). Mark's μνημεῖα are to be understood as caverns, as indicated by 15:46's reference to a "tomb hewn out of rock" (μνημεῖον λελατομημένον ἐκ πέτρας).[40]

(2) In both stories, the monstrous savage has herdsmen for neighbors who fail to help him and bear witness to their inability to challenge the heroic invader's disturbance of their territory.[41] The other Cyclopes, falling for Odysseus's ruse, conclude that Zeus must be responsible for Polyphemus's complaint and that there is nothing they can do for him (*Od.* 9.399–412).[42] The Gerasenes initially fail to assist their countrymen (Mark 5:3–4). Later, prompted by their swineherds, they meekly beg Jesus to depart after his liberation of the possessed man incidentally destroys their livestock (5:14–17).

(3) In both stories, the hero's defeat of the monster involves a treacherously ambiguous moment of naming.[43] Odysseus famously identifies

---

and Margaret Froelich, CSNTCO 3 (Claremont, CA: Claremont, 2018), 71–112. The pattern becomes even more significant insofar as Philostratus, like Mark, figures distinctively Roman enemies of his hero as the Odyssean Cyclops: the emperors Nero and Domitian (*Vit. Apoll.* 4.36; 7.28).

39. See n. 51.
40. MacDonald, *Homeric Epics*, 67–69; MacDonald, *Gospels and Homer*, 213–14.
41. MacDonald, *Homeric Epics*, 71; MacDonald, *Gospels and Homer*, 217.
42. If the Cyclopes imply that Polyphemus is going mad—a standard interpretation of νοῦσον ... Διὸς μεγάλου ἀλέασθαι (9.411)—then the parallel with Mark is stronger. See W. Walter Merry and James Riddell, eds., *Homer's Odyssey*, 2nd rev. ed. (Oxford: Clarendon, 1886), 1:387; cf. Sophocles, *Aj.* 186. Neither Polyphemus's fellow Cyclopes nor the Gerasenes can assist one whom they understand to be mentally deranged because of divine/demonic manipulation.
43. MacDonald, *Homeric Epics*, 69–70; MacDonald, *Gospels and Homer*, 216.

himself as Οὖτις, "Nobody" (9.366–367), thereby undermining Polyphemus's cry for help from his herdsman neighbors: ὦ φίλοι, Οὖτίς με κτείνει δόλῳ οὐδὲ βίηφιν (9.408). Homer's name play involves a grammatical anomaly. Although Polyphemus understands οὖτις as a proper name, he says not Οὖτίς με κτείνει δόλῳ καὶ βίηφιν, but rather δόλῳ οὐδὲ βίηφιν, with οὐδὲ picking up on οὖτις as the negative pronoun rather than a homonymic proper noun. To capture the effect in English, Polyphemus might say "nobody harms me by treachery nor by violence," instead of "Nobody harms me by treachery and violence," only the latter of which a reader would expect from a character understanding "Nobody" as a proper noun. The inconsistency makes plausible the neighboring Cyclopes' misunderstanding of Polyphemus's declaration and gives voice to this Cyclops's befuddlement. Regardless of what he means to say, since Polyphemus begins with οὖτις, his tongue carries him mindlessly through the sentence as if he meant to employ the word as an indefinite negative pronoun, instead of as the identically sounding name Odysseus has just given him.[44]

In Mark 5, the demons, presumably to evade the power Jesus would have over them were he to learn their names,[45] ambiguously respond to his inquiry about their identity with the moniker *Legion*: "my name is Legion, for we are many" (λεγιὼν ὄνομά μοι, ὅτι πολλοί ἐσμεν, 5:9). This deceptive self-identification also displays a grammatical irregularity, for the first-person singular pronoun μοι ("my") gives way to the first-person plural verb ἐσμεν ("we are"), creating a miniature anacoluthon. This grammatical irregularity too is most expeditiously interpreted as a product of the man's befuddlement—the confusion of identities in a person possessed by many spirits.[46]

(4) In both stories, the hero's defeat of the monster relies on a trick involving livestock that complements the deceptive naming. After Odysseus blinds him, Polyphemus blocks the entrance to the cave with his body.

---

44. Alternatively, see Merry and Riddell: "Polyphemus intended to signify, 'he is slaying me by craft, *and not* by violence'" (*Homer's Odyssey*, 1:387). Seth L. Schein adopts this interpretation. See Schein, "Odysseus and Polyphemus in the Odyssey," *GRBS* 11 (1970): 79–80. However, the idea that Polyphemus would deny Odysseus's use of force is difficult to square with the fact that he has just put out his eye.

45. Campbell Bonner, "The Technique of Exorcism," *HTR* 36 (1943): 44–45.

46. Gundry attempts to sort out this grammatical confusion, found in other Markan stories of possession as well (see 1:23–24; *Mark*, 261).

In the morning he must allow his sheep out to pasture and so inspects the exiting flock for human contraband by feeling their backs with his hands. Unbeknownst to him, Odysseus has tied his men to the sheep's bellies, so that they evade the monster's inspection and escape (*Od.* 9.413-463). Analogously, the Markan demons, in an attempt to avoid expulsion from the land, request entrance into a nearby herd of pigs that swineherds are watching (Mark 5:10-12).[47] Jesus grants their wish, but their plan of escape fails, for instead of sheltering the demons, the pigs immediately rush into the sea and drown (5:13).[48]

Attention to parallels (3) and (4) reveals a meaningful transposition. Mark's demons, in their futile attempt to avoid defeat at Jesus's hands, employ treacherous tactics like those Odysseus uses to defeat Polyphemus, which include identifying themselves with ambiguous names and hiding among livestock. Mark thus displaces deception from Jesus, its analogue to the Homeric hero, onto the story's monsters.[49] The evangelist at the same time ensures the deceit fails rather than succeeds. Though the demons avoid revealing their true identities to Jesus, that development will not thwart his power. And though they carry the day in their negotiation to enter the herd of swine, they nonetheless end up drowned along with the pigs. This initial interpretive inference requires complication, but from at least one angle, Mark cleanses the Homeric Cyclopeia of some of its dubi-

---

47. MacDonald observes this parallel, but he seems more interested in connecting Mark's swine with the Circe episode from *Od.* 10 than in understanding them with reference to the Cyclopeia (*Homeric Epics*, 70; *Gospels and Homer*, 216-17).

48. The sudden introduction of the pigs into the story has confounded readers since antiquity, as has as their destruction after Jesus allows the demons entrance into them. For instance, Nineham suggests that Jesus cleanses the gentile land of unclean beasts, as he does the man of unclean spirits (a detail amenable to the allegorical interpretation Robert H. Lightfoot proposes). See Nineham, *Saint Mark*, 154; Lightfoot, *History and Interpretation in the Gospels* (London: Hodder & Stoughton, 1935), 88-90. Marcus emphasizes the episode's martial connotations, likening the horde of demons to an invading army, in particular Pharaoh's, which was also drowned (*Mark 1-8*, 348, 352). See also J. Duncan M. Derrett, "Contributions to the Study of the Gerasene Demoniac," *JSNT* 2 (1979): 2-17; Rikki E. Watts, *Isaiah's New Exodus and Mark*, WUNT 88 (Tübingen: Mohr Siebeck, 1997), 159-60. Collins speculates that the story incorporates ancient traditions of illness transferred to animals (*Mark*, 270). However, it may be that Mark does not so much generate its own narrative logic in introducing the swine as adapt and revise interrelated Homeric motifs in a thematically strategic manner.

49. See MacDonald, *Homeric Epics*, 74.

ous heroic deception, much as Jesus purifies the gentile man of unclean spirits and the area of the Decapolis in which he dwells of impure animals.

However, amid this refinement, Mark's Jesus still reveals himself to be an Odyssean trickster. This becomes evident in Jesus's grant of the demons' request to enter the nearby swine so that they might remain in the land. He thereby ensures their destruction even as he plays at allowing them to stay in safety, for the pigs, presumably shocked and tormented by their sudden demonic possession, promptly kill themselves. Jesus may not actively deceive the demons, but he does facilitate their self-deception by allowing them to imagine they have negotiated with a "son of the most high God" (5:7) to limit the scope of the expulsion he commands. Demonic forces think they can take advantage of Jesus by negotiating another deal with him later in Mark, at which point Jesus again encourages their false belief that they have the upper hand.

(5) Both stories close on a similar note. Once the Cyclops is defeated and Odysseus is safe on his ship, Homer's hero proclaims his true identity, foolishly boasting so that the monster knows just who vanquished him (*Od.* 9.502–505) and thereby allowing Polyphemus to curse him (9.526–536). Analogously, just before embarking, Mark's Jesus eschews his penchant for secrecy and orders the man from whom he had driven the demons to tell his friends "how much the Lord has done for you" (Mark 5:19). The man "began to proclaim in the Decapolis how much *Jesus* did for him, and all were amazed" (5:20). Jesus deferentially refuses to grasp after glory in Mark, unlike Odysseus in Homer (with disastrous results), but he is identified and receives it nonetheless.[50] Once again, even as it establishes parallels between Jesus and Odysseus, Mark's adaptation of Homer reduces or redeems the more troubling traits the Homeric hero displays.

(6) Mark 5 relates to Mark 16, where the hero Jesus again confronts an evil entity associated with cavernous tombs and likened to Polyphemus. In chapter 5, the horde of demons orchestrates its victim's social destruction, ensuring his alienation by settling him among the caves of the dead. In Mark 16, death is literal, not figurative; its power, exercised through Joseph, Pilate, and especially the centurion, who are all involved in his death and burial, shuts Jesus's corpse within a grave cave. This is the problem the women coming to anoint Jesus's body acknowledge when

---

50. MacDonald, *Homeric Epics*, 72; MacDonald, *Gospels and Homer*, 218.

they ask, "Who will roll away for us the stone from the entrance of the tomb" (16:3). As MacDonald observes, it is the same problem Odysseus and his men face in *Od.* 9, when the monster traps them in a cave by rolling in front of it a great stone they are incapable of removing (*Od.* 9.240–243), before he begins to kill and eat them.[51] In the *Odyssey*, the hero and his men escape from the Cyclops's cave through a clearly delineated plot. In Mark, the removal of the stone and opening of Jesus's tomb constitute a mystery (16:4), but Jesus evidently is still liberated from the power of death. So perhaps are many of his followers (see 10:45), at least when one considers that earliest believers understood Jesus's resurrection as the firstfruits of God's general resurrection of the dead (1 Cor 15:23; see Matt 27:53).

To grasp the sense these interrelated Homeric echoes make in their Markan context, it will be useful to survey how Polyphemus tended to function in Greco-Roman writing. This anthropophagic savage was so well-known a terror in classical antiquity that he frequently became an object of burlesque. Euripides used the Odyssean episode as the basis of his satyr play *Cyclops*, and in the Hellenistic period Theocritus represented Polyphemus as the violently buffoonish suitor of the nymph Galatea (*Id.* 6, 11).[52] He is even mentioned in the Armenian *Names, Works and Deaths of the Holy Prophets*, an ancient Christian work that ends with a statement summarizing *Od.* 9.507–512: "T'ilemaw [i.e., Telemos], the Cyclops, the pagan son of Neptune, prophesied to Baelifemōi [i.e., Polyphemus] that Ulysses was destined to put out his eye" (17).[53] This reference—a strange

---

51. MacDonald, *Homeric Epics*, 74–76; MacDonald, *Gospels and Homer*, 200–204. MacDonald notes that a variant reading of Luke 23:53, a revision of the reference in Mark 15:46 to Jesus's cavernous tomb and the stone rolled in front of it, assimilates this stone to the one guarding Polyphemus's cave by describing it with the relative clause ὃν μόγις εἴκοσι ἐκύλιον (*Gospels and Homer*, 201–3; cf. Metzger, *Textual Commentary*, 156). The phrase echoes Homer's claim that οὐκ ἂν τόν γε δύω καὶ εἴκοσ' ἄμαξαι / ἐσθλαὶ τετράκυκλοι ἀπ' οὔδεος ὀχλίσσειαν (*Od.* 9.241–242). MacDonald also observes that recension 2 of the Byzantine Homeric *Centos* uses the same Homeric lines to describe the stone rolled in front of Jesus's tomb (1.2092–2094; *Gospels and Homer*, 203–4). Scribes recognized and amplified allusions to the Cyclopeia in the account of Jesus's empty tomb, which first appears in Mark's *commentarii*.

52. On the comic Polyphemus tradition, see Shirley Clay Scott, "Man, Mind, and Monster: Polyphemus from Homer through Joyce," *CML* 16 (1995): 29–42.

53. Michael E. Stone, ed., *Armenian Apocrypha Relating to the Patriarchs and Prophets* (Jerusalem: Israel Academy of Sciences and Humanities, 1982), 173. On the

concluding tag to an already-obscure text—serves to acknowledge that prophecy was not restricted to Israel but known among pagan nations as well,[54] though the mention of Polyphemus may have originated as a scribal jape.

Foundational to this parodic impulse is the ancient literary tradition that follows Homer in depicting Polyphemus as a ghastly figure. Virgil deploys him with eerie effectiveness at the end of *Aen.* 3, when Aeneas and his crew rescue Achaemenides, whom Odysseus had left behind on Sicily (the location of the events of *Od.* 9, in a popular ancient construal).[55] Virgil's description of Polyphemus's violence is gruesome—more disturbing than Homer's (compare *Od.* 9.288–293 and *Aen.* 3.621–627).[56] Moreover, Virgil figures Polyphemus and his companions not merely as monsters but as chthonic divinities. After departing from Sicily, Aeneas and his men hear Polyphemus's roar and turn back to see an unnerving "dreadful assembly" (*concilium horrendum*, *Aen.* 3.679) of Cyclopes having rushed to the beach, reaching with their heads to the sky like the tallest of trees, their lone eyes scowling (3.675–681). At this point, a "boundless cry" (*clamorem immensum*) bellows within Aetna's caves, shakes the waves of the sea, and is felt as far away as Italy (3.672–674). The poet thereby mythologizes seismic activity associated with the Sicilian volcano Etna by attributing it to bellowing Polyphemus and his chthonic cyclopean companions.[57]

In the context of the emulative relationship Virgil establishes between the Achaemenides episode of his *Aeneid* and the Homeric Cyclopeia,

---

"slightly confused" relationship of the statement to the passage from the *Odyssey*, see Howard Jacobson, "Polyphemus in an Armenian Apocryphal Work," *VT* 37 (1987): 490–91.

54. In both manuscripts preserving the text, a work on the Sibyls follows the final reference to Polyphemus, making a similar point (Stone, *Armenian Apocrypha*, 159).

55. Attempting to align the imagined Odyssean geography with actual places is a problem whose indissolubility readers since antiquity have recognized (see the statement of Eratosthenes quoted in Strabo, *Geogr.* 1.2.15). One prominent view, which Strabo traces to Polybius, located Odysseus's wanderings around Sicily (*Geogr.* 1.2.16).

56. As recognized by Justin Glenn, "Virgil's Polyphemus," *GR* 19 (1972): 58–59 (even as he attempts to do justice to the pathetic elements of the Virgilian depiction).

57. See Alwyn Scarth, "Volcanic Origins of the Polyphemus Story in the *Odyssey*: A Non-classicist's Interpretation," *CW* 83 (1989): 89–95. Scarth interprets the Homeric Cyclopeia as an allegorical representation of Mount Etna's volcanic activity. Possibly because they live in caves in Homer's early treatment, Cyclopes come to be associated with the chthonic world in Greco-Roman myth.

Aeneas's escape from Polyphemus with all his men, and a sailor Odysseus had abandoned to boot, signals the heroic superiority of Virgil's protagonist to Homer's. While Odysseus returns home to Ithaca alone, having left all his followers to die at the hands of monsters such as Polyphemus, Aeneas saves his people (and one of Odysseus's) from Polyphemus and other monsters worse than that, in the process leading many to their new home in Italy.

Mark's allusive integration of the Cyclopeia in the Legion episode displays elements of the humor associated with the tradition of literary burlesque surrounding Polyphemus. The demons' bizarre destruction via mass porcine suicide is grotesquely humorous. Mark may imply the spirits are so unclean that that even swine would rather be dead than possessed. Mark's treatment of the Homeric material also leverages the same emulative power as the *Aeneid*'s more horrid revision of the scene. The Odyssean echoes emphasize the heroic magnitude of Jesus's defeat of the demonic horde that had kept its mutilated victim chained and tortured among tombs. On the one hand, these parallels help explain the consequence of Jesus's final liberating endeavor, when he gives his own life to free others from the power of death. Jesus's liberation from the cavernous tomb in which his own body is trapped, like Odysseus within Polyphemus's cave, gestures at the liberation from death that he brings to many (Mark 10:45; see 1 Cor 15:20–23). On the other hand, by evoking the salvation Odysseus provides for too few of his followers (and, in the end, for none), Mark seizes for the hero Jesus the same kind of emulative advantage vis-à-vis Odysseus that Virgil seized for Aeneas.

Within the mythologically allusive matrix I have been exploring, Mark's figuration of Jesus's resurrection from the dead as release from a cavernous tomb has a complementary intertextual resonance. The Homeric Cyclopeia itself seems to invoke another famous myth from ancient Greek literature, first extant in Hesiod (*Theog.* 453–506) but known from other sources as well. According to it, Zeus's mother, Rhea, and Gaia save the god Zeus from his father, the cannibalistic Titan Cronos, who devours all of Zeus's siblings to secure his cosmic reign from potential rivals. Rhea and Gaia hide the infant Zeus away in a cave until he matures and then trick Cronos into mistaking a great stone for the young god. The Titan consumes and later vomits it, along with the other gods, in connection with Zeus's mature emergence from that cave. Zeus then defeats Cronos, liberates the other Olympians, and assumes monarchical authority in Cronos's place.

The well-known myth's parallels with the Cyclopeia are extensive; they have frequently been noted, and there is no need to elaborate them here.[58] The account known from Hesiod and elsewhere adds the theme of divine, paternal salvation to the mythical paradigm Mark adapts. Zeus's mother, Rhea, alongside Gaia, initially hides Zeus away, and both also play a role in bringing him out of the cave to defeat Cronos (see *Theog.* 493–496), although precisely how Gaia deceives the Titan to ensure that he "vomited up his offspring" (γόνον ἂψ ἀνέηκε, 495) remains unclear.[59]

Similar parallels obtain between Jesus and Odysseus as between Jesus and Zeus, who, like the Homeric hero, saves himself and his comrades from a cannibalistic enemy in conjunction with his emergence from a cavern. As Zeus's mother, Rhea, saves her son, so Mark's repeated prophecies that Jesus or the Son of Man will rise gesture at his father God's role in saving him (8:31; 9:9, 31; 10:34; 14:28). Moreover, just as Zeus emerges from his cave to defeat powerful Cronos and rule the gods, so too will the risen Son of Man ultimately rule at God's right hand, with all the heavenly powers trembling when he assumes that position of authority (13:24–26; see also 8:38–9:1). It therefore seems plausible that Mark was familiar not only with the Homeric episode but also with the Hesiodic one (or with myths lying behind it). The evangelist crafted Mark's conclusion so that these diverse literary-mythological resonances would mutually reverberate within the contours of its narrative, amplifying the theological timbres of its account of Jesus's death, burial, and finally resurrection.

Recognition of these allusive resonances helps to clarify the redemption myth latent in Mark's account of Jesus's ministry, death, and resurrection. Jesus's Galilee ministry begins in opposition to Satan (1:12–13) and involves Jesus's liberation of victims from monstrous demonic forces by means of discrete confrontations with them (see 3:27), including Jesus's dramatic defeat of Legion (5:1–20). At a certain point, Jesus

---

58. Justin Glenn, "The Polyphemus Myth: Its Origin and Interpretation," *GR* 25 (1978): 141–55; Pura Nieto Hernández, "Back in the Cave of the Cyclops," *AJP* 121 (2000): 345–66.

59. Citing and quoting Glenn W. Most, ed., *Hesiod: Theogony, Works and Days, Testimonia*, LCL (Cambridge: Harvard University Press, 2006). Other versions of the myth remove Gaia or replace her with Metis: Zeus emerges from the cave full-grown, and he and Metis give Cronus a drug that induces vomiting to save the consumed Olympians (see Apollodorus, *Library* 1.1–2). This recalls Odysseus serving alcohol to the Cyclops, which not only induces sleep but leads to his vomiting up bits of the hero's devoured comrades (*Od.* 9.371–374).

shifts tactics: his exorcisms end (the last reference to one comes at the end of ch. 9) just before he heads to Jerusalem (10:1, 32), where he will give himself as a ransom to these forces in return for the freedom of their many thralls (10:45). Upon arrival, he delivers himself by means of voluntary death to the demonic powers, represented by or perhaps possessing the Roman centurion who oversees his execution and plays a role in his entombment. After observing Jesus's death, this figure utters a shout of diabolical triumph that echoes and reverses the terror of Legion and the other demons when Jesus defeats them earlier in his ministry (15:39; cf. 5:7). The many whom Jesus's death ransoms would logically be freed at this point, though Mark will no more guarantee or explain this development than Jesus's resurrection. Matthew's revision of Mark's *commentarii*, however, offers a mythological finalization sensitive to the implications of Mark's open-ended gesture.

The authority the hostile powers acquire over Jesus under the auspices of death may explain why Jesus, just before he dies, declares that God has forsaken him (15:34). Jesus finds himself abandoned by God when he falls into the hands of the enemies of God's kingdom. The power they exercise over him reveals itself in the cooperation of the demonic centurion attending Jesus's execution with the Roman ruler Pilate and the Sanhedrin's Joseph of Arimathea, who conspire to trap Jesus's corpse in a cave (15:44–45), like Legion did his victim.

Mark's deployment of the motif of Jesus's empty tomb to signal his resurrection may have been an innovation arising from Mark's engagement with Homer. The other New Testament gospels clearly depend on Mark's *commentarii* at this point in the story. Moreover, Paul, though he mentions that Jesus was buried (1 Cor 15:4), says nothing about his tomb. He may merely have presumed burial on the basis of the general tradition that he elaborates in 1 Cor 15:3–7, namely, that Christ was crucified, rose on the third day, and then appeared to his followers. Since Jesus rose, Paul imagines, he must have been lying in a tomb somewhere. Some scholars have argued that the historical Jesus would have had no tomb at all; his body would have been left for prolonged exposure on the cross, the conventional fate of crucifixion victims in the Roman world.[60]

---

60. Bart D. Ehrman, *How Jesus Became God: The Exaltation of a Jewish Preacher from Galilee* (New York: HarperCollins, 2014), 151–69.

I will not wade very deep into debates about the historicity of Jesus's entombment here or argue that Mark invented from whole cloth the story of his burial by Joseph of Arimathea and his tomb found empty, though that is possible. Perhaps more likely, as proposed earlier, the empty-tomb tradition arose before Mark wrote as part of a rhetorical program supporting Jesus's heavenly apotheosis, with Mark later leveraging it for equivocal evidence of Jesus's resurrection in the *commentarii*. In any case, Mark's employment of it as a literary motif suggests that in dying Jesus has given his life as a ransom to chthonic demons, including Death itself, in exchange for their release of many from bondage. In the Homeric and Hesiodic mythological-literary traditions that influenced Mark, being trapped in a cave signifies captivity to monstrous beings who have the upper hand, or the temporary retreat of a god hiding from such beings' power. Against this background, when Mark depicts the giant stone mysteriously removed from the cave of death that entombs God's son Jesus, and the cave itself found empty, this symbolizes Jesus's escape from and victory over the monstrous demonic powers he has been battling throughout the gospel.[61]

Jesus's Deceptive Weakness

Several interpretive cruxes resolve themselves within the context of the Markan redemption myth that comes into relief when the Second Gospel's account of Jesus's death and resurrection is interpreted against the background of the Greco-Roman mythical-literary traditions discussed above. I have already analyzed Mark 10:45 (the ransom logion) and 15:39 (the centurion's confession). In what follows I complicate the brief comments offered about Jesus's cry of dereliction (15:34) in the previous chapter and then turn to Mark's account of the Last Supper (14:22–25).

Holly Carey's monograph on the relationship between Mark 15:34 and Ps 22 makes it no longer feasible to claim that Mark's quotation of Ps 22:1

---

61. The Cyclopeia's relevance to the story of Jesus's death, burial, and resurrection is even more plausible when one recognizes that in Homer, Odysseus's escape from Polyphemus's cave symbolizes the hero's rebirth. See George E. Dimock Jr., "The Name of Odysseus," in *Essays on the Odyssey: Select Modern Criticism*, ed. Charles H. Taylor Jr. (Bloomington: Indiana University Press, 1963), 59; Schein, "Odysseus and Polyphemus," 82–83; Hernández, "Back in the Cave," 352–53; cf. Rick M. Newton, "The Rebirth of Odysseus," *GRBS* 25 (2004): 5–20.

alludes only to that verse rather than to the entire psalm, which encompasses deliverance (see esp. 22:24) as well as the suffering the quoted line articulates.[62] Mark's allusive procedure frequently involves contextual citation, which one might define as referring to an entire literary passage by echoing a single resonant part of it—in the case of this psalm, its incipit, or first, titular line.[63] Beyond that, Carey's argument shows that Mark as a rule anticipates Jesus's vindication through resurrection whenever his death is prophesied.[64] Readers recognizing the incipit allusion to Ps 22 at Mark 15:34 may thus be driven to interpret that allusion contextually, searching the psalm for evidence of the expected salvation. The psalm obliges by describing the poetic voice's final deliverance (Ps 22:22–31).

The interpretation of Jesus's last words offered at the end of chapter 2 and elsewhere in this study therefore requires modification. Superficially construed, Mark 15:34's declaration that God has forsaken Jesus does amount to a repudiation of his expectation that God will save him from death. Jesus's reluctance to die in 14:36 already anticipates this disavowal. According to this reading, the young man's faithful confession of Jesus's resurrection at the empty tomb in chapter 16 constitutes a positive dialogic rejoinder not only to the disciples' faithless flight, and not only to Peter's denials and curse, but above all to Jesus's own final abandonment of faith that God would resurrect the Son of Man.

But recall that the young man's faithful confession finds its own dialogic response in the women's terrified refusal to reiterate the message he transmits. Like Mark's closing verses, Jesus's final declaration in 15:34 itself encompasses faithful trust (when interpreted as a comprehensive allusion to Ps 22) and faithless despair (when interpreted atomistically). It encapsulates the dialogue between those two prospects that animates Mark throughout, most clearly in the paradoxical formulation of Mark 9:24 ("I have faith; help my lack of faith") and most dramatically in Mark's closing depiction of the young man's faithful confession and the female disciples' failure to believe and repeat it. Mark's double report of Jesus's own last words—once in Aramaic and once in Greek—linguistically emblematizes this internal dialogization. Jesus's cry communicates not one but two ideas,

---

62. Holly J. Carey, *Jesus's Cry from the Cross: Towards a First-Century Understanding of the Intertextual Relationship between Psalm 22 and the Narrative of Mark's Gospel*, LNTS 398 (London: T&T Clark, 2009).

63. Carey, *Jesus's Cry from the Cross*, 70–93, 107–11.

64. Carey, *Jesus's Cry from the Cross*, 45–69.

which converse with each other, as it were. The evangelist poises Jesus, at the moment of his demise, on the threshold of faith and doubt, trust in and skepticism about God's willingness or ability to rescue him from death.

The complexity that Carey's reading of 15:34 makes visible complements the dialogic interpretation of resurrection proposed elsewhere in this study. However, her discussion largely neglects to consider an important aspect of the scene in which Jesus speaks his hermeneutically capacious last words. Mark transliterates what Jesus says in Aramaic in part to signal an alien intrusion inviting examination of his words in their original literary context, rather than their straightforward assimilation to immediate narrative circumstances. At the same time, though, the inserted foreign language clarifies how Jesus's words are (mis)understood by the Markan characters observing his crucifixion. Bystanders construe his cry of ελωι, ελωι (i.e., "My God, my God"; 15:34) as a cry for Elijah (ἴδε Ἠλίαν φωνεῖ, 15:35), whose name sounds similar. This prompts from them ignorant mockery: "Let's see if Elijah comes to lead him down!" (15:36).[65] Although Jesus's words themselves, insofar as they allude to Ps 22, encompass hope in God's deliverance as well as despondency at death, the bystanders' response brutally dismisses such hope as a ridiculous cry for help from an unsympathetic party, or one impotent to assist.[66] More subtly, given Mark's affirmation that the resurrection depends on Elijah's eschatological arrival (see Mark 9:9–13), these bystanders' mocking invocation of an absent Elijah implies the futility of any hope for resurrection that Jesus maintains.

The ambiguity of Jesus's final words collapses into the bystanders' gloating mockery of the eschatological Elijah's presence, which cynically insists on the finality of Jesus's impending death. Similar mockery has been going on since 14:65, where those present at the high priest's interrogation ridicule what they view as his pretentious claims to prophetic power, and it continues throughout the passion narrative, with various parties participating (15:16–20, 23, 29–32). Through all this, Jesus remains silent—apart from "so you say" at 15:2, in response to Pilate's question as to whether he is king of the Jews (probably itself posed in mocking contempt). Jesus's decision to speak again in 15:34 may thus be construed as a carefully measured announcement (after all, he recites the first line of a poem!) that

---

65. Brown, *Death of the Messiah*, 2:1061–63.
66. On the logic underlying their mockery, see Davies and Allison, *Gospel according to Saint Matthew*, 3:626.

provokes bystanders and executioners to continue their derision. This is precisely what happens in the subsequent verse, in response to Jesus's conveniently misunderstandable Aramaic, and climactically in 15:39, when the demonic centurion "seeing that in this way he breathed his last, said 'Really? This man was a son of God!?'"

Earlier in Mark demonic forces fear the power that Jesus exercises. That power, combined with Jesus's confidence that God would save him from death, may make them reluctant to take the bait his life represents in exchange for their captives' freedom. Once fearsome to the legion of demons that had trapped their host within tombs, "Jesus, son of God most high" (5:7) now allows himself to be reduced to a contemptable failure in the eyes of the infernal centurion overseeing his crucifixion. His guise of despairing weakness, which encourages his enemies to take the bait of his life (see 1 Cor 2:6–8) and lay his body away in a tomb, becomes an important element of the redemptive plan at which Mark's narrative gestures. Those attending his execution, including the centurion and the demonic forces he represents, do not know—or perhaps better, because of Jesus's last words and ostentatious cry of despair, choose not to credit—what the readers may themselves recognize. Jesus's diminution is fleeting. After he pays the price of freedom for many, God will vindicate him too by raising him from the dead so that he will come to judge his unjust enemies, as he prophesied.

The proposal I advance, namely, that Jesus's utterance in Mark 15:34 misleads those attending his crucifixion as well as the demonic authorities overseeing it, is not unknown in early Christian literature. The Gospel of Philip saying 64 (in Layton's division) interprets Jesus's final words from Mark 15:34 (par. Matt 27:46) as signifying that the spiritual Christ had already departed from the human Jesus at the time of his death (Gos. Phil. 68.26–29).[67] Since Jesus is said to deceive everyone in saying 23 (ⲁⲓⲥ ϥⲓⲧⲟⲩ ⲛ̄ϫⲓⲟⲩⲉ ⲧⲏⲣⲟⲩ, 57.29–30), and since the demonic powers' state of perpetual deception by the Holy Spirit is stressed in sayings 12 (55.14–19) and 30 (59.18–24), the cry of derelication in the Gospel of Philip culminates an elaborate pattern of trickery that Christ perpetrates on his diabolical

---

67. Citing the Coptic from Bentley Layton, ed., *The Coptic Gnostic Library: Nag Hammadi Codex II, 2–7 Together with XIII,2*, Brit. Lib. Or. 4926 (1), and P. Oxy. 1, 654, 655*, vol. 1, NHS 20 (Leiden: Brill, 1989). The sayings numbers come from Layton, *The Gnostic Scriptures: A New Translation with Annotations and Introductions*, ABRL (New York: Doubleday, 1987), 325–53.

enemies. In Philip, this deceptive cry functions differently from Mark. It signals the escape of the divine Christ from the human Jesus, who is left to suffer alone at his unwitting enemies' hands. However, as in Mark, Jesus's cry of dereliction in Philip simultaneously encourages the demonic enemies in their futile attempt to harm Christ and reveals—at least to the initiated reader—Christ's ingenious escape from their power.

A similar interpretation of Jesus's death appears in Basilides's treatment of the crucifixion, though for this Christian teacher it hinges on the figure of Simon of Cyrene rather than on Jesus's last words. The narrative detail included in Mark 15:21 suggests to Basilides that Simon and Jesus had exchanged places: the former transformed into the latter and was "crucified in accordance with ignorance and error," so that the despairing words of 15:34 are spoken by Simon. Jesus, assuming his substitute's appearance, "laughs at" (*irrisisse*) and "mocks" (*deridentem*) his thoroughly deceived enemies before ascending to heaven (Irenaeus, *Haer.* 1.24.4).[68]

It is not only heretical Christians who interpret Jesus's crucifixion as divine deception. Origen emphasizes Jesus's feigned weakness in his subtle response to Celsus's critique of Jesus's unmanliness in the face of death (*Cels.* 2.24), and more directly elsewhere.[69] I will later trace a related manifestation of the deception motif in ancient Christian literature to Mark's mythologically allusive *commentarii*, which late antique writers finalized directly or indirectly (via the other gospels) and elaborated in more-or-less fanciful ways, probably through the interpretive lens offered by 1 Cor 2:6–8.

Thus, in addition to condensing a dialogized theological theme, the Markan Jesus's carefully chosen final words advance Mark's mythological account of Jesus's redemptive death. They falsely project a persona of despondency and defeat as Jesus hangs on the cross, egging on the gloating

---

68. Citing and quoting Adelin Rousseau and Louis Doutreleau, eds., *Irénée de Lyon: Contre les hérésies livre 1*, SC 264 (Paris: Cerf, 1979).

69. Citing the text in Miroslav Marković, ed., *Origenis Contra Celsum libri VIII*, VCSup 54 (Leiden: Brill, 2001). See also Origen, *Comm. Matt.* 16.8 and *Comm. Rom.* 5.10, with Greek text quoted in Hastings Rashdall, *The Idea of the Atonement in Christian Theology, Being the Bampton Lectures for 1915* (London: MacMillan, 1919), 259–60 n. 2 and 260–61 n. 2. Rashdall blames Origen for most prominently developing the "monstrous" belief in God's deception of the devil through Jesus's crucifixion, which became a constitutive element of patristic theories of the atonement, even as he tries to exonerate Origen of responsibility for the features of that doctrine he found offensive (*Idea of the Atonement*, 259–64).

bystanders who watch him die—including the enemies who take his life. Encouraged by Jesus's feigned despair (Mark 15:34) and by other signs of agony evident in his death (e.g., 15:37), the centurion's declaration (15:39) revels in a demonic victory over the Son of God that reverses the humiliating defeats Jesus has been dealing demons throughout the gospel. Mark 5:1-20 is particularly important in this regard, since the centurion's words echo the exorcised Legion's terrified cry from 5:7, transforming it into a scornful shout of triumph. Moreover, Mark's account of Jesus's liberation of the possessed man from the many demons anticipates the deceptive tactics Jesus will employ in his final liberation of many from demons through the ransom payment of his life.

Deception also plays an important role in the Greco-Roman mythical paradigm I have argued Mark adopts in chapter 5 and in the passion and resurrection narrative, as evident in Homer's Odysseus deceiving Polyphemus and Hesiod's Zeus, Cronos. Jesus feigns powerlessness and despair as he gives himself over to the powers that hold many in thralldom, including Death. Readers attentive to the original literary context of Jesus's final cry of dereliction (Ps 22) will grasp that, even as it expresses despair, it also anticipates God's deliverance from death—an expectation which Jesus's multiple prophecies of resurrection have articulated. Mark's mythically resonant notice of the great stone rolled away from the cave in which Jesus's enemies bury him, and this cavernous tomb mysteriously left empty, gesture at Jesus's salvation and point to his final victory over chthonic demonic enemies including Death, although Mark guarantees neither.

Jesus's Death as an Anthropophagic Meal

The possibility of Jesus's deceptive weakness in death is buttressed by and itself supports a related mythological parallel between Mark's passion narrative and the epics discussed above. In Homer, Odysseus serves wine to Polyphemus for the monster to consume along with the bodies of Odysseus's slain men. The hero makes the Cyclops drunk as part of his plan to escape being eaten (*Od.* 9.345-374). In Hesiod, Gaia deviously feeds a rock to Cronos, which this Titan, at her prompting, mistakes for Zeus as he devours all the new gods. She thereby facilitates Zeus's hidden maturation and ultimate emergence to defeat Cronos and liberate his consumed siblings (*Theog.* 485-492).[70] In a surprising

---

70. In Apollodorus, Rhea, Zeus's mother, perpetrates this deceit (*Library* 1.1).

inversion of this anthropophagic paradigm, Jesus's treachery involves not his salvation from consumption through the substitution of an alternative feast but instead his self-offering as a (symbolic) meal for his enemies to eat in exchange for the many they hold thrall. Mark initiates this provocative development as early as 6:14–29, when he depicts the corpse of Jesus's predecessor, John the Baptist, as the main course of a cannibalistic banquet at which the prophet's enemies feast on his decapitated head (6:25–28) before his body is buried. Mark brings the theme to maturation in the scene of the Last Supper from chapter 14, preceding Jesus's own execution and burial.

This Markan transformation of the Cyclopeia resolves the same problem Virgil addresses in his revision of the episode. Odysseus fails to save several of his men (ultimately all) and, in fact, uses their deaths in Polyphemus's cave to save himself, since his plan of escape involves inebriating the Cyclops during one of the monster's anthropophagic meals. Virgil underscores and exaggerates Odysseus's callousness toward his fellows by having Achaemenides survive to accuse him of abandoning him in the Cyclops's cave while he escaped (*Aen.* 3.616–618). Virgil's Aeneas remediates Odysseus's shameful behavior by rescuing the man the Homeric hero had left behind (3.666–667); Mark's Jesus undoes Odysseus's selfishness even more radically. Jesus saves his followers by himself becoming the anthropophagic monster's meal, an act of self-sacrificial service symbolized by his distribution to the disciples of his soon-to-be crucified body as bread and his shed blood as wine (Mark 14:22–25). He does this just before the disciples flee and survive, and he is captured, killed, and entombed in a cave on their behalf.

This intertextual or mythological context, which amplifies and explains the anthropophagic theme that Mark develops, is often ignored. Scholars tend instead to situate Jesus's words to the disciples at the Passover meal against an Isaianic background that encourages readers to imagine Jesus's death as a sacrificial offering to God,[71] much as they do his words in 10:45, which this passage echoes. Discrete biblical allusions do operate in the scene, but when Jesus identifies the wine he serves as "my blood of the covenant poured out for many" (τὸ αἷμά μου τῆς διαθήκης τὸ ἐκχυννόμενον ὑπὲρ πολλῶν, 14:24), the dominant reference is not to Isaiah but to Zech 9:11, with a secondary reference to Exod 24:8, which the Zechariah passage itself echoes.[72] The biblical background suggests an interpretation of

---

71. Watts, *Isaiah's New Exodus*, 351–62; Marcus, *Mark 8–16*, 966–67; etc.
72. As Marcus, for instance, acknowledges, even though he goes on to interpret

Jesus's voluntary death consonant with the one I have been pressing. Jesus offers himself in death not to his father God as a kind of sacrifice, but to his enemies as a kind of anthropophagic meal, as part of a plan to deceive and defeat them and liberate their captives.

Mark has already alluded to the Zechariah passage a few chapters before the Last Supper, when Jesus completes the journey into Jerusalem by riding a colt into the city while being greeted as its liberator (Mark 11:1–11). As the Matthean parallel makes explicit (see Matt 21:4–5), this event allusively fulfills Zech 9:9 LXX: "Rejoice greatly, daughter of Zion. Cry out, daughter of Jerusalem. Behold, your king comes to you, righteous and himself a savior, humble and riding on a donkey, and a young foal." The Zechariah passage goes on to forecast the defeat of Israel's enemies and the establishment of its king's authority (9:10). It vividly figures that messianic victory as the liberation of captives from a pit in fulfillment of God's covenant with Israel at Sinai: "and in the blood of the covenant you [i.e., the 'daughter of Zion/Jerusalem' apostrophized in v. 9] have discharged your captives from the pit" (καὶ σὺ ἐν αἵματι διαθήκης ἐξαπέστειλας δεσμίους σου ἐκ λάκκου, Zech 9:11 LXX).

That is the verse with which the Markan Last Supper scene rhetorically connects Jesus's death. Mark 14:24 echoes Zechariah's insistence that the salvation the Messiah brings fulfills God's covenant with Israel by paralleling "my *blood of the covenant* poured out for many" with Zechariah's "in the *blood of the covenant* you have discharged your captives." The interrelated allusions to Zech 9:9–11 invite the reader to understand the Messiah Jesus's death upon arriving in Jerusalem as the fulfillment of God's covenantal obligation to save his people from their captivity to foreign enemies. The many on whose behalf Jesus's blood is shed in Mark 14:24 are the same many for whom Jesus's gives his life as a ransom payment in 10:45, where foreign enemies likewise feature (see 10:33, 42).

These many are identified in the Zechariah passage as "discharged ... captives," in recognition that the covenant whose messianic fulfilment it anticipates originated in God's deliverance of Israel from Egypt. In fact, the phrase "the blood of the covenant" occurs in Exod 24:8 as well as in Zech 9:9–11, and Mark 14:24 echoes this passage as well. The Exodus episode recounts the sealing of the covenant into which God's people entered at Sinai, immediately upon deliverance from Egypt—an act of divine liber-

---

the reference to Jesus's death as an expiatory or atoning sacrifice and keeps Isa 53:12 in view (Marcus, *Mark 8–16*, 966–67).

ation that the Passover meal Jesus and his disciples share commemorates. In the Exodus passage, Moses sacrifices oxen to God (see Exod 24:5–6), whose blood he splatters on the people after they vow obedience to the stipulations he reads (24:7–8). As William Propp observes, the blood from Exod 24 complements the blood from the original Passover: "The blood ritual in Exodus 12 initiates Israel's freedom; the blood ritual of Exodus 24 terminates it. Released from involuntary servitude to Pharaoh, Israel voluntarily enters Yahweh's servitude."[73] On a more basic level Moses's symbolic act establishes a contractual condition on God's judgment, whose terms Propp explicates: "if you do not keep [your side of] the Covenant, your blood is forfeit like this blood," a symbolic threat recalling the shed blood of the firstborn who stood outside God's protection in Egypt.[74] By invoking this covenantal blood sacrifice at a meal commemorating the Passover, just as the blood from Exod 24 itself recalls the Passover's blood ritual, Mark suggests that Jesus's death liberates God's people from foreign enemies in fulfillment of his covenantal promises. As a complement, Jesus's shed blood implies the establishment of a new covenant between God and the people whom Jesus's death frees, or perhaps the renewal for them of the covenant originally established with Israel at Sinai.[75]

Mark acknowledges but does not stress the covenant-establishing aspect of Jesus's death. Unlike Luke's Jesus (22:24–27), Mark's offers no generalized behavioral or ethical guidance to his disciples at the Last Supper; unlike Paul, Mark associates it with no requirement of ethical self-inspection or warning of judgment for unworthy behavior (1 Cor 11:27–34). This may relate to Mark's refusal to presume that Jesus's followers were, in fact, among the many redeemed to partake in the divine covenant Jesus (re)establishes through his death, as Israel was in Exod 24. The Last Supper scene's recollections of anthropophagic feasts may implicitly align Jesus's disciples, who symbolically feed on his body, with the hero's enemies such as Polyphemus, Cronos, and Herod (see 6:25). After all, Mark contextualizes the scene between prophetic warnings of Judas's betrayal (Mark 14:18–21), on the one hand, and Peter's satanic denials and his other students' faithless abandonment (14:26–31), on the other. As

---

73. William Henry Propp, *Exodus 19–40: A New Translation with Introduction and Commentary*, AB 2A (New York: Doubleday, 2006), 309.
74. Propp, *Exodus 19–40*, 308.
75. Early Jesus-believers seemed to disagree on this point; compare Mark 14:24 and Luke 22:20, which replaces Mark's reference to the "covenant" with "new covenant."

argued in the previous chapter, Mark neglects to guarantee the redemption of Jesus's disciples and Peter as the gospel draws to a close, which tends to confirm that troubling alignment. At the very least, then, the Last Supper in Mark would not seem an auspicious occasion on which to dwell on the sacrificial death of Jesus as (re)establishing a divine covenant in which his disciples participate. A covenant obliges faithfulness from both parties entering into it.[76] Mark, however, interrogates the faithfulness of Jesus's disciples and of God throughout the passion narrative.

From a related interpretive angle, Mark's focus on resurrection might stand in such indissoluble theological tension with an understanding of Jesus's death as a covenantal sacrifice that Mark will not emphasize the interpretive possibility. If Jesus immediately regains the lifeblood he sheds to (re)establish such a covenant, then that covenant's legitimacy comes into question—much as would a contract's validity were one party to sign it in pencil and then immediately erase the signature.[77]

All this interpretive tension might represent only the tip of a hermeneutic iceberg. Mark's Gospel may actively interrogate not only salvation by resurrection but an emergent theological conviction that the community of Jesus-believers participated in Israel's covenant with God, or in one related to it. Mark is not shy about critiquing this covenant's stipulations (see 7:19; 10:2–9; etc.). Perhaps the Second Gospel also raises questions about whether the death of Jesus effectively renews God's covenant with Israel at all. Mark's contextualization of words from early eucharistic celebrations (see 1 Cor 11:23–26) within a section of narrative emphasizing his disciples' perfidy could certainly be interpreted as a provocative questioning of covenantal theology as the appropriate framework for understanding Jesus's commemorated death. Mark's sustained emphasis on Jesus's recovery by resurrection of the lifeblood he sheds might likewise raise questions about the solemnity of the covenant that blood suppos-

---

76. Although, it must be acknowledged, Israel likewise violated the original covenant soon after its initiation (Exod 32).

77. Mark may also downplay the covenant-establishing significance of Jesus's death to reduce potential ideological incoherence between its emphasis on Jesus's liberation of God's people from enslavement to demonic forces and the suggestion at the Last Supper that this deliverance's goal is a covenant of servitude to God like the one established at Sinai. Though largely benevolent, the Sinai covenant was maintained through coercive threats of divine violence, as Propp's interpretation of the Exodus intertext makes clear (Propp, *Exodus 19–40*, 308).

edly sanctifies. Mark's theological reflection on Jesus's death thus might anticipate Marcion's and other radical Paulinists' critiques of covenantal theology, much as the Second Gospel's reflection on martyrdom and flight anticipates later ancient Christian controversies.

Jesus's Deceptive Redemption in Early Christian Writings

Mark's theology of deceptive redemption, as I have charted it in interpretive dialogue with other ancient literature, has several analogues in post–New Testament ancient Christian writing. The idea that Jesus deceives through his death anthropophagic demons set on consuming him remains implicit in Mark. However, that mythological theme surfaces explicitly in early elaborations of the meaning of Jesus's redemptive death and resurrection at which Mark's christological statements gesture (3:27; 10:45; 14:24). Gregory of Nyssa, to offer one example, explains how Jesus's death and resurrection defeats the devil, whom he describes as a hypostasized anthropophagic power opposing God.

> In order to secure that the ransom on our behalf [εὔληπτον ... ὑπὲρ ἡμῶν] might be easily accepted by him who required it, the Deity was hidden [ἐνεκρύφθη] under the veil of our nature, so that, as with ravenous fish, the hook of the Deity might be gulped down [συγκατασπασθῇ] along with the bait of flesh, and thus, life being introduced into the house of death, and light shining in darkness, that which is diametrically opposed to light and life might vanish; for it is not in the nature of darkness to remain when light is present, or of death to exist when life is active. (*Or. cat.* 65 M)[78]

Gregory alludes to Job 41:1 (40:25 LXX): "will you catch a serpent [δράκοντα] on a fishhook?" Elsewhere he formulates a similar interpretation of the atonement that makes the allusion more explicit (*Trid. spat.* 608 M).[79] That same interpretive line appears in other late antique Christian writers, including Gregory the Great (*Moral.* 33.7). John of Damascus,

---

78. Quoting William Moore and Henry Austin Wilson, trans., *Select Writings and Letters of Gregory, Bishop of Nyssa*, NPNF² 5:494, with reference to the Greek text from Ekkehard Mühlenberg, ed., *Gregorii Nysseni oratio catechetica*, GNO 3.4 (Leiden: Brill, 1996), 62, ll. 6–14, occasionally quoted.

79. Günter Heil et al., eds., *Gregorii Nysseni sermones*, GNO 9.1 (Leiden: Brill, 1967), 280, l. 16–281, l. 16.

though he follows Gregory of Nyssa closely, has a hypostasized Death take the bait rather than Satan (*Fid. orth.* 3.27). Likewise, in Cyril of Jerusalem, Jesus's body becomes a deadly bait so that Death, again figured as Job's δράκων, might in its desire to devour Christ be tricked into disgorging those whom it has already consumed: "Therefore, his body became a bait for death, in order that the serpent [δράκων], having expected to devour [καταπιεῖν] him, might vomit forth those it had already gulped down" (*Catech.* 12.15).[80] Augustine agrees in interpreting Jesus's death as deceptive bait aimed at trapping a demonic enemy, but prefers the metaphor of the mousetrap over that of the fishhook (see *Serm.* 130, 134, 265d).[81]

These and other ancient Christian writers agree in figuring Satan or Death as an anthropophagic beast that devours divinity hidden within Jesus's human body and is thereby destroyed by the resurrection of the Lord of life it had been tricked into consuming, forced to disgorge not only Christ but others it had devoured as well.[82] This mythological development imaginatively manifests the Christus Victor theory of the atonement, which Gustav Aulén's study demanded that theologians and historians of ancient Christianity take with renewed seriousness.[83] Some have argued for the model's centrality to Mark.[84] However, none that I know has attempted to trace to the Second Gospel the imaginative figuration of Christ's crucifixion and restoration to life as demonic enemies' feasting on his deceptively weakened body (death), giving way to their

---

80. Translating Wilhelm C. Reischl and Joseph Rupp, eds., *Cyrilli Hierosolymarum archiepiscopi opera quae supersunt omnia* (Hildesheim: Olms, 1967), 2:20.

81. For discussion of the passages from Augustine, see David Scott-Macnab, "St. Augustine and the Devil's 'Mousetrap,'" *VC* 68 (2014): 409–15, esp. 413–14.

82. For discussions of this literary-theological theme in early Christian writing and its relationship to ransom theology, see Nicholas P. Constas, "The Last Temptation of Satan: Divine Deception in Greek Patristic Interpretations of the Passion Narrative," *HTR* 97 (2004): 139–63; Linda Munk, *The Devil's Mousetrap: Redemption and Colonial American Literature* (Oxford: Oxford University Press, 1997), 3–23, esp. 17–23; cf. Aulén, *Christus Victor*, 47–55; J. N. D. Kelly, *Early Christian Doctrines*, rev. ed. (San Francisco: Harper & Row, 1978), 382–84, 390–92.

83. See, e.g., Darby Kathleen Ray, *Deceiving the Devil: Atonement, Abuse, and Ransom* (Cleveland: Pilgrim, 1998), 118–45; J. Denny Weaver, *The Nonviolent Atonement*, 2nd ed. (Grand Rapids: Eerdmans, 2010); Richard H. Bell, *Deliver Us from Evil: Interpreting the Redemption from the Power of Satan in New Testament Theology*, WUNT 216 (Tübingen: Mohr Siebeck, 2007).

84. E.g., Dowd and Malbon, "Significance of Jesus's Death," which has proven controversial.

5. A Ransom for Many 215

disgorgement of the divine man with his followers (resurrection). Yet points of contact abound, including Mark's relation of Jesus's death and resurrection to his earlier conflicts with monstrous demons likened to anthropophagic monsters; the metaphorical transformation of Jesus's death at his enemies' hands into a cannibalistic feast; the dying Jesus's deceptive adoption of a posture of feeble desperation; the figuration of his resurrection with an empty cave, which signals the hero's escape from an anthropophagic enemy against the Greco-Roman literary background; and so on.

Beyond these parallels, the same literary traditions underlying Mark's inchoate conceptualization of Jesus's redemptive death and resurrection also surface in later Christian writings that elaborate, probably at more than one remove, the Markan *commentarii*'s relevant mythological and theological gestures. For example, a sermon attributed to Athanasius twice compares Christ vanquishing the devil through his deceptive death and resurrection to Odysseus disguised as a beggar in the Homeric scene in which the trickster outwrestles *Odyssey* 18's Irus, an unsuspecting representative of the suitors who consume Odysseus's property:[85] "But now, having made bold against our Lord, [Satan] saw that he himself had become Irus, and having been cast out from all he was trampled upon by everyone.... The dragon, having boasted that he was rich, was stripped naked and now he is a naked and impoverished Irus, having been despoiled by everyone" (*Pass. cruc. Dom.*, 28–29; PG 28:233a, 236a). Nicholas Constas connects the Homeric allusions to an earlier passage from the sermon where the preacher proclaims Christ's deceptive defeat of the devil through his death and resurrection.[86]

> The Lord, having provoked the enemy by means of human weakness, strengthened humanity against him. Therefore, at the time of his death, he both was troubled and began to be sad. And he begged that that cup pass by, and he cried "the spirit is willing but the flesh is weak," in order that our opponent, coming as to a man, might make a trial of divine power. Having been guided by these things, certainly, the wretch was fooled and came to the Lord. Then, seeing his courage, he crouched in

---

85. Daniel B. Levine helps explain why (Pseudo-)Athanasius refers to Irus in particular, showing that his challenge and downfall concretize the outrage and the fate of all those consuming Odysseus's home. See Levine, "*Odyssey* 18: Iros as Paradigm for the Suitors," *CJ* 77 (1982): 200–204.

86. Constas, "Last Temptation of Satan," 152.

fear; but seeing the weakness of his body, he again took heart. And it remained to see, on the one hand, the devil fleeing with his whole army, and the rulers, and his authorities; and, on the other, the Lord pursuing the satanic battle line with human weapons. (*Pass. cruc. Dom.* 14–15; PG 28:212a–b)

Just as the Homeric hero Odysseus adopts the guise of a weak beggar to provoke his opponents into challenging him, so too does the Lord, by disguising himself as a weak and despairing man, provoke Satan to destroy him on the cross. Odysseus wins a surprise victory that leads to the violent liberation of his home from the suitors' possession. Jesus's feigned weakness likewise catches the devil off guard, for Jesus immediately rises from the dead to free himself and many of his followers from the fleeing demons' power. (Pseudo-)Athanasius's invocation of the trickster Odysseus's defeat of Irus to explain Jesus's death and triumphant resurrection amounts to more than a learned rhetorical flourish, *pace* Constas.[87] On the contrary, Odysseus's heroic deceit constitutes a vital element of the theological and mythological matrix on which the preacher draws in explaining Christ's redemptive victory over demonic enemies. Odyssean deceit is likewise part of the evangelical tradition that Mark sets in motion in the *commentarii*'s theologically suggestive engagements with Greek mythological narratives. Later Christian writers draw out and finalize Mark's inchoate allusive gestures, constructing on their foundation a coherent redemptive myth that is different from what one finds in the Second Gospel but not altogether foreign to it.

Peter's Redemption

In the previous chapter I argued that Mark's concluding reference to Peter (16:7) could be read as anticipating Christ's final judgment. It withholds from him the moniker *disciple* as it looks forward to the risen master's possible meeting with him in Galilee, with 8:38–9:1 suggesting that the expected reunion will involve condemnation rather than restoration. But I also noted that there is reason for hope and gestured at its grounds. I bring this chapter to an end by charting the terrain of that hope, which turns out to be coterminous with Mark's conceptualization of Jesus's death and resurrection as ransoming Satan's thralls. In this context, I make a positive

---

87. Constas, "Last Temptation of Satan," 151–52.

case for Peter's redemption in Mark, and in my study's conclusion I briefly consider its implications for a broader understanding of the role doubt about resurrection plays in Mark's *commentarii*.

It is important to acknowledge the scope of the problem Peter's behavior in the passion narrative presents. Mark's account of his triple denial and curse of Jesus carries with it the possibility of damnation. Many ancient Jesus-believing writers believed unforgiveable the sin of apostasy to which Peter's denial may be analogized. Early writings, including Heb 6:4–6, articulate this position clearly.[88] For Mark itself, "blasphemy against the Holy Spirit" is the only unforgiveable sin (Mark 3:29), but ancient Christians could equate such blasphemy with apostasy, by contrasting it to the Spirit-inspired confession Jesus demands of his disciples in Mark 13:11, Matt 10:19–20, and elsewhere.[89] This development relates to the emergence of a Christian ideology of martyrdom to which, as Lampe observes, "the belief that the confessor who testifies before his persecutors is pre-eminently Spirit-possessed is central."[90] How the Second Gospel itself understands blasphemy against the Spirit remains an open issue. On this question, as others, Mark's *commentarii* offer rhetorical and thematic gestures open to competing interpretive construals. However, Peter's denial and curse of Jesus in Mark 14 could qualify, thereby situating Mark near the beginning of the theological tradition that viewed apostasy as unpardonable.

The discursive context of Mark 3:29 suggests that slandering the Holy Spirit involves satanic disparagement of Jesus in his capacity as liberator of people under demonic power (see 3:22, 30). Such blasphemy makes a mockery of Jesus's mission to defeat Satan and save people from his dominion. The Markan Peter's denials and curse of Jesus constitute a similarly seditious rejection of Jesus's identity and liberative mission (14:66–72), for Mark juxtaposes them to Jesus's contrasting confession that he is the Son of Man, which seals his redemptive death (see 14:61–64). Peter's simultaneous denials and curse travesty Jesus's self-confession while also confirming

---

88. Brent Nongbri shows that both plain sense and rhetorical structure invite the most severe interpretation. See Nongbri, "A Touch of Condemnation in a Word of Exhortation: Apocalyptic Language and Graeco-Roman Rhetoric in Hebrews 6:4–12," *NovT* 45 (2003): 265–79; see also Middleton, *Radical Martyrdom*, 157–58.

89. See Lampe, "St Peter's Denial," 130–31, on Jerome's argument against Novatianists in *Ep.* 149; C. K. Barrett, *The Holy Spirit and the Gospel Tradition* (London: SPCK, 1947), 105–7; Van Iersel, "Gospel according to St. Mark," 27–28.

90. Lampe, "St Peter's Denial," 121.

his own alignment with Satan (see 8:31–33; 14:38), as argued in the previous chapter. His satanic blasphemy subverts the liberating death Jesus's confession secures: instead of denying himself and proclaiming an association with Jesus that would result in crucifixion and resurrection at his side, blasphemous Peter denies and curses Jesus in order to preserve his own life (cf. 8:34–37). Therefore, he finds himself in jeopardy of eternal alienation from the liberating effects of Jesus's redemptive death and resurrection (8:35–38; cf. 3:28–29).

I am not the first to suggest that Mark's Peter commits blasphemy against the Holy Spirit,[91] and it is not difficult to discover evidence supporting the interpretive possibility. Note, for instance, that the high priest ironically echoes the Markan discussion about such blasphemy (3:28–29) at the very moment he dismisses Jesus's true confession as "blasphemy" and condemns him to die on its basis (see 14:61–64).[92] The point of that irony becomes sharper when one recognizes that it is Satan-inspired Peter's coincident denials and curse of Jesus that in fact blaspheme the Spirit.[93]

The possibility that Peter blasphemes the Holy Spirit by denying Jesus finds its most decisive confirmation in the prophetic assurance Jesus offers Peter and three other followers in Mark 13 about what should happen if they are interrogated in the context of persecution.[94] "When they lead you to trial, having given you over, do not worry beforehand what you will

---

91. See Middleton, "Suffering and the Creation," esp. 186. T. A. Burkill observes that Mark seems to require Peter's denial of Jesus to constitute such blasphemy. But he is convinced that the reference in 16:7 to Peter assures his forgiveness. Mark therefore "allow[s] his lively interest in the presentation of dramatic contrasts to violate the rigorous demands of logical coherence." See Burkill, "Blasphemy: St. Mark's Gospel as Damnation History," in *New Testament*, part 1 of *Christianity, Judaism and Other Greco-Roman Cults: Studies for Morton Smith at Sixty*, ed. Jacob Neusner, SJLA 12 (Leiden: Brill, 1975), 69–73, quoting 71; see also Jerry Camery-Hoggatt, *Irony in Mark's Gospel: Text and Subtext*, SNTSMS 72 (Cambridge: Cambridge University Press, 1992), 172–73.

92. Scholars occasionally observe this ironic contrast or something akin to it. See, e.g., Adela Yarbro Collins, "The Charge of Blasphemy in Mark 14.64," *JSNT* 26 (2004): 379–401, esp. 381 and 401; Burkill, "Blasphemy," 59.

93. Geddert observes this irony (*Watchwords*, 100–101). (However, there is no hint that Jesus, in falsely being accused of blasphemy, exchanges his innocence for Peter's guilt of blasphemy.)

94. For the connection between 3:28–29 and 13:11, see Van Iersel, "Gospel according to St. Mark," 27–28: "'blaspheming Jesus against the Holy Spirit' is 'abjuring him in court against the voice of the Holy Spirit.'"

speak, but speak whatever is given to you in that hour. For you are not the ones who speak, but rather the Holy Spirit" (Mark 13:11). As throughout the hermeneutically capacious Olivet discourse, Jesus's words anticipate at once the eschatological future and the events of Mark's succeeding passion narrative, although here their meaning is consistent across interpretive horizons. Read with this passage in mind, Mark's account of Peter denying and cursing Jesus in an interrogative context in which he should experience the Holy Spirit's inspiration to speak the truth suggests he blasphemes the Spirit. While Jesus's true confession leading to martyrdom points toward the Spirit's guidance, Peter's juxtaposed false denials and blasphemous curse of his master to avoid death confirm his satanic possession.[95]

The Second Gospel gestures at this interpretation of Peter's speech instead of spelling it out, as it does the definition of blasphemy against the Holy Spirit, which remains frustratingly vague. However, the gesture is clear enough when one examines Mark retrospectively from the vantage of Luke's finalization of the Second Evangelist's *commentarii*, for Luke systematically eliminates the possibility Mark raises that Peter blasphemed the Holy Spirit as part of its pro-Petrine agenda.[96] Luke combines the three Markan passages relevant to Peter's condemnation (Mark 3:28–29; 8:34–9:1; 13:11), and/or parallel material from Q (see Matt 10:32–33; 12:32; 10:19–20), into an exhortation indicating that refusal to confess one's allegiance to Christ constitutes an unforgivably blasphemous rejection of the Spirit's confessional guidance *only when that refusal occurs under official, formal questioning* (see Luke 12:8–12).[97]

---

95. Pudussery suggests that Mark 13:11 recalls stories of God's Spirit coming upon the judges "to help Israel judge rightly, to gain victory over its enemies (cf. Judg 3,10; 6,34)" ("Discipleship," 185). Instead of divine possession allowing Peter heroically to speak the truth under hostile pressure, Satan possesses him, provoking blasphemy.

96. Smith, *Petrine Controversies*, 160–62; cf. Raymond E. Brown, Karl P. Donfried, and John Reumann, eds., *Peter in the New Testament: A Collaborative Assessment by Protestant and Roman Catholic Scholars* (Minneapolis: Augsburg, 1973), 109–28. If Robert H. Gundry compels assent and one finds the Farrer hypothesis plausible, it is possible that Luke revises Matthew on the same score. See Gundry, *Peter: False Disciple and Apostate according to Saint Matthew* (Grand Rapids: Eerdmans, 2015).

97. The source-critical issues are complex. For supporters of the two-source hypothesis, the agreement of Luke 12:2–9 with Matt 10:26–33 in order, against similar material found in Mark, suggests a primary reliance on Q, which would overlap with Mark. For discussion, see François Bovon, *Luke 2: A Commentary on the Gospel of Luke 9:51–19:27*, ed. Helmut Koester, trans. Donald S. Deer, Hermeneia (Minneapolis:

Luke's Jesus initially promises eschatological acknowledgment to the one who confesses him "before people" (ἔμπροσθεν τῶν ἀνθρώπων, 12:8), and then issues a related threat: "whoever denies [ἀρνησάμενος] me in front of people will be denied [ἀπαρνηθήσεται] in front of God's angels" (12:9). Luke 12:10b amplifies the warning. Jesus issues a related threat about blasphemy against the Holy Spirit that recalls Mark 3:29: "one who blasphemes the Holy Spirit [τὸ ἅγιον πνεῦμα βλασφημήσαντι] will not be forgiven." The implication is that unforgivable slander of the Holy Spirit is public denial of Christ, which issues in eschatological condemnation. The Lukan complex tightens the thematic connection between Mark 3:28–29 and 8:34–38 discussed above. It potentially implicates Peter, who clearly denies Jesus in front of people (ἠρνήσατο, Luke 22:57), in blasphemous spiritual slander.

However, Luke's equation of public denial of Christ with blasphemy of the Holy Spirit receives a qualification in 12:10a, which "intends to add an escape clause to the strict rule of 12:9":[98] "everyone who speaks a word against the Son of Man [ἐρεῖ λόγον εἰς τὸν υἱὸν τοῦ ἀνθρώπου] will be forgiven." Scholars suppose that this "escape clause" lets Peter off the hook, but without adequately explaining how. Henk de Jonge thinks it assures readers that the strictures of 12:9 and 10b refer only to negative speech directed at the risen Jesus, with the result that those, like Peter, "who failed to acknowledge him before Easter may still convert after Easter and be saved."[99] De Jonge offers no support for this explanation, but the interpretive claim is comprehensible against the background of a scholarly debate that John Kloppenborg summarizes.[100] I will bypass this deliberation to

---

Fortress, 2013), 172–73. Luke might have redacted Q under the influence of Mark. However, Henk J. de Jonge does not find Mark's influence on Luke extensive here, though the scope of his analysis is limited, focused on linguistic rather than literary or thematic points of contact. See de Jonge, "The Sayings on Confessing and Denying Jesus in Q 12:8–9 and Mark 8:38," in *Sayings of Jesus: Canonical and Non-canonical; Essays in Honour of Tjitze Baarda*, ed. William Lawrence Petersen, Johan S. Vos, and Henk J. de Jonge, NovTSup 89 (Leiden: Brill, 1997), 105–21.

98. De Jonge, "Sayings on Confessing," 117.

99. De Jonge, "Sayings on Confessing," 117; cf. Lampe, "St Peter's Denial," 122.

100. John S. Kloppenborg, *The Formation of Q: Trajectories in Ancient Wisdom Collections*, SAC (Philadelphia: Fortress, 1987), 213–16. For development of de Jonge's position, see Dennis M. Sweetland, "Discipleship and Persecution: A Study of Luke 12,1–12," *Bib* 65 (1984): 72–74. This interpretation is not necessarily opposed to mine. Part of Luke's attempt to preserve Peter from Mark's charge of apostasy may have been a suggestion that apostasy constitutes denial of Jesus after the Holy Spirit's empow-

5. A Ransom for Many 221

construct an interpretation that connects the passage to Luke's account of Peter's denials in a way that attends more carefully to the Third Gospel's narrative dynamics.

Luke 12:11–12 clarifies the escape clause of 12:10a by identifying a specific setting in which generally condemnable but still forgivable public denial of Christ goes a step beyond to become unforgiveable blasphemy against the Holy Spirit, namely, interrogations before official authorities. Luke's identification of this setting in 12:11–12 and the distinction it implies between that and the more general contexts of public speech 12:8–10a envision correspond to the distinction Luke will later draw between the settings of Jesus's praiseworthy self-confession and Peter's shameful denial of Christ.

Luke 12:11–12 promises the Holy Spirit's discursive guidance only to those called to confess while under interrogation before representatives of religious and governmental authorities:[101] "When they bring you before the assemblies and the rulers and the authorities, do not be anxious how or what you will respond or what you will say, for the Holy Spirit will teach you in that very hour what it is necessary to say" (Luke 12:11–12). This passage, adapted from Mark 13:11, affirms that when Jesus's followers find themselves formally interrogated about allegiance to Jesus in official proceedings, the Spirit will intervene and give them words to speak. Coming on the heels of Luke 12:10, it also implies that if they insist on denying Jesus in such situations, wherein the Holy Spirit's inspiration and empowerment are guaranteed, they should not expect forgiveness. Their public recantation goes beyond a pardonable "word spoken against the son of Man" to become "blasphemy of the Holy Spirit."

---

erment at Pentecost (Acts 1:8; 2:1–36). Certainly, the specific setting in which Luke locates unforgiveable denial (to be discussed below) would be relevant to the period following Pentecost.

101. Scholars have noted the problematic relationship between Luke 12:8–9 (or 10) and 12:(10 or) 11–12, sometimes in the context of speculation about which parts of 12:8–12 originated with the historical Jesus. Philipp Vielhauer argues for the inauthenticity of Jesus's reference to himself as Son of Man in Luke 12:8–10 on the basis of its connection with 12:11–12. See Vielhauer, "Gottesreich und Menschensohn in der Verkündigung Jesu," in *Aufsätze zum Neuen Testament*, TB 31 (Munich: Kaiser, 1965), 51[55]–79[91], esp. 69[77]–71[79]. If the latter verses deal with confession or denial of Christ in the context of persecution, then the entire paragraph must have originated in the early church. For a different understanding of the passage, see David R. Catchpole, "The Angelic Son of Man in Luke 12:8," *NovT* 24 (1982): 255–65.

The logic underlying this proposition may take one of at least two forms. Since the Holy Spirit is supposed to instruct believers what to say when they are interrogated by the authorities, others (other believers? the interrogators? curious onlookers?) may attribute to the Spirit denials of Christ uttered in those situations, with the result that such verbal acts constitute de facto travesty of the Spirit, making God's Spirit into an apostate. Alternatively, those who apostatize in the settings wherein the Spirit's support is guaranteed may imply that the Spirit is unwilling or unable to help them persevere. In either case, Luke 12:10a functions as an escape clause for Jesus's earlier condemnations of public denial by clarifying that not in every public setting does denial of Jesus slander the Holy Spirit and result in irrevocable condemnation. That consequence only obtains in formal interrogations wherein the Spirit's confessional instruction is assured.

Luke's diction in 12:8-9 helps clarify this distinction, for these verses speak of acknowledgment and denial of Jesus merely "before people" (ἔμπροσθεν τῶν ἀνθρώπων) or "in front of people" (ἐνώπιον τῶν ἀνθρώπων). The phrases are sufficiently broad to encompass settings both official and not, and thus make room for the possibility of forgiveness 12:10a introduces, where one finds a similarly generic turn of phrase for the forgivable speech act: "to speak a word against [ἐρεῖ λόγον εἰς] the Son of Man." As soon as Luke introduces the unforgiveable sin of "blaspheming" or "slandering the Holy Spirit" (εἰς τὸ ἅγιον πνεῦμα βλασφημήσαντι, 12:10b), however, the evangelist lays out the specific situations in which one might commit it: formal interrogations in official settings, with the interrogating parties identified ("the assemblies and the rulers and the authorities"; 12:11). Only in contexts such as these does denial of Jesus (12:8-9) transcend its status as a public word spoken against the Son of Man (12:10a) to become blasphemy against the Holy Spirit (12:10b), for only in these particular confessional contexts is the Holy Spirit's guidance guaranteed to the confessor (12:11b-12).[102]

This distinction maps onto Luke's revision of the Markan Peter's denial (Luke 22:54-62). Like Mark, Luke juxtaposes an account of Peter's triple denial of Jesus, which would seem to place him in jeopardy of

---

102. Although ignoring Luke 12:10—at least in the fragment preserved in Clement, *Strom.* 4.70.1-72.4—Herakleon's interpretation of the passage observes a similar distinction between more generalized confession (or denial) in Luke 12:8-9, and confession leading to martyrdom (12:11-12). See Winrich Löhr, "Valentinian Variations on LK 12,8-9/Mt 10,32," *VC* 57 (2003): 437-55.

eschatological condemnation (see esp. Luke 12:9), to an account of Jesus's self-confession (22:63–71). Luke goes further than Mark in underscoring that juxtaposition by having the arrested Jesus turn to fix his eyes on Peter at a moment of narrative transition from the latter's denial to the former's proclamation (22:61), thereby linking the episodes' central characters. Luke, though, leverages the juxtaposition to underscore a vital difference in setting between the two, which corresponds to the distinction between 12:8–10a and 12:10b–12 and preserves Peter from damnation.

While in Mark's *commentarii*, the questioning of Jesus and of Peter occur in the same locale (the chief priest's residence) and at the same time (the predawn hours), in Luke's revision they take place in different spatial and temporal settings. After recounting Peter's denial, Luke includes an altered version of Mark's statement that the Sanhedrin "were holding a counsel" (συμβούλιον ποιήσαντες) on the morning following their interrogation of Jesus for the purpose of extraditing him to Pilate (Mark 15:1). The Third Gospel changes this to a report that the council first assembled (συνήχθη) on the morning after Jesus's arrest to lead him away from the high priest's house, where he has been held since his arrest the night before (see Luke 22:54), to their official meeting place for his trial (ἀπήγαγον αὐτὸν εἰς τὸ συνέδριον αὐτῶν, 22:66). Luke therefore indicates that Jesus's interrogation and confession occur at an official daytime meeting of the Sanhedrin at its regular place of assembly, rather than at an ad hoc predawn gathering held at the high priest's house, such as Mark depicts.

Yet Luke leaves in place Mark's notice that it is during the predawn hours that a slave and other bystanders question Peter while he warms himself at a fire in the high priest's courtyard, presumably waiting to learn what will happen to Jesus (22:54–62). Luke eliminates Mark's reference to Peter cursing Jesus and swearing that he did not know him (Luke 22:60; cf. Mark 14:71), which scholars cite as evidence of his attempt to soften Mark's representation of Peter.[103] Luke's revisions of Mark make it clear that Peter's informal questioning in the high priest's courtyard has very little in common with Jesus's formal interrogation at an official meeting of the Sanhedrin held elsewhere on the next morning, though the evangelist recounts the two in quick succession. Peter's curse of Christ, whose point in Mark is to underscore his guilt of spiritually blasphemous apostasy in subversive contrast to Jesus's holy self-confession before the Sanhedrin,

---

103. E.g., Brown, Donfried, and Reumann, *Peter in the New Testament*, 112.

accordingly has no place in Luke's revised account of this disciple's denials of Jesus. Moreover, lest the reader be tempted to conclude that Peter committed an unforgiveable sin in denying his master, Luke's Jesus himself predicts Peter's restoration in 22:32, just before his denial. This prophecy clinches the identification of Peter's sinful denial of Jesus as a forgivable word spoken against the Son of Man rather than unforgiveable blasphemy of the Holy Spirit.

From one interpretive angle, Luke 12:8-12 constitutes a casuistic principle drawn from the understanding of Peter's denial of Jesus that Luke puts forth in narrative form later in the Third Gospel. From another, it provides a juridical scaffolding on which Luke constructs Peter's rehabilitation from the Markan narrative's charge of spiritual blasphemy. In much the same way, Luke's introduction of "daily" in the revision of the related Mark 8:34 (see Luke 9:23) makes the Markan reference to crucifixion symbolic and thereby obviates the threat of eschatological condemnation that Mark's Jesus issues to disciples who refuse to join him on the cross in anticipation of resurrection (Mark 8:35-9:1; see Luke 9:24-27).

Candida Moss has shown that Mark 8:34-9:1, *pace* Luke, was widely interpreted in the early church as a literal call to martyrdom directed not just at Peter and the other disciples but at believers generally.[104] Paul Middleton argues that this is how Mark in fact is meant to be read.[105] As I argued in chapter 3, careful interpretation of the Second Gospel delimits rather than generalizes Jesus's call to follow him to death in anticipation of resurrection. Mark 8:34's "call to martyrdom" provides a mandate only to those identified as Jesus's disciples within Mark's narrative world, as does the related call to confess in the face of coercive threat (13:11). For Mark's later readers, these passages may present confession in the face of death as an ideal of discipleship. They may even invite readers to follow Jesus's example of martyrdom. But they certainly do not require it. On the contrary, Mark leaves open the possibility of flight in the face of persecution for the readers, explicitly directing their attention to it in 13:14.

Even though Mark does not overtly make this option available to Jesus's disciples within the Second Gospel, it is not entirely removed from their table either. Note that Peter, James, John, and Andrew hear the exhortation to flight in 13:14 without the parenthetical tag provided by the

---

104. Moss, *Other Christs*, 28-33.
105. Middleton, *Radical Martyrdom*, 146-58.

narrator limiting its application to Mark's readers. Moreover, though their abscondence flouts Jesus's command that they die with him in anticipation of resurrection, there is evidence in Mark that this failure to meet the ideal Jesus lays out does not finally disqualify them from discipleship or foreclose their eschatological salvation. It is only Peter's Spirit-blaspheming apostasy (and, perhaps, Judas's betrayal) that amount to unforgivable catastrophes—a possibility for Peter that Luke's finalization of Mark's *commentarii* carefully obviates.

Even this requires complication, though. To understand why, it is useful to examine Middleton's dichotomous interpretation of Mark 8:34–9:1. He speculates that "Mark was concerned that members of his community were contemplating following the Way of Satan (the rejection of the road of suffering), rather than the Way of Jesus."[106] Middleton's reference to Satan emerges from his interpretation of Jesus's call to follow him to death (8:34) against the backdrop of 8:31–33, where Jesus rebukes Peter as Satan for resisting the Son of Man's destiny. Middleton also insists that Peter's satanic resistance must be interpreted against the backdrop of Jesus's exorcisms.[107] On these combined bases he relates the ideology and theology of martyrdom implicit in 8:34–38 to a cosmic conflict between God and the devil in which Jesus has been engaged throughout his ministry: "there is a distinct choice to be made: to be on the side of God/Jesus, or on the side of Satan, determined by the acceptance or rejection of the way of the cross."[108] Peter, Middleton's reading implies, ultimately chooses Satan by blaspheming the Spirit in the scene of his denials, and Mark aims to wave readers away from the same disastrous choice.

Though I do not accept his generalization of Mark's call to martyrdom, Middleton's literary analysis is otherwise exemplary, especially in comparison with the work of scholars who, even if they grasp the implications of 8:33's assimilation of Peter to Satan, neglect to read the scene of his denials in the earlier passage's light.[109] However, the particular interpretive conclusion that Middleton draws from 8:33's linkage of Peter to Satan does not follow from his analysis. If Jesus's rebuke of Peter as satanic is of a piece with Jesus's exorcistic ministry, as Middleton understands it to be, then

---

106. Middleton, *Radical Martyrdom*, 155.
107. Middleton, *Radical Martyrdom*, 150–51.
108. Middleton, *Radical Martyrdom*, 151; see also Middleton, "Suffering and the Creation," 180.
109. E.g., Incigneri, *Gospel to the Romans*, 333, 351 n. 12.

Peter's distinct choice as to whether to follow Jesus to death and resurrection is no choice at all—unless one is also to presume that people choose to become possessed by unclean spirits. Mark strongly tells against such a presumption by showing children to be possessed, for instance.

Mark's point, then, is not to warn the audience that Peter or one like him makes a satanic choice when denying or blasphemously cursing Jesus to avoid martyrdom. After all, Mark's passion narrative suggests that Peter apostatizes only after he has already made a contrary choice to follow the master to death (14:31) and, beyond that, has begun to act in accord with his decision by following Jesus into danger even when all the other disciples flee (14:54). Peter does not so much decide to apostatize under interrogation as he is manipulated into it by Satan. One like him is led on Satan's way rather than choosing to follow it oneself, which explains Peter's confusion about what he experiences (14:68). According to Mark, the inverse is true as well: the disciple who confesses when interrogated does not choose to bear witness in expectation of execution; such a one instead speaks under possession of God's Spirit: "when they lead you, handing you over [for trial; see 13:9] ... you are not ... the ones speaking but the Holy Spirit" (13:11).

There is ample room for theological complexity here. Jesus warns Peter of (satanic) testing in 14:38, and it would be otiose to remove Peter's will entirely from the equation. Yet even this warning complements rather than challenges my assessment of Peter's situation in the scene of his denials. Jesus tells Peter not to pray that he might endure or pass Satan's test by resisting sinful cowardice. Contrast Heb 4:15, which says of Jesus that he indeed "was tempted" but remained "without sin" (πεπειρασμένον ... χωρὶς ἁμαρτίας). Rather, Jesus instructs Peter to "pray that [he] might not [even] enter into temptation" (προσεύχεσθε ἵνα μὴ ἔλθητε εἰς πειρασμόν, 14:38). The satanic testing Peter will undergo in the scene of his denials is so intense that safety may only be found in avoidance. Such "testing" is closer to possession than to temptation, to the extent that the two are distinguishable.

Mark thus analogizes satanic Peter (8:33), whose damnable apostasy and curse of Jesus 8:31–9:1 foreshadows, not to a sinner subject to judgment or forgiveness but to a person possessed by a powerful demon requiring exorcism. Condemnation of Peter's failure to confess when interrogated thus constitutes a response no more appropriate or effective than would condemnation of the mute demon-possessed boy of Mark 9:14–29 for refusing to speak, a metaphorical analogue for Peter in his denials and a foil for the spirit-possessed confessor of 13:11. Condemnation of Peter's sin is not the suitable remedy, but neither is the repentance leading to forgiveness that Luke's revision seems to offer (Luke 22:32). Instead, liberation from the devil is required, as indicated by the reference in Mark 13:9–13 to the Holy Spirit's possession of the confessor, which stands in meaningful contrast with the apostate Peter's possession by the unclean spirit. In fact, freedom from Satan and his minions is what Jesus offers throughout his ministry (see 3:27)—to literally every single demon-possessed person he encounters or even hears about (7:24–30) in Mark's Gospel.

From this interpretive vantage, the question of whether Peter has committed the unforgiveable sin by blaspheming the Holy Spirit in Mark is not so much answered in the negative, as it is in Luke, as it is rendered irrelevant. The Second Gospel represents Peter in terms of satanic enslavement requiring spiritual liberation. This character comes to emblematize the fundamental problem Mark's entire narrative features Jesus resolving, in one way or another: demonic thralldom. Peter represents the test case for the redemptive efficacy of Jesus's death and resurrection as the culmination of his exorcistic ministry.[110]

Freedom from death is a necessary corollary to the spiritual liberation Jesus offers—or at least freedom from death's fear, which seems to be what hinders the other disciples from following Jesus's command to "take up the cross and follow" (8:34). Such liberation is the only way out of the paradoxical double-bind in which Mark 8:35–37 situates those who would obey Jesus's call. In that passage, Jesus elaborates 8:34's demand that his disciples die with him by insisting they can make no move to preserve life that does not end in the death they hope thereby to stave off. Since the only hope for human beings lies in salvation from inevitable death by an eternal God who offers everlasting life, choosing to die with the Son of Man in anticipation of divinely granted resurrection constitutes a reasonable expression of faith. Exercising this faith, however, requires faithfully anticipated deliverance from death already to be actualized in present freedom from death's natural fear. Yet debilitating fear of death is precisely what makes Jesus's demand to follow him to crucifixion in hope

---

110. Later accounts of Peter's martyrdom comprehend this in their decision to structure the story of his decision to return to Rome, confess, and be martyred as a reversal of his triple denial and flight from the scene of Jesus's condemnation and execution. They incorporate a spiritually fortifying experience (his triple exchange with the risen Christ) superseding Satan's undermining of his faithfulness (his triple denial; e.g., Pseudo-Linus, Mart. Pet. 6, in Lipsius, *Acta Apostolorum apocrypha* 1:7–8). The early Christian story of Peter's martyrdom is a redeemed story of his apostasy.

of resurrection so difficult for his disciples throughout Mark. The desperate desire to preserve life that Jesus unsuccessfully contests in 8:34–37 cannot be meaningfully distinguished from the craven fear of death the disciples later demonstrate in their flight from his arrest. It is because they cannot overcome their desperate desire to preserve life in the present, in the anticipation of supernatural resurrection in the future, that they abscond instead of joining with Jesus in arrest and crucifixion in hope of resurrection. If Peter, who keeps following Jesus after his arrest only to fall into denial and curses, needs to be freed from Satan, the disciples who flee must be delivered from death's fear.

While Jesus's empty tomb fails to guarantee the eternal life in which Jesus invites his disciples to trust, it at least renders plausible the divine promise of salvation from death's power in which they must put their faith, especially when it is understood against the mythological background this chapter has explored. Through his redemptive death and his own (possible) liberation from monstrous Death by resurrection, Jesus offers a (possible) escape route from the closed loop of fear of death resisting a faith that is necessary to overcome natural trepidation about losing one's life. The female disciples choose not to take it, for instead of taking the risk to proclaim the resurrection of a criminal executed by Rome, they flee from his tomb just as the others do from the scene of Jesus's arrest. But the spiritually fortified disciples might emerge from that vicious circle in the eschatological future prophesied in 13:9–13. Jesus's death and perhaps resurrection potentially offer to them and to many others freedom—both from hostile spiritual powers and from Death itself as the most fearful enemy of all.

The mythical-theological framework that hermeneutically structures Mark's Gospel makes it difficult to deny the possibility, perhaps even the likelihood, that Mark understands Jesus's death and resurrection to free the disciples from their cowardice. This possibility is not only anticipated by 13:9–13 but is emblematized in the anonymous young man who fled in naked panic (14:51–52) but later appears clothed and, upon his own encounter with the empty tomb, faithfully proclaims Jesus's resurrection (16:5–7). Of course, the figure of the empty sepulchral cave, with the multiple intra- and intertextual reverberations explored above, primarily gestures at Jesus's own escape from the demonic powers into whose hands he gives himself on the cross, including Death itself. But Jesus's death and resurrection could likewise free Mark's Peter from the satanic bondage he had suffered in the scene of his apostasy, so that the empty cave comes also to symbolize Peter's deliverance from the satanic manipulation prompting his blasphemous denial of Jesus. In this light, the Second Gospel's final reference to "the disciples and Peter" (16:7) turns out to be no less dialogic than the earlier declaration of the demon-possessed boy's father: "I have faith; help my lack of faith" (9:24). By distinguishing Peter from the disciples, Mark recalls his damnable denials in contrast to their more forgivable flight, implicitly condemning his satanic apostasy. But by singling Peter out, Mark also points to the possibility of even this blasphemer's redemption by Jesus's death and resurrection.

Conclusion: The Redemption of Doubt

The possibility of redemption for the Markan disciples, even in the face of Jesus's clear warnings about the eschatological consequences of their faithless disobedience, has sweeping implications. These disciples emblematize doubt in the face of Jesus's most meaningful promise, namely, that he, or God through him, will defeat Death. They show that they neither understand nor accept that the Son of Man's death will be immediately resolved by his resurrection ("after three days"). They refuse to be crucified with him in anticipation of the eternal life he promises and to proclaim his resurrection when confronted by the empty tomb. Their refusal or failure of resurrection faith finds various analogues throughout Mark's Gospel: in parents who cannot trust that Jesus will restore their dead children, in the Sadducees' skeptical questions about Jesus's resurrection theology, perhaps even in Jesus's last words on the cross. Looking beyond the gospel's textual horizon, the Second Evangelist seems to assume that readers will not possess the kind of absolute faith in resurrection Jesus requires, for the Markan narrator authorizes their flight when faced with the possibility of deadly persecution, in contrast to the multiple requirements Mark's Jesus issues to his disciples that they follow him to death. This authorization finds an explanatory analogue in the skepticism the Second Gospel itself demonstrates regrading resurrection, which it always neglects to certify. In suggesting, then, that even this gospel's most flagrantly disobedient and satanically inspired doubters are liable to be redeemed by Jesus's death and resurrection, Mark in effect redeems doubt itself. The Second Gospel proposes that even Peter's diabolical skepticism, which issues in denials and an unforgivably blasphemous curse of Jesus, does not permanently disqualify him from discipleship. Despite the doubt they show, the Marys, Salome, James, John, and Peter himself are liable to be redeemed by Jesus's death and resurrection, if resurrection indeed occurs.

That final caveat, though, reminds us that in line with virtually every aspect of Mark's thematization of the crucified master's victorious restoration to life, the Second Gospel will not guarantee the doubting disciples' redemption. Although open to a more positive construal, 16:7 is most straightforwardly understood as excluding the apostate Peter from the rolls of Jesus's disciples in anticipation of his final condemnation, especially when his denials and curse are interpreted against the backdrop of 8:34–9:1, let alone 3:28–29. The possibility of redemption for Jesus's fleeing disciples in an eschatological future lying beyond Mark's narrative horizon, while somewhat more assured than for Peter, is still balanced by Jesus's clear threat of eschatological judgment for those who demonstrate shame to be identified with the Son of Man in his execution in 8:38. Mark's *commentarii* guarantee nothing about Jesus's liberating resurrection, either regarding its occurrence or its implications for his disciples' redemption. Nonetheless, to the extent that Jesus's empty tomb plausibly points to the efficacy of God's redemptive plan, it is capable of staving off fear lest skeptical, cynical, or even diabolical doubt about the trustworthiness of the gospel's promises result in exclusion from God's eschatological kingdom. In a sense, Mark's narrative suggests, it finally does not matter whether one trusts in the resurrection Jesus exemplifies. All that matters is whether Jesus's resurrection is real, for if it is, it is capable of redeeming skepticism about it.

In this way, among others I have explored throughout this study, Mark authorizes doubt as a reasonable response to the announcements about and representations of Jesus's resurrection that the Second Gospel offers, and thus to the gospel itself. Mark's narrative embraces a skeptical approach to Jesus's resurrection, despite its central character's multiple demands for resurrection faith, and Mark invites its readers to do the same. This is surely one implication of the provocative transformation in 13:14 of the cowardly flight that virtually all Jesus's disciples demonstrate into the reader's obedience to the Markan Jesus's commands. The authorization of skeptical questions regarding resurrection may seem a strange hermeneutical conclusion at which to arrive about the good news regarding Jesus's defeat of death that Mark inscribes, but it aligns with the Second Evangelist's employment of unfinalized *commentarii* as the preferred generic mode. Mark's emphasis on such questions largely explains the early literary tradition the other New Testament gospels represent, which emerges in finalizing response to Mark's dialogically open-ended treatment of the resurrection theme. As a complement, Mark's suggestive but inchoate pastoral, theological, and mythological reflections related to Jesus's death and resurrection shed light on the early stages of theological debate about flight in the face of persecution and speculation about the atonement, which perpetuate beyond the New Testament into Christian literary history.

Resurrection remains an open question in Mark rather than a settled issue. A faithful reading of the Second Gospel, such as I have attempted here, will therefore embrace doubt about whether anyone, Jesus included, can transcend the ending death represents. Moreover, it will ponder difficult pastoral and theological issues—regarding the demise of children, legitimate responses to violent persecution, and the limitations of God's redemptive power—under the light of this enduring question. For readers whose response to Jesus's promises and demands relevant to eternal life resembles the internally dialogized words of the demon-possessed boy's desperate father ("I have faith; help my lack of faith"; 9:24), the evangelist's willingness to sanction such skepticism is central to understanding Mark as good news. A skeptical and a faithful reading of Mark turn out not to stand in mutual opposition but rather to interrelate so closely as to amount to one and the same thing.

Bibliography

Akin, Danny, Craig Blomberg, Paul Copan, Michael Kruger, Michael Licona, and Charles Quarles. "A Roundtable Discussion with Michael Licona on *The Resurrection of Jesus: A New Historiographical Approach.*" STR 3 (2012): 71–98.
Allen, Thomas W., ed. *Homeri opera*. 2nd ed. 4 vols. OCT. Oxford: Clarendon, 1922.
Allison, Dale C. "Anticipating the Passion: The Literary Reach of Matthew 26:47–27:56." CBQ 56 (1994): 701–14.
———. *Constructing Jesus: Memory, Imagination, and History*. Grand Rapids: Baker Academic, 2010.
———. "The Magi's Angel." Pages 17–41 in *Studies in Matthew: Interpretation Past and Present*. Grand Rapids: Baker Academic, 2005.
Alter, Robert. *The David Story: A Translation with Commentary of 1 and 2 Samuel*. New York: Norton, 1999.
———. *Genesis: Translation and Commentary*. New York: Norton, 1996.
Auerbach, Erich. *Mimesis: The Representation of Reality in Western Literature*. Translated by Willard R. Trask. Princeton: Princeton University Press, 1953.
Aulén, Gustaf. *Christus Victor: An Historical Study of the Three Main Types of the Idea of Atonement*. Translated by A. G. Hebert. New York: MacMillan, 1956.
Bakhtin, Mikhail M. *The Dialogic Imagination: Four Essays*. Translated by Michael Holquist. UTPSS 1. Austin: University of Texas Press, 1981.
———. *Problems of Dostoevsky's Poetics*. Edited and translated by Caryl Emerson. THL 8. Minneapolis: University of Minnesota Press, 1984.
Barnes, Timothy David. "'Another Shall Gird Thee': Probative Evidence for the Death of Peter." Pages 76–95 in *Peter in Early Christianity*. Edited by Helen K. Bond and Larry W. Hurtado. Grand Rapids: Eerdmans, 2015.

Barrett, C. K. "The Background of Mark 10:45." Pages 1–18 in *New Testament Essays: Studies in Memory of Thomas Walter Manson, 1893–1958*. Edited by A. J. B. Higgins. Manchester: Manchester University Press, 1959.

———. *The Holy Spirit and the Gospel Tradition*. London: SPCK, 1947.

Bassler, Jouette M. "1 Cor 12:3: Curse and Confession in Context." *JBL* 101 (1982): 415–18.

Batstone, William Wendell, and Cynthia Damon. *Caesar's Civil War*. OACL. New York: Oxford University Press, 2006.

Bauckham, Richard. "*The Acts of Paul* as a Sequel to Acts." Pages 116–30 in *The Book of Acts in Its Ancient Literary Setting*. Edited by Bruce W. Winter and Andrew D. Clarke. Vol. 1 of *The Book of Acts in Its First Century Setting*. Grand Rapids: Eerdmans, 1993.

———. "The Delay of the Parousia." *TynBul* 31 (1980): 3–36.

———. *Jesus and the Eyewitnesses: The Gospels as Eyewitness Testimony*. Grand Rapids: Eerdmans, 2006.

Baur, Ferdinand Christian. *Apollonius von Tyana und Christus, oder das Verhältniss des Pythagoreismus zum Christentum*. Tübingen: Fues, 1833.

Beasley-Murray, George Raymond. *Baptism in the New Testament*. Grand Rapids: Eerdmans, 1962.

Beavis, Mary Ann. "The Resurrection of Jephthah's Daughter: Judges 11:34–40 and Mark 5:21–24, 35–43." *CBQ* 72 (2010): 46–62.

Becker, Eve-Marie, Troels Engberg-Pedersen, and Mogens Mueller, eds. *For and Against Pauline Influence on Mark*. Part 2 of *Mark and Paul: Comparative Essays*. BZNW 199. Berlin: de Gruyter, 2014.

BeDuhn, Jason David. "'Because of the Angels': Unveiling Paul's Anthropology in 1 Corinthians 11." *JBL* 118 (1999): 295–320.

Bell, Richard H. *Deliver Us from Evil: Interpreting the Redemption from the Power of Satan in New Testament Theology*. WUNT 216. Tübingen: Mohr Siebeck, 2007.

Best, Ernest. *Following Jesus: Discipleship in the Gospel of Mark*. JSNTSup 4. Sheffield: JSOT Press, 1981.

———. "The Gospel of Mark: Who Is the Reader?" *IBS* 11 (1989): 124–32.

———. "The Role of the Disciples in Mark." *NTS* 23 (1977): 377–401.

Beyer, Hermann. "διακνοέω, διακονία, διάκονος." *TDNT* 2:81–93.

Black, Matthew, and Géza Vermès. *An Aramaic Approach to the Gospels and Acts*. 3rd ed. Oxford: Clarendon, 1967.

Bock, Darrell L. "Son of Man." Pages 894–900 in *Dictionary of Jesus and the Gospels*. 2nd ed. Edited by Joel B. Green, Jeannine K. Brown, and Norman Perrin. Downers Grove, IL: InterVarsity Press, 2013.

Bolt, Peter. *Jesus's Defeat of Death: Persuading Mark's Early Readers*. SNTSMS 125. Cambridge: Cambridge University Press, 2003.

———. "Mark 13: An Apocalyptic Precursor to the Passion Narrative." *RTR* 54 (1995): 10–32.

Bond, Helen K. "Was Peter behind Mark's Gospel?" Pages 46–61 in *Peter in Early Christianity*. Edited by Helen K. Bond and Larry W. Hurtado. Grand Rapids: Eerdmans, 2015.

Bonnard, Émile, ed. *Saint Jérôme, Commentaire sur S. Matthieu: Texte Latin, introduction, traduction et notes*. 2 vols. SC 242, 259. Paris: Cerf, 1977.

Bonner, Campbell. "The Technique of Exorcism." *HTR* 36 (1943): 39–49.

Boobyer, George H. "St. Mark and the Transfiguration." *JTS* 41 (1940): 119–40.

Boring, M. Eugene. *Mark: A Commentary*. NTL. Louisville: Westminster John Knox, 2006.

Bovon, François. *Luke 2: A Commentary on the Gospel of Luke 9:51–19:27*. Edited by Helmut Koester. Translated by Donald S. Deer. Hermeneia. Minneapolis: Fortress, 2013.

Boyarin, Daniel. *Socrates and the Fat Rabbis*. Chicago: University of Chicago Press, 2009.

Braun, François-Marie. *Jean le théologien et son évangile dans l'église ancienne*. Vol. 1 of *Jean le théologien*. EBib. Paris: Gabalda, 1959.

Brichto, Herbert Chanan. "Kin, Cult, Land and Afterlife—A Biblical Complex." *HUCA* 44 (1973): 1–54.

Brown, Raymond E. *The Death of the Messiah: From Gethsemane to the Grave; A Commentary on the Passion Narratives in the Four Gospels*. 2 vols. ABRL. New York: Doubleday, 1994.

Brown, Raymond E., Karl P. Donfried, and John Reumann, eds. *Peter in the New Testament: A Collaborative Assessment by Protestant and Roman Catholic Scholars*. Minneapolis: Augsburg, 1973.

Buch-Hansen, Gitte. "The Politics of Beginnings—Cosmology, Christology and Covenant: Gospel Openings Reconsidered in the Light of Paul's Peneumatology." Pages 213–42 in *For and Against Pauline Influence on Mark*. Part 2 of *Mark and Paul: Comparative Essays*. Edited by Eve-Marie Becker, Troels Engberg-Pedersen, and Mogens Mueller. BZNW 199. Berlin: de Gruyter, 2014.

Büchsel, Friedrich. "γενεά." *TDNT* 1:662–65.

Bultmann, Rudolf. *The History of the Synoptic Tradition*. Rev. ed. Translated by John Marsh. Oxford: Blackwell, 1968.

———. *Theology of the New Testament*. Translated by Kendrick Grobel. 2 vols. New York: Scribner's Sons, 1951–1955.

Burkett, Delbert. *The Son of Man Debate: A History and Evaluation*. SNTNMS 107. Cambridge: Cambridge University Press, 2000.

———. "The Transfiguration of Jesus (Mark 9:2–8): Epiphany or Apotheosis?" *JBL* 138 (2019): 413–32.

Burkill, T. A. "Blasphemy: St. Mark's Gospel as Damnation History." Pages 51–74 in *New Testament*. Part 1 of *Christianity, Judaism and Other Greco-Roman Cults: Studies for Morton Smith at Sixty*. Edited by Jacob Neusner. SJLA 12. Leiden: Brill, 1975.

Busch, Austin. "Gnostic Biblical and Second Sophistic Homeric Interpretation." *ZAC* 22 (2018): 195–217.

———. "New Testament Narrative and Greco-Roman Literature." Pages 61–72 in *The Oxford Handbook of Biblical Narrative*. Edited by Danna Nolan Fewell. New York: Oxford University Press, 2015.

———. "Questioning and Conviction: Double-Voiced Discourse in Mark 3:22–30." *JBL* 125 (2006): 477–505.

———. "Resurrection in Mark—or Not?" Paper presented at Annual Meeting of the Society of Biblical Literature. Boston, 22 November 2008.

———. "Scriptural Revision in Mark's Gospel and Philostratus's *Life of Apollonius*." Pages 71–112 in *Classical Greek Models of the Gospels and Acts: Studies in Mimesis Criticism*. Edited by Mark G. Bilby, Michael Kochenash, and Margaret Froelich. CSNTCO 3. Claremont, CA: Claremont, 2018.

———. "*Versane Natura Est*? Natural and Linguistic Instability in the *Extispicium* and Self-Blinding of Seneca's Oedipus." *CJ* 102 (2007): 225–67.

Camery-Hoggatt, Jerry. *Irony in Mark's Gospel: Text and Subtext*. SNTSMS 72. Cambridge: Cambridge University Press, 1992.

Carey, Holly J. "Is It as Bad as All That?: The Misconception of Mark as a Gospel Film Noir." Pages 3–21 in *Mark, Manuscripts, and Monotheism: Essays in Honor of Larry W. Hurtado*. Edited by Chris Keith and Dieter T. Roth. LNTS 528. London: Bloomsbury, 2015.

———. *Jesus's Cry from the Cross: Towards a First-Century Understanding of the Intertextual Relationship between Psalm 22 and the Narrative of Mark's Gospel*. LNTS 398. London: T&T Clark, 2009.

Carlston, Charles Edwin. "Transfiguration and Resurrection." *JBL* 80 (1961): 233–40.
Carter, Warren. "Cross-Gendered Romans and Mark's Jesus: Legion Enters the Pigs (Mark 5:1–20)." *JBL* 134 (2015): 139–55.
Casey, Maurice. *The Solution to the "Son of Man" Problem*. LNTS 343. London: Bloomsbury, 2009.
Catchpole, David R. "The Angelic Son of Man in Luke 12:8." *NovT* 24 (1982): 255–65.
Cohn-Sherbok, Dan M. "Jesus' Defence of the Resurrection of the Dead." *JSNT* 4 (1981): 64–73.
Collins, Adela Yarbro. *The Beginning of the Gospel: Probings of Mark in Context*. Minneapolis: Fortress, 1992.
———. "The Charge of Blasphemy in Mark 14.64." *JSNT* 26 (2004): 379–401.
———. "Finding Meaning in the Death of Jesus." *JR* 78 (1998): 175–96.
———. *Mark: A Commentary*. Hermeneia. Minneapolis: Fortress, 2007.
———. "Mark's Interpretation of the Death of Jesus." *JBL* 128 (2009): 545–54.
Collins, John J. *Daniel: A Commentary on the Book of Daniel*. Hermeneia. Minneapolis: Fortress, 1993.
Constas, Nicholas P. "The Last Temptation of Satan: Divine Deception in Greek Patristic Interpretations of the Passion Narrative." *HTR* 97 (2004): 139–63.
Cook, John Granger. *Empty Tomb, Resurrection, Apotheosis*. WUNT 410. Tübingen: Mohr Siebeck, 2018.
Cozier, Clint L. Review of *Dictionary of Jesus and the Gospels*, ed. Joel B. Green, Jeannine K. Brown, and Norman Perrin. *JSNT* 49 (1993): 125.
Crossan, John Dominic. "Form for Absence: The Markan Creation of Gospel." *Semeia* 12 (1978): 41–55.
———. *In Fragments: The Aphorisms of Jesus*. San Francisco: Harper & Row, 1983.
Crowder, Stephanie R. Buckhanon. *Simon of Cyrene: A Case of Roman Conscription*. StBibLit 46. New York: Lang, 2002.
Damgaard, Finn. "Persecution and Denial—Paradigmatic Apostolic Portrayals in Paul and Mark." Pages 295–310 in *For and Against Pauline Influence on Mark*. Part 2 of *Mark and Paul: Comparative Essays*. Edited by Eve-Marie Becker, Troels Engberg-Pedersen, and Mogens Mueller. BZNW 199. Berlin: de Gruyter, 2014.
D'Angelo, Mary Rose. "Gender and Power in the Gospel of Mark: The

Daughter of Jairus and the Woman with the Flow of Blood." Pages 83–109 in *Miracles in Jewish and Christian Antiquity: Imagining Truth*. Edited by John C. Cavadini. NDST 3. Notre Dame: University of Notre Dame Press, 1999.

Danker, Frederick W. "The Demonic Secret in Mark: A Reexamination of the Cry of Dereliction (15:34)." *ZNW* 61 (1970): 48–69.

Daube, David. "On Acts 23: Sadducees and Angels." *JBL* 109 (1990): 493–97.

Davies, W. D., and Dale C. Allison. *A Critical and Exegetical Commentary on the Gospel according to Saint Matthew*. 3 vols. ICC. Edinburgh: T&T Clark, 1988.

DeConick, April D. "'Blessed Are Those Who Have Not Seen' (Jn 20:29): Johannine Dramatization of an Early Christian Discourse." Pages 391–98 in *The Nag Hammadi Library after Fifty Years: Proceedings of the 1995 Society of Biblical Literature Commemoration*. Edited by John D. Turner and Anne McGuire. NHMS 44. Leiden: Brill, 1997.

———. "John Rivals Thomas: From Community Conflict to Gospel Narrative." Pages 303–11 in *Jesus in Johannine Tradition*. Edited by Robert T. Fortna and Tom Thatcher. Louisville: Westminster John Knox, 2001.

———. *Voices of the Mystics: Early Christian Discourse in the Gospels of John and Thomas and Other Ancient Christian Literature*. JSNTSup 157. Sheffield: Sheffield Academic, 2001.

Deppe, Dean B. "Charting the Future or a Perspective on the Present? The Paraenetic Purpose of Mark 13." *CTJ* 41 (2006): 89–101.

Derrett, J. Duncan M. "Contributions to the Study of the Gerasene Demoniac." *JSNT* 2 (1979): 2–17.

———. "Cursing Jesus (I Cor. Xii. 3): The Jews as Religious 'Persecutors.'" *NTS* 21 (1975): 544–54.

———. "Legend and Event: The Gerasene Demoniac: An Inquest into History and Liturgical Projection." Pages 47–58 in *Midrash, Haggadah, and the Character of the Community*. Vol. 3 of *Studies in the New Testament*. Leiden: Brill, 1982.

———. "Mark's Technique: The Haemorrhaging Woman and Jairus's Daughter." *Bib* 63 (1982): 474–505.

———. "Spirit-Possession and the Gerasene Demoniac." *Man* 14 (1979): 286–93.

Dewey, Joanna. "'Let Them Renounce Themselves and Take Up Their Cross': A Feminist Reading of Mark 8:34 in Mark's Social and Narrative World." *BTB* 34 (2004): 98–104.

Dewey, Kim E. "Peter's Curse and Cursed Peter (Mark 14:53–54, 66–72)." Pages 96–114 in *The Passion in Mark: Studies on Mark 14–16*. Edited by Werner H. Kelber and John R. Donahue. Philadelphia: Fortress, 1976.

Dimock, George E., Jr. "The Name of Odysseus." Pages 54–72 in *Essays on the Odyssey: Select Modern Criticism*. Edited by Charles H. Taylor Jr. Bloomington: Indiana University Press, 1963.

Dinkler, Michal Beth. "Reading the Potentials of Jesus's 'Triumphal Entry' (Luke 19:28–40)." *RevExp* 112 (2015): 525–41.

Dixon, Edward P. "Descending Spirit and Descending Gods: A 'Greek' Interpretation of the Spirit's 'Descent as a Dove' in Mark 1:10." *JBL* 128 (2009): 759–80.

Dodd, C. H. "Review of *Theologisches Wörterbuch zum Neuen Testament*." *JTS* 5 (1954): 244–45.

Dodson, Joseph R. *The "Powers" of Personification: Rhetorical Purpose in the Book of Wisdom and the Letter to the Romans*. BZNW 161. Berlin: de Gruyter, 2008.

Donahue, John R., and Daniel J. Harrington. *The Gospel of Mark*. SP 2. Collegeville, MN: Liturgical Press, 2002.

Dowd, Sharyn, and Elizabeth Struthers Malbon. "The Significance of Jesus's Death in Mark: Narrative Context and Authorial Audience." *JBL* 125 (2006): 271–97.

Dowling, Elizabeth V. "'Do This in Remembrance': Last Supper Traditions in Paul and Mark." Pages 221–41 in *Two Authors at the Beginnings of Christianity*. Part 1 of *Paul and Mark: Comparative Essays*. Edited by Oda Wischmeyer, David C. Sim, and Ian J. Elmer. BZNW 198. Berlin: de Gruyter, 2014.

Downing, F. Gerald. "The Resurrection of the Dead: Jesus and Philo." *JSNT* 5 (1982): 42–50.

Dreyfus, François. "L'argument Scripturaire de Jésus en faveur de la résurrection des morts (Marc, Xii, 26–27)." *RB* 66 (1959): 213–24.

Dulk, Matthijs den. "I Permit No Woman to Teach Except for Thecla: The Curious Case of the Pastoral Epistles and the *Acts of Paul* Reconsidered." *NovT* 54 (2012): 176–203.

Dunn, James D. G. *The Theology of Paul the Apostle*. Grand Rapids: Eerdmans, 2006.

Edwards, J. Christopher. *The Ransom Logion in Mark and Matthew: Its Reception and Its Significance for the Study of the Gospels*. WUNT 327. Tübingen: Mohr Siebeck, 2012.

Edwards, James R. "Markan Sandwiches: The Significance of Interpolations in Markan Narratives." *NovT* 31 (1989): 193–216.
Ehrman, Bart D. *How Jesus Became God: The Exaltation of a Jewish Preacher from Galilee*. New York: HarperCollins, 2014.
Elder, Nicholas A. "Of Porcine and Polluted Spirits: Reading the Gerasene Demoniac (Mark 5:1–20) with the Book of Watchers (*1 Enoch* 1–36)." *CBQ* 78 (2016): 430–46.
Ellis, E. Earle. "Jesus, the Sadducees and Qumran." *NTS* 10 (1964): 274–79.
Engberg-Pedersen, Troels. "1 Corinthians 11:16 and the Character of Pauline Exhortation." *JBL* 110 (1991): 679–89.
Evans, Craig A. *Mark 8:27–16:20*. WBC 34B. Nashville: Nelson, 2001.
Farrer, Austin. *St. Matthew and St. Mark*. ECLectures 1953–54. Westminster: Dacre, 1954.
———. *A Study in St. Mark*. New York: Oxford University Press, 1952.
Fleddermann, Harry. "The Flight of a Naked Young Man (Mark 14:50–51)." *CBQ* 41 (1979): 412–18.
Foerster, Richard, ed. *Libanii opera*. Vol. 2. BSGRT. Leipzig: Teubner, 1904.
Fonrobert, Charlotte. "The Woman with a Blood-Flow (Mark 5.24–34) Revisited: Menstrual Laws and Jewish Culture in Christian Feminist Hermeneutics." Pages 121–40 in *Early Christian Interpretation of the Scriptures of Israel: Investigations and Proposals*. Edited by Craig A. Evans and James A. Sanders. JSNTSup 148. Sheffield: Sheffield Academic, 1997.
Foster, Paul. "A New Dictionary of Jesus and the Gospels," review of *Dictionary of Jesus and the Gospels*, 2nd ed., ed. Joel B. Green, Jeannine K. Brown, and Norman Perrin. *ExpTim* 126 (2015): 195.
France, R. T. *The Gospel of Mark: A Commentary on the Greek Text*. NIGTC. Grand Rapids: Eerdmans, 2002.
———. "The Servant of the Lord in the Teaching of Jesus." *TynBul* 19 (1968): 26–52.
Fridrichsen, Anton. "The Conflict of Jesus with the Unclean Spirits." Pages 71–83 in *Exegetical Writings: A Selection*. Translated by Chrys C. Caragounis and Tord Fornberg. WUNT 76. Tübingen: Mohr Siebeck, 1994.
Fullmer, Paul. *Resurrection in Mark's Literary-Historical Perspective*. LNTS 360. London: T&T Clark, 2007.
Garrett, Susan R. *The Temptations of Jesus in Mark's Gospel*. Grand Rapids: Eerdmans, 1998.
Garroway, Joshua. "The Invasion of a Mustard Seed: A Reading of Mark 5.1–20." *JSNT* 32 (2009): 57–75.

Geddert, Timothy J. *Watchwords: Mark 13 in Markan Eschatology.* JSNTSup 26. Sheffield: JSOT Press, 1989.
Girard, René. "Generative Violence and the Extinction of the Social Order." Translated by Thomas Wieser. *Salmagundi* 63–64 (1984): 204–37.
Glasson, Thomas F. *Greek Influence in Jewish Eschatology; with Special Reference to the Apocalypses and Pseudepigraphs.* BM 1. London: SPCK, 1961.
Glenn, Justin. "The Polyphemus Myth: Its Origin and Interpretation." *GR* 25 (1978): 141–55.
———. "Virgil's Polyphemus." *GR* 19 (1972): 47–59.
Gnilka, Joachim. *Das Evangelium nach Markus.* 2 vols. EKKNT 2. Zürich: Neukirchener Verlag, 1978.
Goulder, Michael D. *St. Paul versus St. Peter: A Tale of Two Missions.* Louisville: Westminster John Knox, 1995.
Guelich, Robert A. *Mark 1–8:26.* WBC 34A. Dallas: Word, 1989.
Gülzow, Henneke. *Cyprian und Novatian: Der Briefwechsel zwischen den Gemeinden in Rom und Karthago zur Zeit der Verfolgung des Kaisers Decius.* BHT 48. Tübingen: Mohr Siebeck, 1975.
Gundry, Robert H. *Mark: A Commentary on His Apology for the Cross.* Grand Rapids: Eerdmans, 1993.
———. *Peter: False Disciple and Apostate according to Saint Matthew.* Grand Rapids: Eerdmans, 2015.
Haber, Susan. "A Woman's Touch: Feminist Encounters with the Hemorrhaging Woman in Mark 5.24–34." *JSNT* 26 (2003): 171–92.
Hachili, Rachel. *Jewish Funerary Customs, Practices and Rites in the Second Temple Period.* JSJSup 94. Leiden: Brill, 2005.
Hagstrom, Andrew Mark. "Philostratus's Apollonius: A Case Study in Apologetics in the Roman Empire." MA thesis, University of North Carolina at Chapel Hill, 2016.
Hamilton, Neill Q. "Resurrection Tradition and the Composition of Mark." *JBL* 84 (1965): 415–21.
Harris, Murray J. "'The Dead Are Restored to Life': Miracles of Revivication in the Gospels." Pages 295–326 in *The Miracles of Jesus.* Edited by David Wenham and Craig L. Blomberg. GP 6. Sheffield: JSOT Press, 1986.
Hatina, Thomas R. "Who Will See 'The Kingdom of God Coming with Power' in Mark 9,1—Protagonists or Antagonists?" *Bib* 86 (2005): 20–34.

Hatton, Stephen B. "Comic Ambiguity in the Markan Healing Intercalation (Mark 5:21–43)." *Neot* 49 (2015): 91–123.

Hedrick, Charles W. "Miracle Stories as Literary Compositions: The Case of Jairus's Daughter." *PRSt* 20 (1993): 217–33.

Heil, Günter, Adrian van Heck, Ernest Gebhardt, and Andreas Spira, eds. *Gregorii Nysseni sermones*. GNO 9.1. Leiden: Brill, 1967.

Hernández, Pura Nieto. "Back in the Cave of the Cyclops." *AJP* 121 (2000): 345–66.

Hodge, Caroline E. Johnson. *If Sons, Then Heirs: A Study of Kinship and Ethnicity in the Letters of Paul*. Oxford: Oxford University Press, 2007.

Hogterp, Albert L. A. "Belief in Resurrection and Its Religious Settings in Qumran and the New Testament." Pages 299–320 in *Echoes from the Caves: Qumran and the New Testament*. Edited by Florentino García Martínez. STDJ 85. Leiden: Brill, 2009.

Holmes, Michael W., ed. *The Apostolic Fathers: Greek Texts and English Translations*. 3rd ed. Grand Rapids: Baker Academic, 2007.

Homer. *The Odyssey*. Translated by Emily R. Wilson. New York: Norton, 2018.

Hooker, Morna Dorothy. *The Gospel according to Saint Mark*. BNTC. Peabody, MA: Hendrickson, 1991.

———. *The Son of Man in Mark: A Study of the Background of the Term "Son of Man" and Its Use in St. Mark's Gospel*. London: SPCK, 1967.

Hubert, Henri, and Marcel Mauss. *Sacrifice, Its Nature and Function*. Translated by W. D. Halls. Chicago: University of Chicago Press, 1964.

Incigneri, Brian J. *The Gospel to the Romans: The Setting and Rhetoric of Mark's Gospel*. BibInt 65. Leiden: Brill, 2003.

Jackson, Howard M. "The Death of Jesus in Mark and the Miracle from the Cross." *NTS* 33 (1987): 16–37.

Jacobson, Howard. "Polyphemus in an Armenian Apocryphal Work." *VT* 37 (1987): 490–91.

Janzen, J. Gerald. "Resurrection and Hermeneutics: On Exodus 3.6 in Mark 12.26." *JSNT* 7 (1985): 43–58.

Jeffery, Peter. *The Secret Gospel of Mark Unveiled: Imagined Rituals of Sex, Death, and Madness in a Biblical Forgery*. New Haven: Yale University Press, 2007.

Johnson, Andy. "The 'New Creation,' the Crucified and Risen Christ, and the Temple: A Pauline Audience for Mark." *JTI* 1 (2007): 171–91.

Johnson, Elliott J. "Mark VIII. 22–26: The Blind Man from Bethsaida." *NTS* 25 (1979): 370–83.

Jones, Christopher P. "The Historicity of the Neronian Persecution: A Response to Brent Shaw." *NTS* 63 (2017): 146–52.

———, ed. *Philostratus: The Life of Apollonius of Tyana*. 3 vols. LCL. Cambridge: Harvard University Press, 2005.

Jonge, Henk J. de. "The Sayings on Confessing and Denying Jesus in Q 12:8–9 and Mark 8:38." Pages 105–21 in *Sayings of Jesus: Canonical and Non-canonical; Essays in Honour of Tjitze Baarda*. Edited by William Lawrence Petersen, Johan S. Vos, and Henk J. de Jonge. NovTSup 89. Leiden: Brill, 1997.

Joynes, Christine E. "A Question of Identity: 'Who Do People Say That I Am?' Elijah, John the Baptist and Jesus in Mark's Gospel." Pages 15–29 in *Understanding, Studying and Reading: New Testament Essays in Honour of John Ashton*. Edited by Christopher Rowland and Crispin H. T. Fletcher-Louis. JSNTSup 153. Sheffield: Sheffield Academic, 1998.

Juel, Donald. *A Master of Surprise: Mark Interpreted*. Minneapolis: Fortress, 1994.

Kalin, Everett R. "Matthew 9:18–26: An Exercise in Redaction Criticism." *CurTM* 15 (1988): 39–47.

Käsemann, Ernst. "On the Subject of Primitive Christian Apocalyptic." Pages 108–37 in *New Testament Questions of Today*. Translated by William J. Montague. Philadelphia: Fortress, 1969.

Kaster, Robert A., ed. *C. Suetoni Tranquilli: De vita Caesarum libros VIII et De grammaticis et rhetoribus librum*. OCT. Oxford: Oxford University Press, 2016.

Kazen, Thomas. "Jesus and the Zavah: Implications for Interpreting Mark." Pages 112–43 in *Purity, Holiness, and Identity in Judaism and Christianity: Essays in Memory of Susan Haber*. Edited by Carl S. Ehrlich, Anders Runesson, and Eileen M. Schuller. WUNT 305. Tübingen: Mohr Siebeck, 2013.

Kee, Howard Clark. "The Transfiguration in Mark: Epiphany or Apocalyptic Vision?" Pages 137–52 in *Understanding the Sacred Text: Essays in Honor of Morton S. Enslin on the Hebrew Bible and Christian Beginnings*. Edited by John Reumann. Valley Forge, PA: Judson, 1972.

Kelber, Werner H. "Hour of the Son of Man and the Temptation of the Disciples (Mark 14.32–42)." Pages 39–60 in *The Passion in Mark: Studies on Mark 14–16*. Edited by Werner H. Kelber and John R. Donahue. Philadelphia: Fortress, 1976.

Kelly, J. N. D. *Early Christian Doctrines*. Rev. ed. San Francisco: Harper & Row, 1978.

Keulen, Wytse Hette. *Gellius the Satirist: Roman Cultural Authority in Attic Nights*. MnemSup 297. Leiden: Brill, 2009.

Kim, Tae Hun. "The Anarthrous Υἱὸς Θεοῦ in Mark 15,39 and the Roman Imperial Cult." *Bib* 79 (1998): 221–41.

King, Karen L. "Which Early Christianity?" Pages 66–84 in *The Oxford Handbook of Early Christian Studies*. Edited by Susan Ashbrook and David G. Hunter. New York: Oxford University Press, 2018.

Kingsbury, Jack Dean. "The 'Divine Man' as the Key to Mark's Christology—the End of an Era?" *Int* 35 (1981): 243–57.

Kloppenborg, John S. *The Formation of Q: Trajectories in Ancient Wisdom Collections*. SAC. Philadelphia: Fortress, 1987.

———. *Q, the Earliest Gospel: An Introduction to the Original Stories and Sayings of Jesus*. Louisville: Westminster John Knox, 2008.

Koester, Helmut. "On Heroes, Tombs, and Early Christianity." Pages 257–64 in *Flavius Philostratus: Heroikos*. Edited by Jennifer K. Berenson Maclean and Ellen Bradshaw Aitken. WGRW 1. Atlanta: Society of Biblical Literature, 2001.

Koskenniemi, Erkki. *Apollonios von Tyana in der neutestamentliche Exegese: Forschungsbericht und Weiterführung der Diskussion*. WUNT 61. Tübingen: Mohr Siebeck, 1994.

Kraus, Christina Shuttleworth. "Hair, Hegemony, and Historiography: Caesar's Style and Its Earliest Critics." Pages 97–115 in *Aspects of the Language of Latin Prose*. Edited by Tobias Reinhardt, Michael Lapidge, and J. N. Adams. Oxford: British Academy, 2005.

Kuhn, Karl Georg. "New Light on Temptation, Sin, and Flesh in the New Testament." Pages 94–113 in *The Scrolls and the New Testament*. Edited by Krister Stendhal. New York: Harper, 1957.

Lampe, Geoffrey W. H. "St Peter's Denial and the Treatment of the *Lapsi*." Pages 113–33 in *The Heritage of the Early Church: Essays in Honor of Georges Vasilievich Florovsky on the Occasion of His Eightieth Birthday*. Edited by David Neiman and Margaret A. Schatkin. OrChrAn 195. Rome: Pont. Institutum Studiorum Orientalium, 1973.

Larsen, Kasper Bro. "Mark 7:1–13: A Pauline Halakah?" Pages 169–87 in *For and Against Pauline Influence on Mark*. Part 2 of *Mark and Paul: Comparative Essays*. Edited by Eve-Marie Becker, Troels Engberg-Pedersen, and Mogens Mueller. BZNW 199. Berlin: de Gruyter, 2014.

Larsen, Matthew D. C. *Gospels before the Book*. New York: Oxford University Press, 2018.

Layton, Bentley, ed. *The Coptic Gnostic Library: Nag Hammadi Codex II, 2-7 Together with XIII,2*, Brit. Lib. Or. 4926 (1), and P. Oxy. 1, 654, 655.* Vol. 1. NHMS 20. Leiden: Brill, 1989.

———. *The Gnostic Scriptures: A New Translation with Annotations and Introductions.* ABRL. New York: Doubleday, 1987.

Leemans, Jan. "The Idea of Flight from Persecution in the Alexandrian Tradition from Clement to Athanasius." Pages 901–10 in *Origeniana Octava: Origen and the Alexandrian Tradition.* Edited by Lorenzo Perrone. BETL 164. Leuven: Peeters, 2004.

Lehtipuu, Outi. *Debates over the Resurrection of the Dead: Constructing Early Christian Identity.* Oxford: Oxford University Press, 2015.

Levine, Amy-Jill. "Discharging Responsibility: Matthean Jesus, Biblical Law, and Hemorrhaging Woman." Pages 70–87 in *A Feminist Companion to Matthew.* Edited by Amy-Jill Levine. FCNTECW 1. Sheffield: Sheffield Academic, 2001.

Levine, Daniel B. "*Odyssey* 18: Iros as Paradigm for the Suitors." *CJ* 77 (1982): 200–204.

Lewis, C. S. *A Preface to Paradise Lost, Being the Ballard Matthews Lectures, Delivered at University College, North Wales, 1941.* London: Oxford University Press, 1942.

Licona, Michael R. *The Resurrection of Jesus: A New Historiographical Approach.* Downers Grove, IL: InterVarsity Press, 2010.

Lightfoot, Robert H. *The Gospel Message of St. Mark.* Oxford: Clarendon, 1950.

———. *History and Interpretation in the Gospels.* London: Hodder & Stoughton, 1935.

Lincoln, Andrew T. "The Promise and the Failure: Mark 16:7, 8." *JBL* 108 (1989): 283–300.

Lindars, Barnabas. *Jesus, Son of Man: A Fresh Examination of the Son of Man Sayings in the Gospels in the Light of Recent Research.* Grand Rapids: Eerdmans, 1984.

Lipsius, Richard, ed. *Acta Apostolorum apocrypha post Constantinum Tischendorf.* Vol. 1. Leipzig: Mendelssohn, 1891.

Loader, William. "The Concept of Faith in Paul and Mark." Pages 423–64 in *Two Authors at the Beginnings of Christianity.* Part 1 of *Paul and Mark: Comparative Essays.* Edited by Oda Wischmeyer, David C. Sim, and Ian J. Elmer. BZNW 198. Berlin: de Gruyter, 2014.

Löhr, Winrich. "Valentinian Variations on LK 12,8–9/Mt 10,32." *VC* 57 (2003): 437–55.

Lunn, Nicholas P. *The Original Ending of Mark: A New Case for the Authenticity of Mark 16:9–20*. Eugene, OR: Pickwick, 2014.
Luther, Martin. *Annotationes in aliquot capita Matthaei*. D. Martin Luthers Werke 38. Weimar: Hermann Böhlau, 1912.
Luz, Ulrich. *Matthew 21–28: A Commentary*. Translated by James E. Crouch. Hermeneia. Minneapolis: Fortress, 2005.
MacDonald, Dennis R. *The Gospels and Homer: Imitations of Greek Epic in Mark and Luke-Acts*. Lanham, MD: Rowman & Littlefield, 2015.
——. *The Homeric Epics and the Gospel of Mark*. New Haven: Yale University Press, 2000.
MacMullen, Ramsay. *Paganism in the Roman Empire*. New Haven: Yale University Press, 1981.
Malbon, Elizabeth Struthers. "Disciples/Crowds/Whoever: Markan Characters and Readers." *NovT* 28 (1986): 104–26.
——. "Fallible Followers: Women and Men in the Gospel of Mark." *Semeia* 28 (1983): 29–48.
Malcovati, Enrica, ed. *M. Tulli Ciceronis, scripta quae manserunt omnia: Fasc. 4. Brutus*. BSGRT. Leipzig: Teubner, 1968.
Marcus, Joel. "Crucifixion as Parodic Exaltation." *JBL* 125 (2006): 73–87.
——. *Mark 1–8: A New Translation with Introduction and Commentary*. AB 27. New York: Doubleday, 2000.
——. "Mark 4:10–12 and Marcan Epistemology." *JBL* 103 (1984): 557–74.
——. *Mark 8–16: A New Translation with Introduction and Commentary*. AB 27A. New Haven: Yale University Press, 2009.
——. "Mark 9,11–13: 'As It Has Been Written.'" *ZNW* 80 (2009): 42–63.
——. "Mark—Interpreter of Paul." *NTS* 46 (2000): 473–87.
Marković, Miroslav, ed. *Origenis Contra Celsum libri VIII*. VCSup 54. Leiden: Brill, 2001.
Markusse, Gabi. *Salvation in the Gospel of Mark: The Death of Jesus and the Path of Discipleship*. Kindle ed. Eugene, OR: Wipf & Stock, 2018.
Marshall, Peter K., ed. *Aulus Gellius noctes atticae*. 2 vols. OCT. Oxford: Oxford University Press, 1968.
Martin, Dale B. *The Corinthian Body*. New Haven: Yale University Press, 1995.
Marx, Frederick, ed. *A. Cornelii Celsi quae supersvnt*. CML 1. Leipzig: Teubner, 1915.
Marxsen, Willi. *Mark the Evangelist: Studies on the Redaction History of the Gospel*. Translated by James Boyce, Donald Juel, William Poehlmann, and Roy A. Harrisville. Nashville: Abingdon, 1969.

Massaux, Édouard. *The Apologists and the Didache*. Vol. 3 of *The Influence of the Gospel of Saint Matthew on Christian Literature before Saint Irenaeus*. Edited by Arthur J. Bellinzoni. Translated by Norman J. Belval and Suzanne Hecht. NGS 5.3. Leuven: Peeters, 1993.

Matera, Frank J. *The Kingship of Jesus: Composition Theology in Mark 15*. SBLDS 66. Chico, CA: Scholars Press, 1982.

Matthews, Shelly. "Elijah, Ezekiel, and Romulus: Luke's Flesh and Bones (Luke 24:39) in Light of Ancient Narratives of Ascent, Resurrection, and Apotheosis." Pages 161–82 in *On Prophets, Warriors, and Kings: Former Prophets through the Eyes of Their Interpreters*. Edited by George J. Brooke and Ariel Feldman. BZAW 470. Berlin: de Gruyter, 2016.

———. "A Feminist Analysis of the Veiling Passage (1 Corinthians 11:2–16): Who Really Cares That Paul Was Not a Gender Egalitarian after All?" *LD* (2015): 1–20.

Matusova, Ekaterina. "The Post-mortem Divisions of the Dead in 1 Enoch 22:1–13." Pages 149–77 in *Evil and Death: Conceptions of the Human in Biblical, Early Jewish, Greco-Roman and Egyptian Literature*. Edited by Beate Ego and Ulrike Mittmann. DCLS 18. Berlin: de Gruyter, 2015.

Mauss, Marcel. *The Gift: Forms and Functions of Exchange in Archaic Societies*. Translated by Ian Cunnison. London: Cohen & West, 1966.

Mayhoff, Karl, ed. *C. Plini Secundi naturalis historiae libri XXXVII*. Vol. 4. BSGRT. Leipzig: Teubner, 1897.

McArthur, Harvey K. "'On the Third Day.'" *NTS* 18 (1971): 81–86.

McKnight, Scot. *Jesus and His Death: Historiography, the Historical Jesus, and Atonement Theory*. Waco, TX: Baylor University Press, 2005.

McLellan, Peter N. "Specters of Mark: The Second Gospel's Ending and Derrida's Messianicity." *BibInt* 24 (2016): 357–81.

McVann, Mark. "Destroying Death: Jesus in Mark and Joseph in 'The Sin Eater.'" Pages 123–35 in *The Daemonic Imagination: Biblical Text and Secular Story*. Edited by Robert Detweiler and William G. Doty. AARSR 60. Atlanta: Scholars Press, 1990.

Meeks, Wayne A. "The Image of the Androgyne: Some Uses of a Symbol in Earliest Christianity." *HR* 13 (1974): 165–208.

Meier, John P. "The Debate on the Resurrection of the Dead: An Incident from the Ministry of the Historical Jesus?" *JSNT* 22 (2000): 3–23.

Merry, W. Walter, and James Riddell, eds. *Homer's Odyssey*. 2 vols. 2nd rev. ed. Oxford: Clarendon, 1886.

Metzger, Bruce M. *A Textual Commentary on the Greek New Testament: A Companion Volume to the United Bible Societies' Greek New Testament.* 3rd ed. London: United Bible Societies, 1975.

Middleton, Paul. "Christology, Martyrdom, and Vindication in the Gospel of Mark and the Apocalypse: Two New Testament Views." Pages 219–37 in *Mark, Manuscripts, and Monotheism: Essays in Honor of Larry W. Hurtado.* Edited by Chris Keith and Dieter T. Roth. LNTS 528. London: Bloomsbury, 2015.

———. *Radical Martyrdom and Cosmic Conflict in Early Christianity.* LNTS 307. London: T&T Clark, 2006.

———. "Suffering and the Creation of Christian Identity in the Gospel of Mark." Pages 173–89 in *T&T Clark Handbook to Social Identity in the New Testament.* Edited by J. Brian Tucker and Coleman A. Stohl. London: Bloomsbury, 2016.

Milgrom, Jacob. *Leviticus 1–16: A New Translation with Introduction and Commentary.* AB 3. New York: Doubleday, 1991.

Miller, Richard C. "Mark's Empty Tomb and Other Translation Fables in Classical Antiquity." *JBL* 129 (2010): 759–76.

Moloney, Francis J. "Constructing Jesus and the Son of Man." *CBQ* 75 (2013): 719–38.

Montgomery, Hugo. "The Bishop Who Fled: Responsibility and Honour in Saint Cyprian." *StPatr* 21 (1989): 264–67.

Morgan, Teresa. *Literate Education in the Hellenistic and Roman Worlds.* CCS. Cambridge: Cambridge University Press, 1998.

Moss, Candida. "The Man with the Flow of Power: Porous Bodies in Mark 5:25–34." *JBL* 129 (2010): 507–19.

———. *The Myth of Persecution: How Early Christians Invented a Story of Martyrdom.* New York: HarperOne, 2013.

———. *The Other Christs: Imitating Jesus in Ancient Christian Ideologies of Martyrdom.* New York: Oxford University Press, 2010.

———. "The Transfiguration: An Exercise in Markan Accommodation." *BibInt* 12 (2004): 69–89.

Most, Glenn W., ed. *Hesiod: Theogony, Works and Days, Testimonia.* LCL. Cambridge: Harvard University Press, 2006.

Muddiman, John. "The Glory of Jesus, Mark 10:37." Pages 51–58 in *The Glory of Christ in the New Testament: Studies in Christology in Memory of George Bradford Caird.* Edited by Lincoln D. Hurst and N. T. Wright. Oxford: Clarendon, 1987.

Mühlenberg, Ekkehard, ed. *Gregorii Nysseni oratio catechetica.* GNO 3.4. Leiden: Brill, 1996.
Munk, Linda. *The Devil's Mousetrap: Redemption and Colonial American Literature.* Oxford: Oxford University Press, 1997.
Myers, Ched. *Binding the Strong Man: A Political Reading of Mark's Story of Jesus.* Maryknoll, NY: Orbis, 1988.
Mynors, R. A. B., ed. *P. Vergili Maronis opera.* OCT. Oxford: Oxford University Press, 1969.
Naiden, F. S. *Smoke Signals for the Gods: Ancient Greek Sacrifice from the Archaic through Roman Periods.* Oxford: Oxford University Press, 2013.
Nardoni, Enrique. *La transfiguración de Jésus y el diálogo sobre Elías segun el Evangelio de San Marcos.* TED 2. Buenos Aires: Editora Patria Grande, 1977.
Neirynck, Francis. "La fuite du jeune homme en Mc 14:51-52." *ETL* 55 (1979): 43–66.
———. "Saving/Losing One's Life: Luke 17,33 (Q?) and Mark 8,35." Pages 295–318 in *Von Jesus zum Christus: Christologische Studien: Festgabe für Paul Hoffmann zum 65. Geburtstag.* Edited by Rudolf Hoppe and Ulrich Busse. BZNW 93. Berlin: de Gruyter, 1998.
Newton, Rick M. "The Rebirth of Odysseus." *GRBS* 25 (2004): 5–20.
Nicholson, Oliver. "Flight from Persecution as Imitation of Christ: Lactantius's *Divine Institutes* IV. 18, 1–2." *JTS* 40 (1989): 48–65.
Nickelsburg, George W. E. "Son of Man." *ABD* 6:137–50.
Nielsen, Jesper Tang. "The Cross on the Way to Mark." Pages 273–94 in *For and Against Pauline Influence on Mark.* Part 2 of *Mark and Paul: Comparative Essays.* Edited by Eve-Marie Becker, Troels Engberg-Pedersen, and Mogens Mueller. BZNW 199. Berlin: de Gruyter, 2014.
Nineham, Dennis E. *The Gospel of St. Mark.* PNTC. Hammondsworth: Penguin, 1969.
Nongbri, Brent. "A Touch of Condemnation in a Word of Exhortation: Apocalyptic Language and Graeco-Roman Rhetoric in Hebrews 6:4–12." *NovT* 45 (2003): 265–79.
Oepke, Albrecht. "βάπτω, βαπτίζω." *TDNT* 1:529–46.
Öhler, Markus. "The Expectation of Elijah and the Presence of the Kingdom of God." *JBL* 118 (1999): 461–76.
Osborne, B. A. E. "Peter: Stumbling-Block and Satan." *NovT* 15 (1973): 187–90.

Pascut, Beniamin. "The So-Called 'Passivum Divinum' in Mark's Gospel." *NovT* 54 (2012): 313–33.
Peppard, Michael. *The Son of God in the Roman World: Divine Sonship in Its Social and Political Context*. Oxford: Oxford University Press, 2011.
Perkins, Judith. *Roman Imperial Identities in the Early Christian Era*. RMCS. London: Routledge, 2009.
Pervo, Richard I. *Acts: A Commentary*. Hermeneia. Minneapolis: Fortress, 2009.
Petersen, Norman R. "When Is the End Not the End: Literary Reflections on the Ending of Mark's Narrative." *Int* 34 (1980): 151–66.
Petrey, Taylor G. "The Resurrection Body." Pages 661–74 in *The Oxford Handbook of New Testament, Gender, and Sexuality*. Edited by Benjamin H. Dunning. New York: Oxford University Press, 2019.
Phelan, James. "Authors, Resources, Audiences: Toward a Rhetorical Poetics of Narrative." *Style* 52 (2018): 1–34.
Pilch, John J. "Flute Players, Death, and Music in the Afterlife (Matthew IX,18–19, 23–26)." *BTB* 37 (2007): 12–19.
Propp, William Henry. *Exodus 19–40: A New Translation with Introduction and Commentary*. AB 2A. New York: Doubleday, 2006.
Pudussery, Paul S. "Discipleship: A Call to Suffering and Glory; An Exegetico-Theological Study of Mk 8,27–9,1; 13,9–13 and 13,24–27." PhD diss., Pontificia Università Urbaniana, 1987.
Rahlfs, Alfred, ed. *Septuaginta*. Stuttgart: Deutsche Bibelgesellschaft, 2006.
Rashdall, Hastings. *The Idea of the Atonement in Christian Theology, Being the Bampton Lectures for 1915*. London: MacMillan, 1919.
Rastoin, Marc. "Simon-Pierre entre Jésus et Satan: la théologie Lucanienne à l'oeuvre en Lc 22,31–32." *Bib* 89 (2008): 153–72.
Ray, Darby Kathleen. *Deceiving the Devil: Atonement, Abuse, and Ransom*. Cleveland: Pilgrim, 1998.
Reardon, Patrick Henry. "The Cross, Sacraments and Martyrdom: An Investigation of Mark 10:35–45." *SVTQ* 36 (1992): 103–15.
Reeder, Caryn A. "Malachi 3:24 and the Eschatological Restoration of the 'Family.'" *CBQ* 69 (2007): 695–709.
Reischl, Wilhelm C., and Joseph Rupp, eds. *Cyrilli Hierosolymarum archiepiscopi opera quae supersunt omnia*. Vol. 2. Hildesheim: Olms, 1967.
Riley, Gregory J. *Resurrection Reconsidered: Thomas and John in Controversy*. Minneapolis: Fortress, 1995.
Robertson, Archibald T. *A Grammar of the Greek New Testament in the Light of Historical Research*. New York: Hodder & Stoughton, 1914.

Robinson, H. Wheeler. *Corporate Personality in Ancient Israel*. Rev. ed. Philadelphia: Fortress, 1980.
Roskam, Hendrika Nicoline. *The Purpose of the Gospel of Mark in Its Historical and Social Context*. NovTSup 114. Leiden: Brill, 2004.
Rossé, Gérard. *The Cry of Jesus on the Cross: A Biblical and Theological Study*. Translated by Stephen Wentworth Arndt. New York: Paulist, 1987.
Rothschild, Clare K. *Baptist Traditions and Q*. WUNT 190. Tübingen: Mohr Siebeck, 2005.
Rousseau, Adelin, and Louis Doutreleau, eds. *Irénée de Lyon: Contre les hérésies livre 1*. SC 264. Paris: Cerf, 1979.
Russell, E. A. "The Gospel of Mark: Pastoral Response to a Life or Death Situation? Some Reflections." *IBS* 7 (1985): 206–22.
Sage, Michael M. *Cyprian*. PMS 1. Cambridge: Philadelphia Patristic Foundation, 1975.
Sanders, E. P. *The Historical Figure of Jesus*. London: Penguin, 1993.
Scarth, Alwyn. "Volcanic Origins of the Polyphemus Story in the *Odyssey*: A Non-classicist's Interpretation." *CW* 83 (1989): 89–95.
Schaberg, Jane. "Daniel 7, 12 and the New Testament Passion-Resurrection Predictions." *NTS* 31 (1985): 208–22.
Schaeffer, Susan E. "The Guard at the Tomb (*Gos. Pet.* 8:28–11:49 and Matt 27:62–66; 28:2–4, 11–16): A Case of Intertextuality?" Pages 499–507 in *Society of Biblical Literature 1991 Seminar Papers*. SBLSP 30. Atlanta: Scholars Press, 1991.
Schein, Seth L. "Odysseus and Polyphemus in the *Odyssey*." *GRBS* 11 (1970): 73–83.
Schreiber, Johannes. *Theologie des Vertrauens: Eine redaktionsgeschichtliche Untersuchung des Markusevangeliums*. Hamburg: Furche-Verlag, 1967.
Schwankl, Otto. *Die Sadduzäerfrage (Mk 12, 18–27 Parr): Eine exegetisch-theologische Studie zur Auferstehungserwartung*. BBB 66. Frankfurt am Main: Athenäum, 1987.
Schweitzer, Albert. *The Mysticism of Paul the Apostle*. Translated by William Montgomery. New York: Holt, 1931.
———. *The Quest of the Historical Jesus: A Critical Study of Its Progress from Reimarus to Wrede*. Translated by William Montgomery. 2nd ed. London: A&C Black, 1911.
Scodel, Ruth. *An Introduction to Greek Tragedy*. Cambridge: Cambridge University Press, 2010.

Scott, Shirley Clay. "Man, Mind, and Monster: Polyphemus from Homer through Joyce." *CML* 16 (1995): 19–75.

Scott-Macnab, David. "St. Augustine and the Devil's 'Mousetrap.'" *VC* 68 (2014): 409–15.

Scroggs, Robin, and Kent Ira Groff. "Baptism in Mark: Dying and Rising with Christ." *JBL* 92 (1973): 531–48.

Seccombe, David P. "Take Up Your Cross." Pages 139–51 in *God Who Is Rich in Mercy: Essays Presented to Dr. D. B. Knox*. Edited by Peter Thomas O'Brien and David Gilbert Peterson. Grand Rapids: Baker Books, 1986.

Seeley, David. "Rulership and Service in Mark 10:41–45." *NovT* 35 (1993): 234–50.

Segal, Moses H., trans. *'Eduyyoth*. In vol. 4 of *The Babylonian Talmud: Seder Nezikin*. Edited by Isidore Epstein. London: Soncino, 1935.

Seim, Turid Karlsen. "Children of the Resurrection: Perspectives on Angelic Asceticism in Luke-Acts." Pages 115–25 in *Asceticism in the New Testament*. Edited by Leif E. Vaage and Vincent L. Wimbush. New York: Routledge, 1999.

Selvidge, Marla J. "Mark 5:25–34 and Leviticus 15:19–20: A Reaction to Restrictive Purity Regulations." *JBL* 103 (1984): 619–23.

Shaw, Brent D. "The Myth of the Neronian Persecution." *JRS* 105 (2015): 73–100.

Shiner, Whitney T. "The Ambiguous Pronouncement of the Centurion and the Shrouding of Meaning in Mark." *JSNT* 22 (2000): 3–22.

Sim, David C. "The Family of Jesus and the Disciples of Jesus in Paul and Mark: Taking Sides in the Early Church's Factional Dispute." Pages 73–99 in *Two Authors at the Beginnings of Christianity*. Part 1 of *Paul and Mark: Comparative Essays*. Edited by Oda Wischmeyer, David C. Sim, and Ian J. Elmer. BZNW 198. Berlin: de Gruyter, 2014.

Simon-Shoshan, Moshe. "Talmud as Novel: Dialogic Discourse and the Feminine Voice in the Babylonian Talmud." *PT* 40 (2019): 105–34.

Singer, Charles, ed. and trans. *Galen on Anatomical Procedures: De anatomicis administrationibus*. PWHMM, NS 7. London: Oxford University Press, 1956.

Skoven, Anne Vig. "Mark as Allegorical Rewriting of Paul." Pages 13–27 in *For and Against Pauline Influence on Mark*. Part 2 of *Mark and Paul: Comparative Essays*. Edited by Eve-Marie Becker, Troels Engberg-Pedersen, and Mogens Mueller. BZNW 199. Berlin: de Gruyter, 2014.

Sloan, David B. "God of Abraham, God of the Living: Jesus's Use of Exodus 3:6 in Mark 12:26–27." *WTJ* 74 (2012): 85–98.
Smith, Daniel A. "Revisiting the Empty Tomb: The Post-mortem Vindication of Jesus in Mark and Q." *NovT* 45 (2003): 123–37.
Smith, Terence V. *Petrine Controversies in Early Christianity: Attitudes towards Peter in Christian Writings of the First Two Centuries.* WUNT 15. Tübingen: Mohr Siebeck, 1985.
Smyth, Herbert Weir, and Gordon M. Messing. *Greek Grammar.* Cambridge: Harvard University Press, 1956.
Starobinski, Jean. "Essay in Literary Analysis: Mark 5:1–20." *ER* 23 (1971): 377–97.
Stein, Robert H. "The Ending of Mark." *BBR* 18 (2008): 79–98.
———. *Studying the Synoptic Gospels: Origin and Interpretation.* 2nd ed. Grand Rapids: Baker Academic, 2001.
Sterling, Gregory E. "Jesus as Exorcist: An Analysis of Matthew 17:14–20; Mark 9:14–29; Luke 9:37–43a." *CBQ* 55 (1993): 467–93.
Stock, Klemens. *Boten aus dem Mit-Ihm-Sein: Das Verhältnis zwischen Jesus und den Zwölf nach Markus.* AnBib 70. Rome: Biblical Institute Press, 1975.
Stone, Michael E., ed. *Armenian Apocrypha Relating to the Patriarchs and Prophets.* Jerusalem: Israel Academy of Sciences and Humanities, 1982.
Swain, Simon. "Defending Hellenism: Philostratus, *In Honour of Apollonius.*" Pages 157–96 in *Apologetics in the Roman Empire: Pagans, Jews, and Christians.* Edited by Mark Edward, Martin Goodman, and Simon Price. Oxford: Oxford University Press, 1999.
Sweetland, Dennis M. "Discipleship and Persecution: A Study of Luke 12,1–12." *Bib* 65 (1984): 61–80.
Swete, Henry Barclay. *The Gospel according to St. Mark: The Greek Text with Introduction, Notes and Indices.* 3rd ed. London: Macmillan, 1913.
Tannehill, Robert C. "Reading It Whole: The Function of Mark 8:34–35 in Mark's Story." Pages 189–99 in *The Shape of the Gospel: New Testament Essays.* Eugene, OR: Cascade, 2007.
Tappenden, Frederick S. *Resurrection in Paul: Cognition, Metaphor, and Transformation.* ECL 19. Atlanta: SBL Press, 2016.
Taylor, Adam. "An Easter Sunday Suicide Bombing Shows Plight of Pakistan's Christians." *Washington Post*, March 28, 2016. https://tinyurl.com/SBL4532a.

Taylor, Vincent. *The Gospel according to St. Mark.* London: Macmillan, 1952.

Theissen, Gerd. *The Gospels in Context: Social and Political History in the Synoptic Tradition.* Translated by Linda M. Maloney. Minneapolis: Fortress, 1991.

———. *The Miracle Stories of the Early Christian Tradition.* Edited by John Riches. Translated by Francis McDonagh. Philadelphia: Fortress, 1983.

Thiessen, Matthew. "A Buried Pentateuchal Allusion to the Resurrection in Mark 12:25." *CBQ* 76 (2014): 273–90.

———. *Jesus and the Forces of Death: The Gospels' Portrayal of Ritual Impurity within First-Century Judaism.* Grand Rapids: Baker Academic, 2020.

———. "The Many for One or One for the Many? Reading Mark 10:45 in the Roman Empire." *HTR* 109 (2016): 447–66.

Thiselton, Anthony C. *The First Epistle to the Corinthians: A Commentary on the Greek Text.* NIGTC. Grand Rapids: Eerdmans, 2000.

Thrall, Margaret E. "Elijah and Moses in Mark's Account of the Transfiguration." *NTS* 16 (1970): 305–17.

Tödt, Heinz Eduard. *The Son of Man in the Synoptic Tradition.* Translated by Dorthea M. Barton. NTL. Philadelphia: Westminster, 1965.

Toensing, Holly Joan. "'Living among the Tombs': Society, Mental Illness, and Self-Destruction in Mark 5:1–20." Pages 131–43 in *This Abled Body: Rethinking Disabilities in Biblical Studies.* Edited by Hector Avalos, Sarah J. Melcher, and Jeremy Schipper. SemeiaSt 55. Atlanta: Society of Biblical Literature, 2007.

Tolbert, Mary Ann. *Sowing the Gospel: Mark's World in Literary-Historical Perspective.* Minneapolis: Fortress, 1989.

Trick, Bradley R. "Death, Covenants, and the Proof of Resurrection in Mark 12:18–27." *NovT* 49 (2007): 232–56.

Trocmé, Etienne. "Marc 9,1: Prédiction ou réprimande." *SE* 2 (1964): 259–65.

Tylor, Edward Burnett. *Primitive Culture: Researches into the Development of Mythology, Philosophy, Religion, Language, Art, and Custom.* 4th ed. 2 vols. London: Murray, 1920.

Tyson, Joseph B. "The Blindness of the Disciples in Mark." *JBL* 80 (1961): 261–68.

Van Iersel, Bas M. F. "Failed Followers in Mark: Mark 13:12 as a Key for the Identification of the Intended Readers." *CBQ* 58 (1996): 244–63.

———. "The Gospel according to St. Mark—Written for a Persecuted Community?" *NedTT* 34 (1980): 15–36.

Vander Stichele, Caroline. "Like Angels in Heaven: Corporeality, Resurrection, and Gender in Mark 12:18–27." Pages 214–32 in *Begin with the Body: Corporeality, Religion and Gender*. Edited by Jonneke Bekkenkamp and Maaike de Haardt. Leuven: Peeters, 1998.

Vanhoye, Albert. "La fuite du jeune homme nu (Mc 14:51–52)." *Bib* 52 (1971): 401–6.

Vielhauer, Philipp. "Gottesreich und Menschensohn in der Verkündigung Jesu." Pages 51[55]–79[91] in *Aufsätze zum Neuen Testament*. TB 31. Munich: Kaiser, 1965.

Viviano, Benedict T., and Justin Taylor. "Sadducees, Angels, and Resurrection (Acts 23:8–9)." *JBL* 111 (1992): 496–98.

Vliet, Johannes van der, ed. *Lucii Apulei Madaurensis Apologia sive De magia liber et Florida*. BSGRT. Leipzig: Teubner, 1900.

Ware, James. "Paul's Understanding of the Resurrection in 1 Corinthians 15:36–54." *JBL* 133 (2014): 809–35.

Waters, Kenneth L. "Matthew 27:52–53 as Apocalyptic Apostrophe: Temporal-Spatial Collapse in the Gospel of Matthew." *JBL* 122 (2003): 489–515.

Watts, Rikki E. *Isaiah's New Exodus and Mark*. WUNT 88. Tübingen: Mohr Siebeck, 1997.

———. "Jesus's Death, Isaiah 53, and Mark 10:45: A Crux Revisited." Pages 125–51 in *Jesus and the Suffering Servant: Isaiah 53 and Christian Origins*. Edited by W. H. Bellinger and William Reuben Farmer. Harrisburg, PA: Trinity Press International, 1998.

Weaver, J. Denny. *The Nonviolent Atonement*. 2nd ed. Grand Rapids: Eerdmans, 2010.

Webb, Geoff R. *Mark at the Threshold: Applying Bakhtinian Categories to Markan Characterisation*. BibInt 95. Leiden: Brill, 2008.

Weeden, Theodore J. *Mark: Traditions in Conflict*. Philadelphia: Fortress, 1971.

Weisberg, Dvora E. "The Widow of Our Discontent: Levirate Marriage in the Bible and Ancient Israel." *JSOT* 28 (2004): 403–29.

Wenham, David, and A. D. A. Moses. "'There Are Some Standing Here…': Did They Become the 'Reputed Pillars' of the Jerusalem Church? Some Reflections on Mark 9:1, Galatians 2:9 and the Transfiguration." *NovT* 36 (1994): 146–63.

Wenham, John W. "How Many Cock-Crowings? The Problem of Harmonistic Text-Variants." *NTS* 25 (1979): 523–25.

Whitaker, Robyn J. "Rebuke or Recall? Rethinking the Role of Peter in Mark's Gospel." *CBQ* 75 (2013): 666–82.

Williams, Guy. "Narrative Space, Angelic Revelation, and the End of Mark's Gospel." *JSNT* 35 (2013): 263–84.

Wills, Lawrence M. *The Quest of the Historical Gospel: Mark, John, and the Origins of the Gospel Genre*. London: Routledge, 1997.

Wimpfheimer, Barry Scott. "The Dialogical Talmud: Daniel Boyarin and Rabbinics." *JQR* 101 (2011): 245–54.

Winer, Georg B. *A Treatise on the Grammar of New Testament Greek: Regarded as a Sure Basis for New Testament Exegesis*. Translated by William F. Moulton. 9th ed. Edinburgh: T&T Clark, 1892.

Winn, Adam. *The Purpose of Mark's Gospel: An Early Christian Response to Roman Imperial Propaganda*. WUNT 245. Tübingen: Mohr Siebeck, 2008.

Wischmeyer, Oda, David C. Sim, and Ian J. Elmer, eds. *Two Authors at the Beginnings of Christianity*. Part 1 of *Paul and Mark: Comparative Essays*. BZNW 198. Berlin: de Gruyter, 2014.

Wrede, Wilhelm. *The Messianic Secret*. Translated by James C. G. Greig. LTT. Greenwood, SC: Attic Press, 1971.

Wright, N. T. *The Resurrection of the Son of God*. COQG 3. Minneapolis: Fortress, 2003.

Zeichmann, Christopher B. *The Roman Army and the New Testament*. Lanham, MD: Rowman & Littlefield, 2018.

Zevit, Ziony. *What Really Happened in the Garden of Eden?* New Haven: Yale University Press, 2013.

Ancient Sources Index

Hebrew Bible/ Old Testament		14:26–15:21	48
		24:5–6	211
Genesis		24:7–8	211
1:27	80	24:8	209–10
2	80–81	32	212
2–3	180		
3:24	87	Leviticus	
4:1	87	3:3	178
6:1–4	80	4	179–80
12:1–3	87–88	12:4–7	50
12:7	87–88	15	52
13:14–15	87–88	15:19–20	50
13:17	87–88	15:19–31	50
17:7–8	87	15:25–27	53
18–19	35	15:28–30	53
18:11–13	82	15:31–33	52
21:5	82	17:10–14	67
21:7	82	17:11	50
22:17	76	17:14	50
23	87–88	21:10	189
25:21	82	24:10–16	189
26:4	76	24:23	189
29:31	82		
30:1	87	Numbers	
30:22	82	5:1–4	50–52
38	75, 77, 82–83, 89	14:22–23	88
38:8	76–77	24:14	55
45:18	178		
		Deuteronomy	
Exodus	182	7:8	182
3:6	82–86, 89	9:26	182
3:15–16	82–86, 88	11:9	85
3:15–17	88	12:23	67
6:6	182	21:22–23	188
12	211	25	75

-259-

Deuteronomy (cont.)		53	181
25:5–6	76	53:10–12	180
25:5–10	77–78	53:12	210
34:6–7	102	62:12	182
		65:1–4	45
Judges		65:2	49
3:10	219	65:4	48–49
6:34	219	66:10–17	48
11:34–40	56		
13:3–6	35	Jeremiah	
		15:21	182
1 Kings		23:20	55
17:1	106	31[LXX 38]:11	182
17:17–24	66	41:4–7	45
18:1	106	48:37–39	45
19:1–3	106		
19:10	106	Ezekiel	
19:14	106	36:16–38	49
		37	49
2 Kings			
1:8	107	Daniel	
2:11–12	42, 102	7	41, 97, 103
4:31–37	66	7:10	10, 102
		7:13–14	102–3, 131–32, 162
Job		9:26–27	133
1–2	180	9:27	132
41:1 [LXX 40:25]	213	11:31–35	132–33
		12	41, 103
Psalms		12:1	102
2:7–8	102	12:1–3	47
22	204–5, 208	12:2	59, 102–3
22:1	165, 203–4	12:2–3	102, 131–32
22:22–31	204		
22:24	204	Hosea	
50 [LXX 49]:17	111	6:1–3	49
75:8	163		
88 [LXX 87]:5–6	59	Micah	
110 [LXX 109]:1	162	4:10	182
		6:4	182
Isaiah			
38:17	111	Habakkuk	
43:1	182	1	182
43:6–7	132		
51:7	163	Zechariah	
52:3	182	2:6	132

9:9	210	Ancient Jewish Writers	
9:9–11	210		
9:10	210	Josephus, *Antiquitates judaicae*	
9:11	209–10	3.261	52
		5.277–279	35
Malachi		13.297	76
4:5–6	104–6, 114	18.16	76
4:6	105–7		
		Josephus, *Bellum judaicum*	
Deuterocanonical Books		2.165	76
		5.227	52
1 Maccabees			
1:54–64	132	Philo, *De vita Mosis*	
2:7–34	132	2.288	42, 102
		2.291	42
2 Maccabees			
3:24–30	35	New Testament	
10:29–31	35		
11:8–14	35	Matthew	
		3:17	186
4 Maccabees		8:5–13	63
6:29	180	9:18	60, 62
7:18–19	85	9:18–19	44, 50
13:15	85	9:18–26	61
16:25	85	9:20–22	50–51
17:22	180	9:23	61–62
18:23	85	9:23–26	44
		9:24	60, 62, 66
Pseudepigrapha		10:5	136
		10:19–20	217, 219
1 Enoch		10:21	137
6–19	80	10:23	109, 137
10.1–6	46	10:26–33	219
15.3–10	80	10:32–33	136, 219
15.6–7	79–80	10:33	116, 135
108.10–15	102	10:38–39	116, 135–36
		12:1–8	94
2 Enoch		12:9–12	94
10	46	12:32	219
		15:16–18	50
2 Baruch		17:14–20	71–72
30	47	17:15	71
82	47	17:21	110
		18:6–7	5
		20:28	191

Matthew (cont.)		1:39	55
21:4–5	210	1:40–45	51
22:33	94	1:43–45	59
23:28–29	189–90	2:10	4, 6
27:46	206	2:13–17	171
27:51–53	189–90	2:23–28	94
27:52	191	2:28	4, 6
27:52–53	43, 57, 192	3:1–12	94
27:53	191–92, 198	3:4	114
27:54	186	3:11	148, 187
27:57	188	3:11–12	112, 184–85
27:57–60	187–88	3:14	135
27:62–66	38	3:14–15	110
27:64	38	3:15	55, 148, 184
28	10	3:22	148, 184, 217
28:1–3	39	3:22–23	55
28:5–7	39	3:22–30	89–90, 184, 189
28:7	39	3:23	163, 184
28:11–15	38	3:25–26	89–90
28:13	38	3:27	90, 177, 184, 201, 213, 227
28:15	38	3:28–29	218–20, 232
28:16–20	39	3:29	173, 217, 220
		3:30	217
Mark		3:31–35	34
1:1	154, 187	3:33–34	165
1:1–11	166–67	4:2	163
1:4	135	4:4	146–47, 154, 169
1:6	107	4:5–6	143, 154, 169
1:8	158	4:7	146, 169
1:9–11	168	4:10	143
1:11	165, 185–87	4:10–11	146
1:12	193	4:11	163
1:12–13	148, 184, 201	4:15	147, 154, 169
1:13	148	4:16–17	144, 154, 169
1:14–15	135	4:17	143
1:16–18	100	4:18–19	169
1:17–18	113	4:19	146
1:18	143	4:35–41	100, 184
1:20	113	4:38	100
1:23–24	195	4:40	100
1:23–28	148, 184	4:43–45	146
1:24–25	112, 185	5	44, 69, 184
1:26	190	5:1	45, 194
1:32–34	184	5:1–20	44, 49, 67, 184–85, 201, 208
1:34	112, 148, 185	5:2	194

Ancient Sources Index

5:2–3	44–45	5:43	58–59, 63
5:3	47, 194	6	106
5:3–4	189, 194	6:3	33–34, 165
5:4–5	45	6:7–13	184
5:5	45	6:14–29	106–7, 209
5:6	190	6:21	107
5:7	185–87, 190, 197, 202, 206, 208	6:22	107
5:7–13	190	6:25	107, 211
5:9	45, 47, 185, 190, 195	6:25–28	209
5:10	48	6:26	107
5:10–12	196	6:27–29	102
5:11–13	45	6:29	108
5:13	48, 196	6:45	123
5:14–17	194	6:53–56	123
5:15	47, 185	7:1	189
5:19	190, 197	7:1–5	123
5:19–20	47	7:1–13	189
5:20	45, 197	7:1–23	51, 93
5:21–24a	43, 49–50, 54, 67, 172	7:6–13	123
5:22–24	54	7:8	108
5:23	54–55, 57, 62, 67, 70, 72	7:8–9	188–89
5:24b–34	49–50	7:13	189
5:25	50	7:14–15	123
5:25–34	50	7:17–23	124
5:26	52	7:18–19	124
5:27	52	7:18–20	51
5:29	50	7:19	124–25, 212
5:29–30	53	7:24–30	37, 184, 227
5:33	52	7:26	55
5:34	37, 53	7:27–28	37
5:35	37, 55–56, 58, 72	7:31–37	24
5:35–36	96	8:22–26	24, 98
5:35–37	62	8:27–31	113
5:35–38	54	8:27–33	112–13
5:35–43	43, 49, 54, 172	8:27–9:1	99, 111
5:36	56, 58, 61, 70, 72–74	8:27–9:29	69
5:37	59	8:29	112
5:38	58, 61	8:29–30	148
5:38–40	55–56, 65	8:29–33	112
5:39	54, 58–63, 65–66, 70, 72	8:30	112
5:40	57–59	8:31	4–6, 36, 49, 89, 96–98, 100–101, 103, 105, 108–9, 111–12, 114, 119, 126, 130, 140, 142, 144, 160, 163, 190, 201
5:40–42	54		
5:41	57, 65		
5:41–42	57, 70, 72		
5:42	57, 63, 70	8:31–32	69, 141, 148

Mark (cont.)
8:31–33 116, 218, 225
8:31–34 163
8:31–9:1 97, 101, 111, 135, 155, 157, 226
8:31–9:13 42
8:32 98, 100–101, 111–12, 160, 163
8:32–33 69, 113, 184
8:33 98–99, 100–101, 104, 111–14, 141, 148, 162, 225–26
8:33–34 114, 148
8:33–9:1 69
8:34 97–98, 101, 111, 113–14, 117–24, 126–27, 135–36, 140–42, 144–45, 147, 150, 163, 166, 224–25, 227
8:34–35 115, 120
8:34–37 109, 111, 113, 116–17, 135, 140–41, 155–56, 162, 218, 228
8:34–38 104, 122, 141–42, 225
8:34–9:1 37, 42, 100–101, 116–17, 121–23, 126, 130, 132, 134, 137–39, 142, 159, 164–65, 170, 219–20, 224–25, 232
8:35 55, 101, 114, 135
8:35–37 15, 97, 101, 114, 136, 140, 218, 227
8:35–9:1 224
8:36–37 114–115
8:38 4, 6, 48, 101–2, 114–15, 121–22, 126, 135–36, 141, 156, 162, 232
8:38–9:1 103, 109, 113–14, 124, 136, 156–57, 160–61, 201, 216
9 98, 202
9:1 101, 103, 114–17, 122, 125–26, 141, 156, 163–64
9:2–8 57, 69, 160
9:2–9 126
9:2–13 101, 109, 111
9:3 102, 155
9:4 108
9:5–6 69
9:7 102, 104, 126, 155, 165, 185–87
9:9 4–6, 102, 105, 201
9:9–10 101, 155
9:9–11 161

9:9–12 102
9:9–13 69, 205
9:10 103–4
9:10–13 126
9:11 103–4
9:11–12 114
9:11–13 105
9:12 4–6, 105–6
9:12–13 104–5, 107
9:13 105–7
9:14 69
9:14–29 37, 69, 72, 109–11, 172, 184, 226
9:17–18 110
9:18 55, 70–72
9:19 110
9:20 70–71
9:21 70
9:21–23 110
9:21–27 191
9:22 70–73
9:22–24 37, 70
9:23 70, 72–73
9:23–24 96
9:24 1, 70, 73, 96, 110, 204, 229, 232
9:25–26 70
9:25–27 2, 70
9:26 69, 70–72
9:26–27 110
9:27 69–70, 72
9:28 55
9:29 110
9:31 4–6, 36, 49, 89, 96–97, 109, 119, 130, 163, 190, 201
9:38 55
9:38–41 184
10:1 183, 202
10:2–9 212
10:21 112
10:23–31 100
10:26 55, 100
10:27 100
10:28 143–44
10:28–29 100
10:29–30 144

10:30	100	13:2	133
10:32	8, 160, 183, 202	13:5–6	83
10:32–34	165, 183	13:6–8	128–30, 133
10:32–45	183–84	13:9	129–32, 226
10:33	4, 130–31, 183, 210	13:9–11	158
10:33–34	4–9, 36, 49, 89, 97, 100, 109, 119, 130–31, 160–61, 163, 182–83	13:9–13	109, 129–34, 157, 166, 169–70, 227–28
		13:10	132
10:34	96, 131, 181, 183, 190, 201	13:11	158, 217–19, 221, 224, 226
10:35	162	13:11–13	159
10:35–40	160–61, 164, 170	13:12	130–31, 169–70
10:37	160, 162, 164	13:13	55, 131, 135
10:38	162	13:14	124, 129, 132–34, 224, 232
10:38–39	163–65, 168	13:14–16	170
10:38–40	166	13:14–18	132
10:39	162, 166–69	13:14–23	128–29, 132, 134
10:40	162, 164–65	13:14–27	131
10:40–41	160–61	13:16	170
10:41–45	161, 182	13:20	55
10:42	161, 181–82, 210	13:24–25	131, 157
10:42–44	161	13:24–26	201
10:42–45	164, 182	13:24–27	48, 132
10:43	162	13:26	4, 6, 156–57
10:43–45	181	13:26–27	131, 156–57
10:44	162	13:27	132, 135
10:45	4, 6, 109, 121, 161, 167, 169, 177–84, 190–91, 198, 200, 202–3, 209–10, 213	13:32	133
		13:32–33	127
		13:32–37	127
10:46–11:10	183	13:33–37	133, 193
11:11	183–84, 210	13:34	127
12:1	163	13:35	127
12:18–27	9–10, 15, 57, 75, 89–90, 93–94	13:36	127
		13:37	121, 128–29, 133–34
12:19	75–77, 92	14	149
12:19–21	75	14:1–9	193
12:20–23	75	14:10–11	140, 146
12:22	77	14:17	127
12:23	77	14:17–27	119
12:24	83, 86, 89	14:18–21	211
12:24–27	89	14:21	4–6
12:25	75–81, 88, 92	14:22–25	115, 167, 203, 209
12:26	76, 82–84, 86, 88–89	14:22–28	36
12:27	84, 94	14:23	167–68,
12:35–37	162	14:23–24	163
13	42, 109, 126, 128, 130–31, 167, 170	14:23–27	182

Mark (cont.)
- 14:24   115, 121, 167, 169, 177, 178, 209–13
- 14:24–25   31, 179
- 14:26–27   31, 115–16
- 14:26–31   211
- 14:27   141–43, 164
- 14:27–28   157
- 14:28   30–31, 39, 57, 89, 96, 141, 154–55, 190, 201
- 14:29   143, 164
- 14:29–31   31, 164
- 14:30   127, 142, 145, 147, 155, 164
- 14:31   142, 226
- 14:32–42   116, 126, 164
- 14:34   127
- 14:36   116, 162–63, 165, 204
- 14:37   127
- 14:37–38   148
- 14:38   145, 147, 218, 226
- 14:39   116
- 14:39–15:39   131
- 14:40   127
- 14:41   4, 6, 127
- 14:43–45   140, 146
- 14:43–16:2   7
- 14:47   142, 144
- 14:50   140, 146, 154, 164
- 14:51   155
- 14:50–52   141, 144
- 14:51–52   29–30, 32–35, 154–55, 170, 228
- 14:52   30, 34, 37, 170
- 14:53   144
- 14:53–54   142
- 14:53–15:39   131
- 14:54   140, 142–44, 146, 154, 226
- 14:55   130, 188
- 14:55–64   189
- 14:57–60   188
- 14:60–61   144
- 14:61   185–87
- 14:61–64   188, 217–18
- 14:62   4, 6, 156–57
- 14:63   189
- 14:63–64   186
- 14:64   188
- 14:65   144, 205
- 14:66   144
- 14:66–72   140–41, 144, 149, 164, 217
- 14:68   141–42, 145–47, 226
- 14:69   144–45
- 14:70   141–42, 144–45
- 14:70–71   146
- 14:71   141–42, 147, 223
- 14:72   127, 145, 149
- 15:1   127–28, 130, 186, 188, 223
- 15:1–11   10
- 15:1–21   149
- 15:2   205
- 15:15   131
- 15:16–20   205
- 15:21   149–50, 164, 207
- 15:23   163–65, 205
- 15:27   164–65, 170
- 15:29–32   33, 205
- 15:33   131, 179
- 15:33–16:8   185
- 15:34   96, 165, 172, 177, 179, 190–91, 202–8
- 15:35   205
- 15:35–36   33–34
- 15:36   116, 163–65, 205
- 15:37   190, 208
- 15:38   186
- 15:39   185–87, 190, 202–3, 205, 208
- 15:40   165
- 15:40–41   33–34, 38, 131, 140, 154
- 15:41   34, 37, 165
- 15:42–43   188
- 15:42–46   187
- 15:43   188
- 15:44–45   185, 202
- 15:46   155, 189–90, 194, 198
- 15:47   38, 140
- 16:1–2   154
- 16:1–3   32
- 16:1–8   1, 8–9, 35, 108, 153–54, 204
- 16:2   34, 128
- 16:3   197–98

16:3-8	7	17:33	116, 135
16:4	32, 198	20:35	81
16:5	30, 32-34, 155	20:36	81
16:5-6	34	20:39	94
16:5-7	170, 177, 228	22:20	211
16:6	30, 32-33, 51, 57	22:24-27	211
16:6-7	9, 39-40, 157	22:31	142, 147
16:7	30-32, 39, 41, 74, 99, 141, 151-58, 171, 216, 218 229, 232	22:31-32	153
		22:32	147, 152, 224, 226-27
16:7-8	141, 153-54	22:40	142
16:8	9, 32, 37, 51, 74, 131, 140, 154	22:54	223
		22:54-62	222-23
Luke		22:57	220
7:1-10	63	22:60	147, 223
7:11-17	43	22:61	147, 223
8:41-42a	44	22:63-71	223
8:42	60, 62	22:66	223
8:49	60	23:46	62-63
8:49-56	44	23:47	186
8:52	63, 66	23:50-51	188
8:52-53	60	23:53	198
8:53	62	24	10, 41
8:54	62	24:4	35, 40
8:55	61-63	24:4-5	35
9:23	136, 124	24:23	35, 40
9:24-27	224	24:28-43	15
9:26	162	24:30	10, 63
9:37-43a	71-72	24:33-34	153
9:39	71	24:34	151-52
9:42	71	24:39	41
12:2-9	219	24:39-42	10
12:8	220	24:41-42	63
12:8-9	221-22		
12:8-10	221, 223	John	
12:8-12	219, 224	4:46-54	63
12:9	116, 220-23	10:31	13-14
12:10	220-22	10:39-40	14
12:10-12	221, 223	11	43
12:11	222	11:1	13
12:11-12	221-22	11:1-16	13
14:25	136	11:8	13
14:26-27	116	11:11	13
14:27	135-36	11:12	13
17:1-2	5	11:15	13
17:4	152	11:16	13

John (cont.)		Romans	
11:23–26	55	4:16–24	83
11:24	77	5–7	183
11:24–27	14	5:9–10	55
11:38	189–90	5:12–6:11	55
11:38–44	14	6:3–6	167–68
11:39–40	14	6:4	168
11:50	189	6:5	77, 168
12:25	116, 135	7:1–3	88
18:10	144	8:29–30	95
18:15	145	9:27	55
18:26	144	11:26	55
18:27	145	16:3	150
19:25–27	34		
19:38	188	1 Corinthians	
20	10	1–2	3
20:1–10	153	2:6–8	206–7
20:24–29	12, 15	3:15	55
20:25	13	7:25–31	79–81
20:27	10	7:31	80
21	151–53	7:39	88
21:15–33	153	10:20–22	183
		10:33	55
Acts		11:2–16	80–81
1:8	220–21	11:7	80
1:10	40	11:8–10	80
1:10–11	34–35	11:10	80
2:1–36	220–21	11:11–12	81
2:17	55	11:16	81
3:19	152	11:23–26	166–67, 212
4:1–2	76	11:27–34	211
5:40	122	12:3	147
6:2	167	13:1–2	80
6:9	150	15	12, 15, 79
7:59	62	15:1–11	10
9:35	152	15:3–7	202
10–11	124	15:4	49, 202
11:19–20	150	15:5	151–52
11:21	152	15:5–8	38, 171
12:1–2	166, 169	15:12	77, 92
13:27–29	188	15:12–13	11
14:15	152	15:13	77
20:10	62	15:17–19	11–12
23:6–8	76	15:18	13
23:8	76	15:19	92

Ancient Sources Index

15:20	55	2 Timothy	
15:20–23	200	2:17–18	15, 92
15:20–28	57	2:18	91–92
15:21	77	3:1	55
15:23	192, 198		
15:24–27	55	Hebrews	
15:26	183	2:14–15	58
15:35–54	11–12, 80	4:15	226
15:39	3	6:2	77
15:42	77	6:4–6	217
15:42–49	79–80	11:35	77
15:51–57	57		
15:54–55	12, 55, 183	James	
		5:3	55
Galatians			
1–2	171	2 Peter	
1:15–24	171	3:7–9	104
2:9	126, 166		
2:11–14	124	Revelation	183
2:11–21	171	1:5	192
2:16	166	2:13	175
2:20	166	6:9–11	108–9
3:19	80	11:6–7	106
3:26–28	168	11:17	187
3:28	80–81	12:1–14:13	183
6:14	3	16:7	187
		17	183
Philippians			
3:11	77	**Rabbinic Works**	
Colossians		Mishnah ʿEduyyot	
1:18	192	8:7	104–5
2:12	168		
		Mishnah Kelim	
1 Thessalonians		1:18	52
4:13	59		
4:13–14	55, 58	Mishnah Sanhedrin	
4:15–17	132	10:1	76
4:16	77		
5:10	59	Babylonian Talmud Taʾan	
		21b	52
1 Timothy			
2:11–15	93		
2:13–15	91		

Early Christian Writings

Acts of Paul and Thecla
14   91–93

Augustine
- Sermones 130   214
- Sermones 134   214
- Sermones 265d   214

Clement of Alexandria, *Stromateis*
4.70.1–72.4   222

Cyprian, *Epistulae*
- 8   137
- 9   137
- 20   137

Cyril of Jerusalem, *Catecheses*
12.15   214

Eusebius, *Historia ecclesiastica*
2.15   18

Gospel of Peter
8.28–11:49   38–39

Gospel of Philip (NHC II 3)
- 55.14–29   206
- 57.29–30   206
- 59.18–24   206
- 68.26–29   206

Gregory the Great, *Expositio in Librum Job, sive Moralium libri xxv*
33.7   213

Gregory of Nyssa, *In tridui spatio*
608 M   213

Gregory of Nyssa, *Oratio catechetica*
65 M   213

Ignatius, *To the Smyrnaeans*
3.2   152

Irenaeus, *Adversus haereses*
1.24.4   207

Jerome, *Commentary on Matthew*, book 3
Ad Matt 22:31–32   84–85

Jerome, *Epistulae*
149   217

John of Damascus, *De fide orthodoxa*
3.27   213–14

Justin Martyr, *Apologia i*
- 5   183
- 64   183

Justin Martyr, *Dialogus cum Tryphone*
108.2   38

Names, Works and Deaths of the Holy Prophets
17   198

Origen, *Contra Celsum*
- 1.49   76
- 2.24   207

Origen, *Commentarium in evangelium Matthaei*
16.8   207

Origen, *Commentarii in Romanos*
5.10   207

Papias, Fragments
3.17   24

(Pseudo-)Athanasius, *De passione et cruce Domini*
- 28–29   215
- 14–15   215–16

Pseudo-Linus, Martyrdom of Peter
6   159, 227

Ancient Sources Index

Tertullian, *Apologeticus*
22.5 — 79

Tertullian, *De fuga in persecutione*
6.1–2 — 137

Tertullian, *De resurrectione carnis*
36 — 92–93

Tertullian, *Scorpiace*
9.3 — 137

Greco-Roman Literature

Achilles Tatius, *Leucippe et Clitophon*
3.15.5–7 — 64
5.19.1–2 — 64
7.3–16 — 64

Apollodorus, *Library*
1.1 — 208
1.1–2 — 201

Apuleius, *Florida*
19 — 64–65

Aulus Gellius, *Attic Nights, praefatio*
3 — 19
12 — 20
13 — 19
13–16 — 21
17–18 — 21
23–24 — 20

Celus, *De medicina*
2.6.15 — 65

Chariton, *De Chaerea et Callirhoe*
1.4.12–9.5 — 64

Cicero, *Brutus*
262 — 22–23

Cicero, *Letters to Atticus*
1.19 — 17–18

2.1 — 17

Euripides, *Cyclops* — 198

Euripides, *Hercules furens*
816–1038 — 149

Galen, *On Anatomical Procedures* — 17, 24

Heliodorus, *Aethiopica*
2.1–5 — 64

Hesiod, *Theogony*
453–506 — 200
485–492 — 208
493–496 — 201
495 — 201

Hirtius, *Letter to Balbus* — 23

Homer, *Iliad*
5.628–698 — 64

Homer, *Odyssey*
3.236–239 — 74
3.437–438 — 178
3.455–463 — 178
9.105–107 — 194
9.114 — 194
9.182 — 194
9.240–243 — 198
9.241–242 — 198
9.288–293 — 199
9.354–374 — 208
9.366–367 — 194–95
9.371–374 — 201
9.399–412 — 194
9.408 — 195
9.411 — 194
9.413–463 — 196
9.502–505 — 197
9.507–512 — 198
9.526–536 — 197
10 — 196
18 — 215

Homer, *Odyssey* (cont.)		Tacitus, *Annales*	
19	193	15.44	174
Julius Caesar, *Civil War*	21–25	Theocritus, *Idylls*	
		6	198
Libanius, *Orationes*		11	198
18.286	163		
		Virgil, *Aeneid*	149
Livy, *Ab urbe condita*		2.270–279	13
1.16	40–41	3.616–618	209
		3.621–627	199
Lucian, *Quomodo historia conscribenda sit*		3.666–667	209
		3.672–674	199
48	17	3.675–681	199
		3.679	199
Philostratus, *Vita Apollonii*		6.565–572	46
4.36	193–94	6.557–558	46
4.45	65		
4.45.1	65–66	Xenophon of Ephesus, *Ephesiaca*	
4.45.2	65–66	3.6–8	64
7.28	193–94		
Plato, *Leges*			
936e	123		
Pliny, *Naturalis historia*			
26.14–15	65		
Plutarch, *Romulus*			
27	41		
Seneca, *Oedipus*	149		
299–383	149		
Sophocles, *Ajax*			
1–133	149		
186	194		
Strabo, *Geographica*			
1.2.15	199		
1.2.16	199		
Suetonius, *Divus Julius*			
56.4	23		

Modern Authors Index

Akin, Danny	191	Bovon, François	219
Allen, Thomas W.	74	Boyarin, Daniel	90
Allison, Dale C.	128, 131, 157, 164, 192, 205	Braun, François-Marie	166
		Brichto, Herbert Chanan	86–88
Alter, Robert	87, 122	Brown, Raymond E.	34, 146, 188, 205, 219, 223
Arndt, William F.	55, 83, 113, 123		
Auerbach, Erich	148	Buch-Hansen, Gitte	168
Aulén, Gustaf	180, 214	Büchsel, Friedrich	114
Bakhtin, Mikhail M.	16, 75, 89–90, 94–95	Bultmann, Rudolf	5, 114, 116, 183
		Burkett, Delbert	97, 102
Barnes, Timothy David	159	Burkill, T. A.	218
Barrett, C. K.	180, 217	Busch, Austin	17, 54, 75, 89–90, 149, 184, 193–94
Bassler, Jouette M.	147		
Batstone, William Wendell	23	Camery-Hoggatt, Jerry	218
Bauckham, Richard	92, 104, 150	Carey, Holly J.	2, 204
Bauer, Walter	55, 83, 113, 123	Carlston, Charles Edwin	126
Baur, Ferdinand Christian	66	Carter, Warren	47
Beasley-Murray, George Raymond	167–68	Casey, Maurice	97
		Catchpole, David R.	221
Beavis, Mary Ann	56	Chatman, Seymour	118
Becker, Eve-Marie	3, 79	Cohn-Sherbok, Dan M.	86
BeDuhn, Jason David	80	Collins, Adela Yarbro	5, 16, 24, 32–36, 40, 56, 59, 65, 70–71, 76, 79–80, 98–99, 106, 114–16, 119, 122, 124, 126, 128–29, 132, 146, 149–50, 152, 160–61, 163, 167, 178, 180, 183–84, 187, 196, 218
Bell, Richard H.	214		
Best, Ernest	99, 123, 129		
Beyer, Hermann	167		
Billerbeck, P.	79		
Black, Matthew	113		
Blass, Friedrich	104, 115, 162	Collins, John J.	97, 102
Bock, Darrell L.	4–7	Constas, Nicholas P.	214–16
Bolt, Peter	47, 128, 130, 157	Cook, John Granger	41
Bond, Helen K.	159	Cozier, Clint L.	4
Bonnard, Émile	85	Crossan, John Dominic	29, 116
Bonner, Campbell	195	Crowder, Stephanie R. Buckhanon	151
Boobyer, George H.	4, 101	Damgaard, Finn	159
Boring, M. Eugene	35, 116	Damon, Cynthia	23

D'Angelo, Mary Rose	50, 52, 60	Geddert, Timothy J.	127–28, 130, 218
Danker, Frederick W.	55, 83, 113, 123, 180, 186	Gingrich, F. Wilbur	55, 83, 113, 123
		Girard, René	45
Daube, David	76	Glasson, Thomas F.	46
Davies, W. D.	192, 205	Glenn, Justin	199, 201
Debrunner, Albert	104, 115, 162	Gnilka, Joachim	48
DeConick, April D.	13–14	Goulder, Michael D.	171
Deppe, Dean B.	128, 130	Groff, Kent Ira	1, 31, 155
Derrett, J. Duncan M.	45, 47–48, 68, 174, 196	Guelich, Robert A.	56, 60
		Gülzow, Henneke	137
Dewey, Joanna	117–20	Gundry, Robert H.	2, 6–7, 9, 31, 33, 56, 59–60, 63, 71, 76, 86, 103, 106, 117, 150, 186, 195, 219
Dewey, Kim	112		
Dimock, George E., Jr.	203		
Dinkler, Michal Beth	120, 136–37	Haber, Susan	50, 52–53
Dixon, Edward P.	186, 193	Hachili, Rachel	190
Dodd, C. H.	113	Hagstrom, Andrew Mark	66
Dodson, Joseph R.	183	Hamilton, Neill Q.	40
Donahue, John R.	55–56, 76, 79, 83	Harrington, Daniel J.	55–56, 76, 79, 83
Donfried, Karl P.	219, 223	Harris, Murray J.	60
Doutreleau, Louis	207	Hatina, Thomas R.	126
Dowd, Sharyn	180–81, 214	Hatton, Stephen B.	54
Dowling, Elizabeth V.	167	Hedrick, Charles W.	60–61, 69, 71
Downing, F. Gerald	85–86	Heil, Günter	213
Dreyfus, François	85	Hernandez, Pura Nieto	201, 203
Dulk, Matthijs den	92	Hodge, Caroline E. Johnson	95
Dunn, James D. G.	167	Hogterp, Albert L. A.	104
Edwards, J. Christopher	178	Holmes, Michael W.	24
Edwards, James R.	49	Hooker, Morna Dorthy	84, 97, 102, 181
Ehrman, Bart D.	202	Hubert, Henri	178
Elder, Nicholas A.	46	Incigneri, Brian J.	16, 119, 133, 175, 225
Ellis, E. Earle	85	Jackson, Howard M.	186
Elmer, Ian J.	3, 79	Jacobson, Howard	198–99
Engberg-Pedersen, Troels	3, 79, 81	Janzen, J. Gerald	77–78, 82–83, 87
Evans, Craig A.	84–85	Jeffery, Peter	31
Farrer, Austin	106, 150	Johnson, Andy	1
Fleddermann, Harry	142	Johnson, Elliott J.	99
Foerster, Richard	163	Jones, Christopher P.	65, 175
Fonrobert, Charlotte	50, 52	Jonge, Henk J. de	220
Foster, Paul	4	Joynes, Christine E.	106
France, R. T.	33–34, 180	Juel, Donald	112, 190
Fridrichsen, Anton	180, 184	Kalin, Everett R.	61
Fullmer, Paul	1, 58, 63–64, 66, 193	Käsemann, Ernst	92
Funk, Robert W.	104, 115, 162	Kaster, Robert A.	23
Garrett, Susan R.	148	Kazen, Thomas	51–52
Garroway, Joshua	47	Kee, Howard Clark	101–3

Kelber, Werner H.	127	Marx, Frederick	65
Kelly, J. N. D.	214	Marxsen, Willi	183
Keulen, Wytse Hette	19–20	Massaux, Édouard	38–39
Kim, Tae Hun	187	Matera, Frank	164
King, Karen L.	96	Matthews, Shelly	41, 81, 192
Kingsbury, Jack Dean	2	Matusova, Ekaterina	46
Kloppenborg, John S.	24, 220	Mauss, Marcel	178
Koester, Helmut	40	Mayhoff, Karl	65
Koskenniemi, Erkki	66	McArthur, Harvey K.	49
Kraus, Christina Shuttleworth	22	McKnight, Scot	3, 6–7, 109
Kuhn, Karl Georg	148	McLellan, Peter N.	29
Lampe, Geoffrey W. H.	152–53, 174, 217, 220	McVann, Mark	47
		Meeks, Wayne A.	81
Larsen, Kasper Bro	93	Meier, John P.	86
Larsen, Matthew D. C.	17–20, 24–25	Merry, W. Walter	194–95
Layton, Bentley	206	Messing, Gordon M.	115, 162
Leemans, Jan	174	Metzger, Bruce M.	145–46, 198
Lehtipuu, Outi	93	Middleton, Paul	113, 136, 141, 173–75, 217–18, 224–25
Levine, Amy-Jill	50–51		
Levine, Daniel B.	215	Milgrom, Jacob	51, 67, 178
Lewis, C. S.	18	Miller, Richard C.	1, 40–41, 193
Licona, Michael R.	191	Moloney, Francis J.	97–98
Lightfoot, Robert H.	127, 196	Montgomery, Hugo	137
Lincoln, Andrew T.	1, 29, 55	Moore, William	213
Lindars, Barnabas	5	Morgan, Teresa	193
Lipsius, Richard	91, 159, 227	Moses, A. D. A.	126
Loader, William	168	Moss, Candida	53, 102, 119, 136, 174, 224
Löhr, Winrich	222		
Lunn, Nicholas P.	152	Most, Glenn W.	201
Luther, Martin	62	Muddiman, John	164
Luz, Ulrich	38	Mueller, Mogens	3, 79
MacDonald, Dennis R.	193–94, 196–98	Mühlenberg, Ekkehard	213
MacMullen, Ramsay	12	Munk, Linda	214
Malbon, Elizabeth Struthers	37, 120–22, 125, 128, 180–81, 214	Myers, Ched	47, 181
		Mynors, R. A. B.	46
Malcovati, Enrica	22	Naiden, F. S.	178–79
Marcus, Joel	3, 6–8, 16, 32–35, 45, 48, 55, 59–60, 63, 70–71, 80, 98–99, 102, 105–6, 111, 115–17, 119, 122–23, 129, 132–33, 146, 148, 150–52, 163, 186–87, 196, 209–10	Nardoni, Enrique	106
		Neirynck, Francis	31, 116
		Newton, Rick M.	203
		Nicholson, Oliver	174
		Nickelsburg, George W. E.	4–5
		Nielsen, Jesper Tang	167–68
Marković, Miroslav	207		
Markusse, Gabi	99, 158	Nineham, Dennis	85, 99, 106, 196
Marshall, Peter K.	20	Nongbri, Brent	217
Martin, Dale	12, 79–80	Oepke, Albrecht	163

Öhler, Markus	104	Seccombe, David P.	120
Osborne, B. A. E.	112	Seeley, David	161, 181–82
Pascut, Beniamin	162	Segal, Moses H.	104
Peppard, Michael	187	Seim, Turid Karlsen	81
Perkins, Judith	64	Selvidge, Marla J.	50
Pervo, Richard	166	Shaw, Brent	119, 175
Petersen, Norman R.	29	Shiner, Whitney T.	187
Petrey, Taylor G.	81	Sim, David C.	3, 79, 159, 171
Phelan, James	118–20	Simon-Shoshan, Moshe	90
Pilch, John J.	61	Singer, Charles	17
Propp, William Henry	211–212	Skoven, Anne Vig	171
Pudussery, Paul S.	16, 114–15, 117, 122, 135, 175, 219	Sloan, David B.	85
		Smith, Daniel A.	40–41
Rahlfs, Alfred	49	Smith, Terence V.	99, 112, 115, 140–41, 150, 152, 155, 219
Rashdall, Hastings	207		
Rastoin, Marc	147	Smyth, Herbert Weir	115, 162
Ray, Darby Kathleen	214	Starobinski, Jean	45
Reardon, Patrick Henry	163	Stein, Robert H.	152–53, 155, 158
Reeder, Caryn A.	107	Sterling, Gregory E.	72
Reischl, Wilhelm C.	214	Stock, Klemens	150
Reumann, John	219, 223	Stone, Michael E.	198–99
Riddell, James	194–95	Strack, H. L.	79
Riley, Gregory J.	12–13	Swain, Simon	66
Robertson, Archibald T.	33	Sweetland, Dennis M.	220
Robinson, H. Wheeler	86	Swete, Henry Barclay	111, 113
Roskam, Hendrika Nicoline	16, 116, 119, 135, 175	Tannehill, Robert C.	120, 136
		Tappenden, Frederick S.	11–12, 44, 168
Rossé, Gérard	165	Taylor, Adam	125
Rothschild, Clare K.	102, 108	Taylor, Justin	76
Rousseau, Adelin	207	Taylor, Vincent	56, 79
Rupp, Joseph	214	Theissen, Gerd	72, 150
Russell, E. A.	173	Thiessen, Matthew	50–53, 76, 161, 181
Sage, Michael M.	137	Thiselton, Anthony C.	92
Sanders, E. P.	189	Thrall, Margaret E.	102, 108
Scarth, Alwyn	199	Tödt, Heinz Eduard	4–5
Schaberg, Jane	97, 102	Toensing, Holly Joan	45
Schaeffer, Susan E.	38–39	Tolbert, Mary Ann	143, 193
Schein, Seth L.	195, 203	Trick, Bradley R.	85, 88
Schreiber, Johannes	150	Trocmé, Etienne	122
Schwankl, Otto	86	Tylor, Edward Burnett	178
Schweitzer, Albert	109, 132, 168	Tyson, Joseph B.	2
Scodel, Ruth	149	Van Iersel, Bas M. F.	16, 31, 114, 119, 175, 217–18
Scott, Shirley Clay	198		
Scott-Macnab, David	214	Vander Stichele, Caroline	82
Scroggs, Robin	1, 31, 155	Vanhoye, Albert	31, 34, 37, 155

Vermès, Géza	113
Vielhauer, Philipp	221
Viviano, Benedict T.	76
Vliet, Johannes van der	65
Volkmar, Gustaf	171
Ware, James	11
Waters, Kenneth L.	192
Watts, Rikki E.	180, 196, 209
Weaver, J. Denny	214
Webb, Geoff R.	146
Weeden, Theodore J.	2
Weisberg, Dvora	77–78
Wellhausen, Julius	105
Wenham, David	126
Wenham, John W.	145–46
Whitaker, Robyn J.	111–12
Williams, Guy	29
Willson, Emily R.	63
Wilson, Emily R.	74
Wilson, Henry Austin	213
Wimpfheimer, Barry Scott	90
Winer, Georg B.	187
Winn, Adam	16, 99, 101, 122, 175
Wischmeyer, Oda	3, 79
Wrede, Wilhelm	58–59, 112
Wright, N. T.	47, 76, 81, 86, 108, 152, 154
Zeichmann, Christopher B.	47–48
Zevit, Ziony	87

Subject Index

Andrew, 113, 126–31, 143, 158, 224
angel(s), 48, 162, 187, 220–21
　as divine mediators, 80–81
　as stars, 76, 157
　bodies of, 79
　fallen, 46, 80
　in Matt 28, Luke 24, and Acts 1, 35–36, 39–40, 191
　interpreting angels, 35–36
　Sadducees' beliefs about, 76
　sexuality of, 80–82
　young man of Mark 16 as, 32–36
anthropophagy/cannibalism, 107, 115, 167–68, 194, 198, 200–201, 208–15
Apollonius of Tyana, 65–66
apostasy, 136–37, 160, 169, 171, 174, 217, 220, 222. *See also* Holy Spirit, blasphemy of
　Peter's denials as, 141, 146, 155, 158–59, 174–75, 217, 220–21, 223, 225–29
Asclepiades, 65–66
bandits (crucified by Jesus's side), 164–65, 169
baptism,
　Jesus's, 166–67, 184, 186
　Jesus's death as, 8, 162–63, 166, 168–69
　rite of initiation, 167–69
betrayal
　of fellow-believers, 129, 137, 169–70, 174
　of Jesus (by Judas), 6–7, 97, 116, 140–41, 146, 159, 170–71, 174–75, 211, 225

burial, 65, 87–88, 190. *See also* tombs; empty tomb
　Jesus's, 7, 31, 36–38, 42, 48, 140, 168, 172, 187–91, 197–98, 201–3, 206, 208–9
　John the Baptist's, 102, 108
　sepulchral inscriptions, 12
centurion, 48, 182, 185, 206. *See also* legion: as Roman military term; Rome/Roman (gentile) rule
　declaration of (in 15:39), 185–87, 190, 202–3, 206, 208
　in league with demons, 186–87, 190, 202, 206, 208
　participation in Jesus's burial, 187–90, 197, 202
children
　deaths of, 55–56, 58, 70–74, 96, 110, 165, 172, 191, 231, 233
Christus victor atonement theory, 10, 213–16
commentarii (Gk. *hypomnêmata*), 17–26, 29, 32, 36, 38–40, 43, 60, 63, 75, 94–95, 108, 112, 135, 137–38, 144, 153, 173, 179, 191–92, 202–3, 215–17, 219, 223, 225, 232
　primary versus secondary, 18–25
confession (of Jesus), 136–37, 147, 219–20, 222, 224
　demons', 112, 148, 186
　inspired by Holy Spirit, 158–59, 169, 219, 221–22, 226–27
　Jesus's self-confession, 144, 156, 217–19, 221, 223
　Peter's (Mark 8:29), 112, 148

Council/Sanhedrin, 130, 188, 223
  condemns Jesus, 188–89
covenant (Sinai), 209–11
  critiqued, 212–13
  renewed by Jesus's death, 211–12
Cronos, 200–201, 208, 211
crowd, 114, 120–25, 130, 136
  conflated with Mark's readers, 120–21
Cyprian, 137, 174
death
  apparent versus actual, 59, 61, 64–66, 70–73
  defeat of demonic Death, 27, 48, 55, 57–58, 95, 110, 183, 191, 194, 198, 200, 203, 208, 213–15
  existential problem, 11–15, 36, 74, 172–73, 175
  fear, 8, 27, 58, 169, 175, 227–28
  genital discharges (esp. blood) as symbol of, 50–54, 67–68
  Mark's supposed emphasis on Jesus's, 1–9, 99–100, 160–61
  social, 44–46, 52–54, 64, 197
Decapolis, 45–49, 185, 197
deception
  heroic (esp. Odyssean), 194–97, 201, 208, 215–16
  Jesus's feigned death (in gnostic writings), 206–7
  Jesus's feigned weakness in death, 205–6, 208, 210, 213–16
demons (including Satan), 61, 183, 187. See also disciples: failure to exorcise demon; legion; monster
  as anthropophagic monsters, 213–16
  deceived by Jesus, 197, 205–6, 208, 210, 213–16
  demonic possession/manipulation, 1–2, 44–49, 70–72, 110, 184–85, 194–95, 197, 200, 202, 226–27
  influence over/possession of Peter, 98–101, 111–15, 141, 147–49, 156, 158–59, 169, 173, 211, 218–19, 225–30
  Jesus silences/rebukes, 112, 114, 148

demons (cont.)
  Jesus's power over (esp. in exorcism), 6, 44–45, 48, 53, 55, 57, 67–70, 89–90, 110, 141, 148, 158–59, 180, 184–85, 190, 195–97, 201–2, 206, 208, 213–17, 225–27
  testing by, 145, 147–48, 180, 184, 201, 226
desolating sacrilege (from Daniel), 132–33
dialogue/dialogization, 2, 16–17, 27, 67, 73–75, 89–91, 93–96, 118, 139–40, 168, 204–5, 229, 232–33
disciples, 10, 13–15, 29–30, 32, 34, 37–40, 42, 69, 95, 101, 109, 112, 115, 183, 188, 209, 211, 217. See also Andrew; doubt/skepticism: disciples'; female disciples; James; John; Peter; young man
  abandon Jesus, 26, 30, 116, 127, 131, 134, 139–44, 146, 148, 164–65, 170–71, 173–75, 177, 182, 204, 209, 211, 225–26, 228. See also persecution, flight
  aligned with Jesus's enemies, 211–12
  commanded to die and rise with Jesus, 8, 42, 97, 101, 103–4, 110–11, 114, 117–20, 122, 124, 126, 129–30, 132–33, 135–36, 140–42, 144, 150, 157, 159, 161–66, 168, 175, 227–28, 231. See also martyrdom
  conflated with readers, 116–21, 125, 127, 130, 135–36, 224
  confused regarding Jesus's teaching, 10, 69, 99, 103–5, 108, 133, 136, 138, 161–62. See also eschatological timetable: disciples' misunderstanding of
  distinguished from readers, 98, 117, 119, 121–25, 128–30, 132–38, 170, 175, 224–25
  eschatological condemnation, 97, 111, 114–17, 122–23, 125–26, 139, 141, 155–57, 160, 164, 175, 179, 224, 232
  failure to exorcise demon, 110–11

disciples (cont.)
Jesus dies for, 109, 115, 165–67, 169, 177–78, 182, 209. *See also* ransom/redemption
possibility of future martyrdom, 42, 109, 127, 130–34, 136, 139, 156–59, 166, 169–70, 228
possibly forgiven/redeemed, 25, 99, 139, 152–53, 159, 165–66, 169, 173, 177, 225, 231–32
refuse to obey Jesus's command to die and rise with him, 10, 27, 37, 42, 98–99, 109, 111, 114–16, 126–28, 130, 133–34, 136, 138–40, 148, 157, 160, 164–65, 168–71, 173–74, 177–78, 182, 227, 231
double tradition. *See* Q
doubt/skepticism (esp. regarding resurrection), 1–2, 9–15, 26–27, 56, 73–75, 77–78, 82–84, 89, 92–95, 97–98, 134, 136, 138, 172–75, 177, 217, 231–33
disciples', 10, 12–15, 27, 37, 42, 97–98, 100–102, 104, 108, 110–11, 134, 136, 139–40, 154, 160, 165, 172–75, 177
Jesus's, 10, 27, 95–96, 109, 165, 172, 177, 190–91, 203–5
Elijah, 41–42, 66, 102, 205
as John the Baptist, 102, 105–8
eschatological, 103–5, 126, 161, 205
Elisha, 66
empty tomb, 7, 10–11, 29–32, 34, 36–43, 73, 131, 140–41, 154–55, 169–73, 175, 190, 192, 197–198, 200–203, 208, 215, 228, 232
indicating Jesus's translation to heaven, 40–43, 192
sham rumors explaining in Matthew, 38–39
epic, 18–19, 21. *See also* Hesiod; Homeric epic
eschatological afflictions, 128–34, 157
eschatological delay, 42, 103–4, 108–9, 132–34, 139, 157

eschatological parousia, 55, 128, 131–32, 156–57, 162. *See also* risen Christ: eschatological glory/authority/judgment
eschatological timetable, 114–15
disciples' misunderstanding of, 103–4, 108–9, 122, 138, 161
Eucharist, 166–68, 212. *See also* Last Supper
excommunication, 169, 171
faith/trust (esp. in resurrection), 1–2, 13–14, 17, 26–27, 31–32, 34, 36–38, 51, 54–56, 58, 60–61, 70, 72–75 77, 83, 93–97, 101, 103–4, 110–11, 113, 115, 138–40, 155, 157, 162, 165–66, 172–77, 181–82, 204–5, 208, 227–28, 232
Farrer hypothesis, 39–40, 71, 219
female disciples (Marys and Salome), 8–9, 31–34, 36–37, 39, 51, 128, 131, 139, 142, 154, 159, 165, 172–73, 175, 197–198, 231. *See also* disciples; young man
compared to male disciples, 36–37, 140, 154
flight from empty tomb, 9, 11, 26, 32, 36–37, 128, 131, 140–41, 154, 169, 171, 173, 228
refusal to proclaim resurrection, 9, 11, 36–37, 73–74, 128, 140–41, 151, 154–55, 158, 172–73, 179, 204, 228
fertility, 51, 67–68, 82–84
following Jesus, 37, 100, 113–14, 123, 140, 142–44, 146
food and drink (consumption of), 114–15, 162–68, 200, 208–9, 211–15
foreign enemies, 133, 181, 185, 194, 202
Israel's liberation from, 47–49, 183–84, 210–11, 219
Galilee ministry, 34, 148, 165, 184
movement from/to Jerusalem, 183–84, 210
healing as ambiguous resurrection, 2, 43–44, 58–61, 63–72, 110. *See also* resurrection: figurative

282   Risen Indeed?

heavenly translation traditions, 40–43, 102, 193
Herod Antipas and/or daughter, 106–7, 211
Hesiod, 200–201, 203, 208–9
high priest, 185–86, 188, 205, 218
  hypocritical piety of, 189
Holy Spirit, 147, 158–59, 169, 186, 193, 206, 217–19, 228. *See also* confession of Jesus
  blasphemy of (unforgiveable sin), 173, 217–26
Homeric epic, 19, 21, 64, 67, 74, 178, 192–93, 215–16
  Cyclopeia (*Od.* 9), 193–98, 200, 202–3, 208–9
impurity, 45, 48–54, 67, 188–89, 196–97, 200
irony, 36–37, 47, 53, 110, 126, 131, 134, 149–51, 164–65, 190, 218
Jairus (and/or daughter), 37, 44, 49–51, 53–74
James (son of Zebedee), 37, 57, 69, 97–98, 102–4, 108, 116, 126–31, 139, 155, 158–74, 224, 231. *See also* disciples
  martyrdom of, 166, 169–70
Jephthah (and/or daughter), 56–57
John (son of Zebedee), 37, 57, 69, 97–98, 102–4, 108, 116, 126–31, 139, 155, 158–73, 224, 231. *See also* disciples
John the Baptist, 109, 135, 168
  anticipates Jesus's death and resurrection, 108–9, 209
  as Elijah, 102, 105–8
Joseph of Arimathea, 187–89, 197, 202–3
  hypocritical piety of, 188–89
Judah, 77–78, 82–83
Last Supper, 30–31, 115, 141–42, 163, 167–68, 180, 212. *See also* Eucharist
  as anthropophagic meal, 163, 209–11
  as Passover celebration, 127, 163, 167, 209, 211
Lazarus, 13–15, 43, 55
Legion, 44–49, 51, 53–54, 64, 68, 184–87,

Legion (*cont.*) 189–90, 193–97, 200–202, 206, 208
  as Roman military term, 45, 47–48, 184–85
  confusion of identities, 45, 195
  livestock, 44–49, 195–97
Mark
  christological statements, 178–79, 213
  finalized/remediated by later scribes (esp. Matt and Luke), 18, 24–27, 32, 36, 38–40, 43, 60–63, 71–72, 94, 110, 136, 140, 144–47, 153, 173, 186–88, 191–92, 202, 219, 222–25, 232
  genre, 17–18, 23–25
  influenced by Paul, 3, 55, 58, 79–80, 83 91–94, 152, 159, 167–68, 171, 175, 213
  narrative voice(s), 32–33, 118–20, 124–25, 135–38, 175, 205
  neglects to guarantee resurrection, 2, 9, 11, 26, 29, 37–38, 42–44, 49, 58–61, 63, 66–69, 71–75, 90, 94, 108, 125, 130, 133–34, 136–38, 140, 148, 151, 171–72, 191–92, 203, 208, 230
  (original) readers of, 10, 15–16, 27, 31, 40, 51, 98, 103–4, 116–22, 124–25, 127–30, 132–38, 166–67, 169–70, 173–77, 193–94, 224–25, 231–32. *See also* disciples: distinction from readers; disciples: possible conflation with readers; persecution: original readers' fear of; persecution: readers' flight from legitimized
  supposed lost ending, 152–53
marriage
  Levirate marriage law, 75, 77–78, 82–83, 86, 88–89, 93
  eschatological obsolescence (perhaps including gender), 79–82, 93
  covenant ends with death, 88
martyrdom, 42, 119, 129–38, 156, 159, 166, 169, 173–76, 217, 219, 222, 224–27.

martyrdom (cont.)
See also disciples: commanded to die and rise with Jesus; confession of Jesus
Maccabean martyrs, 180
Mary (mother of James and Joses). See also female disciples
as Jesus's mother, 33–34, 165
messianic secret, 58–59, 65, 185–86
mockery of Jesus, 15, 58, 65, 205, 217
Jesus mocked on cross, 33, 165, 205–6, 208
Jesus mocks enemies, 207
monster, 193–94, 203
cannibalistic/anthropophagic divinities/monsters, 198, 200–201, 208–9, 211, 213–16
chthonic divinities/monsters 46–47, 199
cyclops/cyclopes (Polyphemus), 194–200, 208–9, 211
Death/demonic powers as, 197–98, 213–16
Legion as, 46–47, 194–97
Moses, 42, 76, 84–85, 88, 102–3, 106, 108, 211
mourning, 45, 47, 55–58, 61–62, 65, 72, 189
Olivet discourse, 125–135, 156–58, 167, 169–70, 173, 219
patriarchs/matriarchs (Abraham, Isaac, Jacob; Sarah, Rebekah, Leah, and Rachel), 76, 95
as evidence of resurrection, 83–85
supernatural generation of, 82–84, 89
survival in their descendants, 86–89
persecution, 26, 100, 108, 117–19, 125, 132–33, 143–44, 159, 169, 171, 173–75, 218, 220–21, 231, 233
flight in response to, 26, 132, 134–35, 137, 143, 156, 160, 170–71, 174, 233
original readers' fear of, 15–16, 119–20, 133, 135, 174–75
readers' flight legitimized, 121, 129, 132–34, 170, 173, 176–77, 224, 231

Peter, 10, 24, 30, 37, 57, 69, 94, 102–4, 108, 116–17, 126–31, 143, 154–55, 160–665, 172–73, 212. See also disciples
blasphemes the Holy Spirit in Mark, 217–19, 225–27
blasphemy remediated in Luke, 222–25, 227
denied appellation of "disciple," 31, 141, 171, 216, 232
denies/curses Jesus, 31, 116, 127, 139–42, 144–48, 151, 155–56, 158, 164, 169–71, 173–75, 204, 211, 217–22, 225–26, 228, 231
eschatological condemnation, 113–15, 126, 139, 141, 155–59, 170–71, 179, 216–18, 229, 232
follows Jesus, 100, 113, 140, 142–44, 146, 154, 226, 228
influenced/possessed by Satan, 98–101, 111–15, 141, 147–49, 156, 158–59, 169, 173, 211, 219, 225–28
possible redemption, 98–99, 139–40, 151–53, 158–59, 166 171, 173, 179, 216–18, 224, 227–29
psychological depth of Mark's characterization, 148–49
resists Jesus's prophecy of death and resurrection, 98–101, 104, 111–12, 115, 141, 148, 160, 225
Pontius Pilate, 128, 149, 182, 186, 197, 205, 223. See also Rome/Roman (gentile) rule
participates in Jesus's burial, 38, 187–90, 197, 202
postmortem punishment, 46
prophecies/predictions, 102–3, 105–8, 131–32, 134, 148, 156–57, 159, 166, 173, 218, 228
of Jesus's death and/or resurrection, 4–8, 31–32, 36–38, 41–42, 44, 49, 69, 73, 89, 97–98, 100–101, 103–9, 111–13, 115, 119–20, 130–31, 134, 144, 148, 154–57, 160–61, 163, 201, 204, 206, 208. See also Son of Man sayings

prophecies/predictions (cont.)
   of the disciples scattering and/or Peter's denial, 115, 127–28, 133, 141–43, 145, 147–48, 155, 158, 164, 211
purification
   of hemorrhaging woman, 53
   of Israel from cultural contaminants, 48–49, 196–97
Q, 24, 39, 63, 71–72, 116, 135–36, 219–20
ransom/redemption, 167, 177
   Jesus's death as ransom to God, 182
   Jesus's death as ransom to Satan and/or Death, 179–85, 191, 194, 200, 202–3, 206, 210–16, 217–18, 227–28
   Matthew mythologizes Jesus's death as ransom payment, 191–92, 202
resurrection. *See also* empty tomb; risen Christ
   ambiguous in Greco-Roman literature, 63–67
   as angelic transformation, 78–82
   as freedom from demons/Death, 190–92, 194, 197–98, 202–3, 206, 208, 214–15
   as heavenly translation, 14, 40–43, 193, 203
   as raising up of offspring, 77–78, 81–84, 86–89, 91–93
   conceptualizations of risen body, 11–15, 79–81
   eschatological, 14, 41–42, 47–49, 54–57, 75, 77–82, 84, 86, 89, 92–93, 95, 101–4, 108–9, 111, 115, 131–32, 168, 192
   figurative, 9, 44–50, 52–54, 67–71, 75
   immediate (as opposed to eschatological), 14, 55, 103–4, 108–9, 115, 156. *See also* eschatological timetable
   of demon-possessed boy (Mark 9), 1–2, 69–73, 110. *See also* demons (including Satan): demonic possession/manipulation; disciples: failure to exorcise demon

resurrection (cont.)
   of disciples, 114–15, 131–32, 156
   of holy ones, 57, 191–92
   of Jairus's daughter, 54–67. *See also* Jairus and/or daughter
   of Jesus, passim
   of Lazarus, 13–15
   synecdoche for personal eternal life, 15, 41, 114, 172
returning master (parable of), 127–30, 133–34
risen Christ
   appearance accounts/traditions, 13–14, 43, 140, 151–53, 156
   assumption to heaven, 35, 40–42, 102, 192–93, 203, 207
   body of, 11–15, 57, 79
   does not appear in Mark, 1, 3, 7, 11, 26, 29, 38, 43, 140, 151–52, 171
   eschatological glory/authority/judgment, 6, 101–3, 113–15, 121–22, 126, 155, 141, 156–57, 160–62, 164–65, 201, 206, 216, 232. *See also* eschatological parousia
   may head to Galilee to meet disciples, 29–30, 39–40, 99, 141, 154–58, 171, 216
   prototype of eschatologically risen ones, 192, 198
Rome/Roman (gentile) rule, 22, 64, 117, 119, 131, 161, 174–75, 181–82, 187–89, 202. *See also* Pontius Pilate
   associated with demons/monsters, 47–48, 183–86, 194, 202
   Roman soldiers/military, 38, 45, 47–48, 133, 149, 185, 187, 189. *See also* centurion; legion
sacrifice, 46–47, 56, 178–79
   Jesus's death as, 163, 178–80, 209–13
Sadducees
   skepticism about eschatological resurrection, 75–76, 78, 83–84, 89, 94, 230. *See also* doubt
   understanding of resurrection as raising up offspring, 75–81, 86–89, 94

scribes (esp. "from Jerusalem"), 89–90, 93, 104, 108, 123–24, 130–31, 189
Secret Gospel of Mark, 31
Sheol, 87
Simon of Cyrene, 149–51, 164–65, 207
sleep, 48–49, 58, 60–62, 66, 72, 201
    as metaphor for death, 11–12, 55, 59–60, 62–63, 131–32, 191
    disciples' (in Gethsemane), 116, 126–27, 130, 164
soil, types of in parable of the sower, 143–44, 146–47, 154, 169–70
Son of Man, 27, 69, 96–98, 103, 106–9, 113–15, 122, 126–28, 130–33, 139, 141 144–45, 156–57, 161–62, 165, 167, 171, 178–79, 181–82, 201, 221–22, 224–25, 227–28, 232
Son of Man sayings, 1–8, 36, 41, 44, 49, 57, 69, 97–98, 100–105, 109, 111–12, 126, 130–31, 140–41 144, 148, 155, 156, 160, 163, 181, 184, 217, 220–22. *See also* prophecies/predictions: of Jesus's death and/or resurrection
    as elaborating Daniel 7 and 12, 41, 97, 102–3, 162
soul, 163
    disembodied/immortal soul, 12, 15, 61–62, 85–86, 114
sower, parable of. *See* soil, types of in parable of the sower
suffering servant (from Isaiah), 8, 180
Tamar, 75, 77–78
Thomas, 12–15
Thomasine Christianity, 12–15, 96
tombs, 40, 43, 45–48, 53, 57, 67, 88, 102, 108, 187, 189–92. *See also* empty tomb
    as caves, 48, 187, 190, 192, 194, 197–98, 200, 202–3, 208–9, 215, 228
transfiguration, 69, 101–3, 106, 108, 125–26
    anticipates resurrection, 101–3, 106, 108, 126, 155, 160
veiling of women (in Corinth), 80–81, 93

young man (from Mark 16). *See also* disciples; female disciples
    flees (naked) from Jesus's arrest, 30, 34, 37, 142, 154–55, 170, 228
    infers/believes Jesus's resurrection, 30–32, 36–37, 73, 155, 172, 177, 228. *See also* faith
    proclaims Jesus's resurrection, 9, 11, 29, 73–74, 155, 173, 204, 228
    reclothed, 30–31, 34–35, 155, 228
    same as young man from 14:51–52, 29–31, 154–55
    theory that he is an angel, 32–36
    transformation into angel(s) in Matt and Luke-Acts, 32, 36, 39–40. *See also* angel(s): young man of Mark 16 as
Zeus, 64, 182, 194, 200–201, 208

www.ingramcontent.com/pod-product-compliance
Lightning Source LLC
Chambersburg PA
CBHW021347300426
44114CB00012B/1119